T0329101

CHALLENGES IN CENTRAL BANKING

Changes in the field of central banking over the past two decades have been nothing short of dramatic. Moreover, they have spanned the globe. They include the importance of central bank autonomy, the desirability of low and stable inflation, and the vital role played by how central banks communicate their views and intentions to the markets and the public more generally. Nevertheless, there remains considerable diversity in the institutional framework affecting central banks, the manner in which the stance of monetary policy is determined and assessed, and the forces that dictate the conduct of monetary policy more generally. The global financial crisis, which began in the United States in 2007, only serves to highlight further the importance of central bank policies. The aim of this volume is to take stock of where we are in the realm of the practice of central banking and to consider some of the implications arising from the ongoing crisis.

Pierre L. Siklos is Professor of Economics and Director of the Viessman European Research Centre at Wilfrid Laurier University, Canada. He is the managing editor of the *North American Journal of Economics and Finance*, author of *The Changing Face of Central Banking* (Cambridge University Press, 2002), and coeditor with Richard Burdekin of *Deflation: Current and Historical Perspectives* (Cambridge University Press, 2004). In 2008 Professor Siklos was named to the C.D. Howe Institute's Monetary Policy Council, became chairholder of the Bundesbank Foundation of International Monetary Economics at the Freie University Berlin, and became a Senior Fellow at the Centre for International Governance Innovation. His research in macroeconomics emphasizes the study of inflation, central banks, and financial markets.

Martin T. Bohl is Professor of Economics, Centre for Quantitative Economics, Westfaelische Wilhelms University Muenster. From 1999 to 2006 he was a professor of finance and capital markets at the European University Viadrina Frankfurt (Oder), where he was also spokesman for the Ph.D. program Capital Markets and Finance in the Enlarged Europe. Professor Bohl focuses on monetary theory and policy as well as financial market research. He has published in many international macroeconomics and finance journals and has been a visiting scholar at several universities in Europe and North America.

Mark E. Wohar is the UNO CBA Distinguished Professor at the University of Nebraska–Omaha, where he is director of the Division of Economic and Financial Analysis. Professor Wohar has published more than 85 refereed journal articles, including those in the *American Economic Review, Journal of Finance, Review of Economics and Statistics, Economic Journal,* and the *Journal of International Economics*. He is an associate editor of the *Journal of Economics and Applied Economics* and serves on the editorial board of *Economic Inquiry* and on the Editor Council of the *Review of International Economics*. The recipient of several awards for research excellence, his areas of investigation include domestic and international macroeconomics, international finance, monetary theory, and financial institutions.

Challenges in Central Banking

*The Current Institutional Environment and
Forces Affecting Monetary Policy*

Edited by

PIERRE L. SIKLOS

Wilfrid Laurier University, Canada

MARTIN T. BOHL

University of Muenster

MARK E. WOHAR

University of Nebraska, Omaha

CAMBRIDGE UNIVERSITY PRESS
Cambridge, New York, Melbourne, Madrid, Cape Town,
Singapore, São Paulo, Delhi, Mexico City

Cambridge University Press
The Edinburgh Building, Cambridge CB2 8RU, UK

Published in the United States of America by Cambridge University Press, New York

www.cambridge.org
Information on this title: www.cambridge.org/9781107616493

First published 2010
Reprinted 2011
First paperback edition 2013

A catalogue record for this publication is available from the British Library

Library of Congress Cataloguing in Publication Data
Challenges in central banking: the current institutional environment and forces affecting
monetary policy / edited by Pierre L. Siklos, Martin T. Bohl, Mark E. Wohar.
p. cm.
ISBN 978-0-521-19929-2 (hardback)
1. Banks and banking, Central. 2. Monetary policy. I. Siklos, Pierre L., 1955–
II. Bohl, Martin T. III. Wohar, Mark E. IV. Title.
HG1811.C4785 2010
332.1′1–dc22 2010000464

ISBN 978-1-107-61649-3 Paperback

From PLS to Nancy, James, and Patrick, as always.

From MTB to Melanie, Hannah, and Alexander.

From MEW to my parents, who have provided me with constant encouragement throughout my life.

Contents

Tables, Figures, and Appendices

TABLES

FIGURES

APPENDICES

Contributors

Martin T. Bohl, Westfälische Wilhelms-Universität, Münster

Georgios E. Chortareas, University of Athens, Athens

Carin van der Cruijsen, De Nederlandsche Bank and University of Amsterdam, Amsterdam

Sylvester C. W. Eijffinger, CentER, Tilburg University, Tilburg

Vitor Gaspar, Banco de Portugal, Lisbon

Charles A. E. Goodhart, London School of Economics, London

Bernd Hayo, Philipps University, Marburg

Carsten Hefeker, University of Siegen, Siegen

Corrinne Ho, Bank for International Settlements, Basel

Philipp Maier, Bank of Canada, Ottawa

Donato Masciandaro, Bocconi University, Milan

David G. Mayes, University of Auckland, Auckland

Stephen M. Miller, University of Nevada, Las Vegas

Marc Quintyn, International Monetary Funds, London

Pierre L. Siklos, Wilfrid Laurier University

Frank Smets, European Central Bank, Frankfurt

Michael W. Taylor, Hong Kong Monetary Authority, Hong Kong

Dimitri P. Tsomocos, Oxford University, Oxford

David Vestin, European Central Bank, Frankfurt

Mark E. Wohar, University of Nebraska–Omaha, Omaha

Geoffrey E. Wood, Cass Business School, London

Preface

The chapters in this collection attempt to survey and analyze some of the key issues in central banking as of early 2009. Clearly, the ongoing global financial crisis has, as this is written, raised a whole set of new questions that are likely to be debated for years to come. Nevertheless, readers will notice that, in 2007, when a conference entitled "Frontiers in Central Banking" was held in Budapest at the National Bank of Hungary, the various papers, most of which appear in the present volume, already began to debate the larger questions of concern to central banks then and to monetary policy more generally today. Issues thought to be resolved, such as the role of central bank independence, have again resurfaced, as demonstrated by debate in the U.S. Congress over Federal Reserve Bank actions in 2008 and 2009, and how to hold that institution more accountable. As this book went to press, a bill was making its way through the U.S. Congress requiring the Fed to become more transparent. The state of the art as it pertains to central bank transparency is also addressed in the present volume. Other "big" questions, still unresolved, such as how to think about financial-system stability, its measurement, and its implications, are also front and center in this volume, as is the future of a monetary policy strategy focused on delivering low and stable inflation and the prospects of replacing it with price-level targeting. Finally, to name one more pressing issue on the minds of academics and politicians everywhere, how to regulate and supervise banks, and the tension between the aims of preserving national sovereignty over these issues while acknowledging the push for global reforms, is also considered in some of the chapters in this book.

It would be presumptuous, of course, to suggest that the editors and contributors were prescient about all the dilemmas that face policymakers today in the area of monetary policy. That would be asking too much. Nevertheless, the contents of this volume provide material that should permit

interested readers to better understand which major issues currently challenge central banks and monetary policy more generally, to get a glimpse of
where we stand, and to become more aware of several of the larger questions
that need to be addressed in future research. Hopefully, this is a modest goal
that has been met.

There are, of course, too many people to thank for ensuring that this
book saw the light of day. Scott Parris of Cambridge University Press was
steadfast in his support for the topics covered and ensured that the necessary
and helpful reviews took place. The many referees were constructive in
their criticisms. The editors can only hope that the end product meets their
approval and that we can expect the same from the rest of the profession.
The editors are also grateful to various institutions, including the National
Bank of Hungary (NBH) and, especially, György Szapári, former Deputy-
Governor of the NBH, for helping underwrite an international conference
where early drafts of the chapters in this book could be presented and
debated. Last, but not least, many thanks to Susanne Thiemann, who has
helped us with the reference lists, the index, and the galleys.

Pierre L. Siklos, Waterloo, Canada, June 2009
Martin T. Bohl, Wallersdorf, Germany, June 2009
Mark E. Wohar, Omaha, U.S.A., June 2009

The State of Play in Central Banking and the Challenges to Come

Pierre L. Siklos, Martin T. Bohl, and Mark E. Wohar

1.1 Introduction

In 2006, the editors conceived the idea of holding a high-level conference to assess the state of play in central banking. At the time, the world economy was in the midst of what has come to be called the "Great Moderation" (Bernanke 2004). We felt that it was high time to take a step back and consider how central banking evolved over the past 20 years or so and the challenges that lay ahead for monetary policy. Little did we know that, soon after the conference – which was co-organized with the National Bank of Hungary – ended, we would enter a global financial crisis, which, as this is written, is still ongoing.[1] Therefore, it is perhaps even more appropriate now not only to take stock of what has been accomplished and the lessons learned, but, perhaps equally importantly, to look ahead and consider what the future of monetary policy might be governed by.

At no time has the performance of central banks been more in evidence than in the last decade. Many central banks have embraced inflation targeting. Nevertheless, central bank behavior around the world differs in a number of respects (e.g., Siklos 2008, and references therein). These differences call for an up-to-date assessment of central banking. This book brings together some of the top researchers in the area of central banking; the chapters emphasize some of the most pressing issues in monetary policy today. The topics covered include the present challenges facing central banks, namely the role of price stability, transparency, governance,

---

[1] Details about the original papers presented at the conference are available at http://www.wlu.ca/viessmann/html_pages/MNB.htm. The conference was jointly organized by the Viessmann European Research Centre at Wilfrid Laurier University, the Chair of Monetary Economics at the Westfälische Wilhelms-University, Münster, and the National Bank of Hungary, which graciously hosted the conference in May 2007.

central bank independence (CBI), the conduct of monetary policy, financial stability, the importance of monetary policy rules, and supervision.

The book is divided into three parts. Part I examines the conduct of monetary policy in the past, present, and future. Part II considers the scope and limits of central banking. Part III explores transparency and governance in central banking. This book takes a comprehensive look at and debates some of the most important questions in the economics of modern central banking. The various chapters offer a mix of new research and a general survey of issues faced by central banks today. It is also hoped, of course, that the contents of this book will provide a launching pad for future scholarly research in this field.

1.2 Part I: Past, Present, and Future in the Conduct of Monetary Policy

Vitor Gaspar, Frank Smets, and David Vestin provide an overview of the case for price-level path stability (PLPS), also referred to as the policy of price-level targeting, in Chapter 2. A number of authors have argued that price-level stability induces increased volatility in inflation and in the output gap when compared with a regime of inflation targeting. However, Svensson (1999) shows that, under rational expectations, price-level targeting can lead to lower inflation and output variability. Clarida et al. (1999) and Svensson and Woodford (2005) have shown that in a new Keynesian model, optimal monetary policy under commitment leads to a stationary price level. The idea here is that when a central bank commits itself to price-level stability, rational expectations become an automatic stabilizer.

Using a standard hybrid new Keynesian model similar to that described in Woodford (2003), Gaspar, Smets, and Vestin argue that price-level stability provides a framework for monetary policy under commitment. Gali and Gertler (1999) and Gali, Gertler, and Lopez-Salido (2001) show that such a hybrid new Keynesian–Phillips curve fits the actual inflation process in the United States and in the euro area quite well. Gaspar, Smets, and Vestin present two main arguments in favor of a PLPS regime. First, under rational expectations, price-level stability leads to macroeconomic stability in general by making expectations operate like automatic stabilizers. Second, a PLPS regime implies that changes in the price-level act like an intertemporal adjustment mechanism, reducing the magnitude of required changes in nominal interest rates. The commitment to price-level stability helps to lessen the restrictions posed by the lower bound on nominal interest rates. The arguments made in favor of PLPS are dependent on endogenous expectations. The stabilizing effect of PLPS on nominal interest rates stems from the fact that fewer adjustments to policy rates are necessary. Consequently, the frequency with which the lower bound on nominal interest rates is attained for a given inflation target is also diminished. When the nominal rate is at zero, the price level will continue to operate as an automatic stabilizer.

Gaspar, Smets, and Vestin also review the arguments against PLPS. First, PLPS is costly when there is imperfect credibility. It has been argued that the determination of whether PLPS is beneficial depends on the credibility of the reversion to the price level. Numerous papers have argued that the benefits of price-level stability are close to zero when the degree of credibility of the monetary policy regime is low, or expectations are backward looking rather than forward looking. A related argument against PLPS is that the transition costs of moving to such a regime are too large in the presence of private sector learning. A second argument against PLPS stems from uncertainty and ongoing learning about the economy by the central bank. Policymakers make mistakes that lead to greater volatility in the price level. Hence, price-level stability makes past policy mistakes very costly to reverse. Gaspar, Smets, and Vestin point out, however, that the above argument does not take into account the positive effects that PLPS may have on expectation formation by the private sector in response to central bank mistakes. They point out that Aoki and Nikolov (2005) find that the benefits of price-level targeting are increased rather than reduced when the central bank faces uncertainty about the economy. These results are also confirmed by Orphanides and Williams (2007).

In spite of the obvious desirability of adopting a monetary policy strategy geared toward achieving price-level stability, there are few indications that any central bank will adopt such a regime any time soon. Although the topic of PLPS is on the research agenda at the Bank of Canada, as it prepares to discuss the renewal of the inflation control objective in 2011, there exists a number of practical hurdles that stand in the way of adopting such a policy. First, the case for PLPS is less well analyzed in the open economy case and, as Parkin (2009) points out, it is unclear whether there is sufficient consensus among politicians, let alone economists, on the inherent superiority of this monetary regime. Second, it is unclear what the implications would be for a country that ends up being the first adopter of this form of price-level targeting while the rest of the world does not. Third, much though not all (as the authors make clear) of the theoretical rationale is based on the current canonical new Keynesian model that lacks a financial sector, let alone allowing for the possibility of a financial crisis. Although some advances have recently been made in this direction (e.g., Cúrdia and Woodford 2008), it is still generally the case that financial crises are only permitted to exogenously influence existing models.

In Chapter 3, Georgios E. Chortareas and Stephen M. Miller point out that recent studies of central banking have raised the issue of the endogeneity of the central bank's decision-making process. This work has focused on institutional structure and incentive constraints. A large body of research deals with attempts to lessen the time-inconsistency problem and related political-economy problems. This research has implications for the institutional framework of central banks (e.g., accountability, transparency) and the delegation process (e.g., inflation targeting, conservatism, incentive contracts). Berger et al. (2001) discuss the difference between CBI and central bank conservatism. Conservatism reflects the weight that the central bank places on controlling inflation relative to output fluctuations. Independence reflects the importance of central bank preferences (as opposed to society's preferences) in determining monetary policy. Chortareas and Miller adopt the principal-agent approach to central banking and discuss its relationship to other institutional designs that attempt to eliminate the time-inconsistency problem, where the principal is the government and the society and the agent is the central bank. They also present an extensive review of the literature on central bank contracts and discuss the related equivalence propositions, as well as presenting some new approaches that focus on the optimality of delegation versus the consistency of delegation.

Chortareas and Miller review the literature that offers proposed solutions to the time-inconsistency problem, which include conservative central bankers, inflation targeting, and explicit contracts. Much of this literature focuses on design of policy rules and shows how these rules dominate discretionary policy. There continues to be an ongoing debate on the issues (e.g., Athey et al. 2005; Persson et al. 2006). Even if a central bank adopts a rule, there is still the problem of commitment. Delegation of such a rule can address the commitment issue.

Chortareas and Miller's modeling framework yields some interesting findings. First, they find that granting independence to the central bank may or may not achieve optimal outcomes. The outcome depends on the objective function of the central bank. Indeed, one aspect of the specification of a central bank objective function not considered is the possibility of interest rate smoothing, evincing a concern for real exchange movements, or even permitting the discount rate of the monetary authority to change. Whereas the broad conclusions of their analysis would doubtlessly remain unchanged, the implications of alternative objective functions remain understudied. Second, the conservative central banking solution alone cannot achieve optimal outcomes. It simply alters the trade off between hitting the inflation and output targets, with greater weight placed on the inflation target. Third, the inflation targeting strategy does not achieve optimal outcomes. That is, the expected values of the target variables are not equal to the optimal outcomes. As a result, the central bank selects targets for output and inflation that are unattainable. Fourth, the explicit contracting solution (either inflation or output incentive contracts) does, in fact, achieve optimal outcomes.

Beyond the issues considered in Chapter 3, it is apparent that summarizing the "contractual" relationship between the central bank and the government omits the possibility that there exists another implicit contract, namely one between the central bank and the public. Few doubt, for example, that a "special" relationship existed between the Bundesbank and the German public while that institution was responsible for the conduct of monetary policy in Germany, and there is a strong sense that the European Central Bank is attempting to follow the same path. Finally, as will be evident to readers of this book, the theoretical apparatus employed by the authors does not explicitly consider the fact that central banks have many roles to play, including the maintenance of financial system stability and banking supervision, and that any maximization exercise will be unable to capture the richness of the calculus that central banks must actually face.

Corrinne Ho examines in Chapter 4 how the day-to-day implementation of monetary policy has undergone significant changes over the past 15 years. Ho presents an in depth and comprehensive discussion of numerous aspects of central banking covering 17 central banks. Monetary frameworks and other aspects of policy making in 14 Asia-Pacific central banks, the European Central Bank, the Bank of England, and the Federal Reserve are considered. One might well ask why a focus on central banks in the Asia-Pacific region versus the usual suspects in the rest of the industrial world. The reason is simple. This is the part of the world that has most recently undergone a fundamental transformation: in part because of the momentum generated by the changes made in the conduct of monetary policy at major central banks, but perhaps more so as a result of the wrenching impact of the 1997–1998 financial crisis. That crisis did not spread worldwide, as did the crisis of 2007–2008, but it nevertheless led to a substantial rethinking about the practice of monetary policy.

Ho finds that a number of trends in the day-to-day operational framework and the choices of instruments have emerged. For example, many central banks now express their official monetary policy stance in terms of an interest rate target. Almost all of the central banks in her study make policy decision announcements at predetermined dates. Central banks have focused on stabilizing some short-term interest rate rather than focusing on a quantity such as reserves. Reserve requirements have played a much smaller role than in previous years. Reserve ratios differ widely among countries. In a number of countries, required reserves no longer act as a tax on the financial institution. Ho finds that among more than half of the sampled central banks that impose reserve requirements, there is explicit remuneration of required reserves. A few of the 17 central banks in the sample still use quantities (e.g., reserves, M2) as operating targets.

Not all of the central banks signal their policy stance with an interest rate. Central banks that are running exchange rate-based regimes with no capital controls cannot use an interest rate. For example, policy in the currency board regimes of Hong Kong and Macao employ the spot exchange rate as anchor. Ho concludes that there are some widely used practices within these central banks, there is no unique "best" way to implement monetary policy. More importantly, central banks in both the developed and developing world continue to refine monetary policy in response to changing economic conditions.

As Ho points out, the events of 2007–2008 make it impossible to keep up with the remarkable new instruments and approaches central banks have taken to stem the implications of the severe credit crunch that has seized the world financial system. However, she helpfully provides a link to some recent developments, and these are likely to need updating as time goes on. It is also notable that Chapter 4 suggests that globalization in financial markets has not led all central banks to adopt a homogeneous set of principles. Considerable diversity remains, and it is possible that, when the dust settles, some elements of central bank operations that were better able to withstand the impact of the crisis will be scrutinized for clues about the set of policies that reflect best practice in the conduct of monetary policy.

1.3 Part II: The Scope of Central Banking Operations and Central Bank Independence

This part of the book deals with the scope and limitations of central banking. In Chapter 5, Charles A. E. Goodhart and Dimitri P. Tsomocos argue that central bankers seem to have developed a consensus about the theoretical framework for analyzing the transmission mechanism of monetary policy, and that there is considerable agreement in the profession about how a central bank should carry out its policies (e.g., an independent central bank and a target for inflation). However, there is no consensus about the theoretical framework for achieving a financial stability objective, a requirement that many central banks also have to meet.

Goodhart and Tsomocos investigate why it has been so difficult to achieve consensus on this point. First, they provide a historical outline of central banks' role in ensuring financial stability. They discuss the reasons why there has been, in recent years, such a diversity of views on the best way to ensure financial stability. They find that the institutional structure of commercial banking supervision is extremely diverse, with central banks sometimes playing no supervisory role and sometimes having full responsibility for commercial bank supervision. The authors also argue that regardless of the supervisory role, central banks must have an operational role in the maintenance of the stability of commercial banking, of the payments system, and in dealing with financial crises. Second, central banks should play a role in designing the regulations under which commercial banks operate, even if the supervision of these banks is conducted by a different agency.

Chapter 5 then investigates how one might go about developing a theoretical basis to address financial stability issues. The first main part of any theory is that a model must be based on the probability of commercial bank default. The authors then outline how such a model might be developed. Their general equilibrium model incorporates heterogeneous banks and capital requirements. In addition, their model contains incomplete markets, money, and default in a two-period framework where all uncertainty is resolved in the second period. In the first period, economic agents either borrow or deposit money into commercial banks in order to achieve a preferred time path of consumption. Banks also trade among themselves. The central bank intervenes in the interbank market to change the money supply and the interest rate. Bank capital adequacy requirements are set by regulators who may or may not be the central bank. Goodhart and Tsomocos conclude by suggesting that banking and finance have become increasingly international in nature, whereas regulation and supervision have to be based on a specific legal structure, which is at the national level. Crises also depend on how they are dealt with nationally.

Clearly, an outline of a model aimed at addressing the issue of financial system stability must omit a number of complications. That these exist will become readily apparent to readers in the next three chapters. In particular, the idea of attaining and maintaining financial system stability is partly a political-economy question. Moreover, there is the issue of how to deal with financial shocks when banks deal with several financial systems simultaneously. Finally, there is the problem of regulation and its diversity around the world – notwithstanding the attempts by the Basel Committee to aim for some international consensus on best practices that has, in spite of their best attempts, now been fundamentally put into question as a result of recent events. The sensibly defined balance sheet the authors rely on, necessitated to keep the analysis at a tractable level, does, however, omit real-world complications that have emerged as central to undermining trust among financial institutions since the summer of 2007. These complications are not easy to deal with, but at least the chapter begins by asking the right questions and providing some initial answers; elsewhere related works do not directly deal with the analysis of financial system stability in such an explicit manner.

In Chapter 6, David G. Mayes and Geoffrey E. Wood note that, for the most part, central banking remains national, while commercial banking has become international. They then investigate the problems this development creates for today's central banks. First, the authors lay out the functions of central banks to better understand which of the functions may be impeded by the internationalization of commercial banking. They focus on two major functions, monetary stability and financial stability. As Goodhart and Tsomocos point out in Chapter 5, there is no single accepted or rigorous definition of financial stability. Mayes and Wood then examine what should be done to deal with how the internationalization of commercial banking impedes central bank policies. They conclude that internationalization of commercial banking does not prevent a national central bank from carrying out the lender of last resort function by which to stabilize the commercial banking system. In addition, bank internationalization does not expose countries to financial crises.

Although explicitly pointing out that cooperation and coordination are not the same thing, Chapter 6 leaves the complications of deciding which is better when a central bank has less than complete jurisdiction over the banking and financial sectors. Moreover, as this is written, governments and central banks have embarked on much more heavy-handed interventions in the financial sector, and there are, as yet, untold implications for central banks and the renewed emphasis on their historical role as lenders of last resort. The authors do make an effort to lay out some of the broad implications of recent developments, a hopeless task under the present circumstances, but one might worry about their "pessimistic" conclusion in the aftermath of the failure of Lehman Brothers. Although AIG was rescued shortly thereafter, this puts paid the notion that central banks can and will solve a problem created by the internationalization of commercial banking.

Bernd Hayo and Carsten Hefeker begin Chapter 7 with the observation that, in the last 20 years, many countries have made their central banks more autonomous. Most economists agree independence is important because it is a device that can assist the central bank in achieving the goal of price stability (Cukierman 2006; Arnone et al. 2007). Hayo and Hefeker present a number of arguments questioning some aspects of the conventional view of CBI, and its beneficial impact on inflation control. They argue that CBI is neither necessary nor sufficient for ensuring monetary stability. CBI is just one monetary policy design instrument among many that can be employed to achieve price stability. Therefore, no one policy instrument is optimal under all conditions. They argue that CBI should not be treated as an exogenous variable, but instead attention should be given to the question of why central banks are made independent.

It is well known that the empirical literature finds CBI to be correlated with low inflation. In this book, Mayes and Wood also argue that CBI is not the only cause of low inflation. By taking the endogeneity of CBI into account, there is little reason to believe that the correlation between CBI and low inflation tells us anything about causality. Their approach is somewhat reminiscent of the argument that the success of the euro area has nothing to do with whether it is an optimal currency area. Rather, once the political will exists to introduce a common currency, the single currency area will eventually become more like an optimal currency area. Hence, the usual optimal currency area criteria are endogenous.

Hayo and Hefeker first review the theoretical foundations of CBI. They outline serious theoretical problems with the conventional argument that CBI is the optimal instrument of monetary design. Next, they show alternative monetary design instruments that can cause low inflation. In particular, they note that these alternatives are fixed exchange rate and currency boards, inflation targeting, and inflation contracts. These have more favorable (or equal) theoretical properties than CBI and have been put into practice. Strictly speaking, this is true. However, what the authors do not emphasize sufficiently is the quite small shelf life of these types of exchange rate regimes. In addition, the world has moved away from rigid exchange rate regimes to ones that permit greater flexibility. The reason seems clear. A central bank with considerable autonomy under a flexible exchange rate regime at least can choose an independent path for its monetary policy. The alternative monetary policy strategies cannot do so, even if they are able to deliver, in theory, the same inflation outcomes. Of course, a more independent central bank does not automatically imply that credibility will be established. Siklos (2002), for example, finds that the linkage between CBI and inflation has been reversed in the 1990s and is negative.

Hayo and Hefeker's main conclusion, then, is that there are alternative means of keeping inflation low other than simply via the granting of CBI. Society has to make two decisions about monetary policy. First, it must decide how important the fight is to keep inflation low. Second, it must choose the best institutional arrangement to achieve price stability. The first decision implies that CBI is not a sufficient condition for price stability because it is one of many instruments to achieve price stability. The second decision makes it clear that CBI is not a necessary condition for price stability, although it might be what some countries need.

In Chapter 8, Donato Masciandaro, Marc Quintyn, and Michael W. Taylor investigate recent trends and determinants of financial supervisory governance with special attention to the role of the central bank as supervisor. A considerable amount of research has been devoted to the relationship between CBI and accountability. Much less, however, has been written about supervision. Indeed, recent work has argued that the supervisory function is, under a variety of circumstances, best delegated to an independent agency.

One issue raised is whether it is beneficial to have monetary policy and commercial bank supervision under one roof. In many countries, the supervisory function is performed by institutions other than the central bank. Building on the work of Quintyn et al. (2007), the authors of Chapter 8 provide ratings for independence and accountability for commercial bank supervisory agencies in 55 countries. Their empirical analysis of the determinants of emerging independence and accountability arrangements indicates that the quality of public sector governance plays a decisive role in establishing accountability arrangements more than independence arrangements. The more mature a democracy is, the more likely it is that a higher degree of independence and accountability will be granted. Their results also show that accountability is driven by crisis experiences, whereas independence is influenced by a kind of "bandwagon" effect. Finally, their findings also indicate that the likelihood for establishing governance arrangements suitable for the supervisory task seems to be higher when the supervisor is located outside the central bank.

It should be clear that rules establishing good governance practices are desirable. What remains unclear is the precise relationship between a central bank on the one hand, the government on the other, and the supervisory body. A further complication that cannot be easily captured by the kind of analysis carried out here is that the financial sector has changed so greatly around the world that it is more difficult to identify firms for which the primary function is a financial one from firms that combine financial and nonfinancial roles. This not only makes the task of supervision more difficult, but it also complicates defining accountability and independence of supervisory institutions.

The authors are surely correct to point out that, whereas there is a large literature that measures every aspect of central bank behavior, there has been noticeably less emphasis on measuring and evaluating the behavior of supervisors. The ongoing global financial crisis not only sheds new light on failures in regulation and supervision but suggests that much is gained by studies of the kind undertaken here. Indeed, in addition to a focus on accountability, future research ought to go where research on central bank performance is now located, namely the role and potential benefits of transparency. Much blame has been laid at the failure of agencies of all kinds in understanding and informing policymakers and the public about the dangers of complex financial instruments and transactions. How supervision can be designed to mitigate the kinds of shocks world financial markets have been experiencing is, of course, unclear, but will be on the agenda for future research. Finally, just as Hayo and Hefeker point out the endogeneity of the CBI criteria, there is similarly an endogeneity in the determinants of good governance in supervision. The authors do mention this as a drawback of their empirical analysis; however, more effort needs to be invested in ascertaining the implications of this possibility for the estimated results presented in this chapter.

1.4 Part III: Transparency and Governance in Central Banking

The final part of this book deals with transparency and governance in central banking. Chapter 9 by Carin van der Cruijsen and Sylvester C. W. Eijffinger arguably represents the first survey of its kind dealing with the large body of literature concerning the economic impact of central bank transparency. As central banks became more independent, transparency emerged as an important issue because, as some have argued, transparency is necessary to ensure accountability. The authors first examine how the theoretical literature in this area has evolved over time. They begin with the seminal work of Cukierman and Meltzer (1986) who argue that the case for accountability is ambiguous. Arguments have been put forth in favor as well as against transparency. van der Cruijsen and Eijffinger rely on a classification of transparency developed by Geraats (2002). Transparency is classified into five categories: (1) Political transparency includes information about central bank goal(s), a formal statement of targets and institutional arrangements such as independence. (2) Economic transparency exists when the central bank reports information about the state of the economy. (3) Procedural transparency concerns the degree of openness about the procedures used to conduct monetary policy, and how the central bank presents its activities through, for example, minutes of committee meetings. (4) Policy transparency concerns how the central bank explains its policy decisions to the public and the extent to which it provides information on future policy actions. (5) Operational transparency considers openness about how well policy actions are implemented.

The findings about the net benefits of economic transparency are mixed. Transparency influences economic outcomes through its effect on the formation of inflationary expectations, which turns out to be the crucial element. The authors also review a new strand of literature that analyzes the effect of transparency on the formation of expectations and is based on coordination games (Morris and Shin 2002). Another strand of literature models decision making within committees to analyze whether more procedural transparency is wanted. On the one hand, the publication of minutes may be desirable if it leads to accountability. On the other hand, the publication of minutes may be harmful as disagreement within the committees would become public, which could threaten central bank credibility.

The most recent literature on central bank transparency examines the implications from learning behavior. This literature takes the view that the rational expectations assumption is too strong and that economic agents need to learn how the economy works. Most of the literature in this area supports more transparency because it improves learning. Hence, more transparency is better (although disagreement still exists about procedural and preference transparency). Blinder (2007) emphasizes that while one type of transparency might work for one type of central bank, it might not work for another.

Van der Cruijsen and Eijffinger then turn their attention to a survey of the empirical literature. A number of different indices for central bank transparency has been developed. All of these indices have a disadvantage in that they were computed at a single point in time and do not measure changes in central bank transparency. Eijffinger and Geraats (2006) constructed time-varying transparency indices. Dincer and Eichengreen (2007) arguably not only improve on the Eijffinger and Geraats classification but also provide a much longer time series. Unfortunately, we know too little about the substantive differences between these indices and their connection with variables, such as inflation, that define central bank performance.

Another strand of literature looks at the long-lasting effects of transparency on macroeconomic variables. With more transparency, the central bank has more flexibility to offset economic shocks because its credibility is not harmed. The empirical literature also finds that increased transparency can reduce interest rate volatility, make forecasts more synchronized, lead to better macroeconomic outcomes, and improve credibility. For the most part, however, the empirical work supports greater central bank transparency.

It remains to be seen how far transparency can go. In particular, van der Cruijsen and Eijffinger do not explore in great detail the controversy over whether the release of forward interest rate tracks represents an improvement in transparency or whether this complicates the task for a central bank in maintaining its credibility. On the basis of the work by Karagedikli and Siklos (2008, and references therein) for New Zeland and the evidence from Norway there is little reason to believe that markets necessarily expect the central bank to deliver the interest rates implicit in these data. Both of these central banks have led the way on reporting future interest rate predictions, conditional on different scenarios for inflation, and other macroeconomic aggregates. Perhaps more worrisome is one implication of the Morris and Shin (2002) hypothesis, which suggests that, as a central bank becomes increasingly transparent, the private sector will invest fewer resources in forecasting the future macroeconomy. Such an outcome is clearly undesirable, but it is too early to tell whether this is indeed the case.

Philipp Maier's contribution (Chapter 10) begins by remarking that the composition of a committee that implements monetary policy, along with the structure of the meeting, can affect the decision-making process in a substantial fashion. He notes that more than 80 central banks make monetary policy decisions under a committee-type structure. When putting together a monetary policy committee, one needs to consider its size, as well as whether voting records should be disclosed.

Maier reviews economic, experimental, empirical, sociological, and psychological studies of committee-based decisions in an effort to identify criteria for the optimal institutional setting of a monetary committee. On the basis of review of empirical and experimental studies, a number of criteria can be derived to explain how monetary policy committees and meetings should be structured. Relying on an investigation of the composition and operation of monetary policy committees at over 40 central banks, Maier finds that some central banks have taken measures that would increase the effectiveness of their monetary committees. Nevertheless, he also reports that a large number of central banks could take measures to improve their committee framework. An important finding is that the monetary policy committee of the Bank of England is the best-practice committee. On the basis of this metric, the committee structure of other central banks could be improved.

It is clear, however, that much remains to be learned about committee behavior and structure. Indeed, Maier's review makes clear that this is an area that is particularly multidisciplinary in nature. There are also a number of unanswered questions. For example, the notion that single decision-maker central banks are more dictatorial understates the governor's desire to maintain, if not improve, their reputation. Hence, it is not obvious that such structures need necessarily be less effective. Moreover, the committee structure at some central banks is more formal than others. The Bank of England's monetary policy committee is an example of a highly formalized committee structure. In contrast, the Bank of Canada, mentioned as a central bank with a monetary policy committee, is one in which the committee structure is not mentioned in the legislation and has no legal standing. In addition, it is the governor who is the sole spokesperson of the central bank. Yet, the Bank of Canada's performance in delivering good monetary policy has been stellar.

Two other considerations not emphasized in Maier's contribution need to be made. First, the adoption of fixed announcement dates has no doubt mitigated the tendency for inertia in decision making. Second, central banks may make actual decisions in the context of a formal meeting, but there is considerable discussion among committee members before the meeting, and this aspect can have a decisive influence on the outcome of a meeting (e.g., Swank et al. 2006; Visser and Swank 2007).

Pierre L. Siklos' chapter (Chapter 11) first reports that there is no clear negative relationship between average inflation and an index of CBI covering a sample of over 100 countries for the period 1990–2004. As is remarked in several chapters of this book, it has been argued that CBI alone is not sufficient to deliver an optimal monetary policy. Consequently, attention has now shifted to the governance of central banks. Siklos reports that good governance should enhance the trustworthiness of a central bank.

Siklos proposes indicators of central bank governance based on an expanded data set complied by Siklos (2005) covering over 100 countries. He uses a large set of quantitative and qualitative variables. With this data set, he empirically evaluates the determinants of trust in central banks. The testable proposition is that governance is partially determined by the particular economic, institutional, and political climate. Siklos defines these by the existence of democratic institutions, the degree of corruption, and the level of economic and political stability. He shows that a linear combination of these factors can serve as an indicator of central bank governance. The measure of trust is defined by the absolute value of accumulated inflation surprises over the period 1990–2004. The empirical evidence supports the view that many principles of good governance matter and that no single indicator of central bank behavior (e.g., its autonomy) suffices to explain inflation performance.

Indeed, Siklos finds some interesting regional differences. For example, cumulative inflation surprises are much larger in European countries that did not join the European Union. Siklos also reports that pegged exchange rates have the smallest absolute value of inflation surprises. This result is compatible with some of the findings reported by Hayo and Hefeker in this book. This implies that pegging an exchange rate regime can, under certain circumstances, increase the confidence one has in the performance of central banks. Institutional and socioeconomic differences across countries mean that one size does not fit all.

There are at least three difficulties with the evidence presented so far. First, as others have noted (e.g., Cukierman 1992), how central banks behave differs greatly, such as between developing versus industrial countries. Hence, it is possible that the relationship, estimated in a linear fashion, may in fact be inherently nonlinear in nature. Second, there have always been questions raised about the accuracy of qualitative determinants of central bank performance. These play a crucial role in the empirical investigation. Finally, data limitations necessitate the resort to forecasts published in the International Monetary Fund's World Economic Outlook. Even if the forecast record of the World Economic Outlook is a good one, the quality and methodologies used to generate these forecasts are likely to be significantly different across the world. It is conceivable, therefore, that it is not, strictly speaking, possible to rely on cross-country comparisons of such forecasts.

References

Aoki, K. and K. Nikolov (2005), "Rule-Based Monetary Policy Under Central Banking Learning," CEPR Working Paper 5056.

Arnone, M. B., L. Segalotto, and M. Sommer (2007), "Central Bank Autonomy: Lessons from Global Trends," IMF Working Paper 07/88.

Athey, S., A. Atkenson, and P. J. Kehoe (2005), "The Optimal Degree of Discretion in Monetary Policy," *Econometrica* 73: 1431–1475.

Berger, H., J. de Haan, and S. C. W. Eijffinger (2001), "Central Bank Independence: An Update of Theory and Evidence," *Journal of Economic Surveys* 15: 3–40.

Bernanke, B. S. (2004), "The Great Moderation," Remarks at the Eastern Economics Association Meetings, 20 February, available at http://www.federalreserve.gov/BOARDDOCS/SPEECHES/2004/20040220/default.htm

Blinder, A. S. (2007), "Monetary Policy by Committee: Why and How?," *European Journal of Political Economy* 23: 106–123.

Clarida, R., J. Gali, and M. Gertler (1999), "The Science of Monetary Policy: A New Keynesian Perspective," *Journal of Economic Literature* 37: 1661–1707.

Cukierman, A. (1992), *Central Bank Strategy, Credibility, and Independence* (Cambridge, MA: The MIT Press).

(2006), "Central Bank Independence and Monetary Policymaking Institutions: Past, Present and Future," *Central Bank of Chile Working Paper* 360.

Cukierman, A. and A. H. Meltzer (1986), "A Theory of Ambiguity, Credibility, and Inflation Under Discretion and Asymmetric Information," *Econometrica* 54: 1099–1128.

Cúrdia, V. and M. Woodford (2008), "Credit Frictions and Optimal Monetary Policy," Working Paper, Columbia University.

Dincer, N. and B. Eichengreen (2007), "Central Bank Transparency: Where, Why, and with What Effects?," NBER Working Paper 13003, March.

Eijffinger, S. C. W. and P. M. Geraats (2006), "How Transparent Are Central Banks?," *European Journal of Political Economy* 22: 1–21.

Gali, J. and M. Gertler (1999), "Inflation Dynamics: A Structural Econometric Analysis," *Journal of Monetary Economics* 44: 195–222.

Gali, J., M. Gertler, and D. Lopez-Salido (2001), "European Inflation Dynamics," *European Economic Review* 45: 1237–1270.

Geraats, P. M. (2002), "Central Bank Transparency," *Economic Journal* 112: F532–F565.

Karagedikli, Ö. and P. L. Siklos (2008), "Explaining Movements in the NZ Dollar – Central Bank Communication and the Surprise Element in Monetary Policy?," Reserve Bank of New Zealand Discussion Paper Series DP2008/02.

Morris, S. and H. S. Shin (2002), "Social Value of Public Information," *American Economic Review* 92: 1521–1534.

Orphanides, A. and J. Williams (2007), "Robust Monetary Policy with Imperfect Knowledge," ECB Working Paper, forthcoming.

Parkin, M. (2009), "What Would an Ideal Monetary Regime Look Like?," C.D. Howe Commentary, 279.

Persson, T., M. Persson, and L. E. O. Svensson (2006), "Time Consistency of Fiscal and Monetary Policy: A Solution," *Econometrica* 74: 193–212.

Quintyn, M., S. Ramirez, and M. W. Taylor (2007), "The Fear of Freedom. Politicians and the Independence and Accountability of Financial Supervisors," in D. Masciandaro and M. Quintyn (Eds.), *Designing Financial Supervision Institutions: Independence, Accountability and Governance* Cheltenham: Edward Elgar.

Siklos, P. L. (2002), *The Changing Face of Central Banking* (Cambridge: Cambridge University Press).

(2005), "Varieties of Central Bank – Executive Relationships," *Current Developments in Monetary and Financial Law*, Washington, International Monetary Fund.

(2008), "Inflation Targeting Around the World," *Emerging Markets Finance and Trade* 44 (November/December): 5–16.

Svensson, L. E. O. (1999), "Price Level Targeting versus Inflation Targeting: A Free Lunch?," *Journal of Money, Credit and Banking* **31**: 277–295.

Svensson, L. E. O. and M. Woodford (2005), "Implementing Monetary Policy Through Inflation-Forecast Targeting," in B. Bernanke and M. Woodford (Eds.) *The Inflation Targeting Debate* (Chicago: University of Chicago Press).

Swank, J., O. Swank, and B. Visser (2006), "Transparency and Premeetings," Tinbergen Institute Discussion Papers 06–054/1.

Visser, B. and O. Swank (2007), "On Committees of Experts," *Quarterly Journal of Economics* **122**(1): 337–372.

Woodford, M. (2003), *Interest and Prices* (Princeton, NJ: Princeton University Press).

PART I

PAST, PRESENT, AND FUTURE IN THE CONDUCT OF MONETARY POLICY

2

Is the Time Ripe for Price-Level Path Stability?

Vitor Gaspar, Frank Smets, and David Vestin

Abstract

In this chapter we provide a critical and selective survey of arguments relevant for the assessment of the case for price-level path stability (PLPS). Using a standard, hybrid new Keynesian model, we argue that price-level stability provides a natural framework for monetary policy under commitment. There are two main arguments in favor of a PLPS regime. First, it helps overall macroeconomic stability by making expectations operate like automatic stabilizers. Second, under a PLPS regime, changes in the price level operate like an intertemporal adjustment mechanism, reducing the magnitude of required changes in nominal interest rates. Such a property is particularly relevant as a means to alleviate the importance of the zero bound on nominal interest rates. We also review and discuss the arguments against PLPS. Finally, we also demonstrate, using the Smets and Wouters (2003) model that includes a wide variety of frictions and is estimated for the euro area, that the price level is stationary under optimal policy under commitment for a particular loss function. Specifically, the results obtained when the quasi-difference of inflation is used in the loss function, as in the hybrid new Keynesian model. Overall, the arguments in favor of or against PLPS depend upon the degree of dependence of private-sector expectations on the characteristics of the monetary policy regime.

For helpful comments and suggestions the authors would like to thank David Andolfatto, Tassos Belesiotis, Larry Christiano, Charles Goodhart, Lars Jonung, Robert King, Andy Levin, Tiff Maklem, Athanasios Orphanides, Pierre Siklos, Pedro Teles, Robert Tetlow, and Tony Yates. The views expressed in this paper are solely our own and do not reflect those of the European Central Bank, the Banco de Portugal or the Eurosystem's. E-mail addresses: vgaspar@bportugal.pt; frank.smets@ecb.int; david.vestin@ecb.int. We thank Rossana Merola for excellent research assistance.

2.1 Introduction

According to the conventional wisdom in central banking circles, PLPS is not an appropriate goal to delegate to an independent central bank. There is strong intuition behind this claim. The idea is that, under a regime of PLPS, a shock to the price level that causes temporary above-average inflation must be followed by a correction implying below-average inflation, and vice versa. The use of monetary policy to move around inflation in order to stabilize the price level implies an increase in the volatility of inflation. Moreover, in the presence of price and wage stickiness, moving around inflation requires pushing output above or below potential, as the case may be. Hence, the intuition goes, PLPS would induce increased volatility of inflation and output gaps, compared to a regime of inflation targeting. The common practice of letting bygones be bygones is, thus, justified. This consensus was, for example, reflected in the paper contributed by Stanley Fisher to the conference celebrating the tercentenary of the Bank of England in 1994, where he said: "Price level targeting is thus a bad idea, one that would add unnecessary short-term fluctuations to the economy." The trade-off between low frequency price (level) variability and higher frequency inflation and output (gap) volatility was also found in a number of small macroeconomic models developed in the 1990s (e.g., Lebow et al. 1992; Fillion and Tetlow 1994; Laxton et al. 1994; Haldane and Salmon 1995).

As noted in the preceding discussion, the main difference between inflation targeting and price-level path targeting is the relevance each gives to past departures from target. Under inflation targeting, bygones are bygones. Past deviations from target are effectively ignored. If there is some impulse leading to a one-off jump to the price level, there is no effort to reverse it. Instead, inflation targeting aims at bringing projected (and actual) inflation back to target. Thus, under an inflation-targeting regime it should be true that over a sufficiently long period, average inflation comes close to target inflation. Such outcome requires symmetric random shocks and a monetary policy authority that consistently and symmetrically aims at the target. Nevertheless, the uncertainty about the price level would rise without limit. This is also illustrated by the recent experience of central banks like the Sveriges Riksbank, the Bank of Canada, and the European Central Bank (ECB), each of which has defined price stability with reference to an annual increase of consumer prices by 2%. Figure 2.1 plots the development of the consumer price level in each of those three economies since 1999 (when the ECB was established). The average inflation rate over the period from 1999

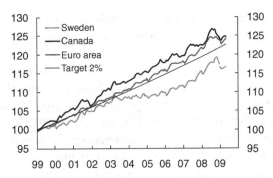

Figure 2.1. Consumer prices in Canada, the euro area, and Sweden since 1999
Note: In each case, the price index refers to the headline index. The solid line is the 2% target; the top line is Canada; the middle line is the euro area; and the bottom line is Sweden.

to 2006 is indeed very close to 2% in each of those economies. However, the uncertainty about the price level over a period of 8 years is much higher, as highlighted by the range of price levels at the end of 2006.

In contrast, under a price-level path target, the monetary authority would consistently aim at correcting deviations from target.[1] In cases where the price level is above the price-level norm, monetary policy aims at a lower than average inflation rate for a period of time; in cases where it is below the norm, monetary policy aims at an above-average inflation rate.[2,3] Under such a regime, both average inflation and the price level would be well anchored at low frequencies. Low uncertainty over long horizons may be crucial for long-term financial planning for home purchase or retirement.

[1] The price-level target can be defined as a deterministically increasing price path. A case for literal price-level stability may be based on the analogy with the system of weights and measures. It relates to the use of money as a unit of account. A very powerful formulation is due to Leblanc (1690): "If there is something in the world that ought to be stable it is money, the measure of everything that enters the channels of trade. What confusion would not be in a state where weights and measures frequently changed? On what basis and with what assurance would a person deal with another, and which nations would come to deal with people who lived in such disorder?"

[2] Average here refers to the average inflation rate implicit in the definition of the normative price-level path.

[3] In a recent report on the Riksbank's monetary policy, Giavazzi and Mishkin (2006) suggest that following the persistent undershooting of the inflation target in Sweden, monetary policy should lean toward more expansionary policy. In his reply, Ingves (2006) stated that a time-varying inflation target would be too difficult to communicate, and that it would complicate inflation expectation formation and may make it more difficult to anchor expectations. A price-level target would be a natural way of implementing such a policy.

Such a line of enquiry would lead to a number of questions such as: How important are the benefits from low, long-term price-level uncertainty? Would price-level stability make a difference for the use of long-term debt contracts or the duration of investment projects?[4] These are interesting and important questions. They are also beyond the scope of this chapter.[5]

Instead, the path that we wish to pursue stems from Svensson (1999), Svensson and Woodford (2005), and Clarida et al. (1999). Svensson (1999) was the first to emphasize that, under rational expectations, price-level targeting might lead to lower inflation and to identical output variability. Price-level targeting would, thus, deliver a free lunch. The intuition is that, within a model that incorporates a Lucas-supply function, delegating a price-level target to a central bank helps solve the time inconsistency problem. The argument put forward by Svensson (1999) is very strong and, hence, persuasive. It implies that, even if society does not care about price stability per se, it may still be well advised to focus on price-level stability. Moreover, Clarida et al. (1999) and Svensson and Woodford (2005) have shown that in a simple new Keynesian model, optimal monetary policy under commitment leads to a stationary price level.[6] The intuition is clear: When the central bank is committed to stabilizing the price level, rational expectations become automatic stabilizers. The mechanism operates as follows. Assume that a deflationary or disinflationary disturbance leads to a fall in the price level relative to target. Economic agents observing the shock understand that the central bank will correct the disturbance through higher inflation than otherwise in the near future. As a result, inflation expectations increase, helping to mitigate the initial impact of the deflationary shock, spreading it over time, and contributing to overall stability. Under a credible regime implying reversion in the price level, inflation expectations operate as automatic stabilizers. The beneficial impact of a credible price-level target on current inflation and inflation expectations was typically lacking in the analysis with the backward-looking models mentioned previously.

---

[4] Similar questions are raised in Bank of Canada (2006).

[5] On July 3, 1933, U.S. President Roosevelt stated his commitment to long-run price stability in no uncertain terms: "The United States seeks the kind of dollar which a generation hence will have the same purchasing power and debt paying power as the dollar we hope to attain in the near future." The address was a wireless communication to the World Economic Conference that had started on June 12, in London (available from http://www.presidency.ucsd.edu/?pid=14679). It is clear from other documents that Roosevelt aimed at inflating the economy after a period of deflation. Such a goal is much easier to attain in case mean reversion is a permanent feature of the policy regime. See McCallum (2005).

[6] See the monumental Woodford (2003) for a complete presentation.

The new Keynesian model is currently the main workhorse for monetary policy analysis. Its relevant friction, leading to monetary nonneutrality, is sticky prices and/or wages. The main alternative, as given in the literature, is sticky information. Ball et al. (2005) explore a model that belongs to this class with foundations rooted in behavioral economics. Interestingly, they find that optimal monetary policy stabilizes the price-level path in response to demand and productivity shocks. In general terms, optimal monetary policy, in their model, may be characterized as flexible targeting of the price level.

Our objective in this chapter is modest. In the next section, we review the case in favor of price-level stability, using a standard, hybrid new Keynesian–Phillips curve, which, following the seminal book by Woodford (2003), has become the workhorse in most monetary policy analysis.[7] We follow Svensson (1999) and assume that society does not care about price stability per se. In this setup, we first explain in Section 2.1 how the optimal monetary policy under commitment is characterized by mean reversion in the price level, and how assigning a price-level stability objective can implement the first-best monetary policy as in Vestin (2006) and Roisland (2006). In Section 2.2.2, we then turn to the argument that anchoring inflation expectations by means of price-level targets could also help to address the problem posed by the zero lower bound on interest rates.[8] This follows the early intuition of Duguay (1994) and Coulombe (1997), that is, announcing a target path for the price level would help promote expectations of a future rebound in inflation, even in the event that the economy should fall into a lower-bound situation, which would in turn help resist deflation and a profound downturn in the first place. Wolman (2003) and Eggertson and Woodford (2003) make this case in the context of a version of the New Keynesian model discussed in Section 2.2.1.[9] Finally, in Section 2.2.3 we use the Smets and

---

[7] For another recent review, see Ambler (2007).

[8] In the context of the renewal of its Inflation Control Target on November 23, 2006, the Bank of Canada (2006) mentions this argument as one of the main reasons for studying the relative merits of specifying a price-level target as opposed to an inflation target.

[9] A related argument that we do not discuss is that price-level stability reduces the risk of a debt-deflation spiral. While deeper and more efficient financial markets allow households and firms to better smooth their expenditure patterns and hedge against the various risks to which they are subjected, they also lead to higher indebtedness of certain agents, making them more sensitive to unexpected changes in both asset and goods prices. If such unexpected asset price collapses lead to deflationary expectations and falling prices, the real debt burden will typically further rise and a Fisherian debt-deflation spiral could start. A focus on price-level stability ensures that the real redistribution due to nominal shocks will be (perceived as) temporary and may thereby reduce the probability of a debt

Wouters (2003) model to show that the price level remains stationary if the central bank minimizes an ad-hoc loss function under commitment, even in a model that includes a wide variety of frictions and is estimated for the euro area. The result obtained with the quasi-difference of inflation is used in the loss function, as in the hybrid new Keynesian model.

In Section 2.3 we then turn to investigating two arguments that have been used against the case for price-level targeting. First, the superior performance of price-level stability crucially hinges on the (assumed) credibility of the reversion in the price level. It is argued that if expectations are mainly backward looking, the additional benefits of price-level stability will be small.[10] Moreover, the transitional costs of establishing the credibility of a regime of PLPS may be too large. We address these issues in Section 2.3.1 by extending the basic new Keynesian framework with adaptive learning. A second argument is that the benefits of price-level targeting depend too much on unrealistic assumptions regarding central bankers' ability to control the price level. The idea here is that, because of uncertainty about the state and the functioning of the economy, policymakers make mistakes and generate volatility in the price level. Under price-level targeting, they will be forced to create additional volatility in the real economy in order to undo the effects of their own mistakes on the price level. In Section 2.3.2, we rely on recent results by Aoki and Nikolov (2006) to address this issue. Finally, Section 2.4 contains our main conclusions.

Before turning to the analyses in Sections 2.2 and 2.3, it is worth recalling that the current focus in central banking on stabilizing inflation rather than the price level is a relatively new phenomenon that arose in the wake of the Great Inflation of the 1970s. One could argue that price-level stability is the natural fiduciary alternative to the commodity standards of the pre-World War II economies.[11] Research on the gold standard shows that in this period, the price level was indeed mean reverting, and that periods of falling prices were not necessarily associated with lower output growth or higher output losses. Indeed, Bordo and Redish (2003) and Bordo et al. (2004) have demonstrated that deflations in the pre-1914 classical gold standard period in the United Kingdom and Germany were primarily driven by productivity-driven increases in aggregate supply. For the United States, these results generally prevail with the exception of a banking panic that induced a

---

deflation spiral. Of course, the importance of this argument will also depend on the source of the shocks.

[10] See, for example, Barnett and Engineer (2000).

[11] The monetary literature of the early days of the twentieth century (Fisher, Keynes, and Wicksell) shows as much.

demand-driven deflation episode in the mid-1890s. Bordo and Filardo (2004) generalize this finding to a panel of over 20 countries for the past two centuries. With the exception of the interwar period, they find that deflation was generally benign. Interestingly, Berg and Jonung (1999) argue that the adoption of a price-level target in Sweden during the Great Depression has alleviated the output losses associated with deflation in this country.

2.2 The Case for Price-Level Stability

2.2.1 The Optimality of Price-Level Stability in the New Keynesian Model

A case for the optimality of price-level stability can be based on the benchmark new Keynesian model, as, for example, in Woodford (2003). This model rests on a number of assumptions. First, the production sector of the economy is composed by a large number of identical monopolistically competitive firms. Monopolistic competition prevails because firms produce differentiated goods that are imperfect substitutes. Second, the monopolistically competitive firms are price setters. They set prices before knowing demand and are committed to satisfy demand at the set price. A proportion of firms are allowed to reset their prices at the end of each period. This proportion is exogenously given and constant over time. Third, firms that are not allowed to reset prices or adjust their prices to offset a fraction of the average price change observed in the period. Such partial indexation to past inflation is justified by the need to match the degree of inflation persistence found in aggregate data, but is not in line with microevidence. Fourth, firms that produce using labor or technology only exhibit diminishing returns. Fifth, all goods contribute in a symmetric way to the utility of the representative consumer.

The model delivers a strong case for price stability (Goodfriend and King 1997, 2001). Given the symmetry of preferences and technology, an efficient equilibrium is characterized by equal production of all goods and unitary relative prices. Owing to staggered price setting, inflation creates inefficiencies, as relative prices and associated quantities will differ across producers. Price stability restores the efficient equilibrium.

In this section, we lay out the basic model and show that optimal monetary policy is characterized by mean reversion in the price level. In other words, price-level stability is implied by optimal policy.[12] As extensively

---

[12] The benefits from price-level targeting in a rational expectations framework were first highlighted by Svensson (1999) in the context of a neoclassical framework. It shows that

discussed in Woodford (2003), under rational expectations, the set of microeconomic assumptions considered in the above gives rise to the following standard new Keynesian model of inflation dynamics:

$$\pi_t - \gamma \pi_{t-1} = \beta(E_t \pi_{t+1} - \gamma \pi_t) + \kappa x_t + u_t, \tag{1}$$

where π_t is inflation, x_t is the output gap, and u_t is a cost-push shock (assumed i.i.d.). Furthermore, β is the discount rate, κ is a function of the underlying structural parameters including the degree of Calvo price stickiness, and α (not explicitly shown) and γ capture the degree of intrinsic inflation persistence due to partial indexation in the goods market. Galí and Gertler (1999) and Gali et al. (2001) have shown that such a hybrid new Keynesian–Phillips curve fits the actual inflation process in the United States and the euro area quite well.

In addition, we assume that the central bank uses the following loss function to guide its policy decisions:

$$L_t = (\pi_t - \gamma \pi_{t-1})^2 + \lambda x_t^2. \tag{2}$$

Woodford (2003) has shown that, under rational expectations and the assumed microeconomic assumptions, such a loss function can be derived as a quadratic approximation of the (negative of the) period social welfare function, where $\lambda = \kappa/\theta$ measures the relative weight on output gap stabilization and θ is the elasticity of substitution between the differentiated goods. We implicitly assume that the inflation target is zero. To keep the model simple, we also abstract from any explicit representation of the transmission mechanism of monetary policy, and simply assume that the central bank controls the output gap directly.

Next, we solve for optimal policy under rational expectations with and without commitment by the central bank.

Defining $z_t = \pi_t - \gamma \pi_{t-1}$, equations (1) and (2) can be rewritten as:

$$z_t = \beta E_t z_{t+1} + \kappa x_t + u_t \tag{1'}$$

$$L_t = z_t^2 + \lambda x_t^2. \tag{2'}$$

Optimal monetary policy under discretion

If the central bank cannot commit to its future policy actions, it will not be able to influence expectations of future inflation. In this case, there are

---

a free lunch also arises when the aggregate supply function has the new Keynesian form with current expectations of future inflation rates.

no endogenous state variables and since the shocks are *i.i.d.*, the rational expectations solution (which coincides with the standard forward-looking model) must have the property $E_t z_{t+1} = 0$. Thus:

$$z_t = \kappa x_t + u_t. \tag{1''}$$

Hence, the problem reduces to a static optimization problem. Substituting (1″) into (2′) and minimizing the result with respect to the output gap, implies the following policy rule:

$$x_t = -\frac{\kappa}{\kappa^2 + \lambda} u_t. \tag{3}$$

Under the optimal discretionary policy, the output gap only responds to the current cost-push shock. In particular, following a positive cost-push shock to inflation, monetary policy is tightened and the output gap falls. The strength of the response depends on the slope of the new Keynesian–Phillips curve, κ, and the weight on output gap stabilization in the loss function, λ.[13]

Using equation (3) to substitute for the output gap in (1″) and the definition of z_t implies:

$$\pi_t = \gamma \pi_{t-1} + \frac{\lambda}{\kappa^2 + \lambda} u_t. \tag{4}$$

Note that in this case, inflation follows an AR(1) process and there is a unit root in the price level:

$$p_t = (1 + \gamma) p_{t-1} - \gamma p_{t-2} + \nu u_t, \tag{5}$$

where $\nu = \lambda/(\kappa^2 + \lambda)$. Under discretionary monetary policy, the price level does not revert to a constant mean.

Optimal monetary policy under commitment.
Under discretion, there is no inertia in policy behavior. In contrast, if the central bank is able to credibly commit to future policy actions, optimal policy will feature a persistent "history-dependent" response. In particular,

---

[13] The reaction function in (3) contrasts with the one derived in Clarida et al. (1999). They assume that the loss function is quadratic in inflation (instead of the quasi-difference of inflation, z_t) and the output gap. They find that, in this case, lagged inflation appears in the expression for the reaction function, corresponding to optimal policy under discretion.

Woodford (2003) shows that optimal policy will now be characterized by the following equation:

$$z_t = -\frac{\lambda}{\kappa}(x_t - x_{t-1}). \tag{6}$$

In this case, the expressions for the output gap and inflation can be written as:

$$x_t = \delta x_{t-1} - \frac{\kappa \delta}{\lambda} u_t, \text{ and} \tag{7}$$

$$\pi_t = \gamma \pi_{t-1} + \frac{\lambda(1 - \delta)}{\kappa} x_{t-1} + \delta u_t, \tag{8}$$

where $\delta = (\tau - \sqrt{\tau^2 - 4\beta})/2\beta$ and $\tau = 1 + \beta + k^2/\lambda$. Comparing equations (3) and (7), it is clear that undercommitment optimal monetary policy is characterized by history dependence in spite of the fact that the shock is temporary. The intuitive reason for this is that undercommitment perceptions of future policy actions help stabilize current inflation through their effect on expectations. By ensuring that, under rational expectations, a positive cost-push shock is associated with a decline in inflation expectations, optimal policy manages to spread the impact of the shock over time.

One can show that, in this case, the optimal reaction function can also be written as a function of past price levels and the cost-push shock:

$$x_t = -(\kappa \delta/\lambda)(p_{t-1} - \gamma p_{t-2} + u_t) \tag{9}$$

Expressing this in words, the central bank tightens policy in response to a positive cost-push shock and in response to positive deviations of past prices from its target. Moreover, the optimal policy under commitment implies a stationary price level, as long as the degree of indexation is not perfect (i.e., γ is less than one). In this case, the solution for the price level can be written as:

$$p_t = (\gamma + \delta)p_{t-1} - \gamma \delta p_{t-2} + \delta u_t, \tag{10}$$

where the expression for δ is given above.

Figure 2.2 plots the response of the price level to a standard-deviation, cost-push shock for different degrees of indexation. The calibration of the other parameters is taken from Gaspar et al. (2006) as in Table 2.1. As also shown by Woodford (2003, 500), the price level may exhibit a hump-shaped response, depending on the degree of indexation. The higher the degree of

Table 2.1. *Calibration parameters for the benchmark case*

β	γ	λ	θ	α	ϕ	κ	σ
0.99	0.5	0.002	10	0.66	0.02	0.019	0.004

Note: We justify our choices in Gaspar et al. (2006).

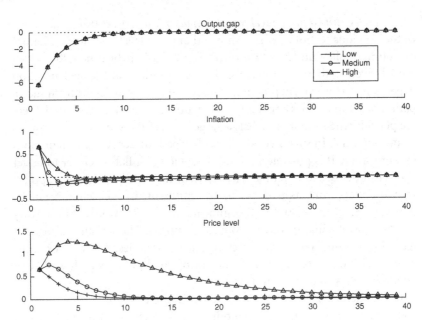

Figure 2.2. Responses to a cost-push shock under different degrees of indexation
Note: Low, medium, and high refer to the degree of indexation of prices to lagged inflation of 0.1, 0.5, and 0.9, respectively.

indexation, the more hump-shaped the response of the price level to a cost-push shock. However, eventually it always returns to baseline as long as the degree of indexation is less than one.

This feature of optimal policy may seem counterintuitive. It is often argued that if one wishes to stabilize inflation and is not concerned with the absolute level of prices, then surprise deviations from the long-run average of inflation rate should not have any effect on the inflation rate for which policy aims subsequently: one should let bygones be bygones, even though this means allowing the price level to drift to a permanently different level. "Undoing" past deviations simply creates additional and unnecessary variability in inflation. This would be correct if the commitment to correct past deviations had no effect on expectations. However, if price setters are forward looking as in this new Keynesian model, the anticipation that a current increase in the general price level will predictably be undone gives firms a reason to moderate the current adjustment of their own prices. As a result, it is optimal to return the price level to its baseline in order to reduce equilibrium inflation variability.

Delegating a price-level target to a discretionary central bank

In the previous section, we have shown that price-level stability is a feature of optimal policy under commitment in the basic hybrid new Keynesian model, even if there is some degree of indexation and lagged inflation dependence. However, in practice, there are incentives to depart from such a path. The temptation is apparent from Figure 2.2. For all cases plotted, there are periods when inflation is below target and, at the same time, output is below potential. In such periods, the policy path under commitment looks inappropriate. It is possible simultaneously to get inflation closer to target and output closer to potential. Hence, according to common sense, policy should depart from its path under commitment. In such circumstances, policymakers face the strains of commitment. In other words, it is not easy for the central bank to commit to optimal policy. There is an incentive to reoptimize as time passes and to let bygones be bygones. This is an example of the well-known time inconsistency of optimal policy, which we like to refer to as the strains of commitment.

In the literature, one of the ways to overcome the suboptimality of discretionary policy is to delegate a modified loss function to the policymaker. Such an act of delegation was initially considered by Rogoff (1985). In our context, under discretion, assigning an explicit price-level target to the central bank may be a transparent way to enforce the appropriate history dependence of monetary policy. Moreover, as pointed out by Svensson (1999), a price-level target would also eliminate any existing inflation bias under discretionary policy. Indeed, Vestin (2006) shows that, when the central bank is operating in a discretionary environment, price-level targeting outperforms inflation targeting in the basic forward-looking new Keynesian model with zero indexation. He shows that when there is no persistence in the cost-push shocks, the commitment equilibrium can be fully replicated. Roisland (2006) extends Vestin's (2006) results of the hybrid case with indexation to past inflation as discussed previously, and shows that, also in this case, it is beneficial to assign a hybrid price-level target to the central bank. In this case, the targeting rule can be written as a modified instantaneous loss function of the form $(p_t - \gamma p_{t-1})^2 + \bar{\lambda} x_t^2$, where γ is the degree of indexation as before, and $\bar{\lambda}$ is a modified weight on the output gap.[14] Finally, Svensson and Woodford (2005) analyze optimal targeting rules in a related model and show that such a rule includes a term in the price level in addition to the more traditional terms in inflation and output gap volatility. The weight on the price-level term in the optimal targeting rule is, in general, time-varying and depends on the shadow price of sticking to past promises. This time-varying weight underlines the notion that, in general, the horizon over which the central bank attempts to revert the price level will depend on the state of the economy and the shocks that have hit the economy in the past.

Intuitively, these results highlight that price-level targeting introduces history dependence and a stationary price level, both of which are characteristics of the commitment solution as mentioned in the preceding discussion.

It is worthwhile to pause to examine how focusing on the price level helps overcome the strains of commitment. The argument becomes intuitive after careful examination of Figure 2.2. Looking simultaneously at the first and third panels, it is apparent that optimal policy under commitment involves keeping output below potential, as long as the price level is above target. Hence, communication of the rationale for optimal policy under commitment becomes easier as soon as one shifts the focus from inflation to the price level. As Figure 2.2 makes clear, the time horizon associated with the return of the price level to target may be very long, particularly in the case of a relatively high partial indexation parameter, γ.

It could be argued that it is difficult to reconcile such a long-time horizon with reasonable confidence that the favorable effects on private expectations will materialize. Given such a long-time horizon it would be difficult for the private sector to figure out whether policymakers' behavior was consistent with their commitments. On this important consideration two remarks are in order. First, clearly the result presented is fully consistent with rational expectations. However, it is still possible to argue that the information and knowledge assumptions underlying rational expectations are particularly demanding under a price-level stability regime. Hence, it is important to add a second remark. Figure 2.2 illustrates how a price-level regime provides an information-rich environment. The idea is that after a cost-push shock, a relatively short period of inflation above target, depending on the degree of partial indexation, should be expected. After that, inflation should remain

---

[14] Roisland (2006) also shows the optimality of inflation targeting when there is full indexation ($\gamma = 1$).

persistently below target in order to ensure correction in the price level. It is precisely because it takes so long to correct the price level that it is possible to monitor the process of adjustment well before the eventual correction materializes. In any case, the reliance of the case for price-level stability on credibility must be taken seriously. Below, in Section 2.3.1, we find that the case for a price stability regime remains intact when the private sector departs from rational expectations and relies instead on adaptive learning. Finally, Figure 2.2 makes it clear that the adjustment path is particularly long when the partial indexation parameter is high (below but close to one). Thus, it is opportune to suggest that it is likely that a price-level stability regime would reduce the degree of indexation. Under such circumstances, the time horizon associated with corrections to the price level would also become shorter.

2.2.2 Price-Level Stability, Zero Lower Bound, and Deflationary Spirals

An important additional argument in favor of a commitment to price-level stability is related to its benefits in alleviating the potentially negative implications for macroeconomic stability of the zero lower bound on nominal interest rates. The argument is very intuitive. As highlighted by Duguay (1994) and Coulombe (1997), under price-level targeting, the price level plays the role of an intertemporal price reducing the need for variations in the nominal interest rate.[15]

To see this, it is instructive to write down the standard forward-looking IS curve that results from intertemporal consumption smoothing. This IS curve links the output gap to the ex-ante real interest rate:

$$x_t - x_T = -\sigma \sum_{i=0}^{T-1} R_{t+i} + \sigma E_t(p_T - p_t) + \varepsilon_t, \qquad (11)$$

where x_t is the output gap as before, R_t is the nominal short-term interest rate, and ε_t is a demand shock.[16] Assume now that there is a negative demand shock that reduces current output and the current price level. Under credible price-level targeting, this will generate an expected increase in the price level ($p_T > p_t$), as the price level is expected to return to its

---

[15] Coulombe (1997) gives the concrete example of his grandfather, who would decide to buy durable goods based on whether the price level was relatively low.

[16] See Svensson (2006) for a similar analysis in the context of Japan's liquidity trap.

target. As a result, for a given nominal interest rate, the real interest rate will fall stimulating current output. This will have an automatic stabilizing effect on the economy. The net outcome of this stabilizing effect is that nominal interest rates need to adjust less and, as a result, the frequency of hitting the zero lower bound for a given target rate of inflation will be less. Moreover, when nominal interest rates are stuck at zero, the price level will continue to operate as an automatically stabilizing intertemporal price.

Eggertson and Woodford (2003) formally analyze the benefits of price-level targeting in a forward-looking new Keynesian model like the one we analyzed in Section 2.2.1. When the degree of indexation is zero, the optimal targeting rule (7) can be written in terms of the price level:

$$x_t = -\frac{\kappa}{\lambda}(p_t - p^*) \qquad (12)$$

Eggertson and Woodford (2003) show that this simple price-level targeting rule does almost as well as the optimal nonlinear rule under a zero lower interest rate constraint. Under the optimal nonlinear rule, the price-level target (p^*) is time varying and depends on the length of time during which the lower zero constraint is binding. Eggertson and Woodford (2003) show that under their calibration the price-level rule (12) creates losses that are only 9% of the losses that would ensue under a zero inflation target, and only one-fifth of the losses that would ensue under a 2% inflation target.[17] Equally important, the alternative policy rule (7), which without zero lower bound would also implement the commitment equilibrium, does much worse than the price-level targeting rule. In fact, this rule does even worse than the zero inflation target rule. The reason for this is that this rule mandates deflation when there is growth in the output gap. This, in turn, implies that the central bank will deflate once it is out of a liquidity trap. However, this is exactly the opposite to what is optimal: In order to get out of the trap, the central bank needs to commit to generating higher-than-average inflation.

Overall, this analysis shows that while in normal times, the alternative ways of implementing the optimal policy under commitment may be equivalent, there are important additional benefits of communicating the optimal

---

[17] Similarly, Wolman (2003) shows in the basic new Keynesian model that a simple rule that targets the price level reduces the cost of the zero lower bound to almost zero even when the inflation target is zero. Price-level targeting rule also works quite well in the U.S. econometric model of the Federal Reserve Board.

policy in terms of a price-level target. In particular, it makes the implementation of such a target in a situation where the zero lower interest rate constraint is binding much more credible, as agents will have experienced the actual implementation of a price-level targeting regime. As highlighted previously, a credible price-level targeting rule is a particularly effective way of reducing the risk of falling into a deflationary trap when nominal interest rates are bound at zero. As highlighted by Berg and Jonung (1999), the Swedish experience with a price-level target during the interwar period may be an example of how those benefits work in practice.

2.2.3 Going Beyond the Basic New Keynesian Model

Woodford (2003, 501) has argued that the result of the optimality of price-level stationarity in the basic new Keynesian model is relatively fragile given that its welfare does not depend at all on the range of variation in the absolute level of prices. However, the intuition that a monetary policy that does not let bygones be bygones has strong stabilizing effects on inflation and economic activity, in particular in the presence of a potentially binding zero lower constraint on nominal interest rates, is very strong and is likely to survive in more general characterizations of the economy as long as expectations matter. While full mean reversion in the price level may not be a feature of the fully optimal policy in more general models, a price-level path targeting regime is a simple, easy-to-communicate way of implementing a policy that ensures an appropriate level of history dependence. Moreover, a flexible regime that allows for a gradual return of the price level to its target depending on the shocks hitting the economy is likely to reduce the costs associated with a stricter implementation.

These findings can be illustrated using a much more elaborate model such as Smets' and Wouters' (2003). This model incorporates a hybrid new Keynesian–Phillips curve like the one analyzed in Section 2.2.1, but also many other frictions, such as nominal wage stickiness, habit formation, and investment adjustment costs, which make it costly to revert the price level. Figure 2.3 shows the impulse response of the output gap, the short-term interest rate, inflation, the price level, and the nominal wage level to a 1% price-mark-up shock, when the central bank optimizes under commitment an ad-hoc loss function in the semidifference of inflation, the output gap, and interest rate changes. It is immediately clear that, in spite of the other real and nominal frictions, the optimal commitment policy again induces a stationary price level. As in the simple new Keynesian model of Section 2.2.1, the higher the degree of inflation indexation, the more hump-shaped the

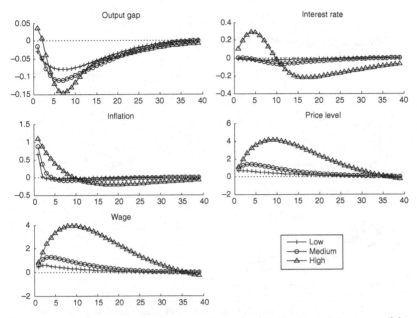

Figure 2.3. Impulse response to a price-mark-up shock in the Smets–Wouters model
Note: Low, medium, and high correspond to different degrees of inflation indexation: 0.1, 0.5, and 0.9, respectively. The impulse responses are derived under the assumption that the central bank minimizes a loss function in the variability of the semidifference of inflation, the output gap, and interest rate changes under commitment. The respective weights are 0.9, 0.1, and 0.05, respectively.

price-level response and the longer it takes before prices revert back to baseline. Note that the medium case depicted in Figure 2.3 corresponds to the empirical estimate of the degree of indexation (i.e., 0.5). Reducing the weight on the variability of the output gap and on interest rate changes shortens the horizon over which the price level is returned to baseline, confirming the analysis of Batini and Yates (2003) and of Smets (2003). Those studies also show that the horizon over which mean reversion in the price level is to be achieved will depend on the structure of the economy. For example, if the Phillips curve of the economy is relatively flat, it is beneficial to have a relatively longer horizon. Figure 2.4 plots the impulse response functions to a price mark-up shock under different degrees of nominal wage rigidity. It is clear that in this case also, higher nominal wage rigidity increases the time it takes for prices to return to baseline.

Finally, a similar reversal of the price level is also obtained in response to other shocks such as a wage mark-up shock as shown in Figure 2.5.

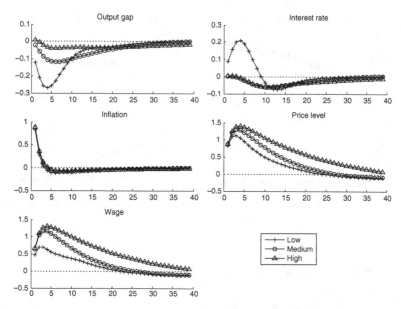

Figure 2.4. Impulse response to a price-mark-up shock under different degrees of nominal wage rigidity
Note: Low, medium, and high correspond to different degrees of nominal wage stickiness: 0.2, 0.7, and 0.9, respectively. See also the note to Figure 2.3.

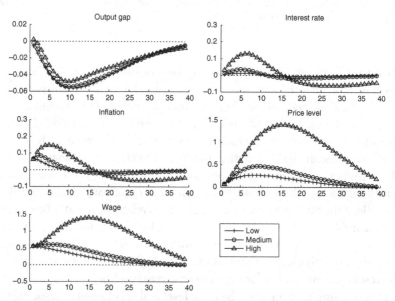

Figure 2.5. Impulse response to a wage-mark-up shock in the Smets–Wouters model
Note: Low, medium, and high correspond to different degrees of inflation indexation: 0.1, 0.5, and 0.9, respectively. See also the note to Figure 2.3.

Taking into account the differences between the basic new Keynesian model and Smets and Wouters' (2003) model, the similarity among the panels of Figure 2.3 depicting the output gap, inflation, and the price level, and those in Figure 2.2 is remarkable. It suggests that the importance of endogenous expectations is still decisive in complex environments. The intuition remains that focusing on the price level allows the monetary authority to spread, over time, the effects of shocks that create a trade-off between low and stable inflation and the maintenance of output close to potential. Many authors have emphasized the importance of lagged inflation dependence for the cost–benefit analysis of price-level path targeting. The preceding results suggest that the issue is not so much whether to focus on price-level path targeting, but how long the mean-reversion process should be allowed to take.

Moreover, it is worth recalling that the automatic indexation of prices to past inflation that underlies the lagged inflation dependence in the hybrid new Keynesian–Phillips curve discussed in Section 2.2.1 is not supported very much by the microdata. Typically, around 80% of observed prices in the consumer price index do not change in a given month. Finally, the degree of indexation is likely to be regime dependent. More specifically, it is likely that the degree of lagged inflation dependence would fall under a price-level path targeting regime.

Before turning to Section 2.3, it is also worth mentioning that a number of studies have analyzed the properties of simple policy rules that include a price-level term in large-scale macroeconometric models. One prominent example is Williams' (2000), which uses the Federal Reserve's FRBUS model and shows that a simple feedback rule applied to the price level also has positive stabilizing effects in such a large, more extensive model.[18]

2.3 Two Objections to PLPS

In this section, we discuss a number of counter arguments. We first discuss the argument that PLPS is too costly when there is imperfect credibility. A related argument is that the transitional costs of moving to a PLPS regime are too large in the presence of private-sector learning. We then examine the argument that, in the face of uncertainty and learning by the central bank, price-level stability is too costly because it forces the central bank to instill volatility in the economy following its own mistakes.

---

[18] Another example is Black et al. (1997). See also Section 3.1.

2.3.1 Unrealistic Reliance on Credibility

A number of papers have argued that the benefits of price-level stability disappear or are greatly reduced when the degree of credibility of the monetary policy regime is limited or expectations are backward looking rather than forward looking.[19] For example, in early studies of simple policy rules in an economy with backward-looking expectations, Haldane and Salmon (1995) and Lebow et al. (1992) find that feedback rules on the price level result in higher short-term variability for both inflation and output growth.[20] In a later simulation study, Black et al. (1997) show that adding a price-level gap term to the monetary policy reaction function can deliver significant reductions in the volatility of output, inflation, and interest rates if there is a small effect of the price-level gap on inflation expectations. MacLean and Pioro (2001) explicitly investigate to what extent the "free lunch" result of Svensson (1999) and others is robust to changes in assumptions about the way in which price expectations are formed and the "degree" of credibility. They model imperfect credibility as a process whereby private sector inflation expectations are a weighted average of forward-looking rational expectations, the inflation target, and past inflation. They find that, with model-consistent expectations, it is possible to reduce the variability in inflation, output, and nominal interest rate. Moreover, incorporating credibility effects specifically tied to the price-level target leads to even greater reductions in variability. At the same time, they confirm that when agents are highly backward looking, introducing a price-level target results in increased output and interest rate variability. Finally, using the policy model of the Board of Governors of the Federal Reserve System, Williams (1999) also finds that targeting the price level rather than the inflation rate generates little additional cost in terms of output and inflation variability. However, the characteristics of efficient policy rules depend critically on the assumption regarding expectations formation. In particular, the policy rule that is most efficient when the model assumes forward-looking expectations turns out to be the worst when fixed adaptive expectations are assumed. The robustness of inflation and price-level rules (or a combination of the two) is explicitly investigated in Jääskelä (2005). He shows that, if the policymaker overestimates the degree of forward-looking expectations, the optimal hybrid rule appears to be the worst performing rule. The standard Taylor rule that fails to introduce inertia avoids bad outcomes and is shown to be the most robust to model uncertainty.

---

[19] This is also the main concern raised in Bank of Canada (2006).
[20] Another relevant study is Fillion and Tetlow (1994).

One criticism of the studies these discussed is that the expectation-formation process is typically assumed to be fixed. In general, expectations formation will respond to the characteristics of the monetary policy regime. Even if expectations are backward looking, in the sense that they are based on regressions using past data as in the adaptive learning literature, the estimated regression model that agents use will change as the monetary policy regime is changed. In such a case, it is important to investigate whether the long-run benefits from moving to a regime of price-level stability and accordingly anchored expectations, outweigh the transitional costs as agents learn about the new regime and adjust their expectation-formation process.

In the rest of this section, we perform this cost–benefit analysis in the context of the basic new Keynesian model of Woodford (2003), discussed in Section 2.2.1. We assume adaptive learning rather than rational expectations, that is, agents form their expectations by running regressions on past inflation and prices. Equations (5) and (10) in Section 2.2.1 show that in both the discretionary and commitment equilibrium of the hybrid new Keynesian model, the price level can be written as a second-order autoregressive process. In a discretionary equilibrium, there is a unit root in the price level, whereas in a commitment equilibrium, prices are mean reverting. We, therefore, analyze the following experiment. Assume that agents start in a discretionary equilibrium. In this equilibrium, the estimated coefficients on the price-level process will be given by equation (5). Under the assumed calibration of Table 2.1, this implies that the first-order autoregressive coefficient is 1.5, whereas the second-order coefficient is -0.5. We then assume that the central bank decides to implement a commitment equilibrium by following a rule such as equation (9), which delivers price-level stability. Several questions can now be answered. Will the equilibrium converge to the rational expectations equilibrium under commitment? If so, how long does it take, and how important are the transitional costs?

We rely on the fact that, under rational expectations, both in the case of commitment and discretion, the stochastic process for the price level can be written as an AR (2) process (see Section 2.2.1). Thus, under adaptive learning we assume that the agents estimate an equation such as:

$$C_t = \alpha_1 p_{t-1} + C_2 p_{t-2} + \varepsilon_t. \tag{13}$$

Turning to the first question, the answer is affirmative. Using the methods of Evans and Honkapohja (2001), one can show that under the baseline calibration assumptions used above (and reasonable alternative assumptions), the dynamic system is indeed e-stable. In other words, one can prove that under recursive least-squares learning, the equilibrium will converge to the rational expectations equilibrium under commitment. This shows that even under adaptive learning (where the agents are completely backward looking), eventually the benefits of price-level stability can be achieved in the long run. This result is illustrated in Figure 2.6 using stochastic simulations for the calibrated model. Figure 2.6 displays mean-dynamics responses for our system.

From equation (10), it is clear that, under rational expectations and commitment, the autoregressive coefficients are 1.15 and −0.35, respectively. Under recursive least squares Figure 2.6 shows the estimated coefficients converging slowly to these values. As a result, the price level becomes stationary eventually.

Figure 2.6 is also informative regarding the latter questions raised above. It shows the convergence process of the estimated autoregressive parameters in the estimated price equation, as well as the mean loss incurred in the convergence process as a function of the initial gain. The initial gain will determine how fast agents learn the new regime. It can be considered as the weight agents put on past data relative to the data in the new regime. If the announcement of a price-level stability regime is credible, agents will put little weight on the past experience and the convergence will be faster.

Figure 2.6 highlights that the speed of convergence will depend strongly on the speed of learning. When a relatively high weight is put on recent new observations, the estimated coefficients converge quite rapidly. The upper left panel shows that, because of learning, there is an initial increase in the loss relative to the discretionary equilibrium (i.e., the horizontal line located at about 1.35), but after a few periods, as agents learn about the new regime, losses start falling and eventually fall below the discretionary outcome, converging to the losses under commitment.

Recursive least-squares learning may not be the most attractive learning scheme when considering possible changes in policy regimes. Figure 2.7 plots a similar experiment in the case of constant gain learning. The constant gains considered vary from 0.01 (slow learning) to 0.04 (fast learning). The size of these gains is consistent with empirical evidence on the speed of learning in the formation of inflation expectations (e.g., Orphanides and Williams 2007). In this case, there is no guarantee that the learning equilibrium converges to the rational expectations commitment equilibrium. However, in each case, the equilibrium loss converges to a loss level that is close to the level under commitment.

Table 2.2 reports the time it takes for the losses to fall below the discretionary losses, as well as the present discounted value of the difference in loss under price-level stability and the discretionary policy, for different initial

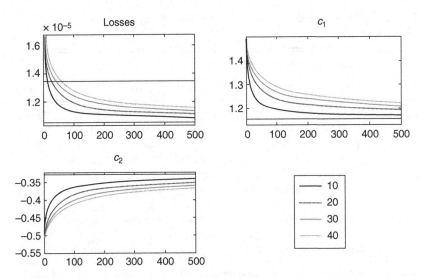

Figure 2.6. Convergence to the commitment regime: losses and estimated autoregressive coefficients

Note: The different convergence paths correspond to different initial estimation periods: $T = 10, 20, 30$, and 40 quarters. C_1 and C_2 are the recursively estimated coefficients of equation (13).

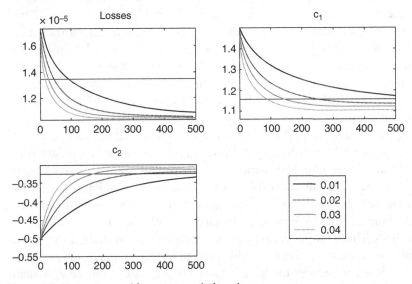

Figure 2.7. Convergence with constant-gain learning

Note: The different convergence paths correspond to different gains in the constant-gain learning algorithm: gain $= 0.001, 0.01, 0.02, 0.03$, and 0.04. C_1 and C_2 are the estimated coefficients in equation (13).

Table 2.2. *The cost–benefit analysis of the transition to PLPS under least-squared leavening*

	Initial estimation period			Constant gain			
	T = 10	T = 20	T = 30	C = 0.01	C = 0.02	C = 0.03	C = 0.04
Baseline	15	27	40	90	44	29	22
	−0.014	−0.007	−0.003	0.006	−0.004	−0.010	−0.014
$\gamma = 0.3$	13	26	38	89	44	29	21
	−0.015	−0.008	−0.003	0.006	−0.004	−0.010	−0.015
$\gamma = 0.7$	16	28	42	93	46	30	22
	−0.013	−0.006	−0.002	0.006	−0.004	−0.010	−0.014
$\alpha = 0.6$	13	22	33	78	37	25	19
	−0.015	−0.009	−0.005	0.003	−0.006	−0.012	−0.016
$\alpha = 0.7$	17	30	44	104	49	32	25
	−0.012	−0.005	−0.001	0.008	−0.002	−0.009	−0.013

Note: The first entry gives the time in quarters it takes before the loss under the price-level stability regime is lower than that under the discretionary regime. The second entry gives the discounted loss with a discount factor of 0.99. A negative number implies it is beneficial to implement a PLPS regime.

estimation periods, constant gains, degrees of indexation, and degrees of price stickiness. It is worth noting that when learning is slow (as, e.g. illustrated by the column with a constant gain of 0.01 in Table 2.2), the transition process may take very long and on balance it may be too costly to move to a price-level stability regime. However, this case is not likely to be empirically relevant for two reasons. First, empirical evidence on the speed of learning suggests that higher gains of 0.02 or above are more appropriate to describe the inflation expectations formation process. Under such gains, the net benefits are positive. Second, communication by the central bank may facilitate the transition by speeding up the learning process. In the benchmark simulation with an initial estimation period of 5 years, it takes about 7 years before the losses fall under those of the discretionary equilibrium. Similar results are obtained with a constant gain of 0.03. In both cases, the net benefit from moving to price-level stability is positive, with a discount factor of 0.99. This learning period can be shortened to 3–4 years if the initial estimation period is shorter or the speed of learning faster. A lower degree of indexation reduces the time it takes for the losses to be smaller than under the discretionary equilibrium, but the sensitivity is limited. In contrast, the duration and the net benefit seem to be more sensitive to changes in the degree of price stickiness. Increasing the degree of price stickiness to an average duration of one year lengthens the break-even period by more than a year. Clearly those calculations also depend on the assumed discount factor.

2.3.2 Uncertainty and Price-Level Stability

When the central bank faces uncertainty about the state and structure of the economy and the monetary transmission mechanism, it may make mistakes and may not be able to control the price level perfectly. One can argue that in such circumstances, price-level stability would increase the cost of such central bank mistakes, as the central bank is forced to undo their effects on the price level. When prices are sticky, this will tend to increase the volatility of the real economy.

Again, this argument is only partially true as it does not take into account the positive ex-ante effects price-level stability may have on expectation formation by the private sector in response to such central bank mistakes. Moreover, one should also take into account the positive effect of the commitment to price-level stability on the central bank's incentive not to make mistakes.

Aoki and Nikolov (2006) evaluate the performance of three popular monetary policy rules when the central bank is learning about the parameter values of a simple new Keynesian model. In particular, both the central bank and the private sector learn about the slopes of the IS and Phillips curves by recursive least squares.[21] This model uncertainty also introduces uncertainty about the state of the economy, such as estimates of the natural real interest rate. The three policies are the optimal noninertial rule, the optimal history-dependent rule, and the optimal price-level targeting rule. Under rational expectations, the last two rules implement the fully optimal equilibrium by improving the output-inflation trade-off. The optimal history-dependent rule is a targeting rule similar to the one exhibited in equation (6), whereas the optimal price-level targeting rule relates the price level to the output gap.

When imperfect information about the model parameters is introduced, Aoki and Nikolov (2006) find that the central bank makes monetary policy mistakes, which affect welfare to a different degree under the three rules. Somewhat surprisingly, the optimal history-dependent rule is the worst affected and delivers the lowest welfare. It turns out that under this rule,

---

[21] The Phillips curve is similar to the one analyzed before, but with no indexation. The IS curve is a forward-looking IS curve as in Woodford (2003).

endogenous persistence due to the rule works as a propagation mechanism of policy mistakes, particularly in response to demand shocks. In contrast, price-level targeting performs best under learning and maintains the advantages of conducting policy under commitment. It turns out that adopting an integral representation of rules designed under full information is desirable because they deliver the beneficial output-inflation trade-off of commitment policy while being robust to implementation errors. Integral control elements improve the performance of feedback rules when, for example, there are errors in estimating the steady state of the system. In the analysis by Aoki and Nikolov (2006), a rule involving integral term performs better because it reverses past policy mistakes. These benefits are even greater in a forward-looking model as they help stabilize inflation expectations.

Importantly, Aoki and Nikolov (2006) show that those benefits of responding to a price-level target continue to dominate when an interest-rate variability term is introduced in the central bank's objective function, or when inflation indexation is included in the Phillips curve. While under perfect information, mean reversion in the price level is no longer fully optimal, a rule implementing it is optimal when the central bank is learning about the model's parameter values.

Overall, the results in Aoki and Nikolov (2006) suggest that the benefits of price-level targeting are enhanced rather than reduced when the central bank faces uncertainty about the structure of the economy. These results are confirmed by Orphanides and Williams (2007). They find that a first-difference rule, which is akin to a price-level targeting rule, is a robust rule with respect to uncertainty about private-sector learning and estimates of the natural interest rate and the natural rate of unemployment. Similarly, Gorodnichenko and Shapiro (2007) argue that a price-level target—which is a simple way to model a commitment to offset errors—can serve to anchor inflation, even if the public believes the central bank is overly optimistic about shifts in potential output. Their paper shows that price-level targeting is superior to inflation targeting in a wide range of situations when potential output is uncertain.

2.4 Conclusions

We have provided a critical and selective survey of arguments that are relevant for assessing the case for price stability, that is, the case for stability around a price-level path. A regime of PLPS is most compatible with the functioning of a market economy. Intuitively, it provides a neutral numeraire allowing the market mechanism to operate fully. Therefore, it is not surprising that such a regime was advocated by classical economists like Knut Wicksell, Irving Fisher, and John Maynard Keynes, as a superior alternative even relative to the gold standard.

In this chapter, we have identified two main arguments in favor of such a regime. First, under rational expectations, price-level stability helps overall macroeconomic stability by making expectations operate like automatic stabilizers. After a positive (negative) shock to the price level, firms, correctly anticipating a persistent policy response, adjust their inflation expectations down (up), thereby mitigating the impact of the shock. Moreover, focusing on the price-level path contributes to circumventing credibility problems that central banks may face. Second, a commitment to a reversion to a price-level path helps to alleviate the zero bound on nominal interest rates. Here the reason is that the changes in the price level operate as an intertemporal adjustment mechanism. The mechanism described in the preceding discussion implies that, after a negative shock to the price level, inflation expectations adjust upward, thereby depressing real interest rates, which in turn contributes to the stabilization of the economy. The magnitude of required monetary policy action is thereby reduced.

Overall, the conventional wisdom that relies on a trade-off between low-frequency uncertainty of the price level and high-frequency volatility of inflation and the output gap disregards the fundamental importance of endogenous expectations for monetary policy making. In this chapter we presented arguments that make the case for price-level stability dependent on the endogenous character of expectations. Such arguments are of general interest as they highlight the importance of endogenous expectations for the conduct of monetary policy.

We have also investigated arguments made against PLPS. A first argument against PLPS is that it relies on the assumed credibility of the regime. Only with unrealistic levels of credibility would expectations operate like automatic stabilizers. Relying on our own recent research in models with adaptive learning, we presented examples that this is not generally the case. We showed that, under adaptive learning on the part of firms, the track record obtained under such a regime leads to a similar case for price-level path targeting. We also showed that the question of regime transition and the associated costs is important but not decisive. A second argument is that price-level stability would make past policy mistakes very costly to unwind. We referred to Aoki and Nikolov (2006), which shows that, in a model where both the central bank and the private sector are learning about the relevant parameters of the economy, price-level targeting automatically corrects past policy mistakes.

We have performed our analysis mostly within the framework of the hybrid New Keynesian–Phillips curve, abstracting from other frictions such as nominal and real labor market rigidities. Such frictions will typically increase the costs associated with reverting the price level following a shock. However, they also increase the benefits of price-level stability to the extent that the impact of inflation shocks on inflation is reduced. In particular, when agents and the central bank are learning and inflation shocks may persist and become costly to control, the benefits of price-level stability may outweigh the costs. Moreover, those costs can be reduced by lengthening the horizon for price-level stability accordingly. Using the model of Smets and Wouters (2003), which incorporates a wide range of frictions including nominal wage stickiness, habit formation and investment adjustment costs, we found that optimal policy under commitment (with an ad-hoc loss function in the semidifference of inflation, the output gap, and interest rate changes) delivers a stationary price level, as it does in the simple new Keynesian model.

Finally, it is frequently argued that a strategy based on price-level stability would be hard to communicate and to explain to the public. In this chapter we have argued that, on the contrary, a focus on the price level allows the central bank to follow a consistent communication strategy that circumvents the strains of commitment. It does seem to us that the public at large finds it much easier to focus on prices rather than on inflation. Working in first differences seems to be a common professional hazard only among economists.

There are many important dimensions that we have omitted. Clearly they are too many to list. Nevertheless, it is useful to comment briefly on two specific examples. First, in the case of constraints on nominal interest on monetary instruments (e.g., zero nominal interest on cash) then mild deflation is optimal. Khan et al. (2003) have shown that these effects induce only small deviations from a stationary price level.[22] Second, we have not dealt with the question about which price index to target.

In the class of models discussed in this paper, Aoki (2001), Benigno (2004), and Erceg et al. (2000) have shown that from a welfare perspective it is optimal to target a weighted price index, where the weights depend on the degree of price stickiness. Our conjecture is that the benefits of PLPS survive once the price index is redefined this way.

References

Ambler, S. (2007), "Price-Level Targeting and Stabilization Policy: A Review," Bank of Canada Discussion Paper 2007–11.

---

[22] We are grateful to Robert King for clarifying this point for us.

Aoki, K. (2001), "Optimal Monetary Policy Responses to Relative-Price Changes," *Journal of Monetary Economics* 48: 55–80.

Aoki, K. and K. Nikolov (2006), "Rule-Based Monetary Policy under Central Banking Learning," CEPR Working Paper 5056.

Ball, L., G. Mankiw, and R. Reis (2005), "Monetary Policy for Inattentive Economies," *Journal of Monetary Economics* 52: 703–725.

Bank of Canada (2006), *Renewal of the Inflation-Control Target*, November.

Barnett, R., and R. Engineer (2000), "When Is Price-Level Targeting a Good Idea?," in *Price Stability and the Long-Run Target for Monetary Policy*, Bank of Canada. Proceedings of a conference held by the Bank of Canada, June 2000: 101–136.

Batini, N. and A. Yates (2003), "Hybrid Inflation and Price-Level Targeting". *Journal of Money, Credit and Banking* 35: 283–300.

Benigno, P. (2004), "Optimal Monetary Policy in a Currency Area," *Journal of International Economics* 63 (2): 293–320.

Berg, C. and L. Jonung (1999), "Pioneering Price Level Targeting: The Swedish Experience," *Journal of Monetary Economics* 43: 525–551.

Black, R., T. Macklem, and D. Rose (1997), "On Policy Rules for Price Stability," in: *Price Stability, Inflation Targets, and Monetary Policy*, Proceedings of a conference held by the Bank of Canada, May 1997: 411–461.

Bordo, M. and A. Filardo (2004), "Deflation and Monetary Policy in a Historical Perspective: Remembering the Past or Being Condemned to Repeat It?," NBER Working Paper 10833, October 2004.

Bordo, M. and A. Redish (2003), "Is Deflation Depressing? Evidence from the Classical Gold Standard," in Burdekin and Siklos (Eds.), *Deflation* (New York: Cambridge University Press).

Bordo, M., J. Lane, and A. Redish (2004), "Good versus Bad Deflation: Lessons from the Gold Standard Era," NBER Working Paper 10329, February 2004.

Clarida, R., J. Gali, and M. Gertler (1999), "The Science of Monetary Policy: A New Keynesian Perspective," *Journal of Economic Literature* 37 (4): 1661–1707.

Coulombe, S. (1997), "The Intertemporal Nature of the Information Conveyed by the Price System," in *Price Stability, Inflation Targets and Monetary Policy*, A colloquium organized by the Bank of Canada.

Dittmar, R. and W. T. Gavin (2000), "What Do New-Keynesian Phillips Curves imply for price-level Targeting?," *Federal Reserve Bank of St. Louis Review* March/April 2000, 82 (2): 21–30.

Duguay, P. (1994), "Some Thoughts on Price Stability versus Zero Inflaton," Paper presented to initiate discussion at a conference on Central Bank Independence and Accountability, Universitá Bocconi, Milan, 4 March 1994.

Eggertson, G. and M. Woodford (2003), "The Zero Bound on Interest Rates and Optimal Monetary Policy," *Brookings Papers on Economic Activity* 1: 139–211.

Erceg, C., D. Henderson, and A. Levin (2000), "Optimal Monetary Policy with Staggered Wage and Price Contracts," *Journal of Monetary Economics* 46 (3): 281–313.

Evans, G. and S. Honkapohja (2001), *Learning and Expectations in Macroeconomics* (Princeton, NJ: Princeton University Press).

Fillion, J. F. and R. Tetlow (1994), "Zero-Inflation or Price-Level-Targeting? Some Answers from Stochastic Simulations on a Small Open-Economy Macro Model," in *Economic Behaviour and Policy Choice under Price Stability*. Proceedings of a conference held by the Bank of Canada, October 1993: 129–166 (Ottawa: Bank of Canada).

Gali, J. and M. Gertler (1999), "Inflation Dynamics: A Structural Econometric Analysis," *Journal of Monetary Economics* **44** (2): 195–222.

Gali J., M. Gertler, and D. Lopez-Salido (2001), "European Inflation Dynamics," *European Economic Review* **45** (7): 1237–1270.

Gaspar, V., F. Smets, and D. Vestin (2006), "Optimal Monetary Policy under Adaptive Learning," ECB Working Paper Series.

Giavazzi, F. and F. Mishkin (2006), *An Evaluation of Swedish Monetary Policy between 1995 and 2005*. Available at http://www.riksdagen.se/Webbnav/index.aspx?nid=45&sq=1&ID=yvqavr7D6_B_1C

Goodfriend, M. and R. King (1997), "The New Neo-Classical Synthesis and the Role of Monetary Policy," *NBER Marcoeconomics Annual* **12**: 231–283.

     (2001), "The Case for Price Stability," in A. Garcia-Herrero et al. (Eds.), *Why Price Stability?* First ECB Central Banking Conference, November 2000. Available at http://www.ecb.int/pub/pubbydate/2001/html/index.en.html#Jun

Gorodnichenko, Y. and M. Shapiro (2007), "Monetary Policy when Potential Output Is Uncertain: Understanding the Growth Gamble of the 1990s," *Journal of Monetary Economics* **54**(May): 1132–1162.

Haldane, A., and C. Salmon (1995), "Three Issues on Inflation Targets," in A. Haldane (Ed.), *Targeting Inflation* (London: Bank of England), pp. 170–201.

Ingves, S. (2006), Comments on "An Evaluation of Swedish Monetary Policy 1995–2005," Available at http://www.riksbank.com/templates/Page.aspx?id=23335

Jääskelä, J. (2005), "Inflation, Price Level and Hybrid Rules under Inflation Uncertainty," *Scandinavian Journal of Economics* **107** (1): 141–156.

Khan, A., R. G. King, and A. L. Wolman (2003), "Optimal Monetary Policy," *Review of Economic Studies* **70** (4, October): 825–860.

Laxton, D., N. Ricketts, and D. Rose (1994), "Uncertainty, Learning and Policy Credibility," in *Economic Behaviour and Policy Choice under Price Stability*. Proceedings of a conference held by the Bank of Canada, October 1993: 129–166 (Ottawa: Bank of Canada).

Leblanc, F. (1690), *Traite Historique des Monnaies en France* (Paris).

Lebow, D., J. Roberts, and D. Stockton (1992), "Economic Performance under Price Stability," US Board of Governors of the Federal Reserve System Working Paper 125.

Maclean, D. and H. Pioro (2001), "Price-Level Targeting—The Role of Credibility," in *Price Stability and the Long-run Target for Monetary Policy*. Proceedings of a seminar held by the Bank of Canada, June 2000: 153–85.

McCallum, B. T. (2005), "A Monetary Rule for Automatic Prevention of a Liquidity Trap," *NBER Working Paper* 11056.

Orphanides, A. and J. Williams (2007), "Robust Monetary Policy with Imperfect Knowledge," ECB Working Paper.

Roggof, K. (1985), "The Optimal Degree of Commitment to an Intermediate Monetary Target," *Quarterly Journal of Economics* **100** (November), 1169–1189.

Roisland, O. (2006), "Inflation Inertia and the Optimal Hybrid Inflation/Price-Level Target," Norges Bank Working Paper 2005/4, *Journal of Money, Credit and Banking* **38**(8): 2247–2251.

Smets, F. (2003), "Maintaining Price Stability: How Long Is the Medium Term?," *Journal of Monetary Economics* **50**: 1293–1309.

Smets, F., and R. Wouters (2003), "An Estimated Dynamic Stochastic General Equilibrium Model of the Euro Area," *Journal of the European Economic Association* **1**: 1123–1175.

Svensson, L. (1999), "Price Level Targeting versus Inflation Targeting: A Free Lunch?," *Journal of Money, Credit and Banking* **31**: 277–295.

(2006), "Monetary Policy and Japan's Liquidity Trap," mimeo, January 2006.

Svensson, L. and M. Woodford (2005), "Implementing Monetary Policy Through Inflation-Forecast Targeting," in B. Bernanke and M. Woodford (Eds.), *The Inflation Targeting Debate* (Chicago: University of Chicago Press).

Vestin, D. (2006), "Inflation versus Price-Level Targeting," *Journal of Monetary Economics* **53** (7): 1361–1376.

Williams, J. (2000), "Simple Rules for Monetary Policy," *Economic Review*, Federal Reserve Bank of San Francisco.

Wolman, A. (2003), "Real Implications of the Zero Bound on Nominal Interest Rates," Federal Reserve Bank of Richmond Working Paper 03–15.

Woodford, M. (2003), *Interest and Prices* (Princeton, NJ: Princeton University Press).

3

The Principal-Agent Approach to Monetary Policy Delegation

Georgios E. Chortareas and Stephen M. Miller

Abstract

Recent research in monetary policy emphasizes the endogenous nature of the central bankers' decision process, shifting focus toward institutional structure and "incentive" constraints. Much of this work attempts to mitigate time inconsistency, credibility, and political problems that emerge from this agenda. In this chapter, we present the principal-agent approach to central banking and discuss its relationship to the other institutional designs. We also provide an extensive review of the existing literature on central bank contracts and discuss the related equivalence propositions that emerge.

3.1 Introduction

In this chapter, we present the view that monetary policy delegation reflects a principal-agent problem between government (society) and the central bank. The principal (government) delegates monetary policy implementation to the agent (central bank). In the 1960s and 1970s, attempts by government to exploit the apparent trade-off between inflation and unemployment along the short-run Phillips curve led to the idea of the time inconsistency of monetary policy (Kydland and Prescott 1977; Calvo 1978). The resulting inflationary bias in the implementation of monetary policy prompted a search for the "holy grail of monetary policy."[1]

We gratefully acknowledge the comments of the Editors, P. L. Siklos, M. T. Bohl, and M. E. Wohar, and three anonymous referees on an earlier draft of this chapter. Nonetheless, we assume responsibility for any remaining errors.
[1] Siklos (2002) provides extensive discussion of the search for what he calls the "holy grail of monetary policy."

More recent practical and theoretical developments shift the focus away from the assumption of an inflationary bias. Monetary policy in the standard dynamic stochastic general equilibrium (DSGE) models can typically achieve full stabilization, but nevertheless the absence of an inflationary bias does not suffice to eliminate issues of monetary policy credibility. A vast literature addresses issues of monetary policy design. In this chapter, we argue that the principal-agent framework proves useful in understanding and interpreting this literature.

Recent research in monetary policy emphasizes the endogenous nature of the central bankers' decision process, shifting focus toward institutional structure and "incentive" constraints. Much of this work attempts to mitigate time inconsistency, credibility, and political problems that emerge from this agenda (e.g., Athey et al. 2005). This research effort entails direct and tangible implications for both the institutional design of central banks (independence, accountability, transparency, etc.) and the delegation process (inflation targeting, central bank conservatism, incentive contracts, etc.).

In particular, the literature on central banker contracts shows that the government can delegate monetary policy in an explicit principal-agent framework to deliver policy outcomes equivalent to those under credible commitment. Typically, an efficient punishment (transfer) mechanism exists that neutralizes the policymaker's tendency to produce high inflation by raising the marginal costs of such attempts.[2] Furthermore, when considering alternative institutional designs, monetary policy delegation schemes that incorporate a combination of contracts with either conservative central bankers or inflation targets perform better than each of them in isolation.

Researchers initially considered the concepts of central bank independence and a conservative central banker (Rogoff 1985). The conservative central banker approach implies, however, that the central banker's objective function differs from the society's.[3] Central bank independence can imply independence of targets and independence of instruments. Concern emerges, however, that the central bank may achieve too much independence unless the government maintains some additional control. That is,

---

[2] We implicitly refer to the inflation bias in monetary policymaking outlined in the classic Barro–Gordon (1983a, b) model.

[3] Several authors examine the trade-off between central banker independence and conservativeness (e.g., Eijffinger and de Haan 1996; Berger et al. 2001; Hughes Hallett and Weymark 2005), where the objective function equals a weighted average of the objective functions of society and the central bank. In our chapter, we assume complete central banker independence, in the sense that the weight on society's objective function equals zero.

the government may want to delegate targets to the central bank. In that case, such delegation must ensure that the central bank objective function differs effectively from society's. As just noted, Rogoff (1985) proposes a conservative central banker who weights the output-inflation trade-off differently. Svensson (1997) delegates an inflation target that differs from the society's target. In a seminal paper, Walsh (1995a) models central banker-incentive contracts that anchor the "compensation" to targets for inflation that differ from society's. In a subsequent contribution, Chortareas and Miller (2003b) the consider similar contracts written in terms of output. Finally, Yuan et al. (2006) delegate an objective function where the output target differs from the society's.

While only a part of the literature dedicated to solving the problem of the time inconsistency of monetary policy involves explicit contracts, the basic nature of the delegation problem requires some form of contract, explicit or implicit. For example, how does the government guarantee or enforce an inflation-targeting regime when the central bank misses the target? New Zealand came close to adopting an explicit central bank contract. They did not do so, however, because of a potential public-relations problem that could emerge if the central banker's salary rose in response to the inducement of a recession.[4] The weak aspect of this theoretical framework emerges with practical issues pertaining to its implementation. Critics frequently object that "it is too good to be true" or "we do not observe contracts, in practice." In this chapter, we argue that this view emerges only under a narrow interpretation of contracts.

We provide a review of the principal-agent approach to central banking and its relationship to the other institutional designs proposed as remedies for the time-inconsistency problem. While we provide a general introduction that summarizes the theory and policy consensus, we raise a number of issues that we partially attempt to address in the subsequent parts of the chapter. In summarizing the existing models, we extend the graphical framework introduced by Walsh (2003) in a way that allows consideration of the effects of alternative institutional designs. We discuss a number of equivalence propositions regarding the above-said forms of central bank

---

[4] For example, in an interview in Federal Reserve Bank of Minneapolis (1999), *The Region*, Donald Brash, Governor of the Reserve Bank of New Zealand, indicates that the New Zealand legislation excludes an explicit performance contract because of the potential "public-relations" problems associated with "... giving Brash a great six-figure bonus for delivering low inflation at the very time unemployment was peaking" (p. 48). In this instance, political considerations obviated performance contracts at the outset.

institutional design. One of the most important pertains to the equivalence result between the principal-agent approach and inflation targeting.

We also provide an extensive review of the existing literature on central bank contracts, covering issues such as asymmetric information between the private sector and the central banks, incomplete information about the central bankers' responsiveness to the contract, the role of contract costs for the principal, the effects of alternative contract targets, the existence of complementarities between various delegation approaches, the role of the institutional framework, and so on.

Finally, in the process of identifying some unresolved issues, we discuss some aspects of monetary policy delegation through contracts and the difficulties that emerge in interpreting some actual delegation formats in the context of the principal-agent approach.

3.2 Background, History, and Context[5]

The first central bank, the Bank of Sweden, opened in 1668 with the assistance of a Dutch businessman. The Bank of England followed some 25 years later in 1694, when the English government needed to finance a war and asked a Scottish businessman, William Patterson, to establish England's central bank. Many other European countries did not establish their central banks until the early part of the eighteenth century—France, Finland, the Netherlands, Austria, Norway, and Denmark, in that order. The United States did not establish the Federal Reserve System until 1914.

As such, central banking entered the economic scene rather late. Central banks typically received their start by financing a country's war effort for government. For most of this period, international monetary arrangements, and especially the gold standard, placed severe constraints on the central bank's ability to affect the domestic economy. In playing by the rules of the game, the central bank kept its currency's price pegged to gold and could not concern itself with the price level or output. The two World Wars and the Great Depression in the first half of the twentieth century saw the demise of the gold standard and its replacement with the Bretton Woods system.

The "inconsistent trinity"[6] among stable exchange rates, free capital mobility (i.e., no capital controls), and monetary policy autonomy provides one useful method of formalizing the constraints that monetary policy

---

[5] Portions of this section rely on Siklos (2002).
[6] Obstfeld and Taylor (2004) refer to this problem as the open economy "trilemma."

faces, given that the monetary authorities can only achieve (any) two of the trinity. The collapse of the Bretton Woods system opened the door for central banks to implement active stabilization in the domestic economy. Since then, the monetary authorities prefer the combination of monetary policy autonomy in an environment of capital movements. The first part of this new policy period experienced excessive turbulence, largely due to the two oil price shocks. The latter part of this new policy period, however, coincided with the "Great Moderation." Regardless of the reasons for Great Moderation (i.e., better policy, structural changes, and good luck),[7] it is difficult to dispute the role of "better policy" and, in particular, better monetary policy.[8] A number of key features that characterize the current institutional framework of monetary policy appeared recently, largely in response to the difficulties of controlling inflation in the late 1970s and early 1980s. Major developments include the trend toward greater central bank independence in the 1990s, and the enhanced emphasis on transparency and accountability in the new millennium.

Either including the central bank within the Ministry of Finance, which implemented fiscal policy, or requiring the central bank to keep the interest cost of the government debt low emasculated the central bank's power. The inflationary environment of the 1970s and early 1980s caused central bankers and governments to recognize the need for an independent central bank. Otherwise, the implementation of successful and proper monetary policy proved difficult, as the central bank experienced pressure from the government to serve its fiscal or political needs.

Central bank independence, however, comes with its own set of potential problems. While several issues arise from independence, we focus on one— the principal-agent problem associated with central bank independence.[9] Central bank independence involves two different, but related, freedoms— target and instrument independence. Target independence means that the central bank chooses the targets for monetary policy (e.g., inflation only,

---

[7] See, for example, Bernanke (2004).

[8] Recent economic events, however, may provide an acid test of the efficacy of monetary decision makers and their monetary policy.

[9] Eijffinger and de Haan (1996) list two objections to central bank independence—lack of accountability and policy coordination. In a democratic society, government remains accountable to the public through the ballot box. If the central bank enjoys independence from government, then it does not experience accountability to the voting public. Further, if the Ministry of Finance includes the central bank, then coordinating monetary and fiscal policy proves much easier to orchestrate. Sargent and Wallace (1981) raised the issue of policy dominance rather than coordination, even when the central bank possesses independence.

both inflation and output targets, etc.). Instrument independence means that the central bank chooses how it attempts to control the economy (e.g., open market operations, interest rate control, etc.).

The government (principal) may not know the type of central banker (agent) that it appoints. Thus, the government may not want to allocate control of both targets and instruments to the central bank. That is, by delegating targets to the central bank, the government regains some control over how the central bank operates, but at the same time, the central bank may escape from heavy-handed control by the government when the needs of government (e.g., fiscal or political) deviate from the requirements of proper monetary policy.

In sum, central bank independence proves the sine qua non of the principal-agent problem. Without central bank independence, no principal-agent problem exists.[10] The rest of our chapter considers this principal-agent problem in central banking.

3.3 Time Inconsistency, Discretion, and Central Banker Contracts

The typical model for principal-agent considerations relates to a variant of the Barro–Gordon model of monetary policy (e.g., Walsh 1995a). For simplicity we adopt a one-period model with complete information. This version of the model incorporates a quadratic social loss function in terms of the inflation rate and employment.[11] That is,

$$L^S = (y - \bar{y})^2 + \beta(\pi - \pi_0)^2 \text{ and } \bar{y} = y^n + k, \text{ with } k \geq 0, \qquad (1)$$

where $\bar{y}$ and π_0 equal the targeted (desired) levels of output and inflation. The term k reflects the expansionary bias of society and the policymaker,

---

[10] The existing literature frequently does not carefully distinguish between central bank independence and central bank conservativeness. Berger et al. (2001) outline the distinctions and develop a model that illustrates the differences. Conservativeness reflects the weight that the central bank places on controlling inflation relative to output fluctuations. Independence reflects the importance of the central bank's preferences, rather than the society's preferences, in determining monetary policy. A conservative central banker may possess no independence, if society's preferences completely determine monetary policy. In other words, conservativeness reflects the type of central banker in office whereas independence, as noted in the text, reflects the central banker's authority in office and leads to the principal-agent problem.

[11] See, for example, Barro and Gordon (1983a), Rogoff (1985), Flood and Isard (1989), Lohmann (1992), Walsh (1995a), Persson and Tabellini (1993), and Svensson (1997).

who want output above the socially optimal level. The term $\beta (\beta \in [0, \infty])$ reflects the conservatism (inflation aversion) of the central banker. A higher β implies a higher weight attached to inflation stabilization as compared to output stabilization. We also assume that the central bank directly controls the inflation rate, π.

The expectations-augmented Phillips curve depends on employment and rationally expected inflation as follows:

$$y = y^n + \alpha(\pi - \pi^e) + \varepsilon, \text{ and} \tag{2}$$

$$\pi^e = E(\pi). \tag{3}$$

For the timing of events, the wage setter and the firm sign a wage contract, where the wage setter sets the nominal wage, w, and the firm sets the labor amount, ℓ, that it hires. After signing the wage contract, a supply shock, ε, may occur. Then the central bank implements its policy decision, π, minimizing the social loss function. Because the contract fixes the nominal wage, the wage setter must set the wage rate, contingent on a rational expectation of the inflation rate [i.e., the wage setter uses behavioral equation (3)]. Finally, given the firm's decision, a certain output level emerges from the firm's behavioral equation (2). Further, we assume that the participants in the economy (i.e., the central bank, the wage setter, and the firm) view the model as common knowledge (i.e., the social loss function and the two behavioral equations of the private sector).

3.3.1 Commitment and Optimal Policy

The benchmark case assumes complete information and decisions made by one person before the game starts. That is, we assume that the optimal policy equals an ex-ante plan made by a social planner with complete information. The optimal policy and outcome for model (4) reduce to the following:

$$\pi^{op} = \pi_0 - \frac{\alpha}{\beta + \alpha^2}\varepsilon; \tag{4}$$

$$y^{op} = y^n + \frac{\beta}{\beta + \alpha^2}\varepsilon; \text{ and} \tag{5}$$

$$E(L)^{op} = \frac{\beta}{\beta + \alpha^2}\sigma^2 + k^2, \tag{6}$$

where *op* means optimal policy (commitment).

3.3.2 Consistent Policy

Given the nominal wage and the supply shock, the central bank chooses π to minimize the social loss function, yielding the following outcomes:

$$\pi^d = \pi_0 + \frac{\alpha}{\beta}k - \frac{\alpha}{\beta + \alpha^2}\varepsilon, \tag{7}$$

$$y^d = y^n + \frac{\beta}{\beta + \alpha^2}\varepsilon, \tag{8}$$

$$E(L)^d = \frac{\beta}{\beta + \alpha^2}\sigma^2 + \left(1 + \frac{\alpha^2}{\beta}\right)k^2. \tag{9}$$

The inflationary bias emerges as $E(\pi^d - \pi_0) = \frac{\alpha}{\beta}k$. With the equilibrium inflation and expected inflation rates, we get the equilibrium employment.

Compared with the optimal policy and outcomes in equations (4) and (6), the consistent policy and outcomes generate an inflationary bias (i.e., a higher inflation rate than the initial one) in equation (7) and a larger social loss in equation (9).

3.3.3 Explicit Contracts as a Remedy for Time Inconsistency

Now, consider a contract that penalizes the central banker for high inflation rates and takes the general form $[t_0 - t(\pi - \pi_0)]$ (Persson and Tabellini 1993; Walsh 1995a; Fratianni et al. 1997), where t_0 equals a constant. Recalling that the inflation rate target equals π_0, this contract penalizes the central banker for inflation rates exceeding π_0. We can write the central bank additively separable utility (rather than loss) function, including the incentive contract, as follows:

$$U^{CB} = -[(y - \bar{y})^2 + \beta(\pi - \pi_0)^2] + \xi[t_0 - t(\pi - \pi_0)]. \tag{10}$$

The relative weight that the central banker attaches to the social welfare function and the incentive contract equals ξ. In other words ξ equals the trade-off between the reward, monetary and/or nonmonetary, to the central banker and the social welfare. We retain the assumption that the central banker exhibits an expansionary bias k, and, therefore, the targeted output level equals $\bar{y} = y^n + k$, with $k \geq 0$. This form of the utility function appears in models where policymakers explicitly care about their monetary rewards. In the trade models by Dixit (1996a), Grossman and Helpman (1994), and Levy (1997), these rewards take the form of contributions to politicians. In this section, we adopt the more explicit form as described by Grossman and Helpman (1994, fn. 5).[12]

Carrying out the optimization leads to the actual inflation rate with a contract as follows:

$$\pi^c = \pi_0 - \frac{\alpha}{\alpha^2 + \beta}\varepsilon + \left(\frac{\alpha}{\beta}\right)k - \left(\frac{\xi}{2\beta}\right)t = \pi_0 - \frac{\alpha}{\alpha^2 + \beta}\varepsilon. \qquad (11)$$

The optimal marginal penalization rate equals the following:

$$t^* = \frac{2\alpha k}{\xi}. \qquad (12)$$

One can easily verify that when $t = t^*$, the corresponding inflation rate and output level as well as the variances of those variables equal those under commitment [i.e., equations (4) and (5)].

The incentive scheme $[t_0 - t(\pi - \pi_0)]$ counteracts the inflationary bias k by working as a Pigovian corrective tax. The penalization rate (t) raises the marginal costs of excessive inflation rates for the central banker. The central banker, in turn, possesses an incentive to internalize the effect of policy on expectations. Note that t^* does not depend upon the degree of the central banker's conservatism (β). The optimal penalization rate decreases in ξ, because the higher the weight put by the central banker on monetary rewards, the greater is the marginal effect of a change in t. Central bankers who deviate from the time-consistent policy, believing that they can improve social welfare, need a stronger incentive scheme not to do so. That is, a central banker with low ξ requires a higher t^* to deliver the optimal results. A high t^*, however, means that a positive inflation rate implies a more severe punishment for the central banker. These two observations imply that in a typical agency model, *the principal prefers an extremely self-interested central banker in equilibrium.* Finally, the contract marginal penalization rate increases in α, which measures the strength of inflation surprises on raising output. That is, more effective monetary policy (in the short run) implies a greater temptation for the central banker. Therefore, the principal must impose a tougher punishment scheme to maintain the minimization of deviations from the targeted inflation rate.

Figure 3.1 modifies a graph by Walsh (2003), depicting the reaction functions of the central bank under commitment and discretion. We use this

---

[12] We also normalize the reservation utility of the central banker to zero and assume that the central banker requires an expected utility from accepting the assignment exceeding or equal to the reservation utility level.

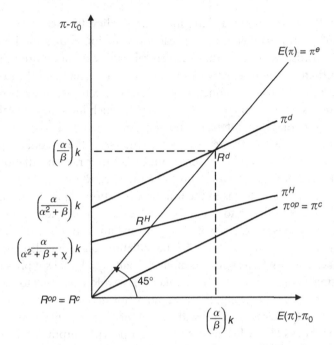

Figure 3.1. Central banker's reaction functions under commitment, discretion, contracts, and delegation to a conservative central banker.

diagrammatic tool to capture delegation to a conservative central banker and offers of central banker contracts.[13] The horizontal axis in Figure 3.1 shows the private sector's expectations about the rate of inflation. The rational expectations equilibrium occurs along the 45-degree line, where the rate of inflation π equals the expected rate of inflation $[E(\pi) = \pi^e]$. The line π^d represents the central banker's reaction function under discretion, which has a slope less than one $([\alpha^2/(\alpha^2 + \beta)])$, as the central banker increases the rate of inflation to raise output. The private sector's expectations rise, along with actual inflation. The equilibrium rate of inflation $[[\alpha/\beta]k]$ under discretion equals the point where the reaction function intersects with the rational expectations equilibrium (i.e., R^d). The term z reflects the inflationary bias and appears in the intercept of the reaction function $[[\alpha^2/(\alpha^2 + \beta)]k]$. Thus, a higher inflationary bias (k) shifts upward the central bank's reaction function, resulting in a higher equilibrium inflation rate.

---

[13] Under certain conditions, central banker contracts prove equivalent to an inflation target. See, for example, Svensson (1997) and Walsh (2003).

When the government assigns monetary policy to a conservative or "hawkish" central banker (H), the reaction function equals the line π^H. In other words, we assume that the central bank exhibits more inflation aversion than the representative agent. Both the intercept and the slope of the central bank's reaction function now fall, as greater weight gets placed on inflation stabilization $(\beta^H = \beta + \chi > \beta)$, which increases the value of the denominator in the intercept and slope parameters. This equilibrium equals the point where the reaction curve intersects the rational expectations equilibrium (i.e., R^H), which produces a lower rate of inflation, but differs from the zero commitment benchmark (i.e., R^c).

As $\beta^H \to \infty$, both terms in the inflation equation [equation (7) minus the stochastic term] tend to π_0, and the π^H reaction function approaches the horizontal axis. In other words, appointing an extremely conservative central banker eliminates not only the inflation bias, but also the central banker's ability to respond countercyclically to adverse supply shocks. Appointing a conservative central banker does avoid payments to the central banker. This cost saving, however, does not necessarily prove socially cheaper. Society's "savings" come with a "cost" of a lower ability to respond to stochastic shocks.[14] The loss of flexibility to cope with output shocks equals the "price" of credibility gains. While acceptable during "normal" times, this "price" may become intolerable when large supply side shocks occur.[15]

The reaction function of the central bank under delegation through incentive contracts (or by assigning the proper inflation target) equals the solid line π^c. The new equilibrium occurs at point R^c, which constitutes a commitment-equivalent outcome for the rate of inflation.[16]

3.3.4 Contracts and the Selfish Central Banker

We noted previously that the political principal wants to appoint a relatively selfish central banker (i.e., a central banker with large ξ). In this context, a number of issues emerge, however. Does the transfer scheme have the same

---

[14] Flood and Isard (1989) and Lohmann (1992) suggest that the appointment of a conservative central banker should include escape clauses.

[15] Lohmann (1992) suggests a nonlinear rule that requires the appointment of a conservative central banker with the possibility of replacement when such shocks occur.

[16] Svensson and Woodford (2005) utilize the Walsh contract in a different way. In particular, they consider monetary policy in the context of a targeting rule according to which the central bank minimizes a loss function through a forecast-based dynamic optimization procedure. To ensure time consistency in the optimal forecasts, they augment the loss function at $t + 1$ by a term that corresponds to a state-contingent linear inflation contract.

effectiveness for all types of candidate central bankers? Does a self-selection issue emerge in the sense that only specific types of central banker will accept such an incentive scheme?

A low t may exert enough power, but a high t may prove counterproductive. Consider the possibility of a high t that makes the net transfer to the central banker (tr) go to 0 quickly. As such, a central banker misses the inflation target early in his term. Suppose that the deviation proves large enough so that he does not believe that he can achieve enough disinflation during the remainder of his term so that the average inflation rate at the end of his term falls within the acceptable range specified by the contract. Then he does not possess any incentive to achieve the outcome consistent with the contract, leading to the discretionary outcome.

The biggest challenge identified by the principal-agent literature in central banking, however, relates to the absence of explicit principal-agent contracts in the real world. Difficulties in implementation and enforcement may explain their absence. Or, rather, the generality of the explicit-contracting approach may prove its main weakness. The equivalency of optimal contract solutions to other optimal institutional design solutions, however, proves useful in designing these other optimal institutional designs ("contracts").

3.4 Selected Literature Review

The following section provides a review of the various proposed solutions to the time-inconsistency problem—conservative central banker, inflation targeting, and explicit contracts—as well as the role of contracts when the decision process reflects incomplete information.

3.4.1 Solutions to Inconsistency of Optimal Plans

One can classify the solutions to the inconsistency of optimal plans into three types: rules, reputation, and delegation. Kydland and Prescott (1977) reiterate the need for "rules rather than discretion," which goes back at least to Simons (1936), developing an argument based on the time inconsistency of optimal plans.[17] That is, rules can provide the commitment technique to achieve optimal policy. And the literature provides many illustrations that economies perform better under rules than under consistent policy (i.e., discretion). As a result, an extant literature exists on the design of policy

---

[17] Calvo (1978) independently raised the issue of the time inconsistency of monetary policy.

rules.[18] Nonetheless, both the issues of time inconsistency and the optimal degree of discretion remain the subjects of continuing academic scrutiny (e.g., see Athey et al. 2005; Persson et al. 2006, respectively), indicating that the matter remains not yet fully resolved. Even if a central bank voluntarily adopts a rule, however, it still faces the commitment issue—time consistency. Delegation of a rule to the central bank can address this commitment issue, but we can achieve the same outcomes by delegating a loss function to the central bank.[19]

The consistent-policy equilibrium often proves Pareto inefficient. Game-theoretic approaches suggest, however, that an equilibrium outcome may prove optimal under certain conditions, if the game repeats and reputation plays a role. That is, reputation can provide a commitment technique to attain optimal policy in repeated games. Barro and Gordon (1983b) construct such a model to show that optimal policy proves implementable and consistent under certain conditions. Backus and Driffill (1985) demonstrate that reputation, based on the concept of Kreps and Wilson's (1982) sequential equilibrium, makes optimal policy credible.

In sum, the delegation of monetary policy to a central bank can occur through the delegation of a loss function or a policy rule. Whether the principal delegates a loss function or a policy rule does not depend on the ability of the loss function or the policy rule to achieve the optimal (second-best) outcomes. That is, the correct loss function or the correct policy rule leads to the same solutions. Rather, the choice of delegating a loss function or policy rule may depend on issues such as monetary policy transparency.

Compared with the outcomes of optimal policy and the social loss in equations (4) and (6), the consistent policy and outcomes generate the inflationary bias (i.e., a higher inflation rate than the initial one) in equation (7) and a larger social loss in equation (9). Two important points deserve comment. First, the two targets in the social loss function, π_0 and k, actually conflict with each other, given the macroeconomic structure in equations (2) and (3). If the central bank wants to achieve full employment, it must inflate the economy, meaning that the central bank cannot achieve the inflation-rate target. If the central bank, on the other hand, wants to hit

---

[18] The concept of a "rule" in the context of monetary policy possesses many interpretations. A "*k*-percent rule" differs from an "instrument rule," and this, in turn, differs from a "targeting rule."

[19] Delegating a loss function to the central bank proves consistent with delegating a specific policy rule. That is, the central banker decision process with a delegated loss function will produce a specific policy rule for optimal outcomes. The mapping, however, does not necessarily prove one-to-one. See Yuan et al. (2006) for more details.

the inflation-rate target, then it cannot raise the employment level above the natural level. So the two targets π_0 and k prove incompatible. Does it make sense to delegate incompatible targets to the central bank? No. Then how can we define compatible targets for the central bank? We assume that compatible targets π^* and y^* exist. Such compatible targets must conform to the structure of the macroeconomic model that underlies the central bank optimization problem.

Second, we observe that the employment target k proves overambitious and unattainable under the assumptions of the macroeconomic model because

$$E(y) = E[y^n + \alpha(\pi - \pi^e) + \varepsilon] = y^n + \alpha[E(\pi) - \pi^e] + E[\varepsilon] = y^n, \tag{13}$$

which means that the level of employment can only equal the natural level, on average. According to equations (7) and (8), we also know that

$$E(\pi) = \pi_0 + \frac{\beta}{\chi}k \neq \pi_0 \text{ and } E(y) = y^n \neq y^n + k, \text{ since } k > 0. \tag{14}$$

The above inequalities mean that, on average, the central bank cannot achieve each of its targets, which seems illogical. Society should not delegate such targets to the central bank. A more sensible approach makes the following assumptions about delegating targets to the central bank

$$\pi^* = E(\pi) \text{ and } y^* = E(y). \tag{15}$$

That is, proper targets should allow the central bank to achieve them. Yuan et al. (2006) call such targets *consistent targets*. In sum, the central bank should not adopt, nor get delegated, the social loss function as its own.

Yuan et al. (2006) developed a two-step optimization problem to determine the delegated central bank loss function. They required, as the key, that the delegated loss function differ from the social loss function, since the latter incorporates inconsistent targets. That is, the delegated loss function must include consistent targets. In the first stage, the central bank chooses the inflation rate to minimize its target-consistent delegated loss function subject to the macroeconomic structure. Then, in the second stage, the government chooses the parameters of the delegated central bank loss function that minimizes the target-inconsistent social loss function.[20]

---

[20] A similar two-stage optimization appears in Hughes et al. (2005), who consider the trade-off between central bank independence and conservativeness.

Carrying out the two-stage optimization process leads to the following relationships between the target inflation (π^*) and output (y^*) rates as well as the weight on the inflation loss (β^*) in the target-consistent delegated loss function:

$$\beta^* = \beta \text{ and} \tag{16}$$

$$\pi^* = \pi_0 - \frac{\alpha}{\beta}(y^* - y^n). \tag{17}$$

Substituting these solutions back into the expected social loss function generates:

$$E(L) = \frac{\beta}{\beta + \alpha^2}\sigma^2 + k^2, \tag{18}$$

which equals the expected social loss associated with the optimal outcome (see equation 6).

The solution in equation (17) implies an infinite number of combinations of target inflation rate and output level that achieve the optimal solution. For a consistent target, the expected inflation rate equals the target inflation rate, π_0. Thus, the target inflation rate will equal the expected inflation rate, a consistent target, only if the output level equals the natural rate. But that makes the output level target consistent as well, since it will equal the expected output level.[21]

Consider, now, the solutions of Rogoff (1985), Svensson (1997), Walsh (1995a), and Chortareas and Miller (2003b). First, Rogoff's (1985) solution proves inconsistent with these findings. That is, he alters the central bank objective function by appointing a conservative central banker. Within the context of the model used previously, he did not adopt consistent targets. Moreover, he also did not adopt an optimal central bank objective function. The findings for optimal monetary policy require that equations (16) and (17) hold. Rogoff (1985) appoints a central banker for whom the trade-off coefficient between the inflation and employment rate stability exceeds that for society. Equation (16) indicates that the trade-off coefficient should not change. Moreover, Rogoff (1985) maintains Barro and Gordon's target values for the inflation and employment rates, which prove inconsistent in this framework.

---

[21] Consistent targets also minimize the central bank's expected loss function. In other words, equations (16) and (17) minimize the expected social loss function, but only consistent targets will also minimize the central banker's expected loss function.

Second, Svensson (1997) delegates an inflation target that differs from society's target. Once again, the central banker possesses a loss function that differs from the social loss function. Svensson's inflation target can completely eliminate the inflation bias, if we simplify Svensson's model to the basic model without employment persistence. That is, consistent policy proves optimal under inflation targeting for the simplified model. But he chooses inflation and employment rate targets that prove inconsistent. His loss function takes the following form:

$$L^{CB}(S) = (y - y^n - k)^2 + \beta(\pi - \pi^*)^2, \tag{19}$$

where π^* equals the inflation target. Svensson (1997) determined that the optimal inflation target π^* equals $\pi_0 - \frac{\alpha}{\chi}k$. Interestingly, his targets $\pi^* = \pi_0 - \frac{\alpha}{\chi}k$ and $y^* = y^n + k$ satisfy the optimal target relationship identified in equation (17), but $\pi^* \neq E(\pi)$ and $y^* \neq E(y)$, which means that he uses inconsistent targets.

Third, Walsh (1995a) introduces an incentive contract, which penalizes the central banker for producing an inflation rate different from its target value. His central bank loss function takes on the following form[22]:

$$L^{CB}(W) = [(y - y^n - k)^2 + \beta(\pi - \pi_0)^2] - \xi[t_0 - t(\pi - \pi_0)], \tag{20}$$

where CB is the central banker, and t_0 and t measure a fixed payment and the penalty (fine) imposed on the magnitude, once the central bank deviates from the inflation-rate target. Walsh determines that the optimal marginal penalty rate t equals $2\alpha k$, where the weight $\xi = 1$. This penalization rate completely eliminates the inflation bias.[23]

Chortareas and Miller (2003b) consider an incentive contract, which penalizes the central banker for producing an employment level different from its target value. Their central bank loss function takes on the following

---

[22] In equation (10), we specified a central bank utility function, which equals the negative of the loss function.

[23] Walsh implicitly assumes in his derivation that the government places no weight on the cost of the incentive contract. Chortareas and Miller (2003b) show that if the government places some weight on such costs, the contract cannot completely eliminate the inflationary bias. In a subsequent paper, Candel-Sanchez and Campoy-Minarro (2004) derive an identical marginal condition for the optimal contract. Finally, in a more recent paper, commenting on Candel-Sanchez and Campoy-Minarro (2004), Chortareas and Miller (2007) reconsider this result and prove that the Walsh contract is optimal after all, once the government can choose both the fixed payment and the marginal penalization rate in the central bank contract.

Table 3.1. *Optimal policy and consistent policy*

Solution method	Optimal outcomes	Consistent targets
Independent central bank	Yes/No*	Yes/No*
Conservative central bank	No	No
Central bank inflation targeting	Yes	No
Central bank inflation of output contract	Yes	Yes
Delegated central bank objective function	Yes	Yes

*If the independent central bank possesses the same objective function as the delegated central bank objective function, then policy is optimal and consistent. Otherwise, it is not.

form in our context:

$$L^{CB}(\text{C\&M}) = [(y - y^n - k)^2 + \beta(\pi - \pi_0)^2] - (tr),^{24} \quad (21)$$

where $tr = f_0 - f(y - y^n)$ equals the incentive scheme, f_0 equals a fixed payment, and f equals the marginal penalization rate for deviations of the employment rate from full employment. Chortareas and Miller (2003b) determine that the optimal incentive scheme takes the form:

$$tr = f_0 - 2k(y - y^n). \quad (22)$$

This penalty rate completely eliminates the inflation bias.

We summarize the various solutions to the time inconsistency of monetary policy in Table 3.1. In each case, we identify whether the individual solution does or does not achieve the optimal outcomes and does or does not imply consistent targets for the central bank. Both inflation or output contracts and the delegated central bank objective function achieve both optimal outcomes and consistent targets. That is, monetary policy proves optimal and consistent. Inflation targeting achieves optimal, but not consistent, policy. The conservative central banker does not achieve either optimal or consistent policy. Finally, the independent central banker will achieve optimal and consistent policy, if and only if, the central banker shares the government-delegated objective function of our last case.

In our context and in monetary models, delegation means that the government assigns a monetary policy objective to the central bank. In a broad

---

[24] In fact, Chortareas and Miller (2003b) use a utility function where the incentive scheme enters with a positive sign and the loss function enters with a negative sign. We multiply by minus one to convert into the loss function used in our work.

sense, delegation implies mechanism or institutional design. When establishing a specific institution (e.g., the central bank), the government must delegate an appropriate objective. Rogoff (1985), Walsh (1995a), Svensson (1997), Chortareas and Miller (2003b), and so on fall broadly into the delegation approach.

3.4.2 Monetary Policy under Contracts and Incomplete Information

In the seminal contribution of Walsh (1995a), the optimal contract can produce outcomes consistent with commitment and full information. The feasibility and the easiness of implementing such a solution, however, can fail in the presence of informational asymmetries. We now discuss information asymmetries pertaining to the model as well as the agent's behavior.

Monetary policy games with incomplete information typically assume that the central bank possesses private information.[25] This private information can generally take one of two forms: (i) the central banker holds information about the structure of the economy that the private sector does not (e.g., a signal about a productivity shock, an estimate of potential output,[26] or an estimate of the natural rate of interest), or (ii) the central banker exhibits a characteristic (e.g., preferences different from the private sector) about which the private sector lacks information.

Cukierman (1992) describes three forms of private information in monetary policy models: private information about the central banker's objectives, about the central banker's ability to commit, and about the central banker's knowledge of the economy. Blanchard and Fisher (1989) distinguish between the private sector's "endogenous" and "exogenous" uncertainty. Uncertainties about the economy, about the information available to the central bank, and about the central banker's tastes prove exogenous, while uncertainty that arises from credibility considerations proves endogenous. The last type, which emerges in reputation models, does not depend on assumptions about private information. In Canzoneri

---

[25] For example, in Herrendorf and Lockwood (1997), the private sector (wage setters) holds private information on the realization of a supply shock.

[26] This does not mean that the central bank's assessment of the economy proves necessarily accurate. For example, Orphanides (2001) argues that the Federal Reserve in the 1970s overestimated potential output, which led subsequently to higher inflation. Nevertheless, in most developed countries, no private sector entity devotes more resources in the analysis of the economy than the central bank.

(1985) and Garfinkel and Oh (1993), the central banker's private information produces better forecasts of velocity shocks. In Walsh (1995b), the central banker's private information reflects an unverifiable forecast of a demand side (velocity) shock that does not prevent the central banker from achieving the optimal policy. One can question whether the central bank holds superior information, because the private sector can probably forecast just as well as the central bank. A number of practical considerations, however, can support the assumption that the central bank may enjoy private information on velocity shocks. Central banks process and analyze the data relevant to monetary aggregates. Moreover, the central bank may produce better information because of the larger resources that it employs. Finally, in principle, the central bank should know better than anybody else about its own control errors.

Other work identifies the different characteristics that a central banker can possess, which define various "types" of central bankers. Cukierman (1992) and Cukierman and Liviatan (1991) distinguish between "strong" and "weak" policymakers in terms of their ability to commit. A strong policymaker proves "dependable." In these models, incomplete information about the ability to precommit produces positive inflation surprises for both strong and weak central bankers. Even the dependable policymaker must accommodate positive inflation expectations to avoid large unemployment losses. Barro (1986) defines a strong policymaker similarly. Vickers (1986) uses "wet" and "dry" to describe weak and strong policymakers, respectively. Backus and Driffill (1985) employ the actions of the policymakers to distinguish between the strong and weak, where strong central bankers choose a zero inflation rate. Rogoff (1985) distinguishes between central bankers with various degrees of conservatism, but under complete information.

In Cukierman and Meltzer (1986), the public faces uncertainty about the policymaker's trade-off between inflation and economic stimulation. This uncertainty intensifies when the economy experiences unanticipated shocks. Crosby (1994) considers a model where the voters do not know the preferences of the policymaker (central banker) and only observe the policymaker's actions with noise. Uncertainty, in this instance, refers to the time-consistent (discretionary) rate of inflation for the policymaker.

Muscatelli (1998) considers uncertainty about the central banker's relative concern for price stability and output in the presence of contracts and inflation targeting. He demonstrates that uncertainty about the central banker's preferences makes optimal policy unattainable and a stochastic inflation bias prevails despite writing contracts or adopting inflation targets.

The trade-off between stabilization and inflation emerges again, but now this trade-off proves stochastic. The coexistence of contracts and targets, however, produces a solution closer to the optimal.

Beetsma and Jensen (1998) also examine uncertainty about the relative weights that the central banker attaches to deviations of inflation and output from their targets. The public, however, knows the preferences of the central banker's political principal (i.e., government) with certainty. Beetsma and Jensen (1998) consider two forms of monetary policy delegation— inflation targeting and inflation contracts. Uncertainty, here, restores the typical trade-off between the efficacy of stabilization and inflation fighting.[27] Optimal contracts display superior performance to optimal inflation targets, but the optimal combination of targets and contracts performs even better. Unless the political principal adopts a quadratic incentive scheme, the outcomes of this optimal combination prove inferior to the outcomes that prevail under a precommitment solution. Beetsma and Jensen (1998) suggest a combination of inflation contracts, inflation targets, and central bank conservatism.

Herrendorf and Lockwood (1997) also argue for a combination of a linear inflation contract, an inflation (or unemployment) target, and a more conservative central banker. If the political principal cannot delegate (through inflation targets or inflation contracts) conditionally on the private sector's private information about supply shocks, then delegation can only bring the mean of the inflation bias to zero, but fails to eliminate the variance of the inflation bias. If the private sector holds private information, then the optimal delegation scheme must include a conservative central banker.

Of course, a meaningful agency framework requires that the principal and the agent exist as two separate and distinguishable entities. In other words, monetary policy delegation that emphasizes incentives requires a central bank sufficiently independent from its political principal. On the other hand, an explicit agency framework does not make sense if the central bank achieves complete independence in both "operational" and political terms. A high degree of "political independence" of the central bank can give rise to a trade-off with accountability.[28] In a recent speech, Tucker (2007), a member of the Bank of England's Monetary Policy Committee

---

[27] This trade-off emerges in Rogoff's (1985) model with a conservative central banker, but disappears in Walsh's (1995a) optimal contract model.

[28] See, for example, the relevant discussion by the panel of experts chaired by Lord Roll (Begg et al. 1993).

(MPC), discusses such concerns that emerged in designing the current U.K. monetary policy framework in the mid-1990s, citing the resentment that some expressed about the possibility that an "overmighty citizen" (p. 5) might emerge as Governor.

Some authors distinguish among central banker types according to the degree of central banker independence. Central banker independence, however, provides a more empirically, than theoretically, tractable approach. Waller and Walsh (1996) note, "the literature has lacked an accepted means of parameterizing independence" (p. 1140). Some authors (Schaling 1995) link central banker conservativeness to central banker independence (or interpret the central banker conservativeness as central banker independence). This linkage, however, appears unsatisfactory, since conservativeness refers to the tastes of the central banker, whereas independence refers to the institutional features of monetary policy delegation. In general, uncertainty can arise regarding the central banker's degree of inflation aversion (an individual characteristic). Uncertainty becomes less plausible when discussing the central banker's legal independence, an institutional characteristic that is public information. Of course, the legislated degree of central banker independence does not provide the only indicator of independence that matters. Actual independence may depend on other factors, including internal developments at the central bank, personalities, and so on. Unquestionably, the central banker's attitudes, including the relative weight placed on inflation and unemployment, appear in these factors. But this provides only one dimension. Moreover, Cukierman et al. (1992) and Cukierman (1992) find that a proxy for the legal definition of central bank independence matters empirically more than a proxy of actual independence in developed countries. Hayo and Hefeker (Chapter 7, this volume) consider the complex nature of the link between central bank independence and inflation.

Cukierman (1992) provides an appropriate framework to define central banker independence by considering macroeconomic policy in its entirety. The fiscal and monetary authorities (e.g., the Treasury and the Federal Reserve in the United States) use different objective functions. Thus, macroeconomic policy maximizes a weighted average of the Federal Reserve's and Treasury's objective functions. The public does not know precisely these relative weights. In other words, uncertainty refers to the balance of power between the two arms of macroeconomic policy. Although this modeling approach boils down to different preferences (because the different weights attached to the Federal Reserve's and Treasury's objectives imply different degrees of inflation aversion), private information refers to the degree of central banker independence or whether fiscal or monetary policy dominates (Sargent and Wallace 1981). An alternative modeling approach, also offered by Cukierman (1992), assumes that the underlying intertemporal utility functions of the two policymakers prove similar except for the discount factor. In particular, the Treasury uses a larger discount factor (i.e., a preference for short-term achievements). Again, private information enters the model by allowing a different balance of power between the two policymakers.

More recently, researchers focus on uncertainty about some aspect or factor of the economy (e.g., productivity) about which the central bank possesses superior information. In Athey et al. (2005), this variable fluctuates randomly, while in Sleet et al. (2001) the central bank receives a signal about future productivity. One can consider also the possibility that the central bank possesses private information about the natural rate of unemployment or the natural equilibrium real interest rate. Such variables typically remain unobservable and the assessment of their value by the central bank becomes pivotal. On the basis of such concerns, one can develop models that incorporate various "misperceptions."

Chortareas and Miller (2003a) consider the importance of different degrees of selfishness by the central banker when contracts exist. In other words, uncertainty enters as to the coefficient on the incentive scheme in the utility function of the central banker. In typical models of monetary policy, selfish policymakers are considered undesirable. Selfishness, however, becomes the sine qua non of the contracting model, because the selfishness of the central banker provides a necessary condition for the effectiveness of the contract. That is, the more selfish the central banker is, the lower is the fixed cost of implementing a contract regime. Knowledge of the central banker's type enables the principal to design the appropriate incentive scheme for each type.

Chortareas and Miller (2003a) show that in the presence of uncertainty about the central banker's selfishness, inflation surprises can occur and output can exceed its natural level. They propose a mechanism design that solves this problem. Can some screening mechanism alleviate this informational asymmetry? Such a solution, however, would require repetition of the game to deliver the intended outcome. In a one-shot game, mimicking (say choosing strategically from a menu of contracts in order to mislead the principal) proves costless for a strategic candidate central banker.

The mechanism that works, providing a focal point of the contracting literature on central banking, involves the possibility of firing the central banker. Central bankers with short terms become more susceptible, in general, to political pressure (Waller and Walsh 1996). O'Flaherty (1990) argues that the incentive to inflate always exerts the most pressure in the first period. This result also proves consistent with the relatively high discount factor of the Federal Reserve versus the Treasury in Cukierman (1992). Waller (1992) and Garcia del Paso (1993) show that lengthy terms in office reduce the probability that new appointees will attempt to generate policy changes.

Central banking practice generally matches these observations. Lengthy terms of appointment to insulate central bankers from political pressure appear in both the governors of the U.S. Federal Reserve System (FRS) (i.e., 14-year terms) and the members of European Central Bank's (ECB) Executive Board (i.e., 8-year terms). In addition, the president of the ECB and the governors of the FRS can only serve one term. Given nonrenewable appointments, non-reappointment threats do not deter central bankers' actions, especially near the end of a term. Chappell et al. (1993), estimating individual Federal Open Market Committee (FOMC) member reaction functions, find that partisan considerations in presidential appointments to the Board of Governors provide the primary channel through which partisan effects arise in monetary policy. Direct presidential pressure on FOMC members emerges with only secondary importance.

Walsh (2002) demonstrates that a contract resembles dismissal rules, which apply when the central baker fails to keep inflation below a particular target level. To fire a central banker before the completion of the term seriously restricts a central banker's independence. For example, Cukierman et al. (1992) and Cukierman (1992) suggest that a high turnover rate of central bankers indicates low central banker independence [also see Hayo and Hefeker (Chapter 7, this volume)]. Empirically, however, high turnover rates significantly explain higher inflation rates only in developing countries. Walsh (1995b) argues that if the central banker cares about holding office and if the reappointment decisions reflect inflation and output performance rather than on realized inflation, then the precommitment outcomes become feasible. The central banker is fired if inflation exceeds a critical rate. This critical rate depends on aggregate supply shocks and the measurement error in the observed inflation rate. Given that the effects of monetary policy on inflation involve long lags,[29] the central banker's performance reflects the policy decided 1 or 2 years ago.

What happens after the central banker's dismissal? Who gets appointed to run the central bank and how will the replacement get chosen? Should the new appointment require an explicit contract or some other institutional

---

[29] For example, Mishkin and Posen (1997) find that the average lag equals 2 to 3 years.

arrangement? Who will decide on the appointment of the replacement central banker? Society may appoint the replacement, but society's appointment policies may also reflect the time-inconsistency problem (McCallum 1995, 1997; Jensen 1997). It is also observes that the principal may not maximize social welfare as a social planner. Partisan or opportunistic incentives may influence the principal. In addition, the principal may face high reappointment costs. Jensen (1997) suggests that when high reappointment costs exist, then the principal should delegate monetary policy. High reappointment costs prevent society from reconsidering its delegation decisions. Monetary policy delegation becomes immune to the principal's (society's) time-inconsistent decisions. If the principal's (society's) preferences, however, prove time invariant, then high reappointment costs make it difficult to override a central banker who does not meet the prescribed policy targets. High reappointment costs may make the political principal hesitant to replace a central banker who breaches the contract. As long as the legislature can override existing central banker legislation, the political principal's decision to change or not to change this legislation will reflect a political calculation. Lohmann (1992), for example, observes that since the legislature can repeal the central bank law at any time in New Zealand, the commitment to the existing monetary regime reflects political, rather than legal, factors.

Finally, the bulk of the existing literature on central banker contracts only considers delegated bilateral agency (i.e., one principal and one agent). Dixit (2000) and Chortareas and Miller (2004) introduce the theoretical possibility of common agency in principal-agent models of monetary policy. Dixit (2000) focuses on the sustainability of the commitment policy of a central bank in a multinational monetary union. Chortareas and Miller (2004) consider the possibility of a second principal with preferences different from government.

3.5 Conclusion

The rule-versus-discretion debate entails a long history. Since the pioneering work of Kydland and Prescott (1977) and Calvo (1978), much attention focuses on the time-inconsistency issue on monetary policy implementation. Barro and Gordon (1983a, b) examined the issue in a simple, tractable model with an inherent inflation bias. Different solutions to the time inconsistency and inflation bias exist—create an independent central bank, appoint a conservative central banker, implement inflation targeting, develop a reputation in a repeated game, adopt central bank incentive contracts, and so on. In the Barro–Gordon type models, the inflation bias emerges because the targets for the policymaker, as expressed in the social loss function, prove inconsistent with each other in the context of the macroeconomy. That is, the structure of the macroeconomic economy does not allow for the targets in the social loss function to obtain simultaneously. Thus, the policymaker can only achieve actual and consistent outcomes by adopting a central banker loss function that differs from society's.

Our analysis considers solutions one at a time and does not entertain combination policies, as is frequently done in the existing literature. We follow this strategy to evaluate the success or failure of individual solutions in addressing the inflation bias. First, giving independence to the central bank may or may not achieve optimal outcomes. That depends on the objective function of the independent central bank. That is, central bank independence in its extreme form cedes the power to determine the targets and instruments of monetary policy, as well as the trade-off between output and inflation. Some additional government control through delegation or assignment of targets militates against the danger of too much central bank independence.

Second, the conservative central banker solution by itself cannot achieve optimal outcomes. It merely alters the trade-off between achieving the output and inflation targets, placing greater weight on achieving the inflation target. As such, the conservative central banker solution still accepts the inconsistent targets for output and inflation embedded in the social loss function.

Third, the inflation-targeting solution does achieve the optimal outcomes, but the implied targets within the central banker's loss function prove inconsistent with the structure of the macroeconomy. In other words, the expected values of the target variables do not equal the optimal outcomes. As a consequence, the central banker adopts targets for both output and inflation that prove unattainable. Delegating targets to the central banker that the central banker cannot attain seems like a poor policy strategy.

Fourth, the explicit contract solution, either an inflation or output incentive contract, does achieve the optimal outcomes. Moreover, the delegated targets in the central banker's loss function prove consistent and attainable within the structure of the economy.

Finally, delegation of a central bank objective function with consistent targets also achieves the optimal outcomes.

All solutions reflect a "contract"—explicit or implicit. For the solutions with implicit contracts, successful implementation of monetary policy requires some enforcement of penalty or incentive system to ensure compliance with the contract.

New Zealand considered an explicit incentive contract but, at the last minute, decided against its adoption, because of the potential public-relations problems associated with tying the Governor's compensation to the economy's performance. A broadened view of contracts makes it easier to reconcile the principal-agent theoretical approach with observed prac-tice of monetary policy delegation. In his survey, Blinder (1998) ranks the potential of "incentives" last (along with "rule constraints") in terms of importance for establishing credibility in the eyes of central bankers and academics.

Will a monetary policy framework based on incentives improve per-formance? Consider, for example, the performance of inflation-targeting countries. Bernanke and Woodford (2005) wonder whether the improved performance of countries that adopt inflation targeting directly results from the change in the policy regime. The U.K. experience hints at answers to this question, suggesting that inflation targeting made the job of central banks easier by reducing the costs of making the right decisions. Indeed, inflation-targeting central banks display, on balance, improved perfor-mance. But, at the same time, other central banks that do not follow explicit inflation targets also perform equally well.[30] Other features of the policy framework may be decisive, such as the communication framework and the enhanced transparency that usually accompanies inflation targeting. Devel-oping such policy framework may endogenize particular delegation schemes that incorporate agency features and emphasize incentives, including the assignment of an explicit inflation target to the central bank.

How one interprets the incentive contract proves crucial in justifying or refuting the above concerns. We argue that interpreting central banker contracts only in terms of monetary value appears too limiting. Focusing only on the pecuniary value of the central bankers' rewards may ignore other dimensions such as the prestige of the position, their reputation in the profession, and so on. Dixit (1996b), for example, suggests that we should interpret the incentives (penalties or rewards) in policymak-ing, whether financial or nonmonetary, broadly to include career concerns and status (power). Brunner (1985) also argues that central bankers care-fully evaluate their actions because they affect their "political status and future market opportunities in the private and public sector" (p. 15). For example, we can interpret the "Open Letter" procedure in the context of the

---

[30] The improved inflation performance may reflect good luck rather than good policy, which are two of the possible explanations for the Great Moderation (Stock and Watson 2003).

Bank of England's inflation-targeting framework as an incentive scheme that imposes a reputation cost on the policymaker when the target falls outside the limits set by a band.[31] One can view such concerns as related to the central banker's human capital. Demonstrating insufficient competency in the conduct of monetary policy affects the reputation of the central banker and his/her future career prospects. The more explicit the delegation scheme (as in a central banker contract) is, the more observable the degree of competency in the conducting monetary policy becomes.

The financial crisis that started in 2007 may lead to a more pronounced role for central banks in the areas of prudential supervision and regulation with the aim of safeguarding financial stability. In monetary policy models, the existing agent-theoretic models give scant attention to the demand side for policy outcomes and relevant institutions models. In other words, they implicitly assume that the government rules the demand side. Once we shift focus to financial stability issues and banking regulation, the rationale for common agency becomes more pronounced, and concerns about regulatory capture may emerge. Financial institutions may want to influence regulators to favor their interests. The possibility of informal contracts, as in Grossman and Helpman (1994) and Spiller (1990), becomes more probable.

The contracting approach, broadly defined, allows enough flexibility for it to prove generally consistent with a number of alternative theoretical formulations and the corresponding attempts to implement them in practice. The existing literature establishes the necessary conditions for alternative solutions to mirror the contracting equilibrium. Moreover, in many ways, monetary policy delegation appears consistent with a contractual arrangement of punishments and rewards. The challenge remaining for the contracting approach to central banking is to analyze and interpret specific institutional arrangements of monetary policy delegation more explicitly and directly.

Finally, all our analysis implicitly assumes a single decision maker for the central bank. In fact, central bank decisions reflect a board that includes individuals with potentially divergent views. Of course, a preference exists for consensus decisions at central banks. Nonetheless, considering the dynamics of group decision making complicates our analysis. But that takes us beyond the intent of this chapter.

---

[31] The Deputy Governor of the Bank of England, however, disagrees with this interpretation of the "Open Letter" procedure as a punishment, suggesting that it should be viewed "as an opportunity for the MPC to explain itself" (Lomax 2007, 111).

References

Athey, S., A. Atkenson, and P. J. Kehoe (2005), "The Optimal Degree of Discretion in Monetary Policy," *Econometrica* **73**: 1431–1475.

Backus, D. and J. Driffill (1985), "Inflation and Reputation," *American Economic Review* **75**: 530–538.

Barro, R. J. (1986), "Reputation in a Model of Monetary Policy with Incomplete Information," *Journal of Monetary Economics* **17**: 3–20.

Barro, R. and D. B. Gordon (1983a), "A Positive Theory of Monetary Policy in a Natural Rate Model," *Journal of Political Economy* **91**: 589–610.

  (1983b), "Rules, Discretion and Reputation in a Model of Monetary Policy," *Journal of Monetary Economics* **12**: 101–121.

Beetsma, R. M. W. J. and H. Jensen (1998), "Inflation Targets and Contracts with Uncertain Central Banker Preferences," *Journal of Money, Credit and Banking* **30**: 384–403.

Begg, D., T. C. Daintith, L. Gleske, C. A. Goodhart, P. Lagayette, P. Middleton, M. Monti, R. Portes, R. Roll of Ipsden, D. Walker, and C. Wyplosz (1993), *Independent and Accountable: A New Mandate for the Bank of England*, Centre for Economic Policy, Research Report.

Berger, H., J. de Haan, and S. C. W. Eijffinger (2001), "Central Bank Independence: An Update of Theory and Evidence," *Journal of Economic Surveys* **15**: 3–40.

Bernanke, B. S. (2004), *The Great Moderation. Eastern Economic Association meetings* (Washington, DC) Available at http://www.federalreserve.gov/boarddocs/ speeches/2004/20040220/default.htm

Bernanke, B. S. and M. Woodford (2005), "Introduction" in B. S. Bernanke and M. Woodford (Eds.), *The Inflation-Targeting Debate* (Chicago: The University of Chicago Press), pp. 1–10.

Blanchard, O. and S. Fisher (1989), *Lectures on Macroeconomics* (Cambridge, MA: The MIT Press).

Blinder, A. (1998), *Central Banking in Theory and Practice* (Cambridge, MA: The MIT Press).

Brunner, K. (1985), "Monetary Policy and Monetary Order," in *Monetary Policy and Monetary Regimes*, Graduate School of Management, University of Rochester.

Calvo, G. A. (1978), "On the Time Consistency of Optimal Policy in a Monetary Economy," *Econometrica* **46**: 1411–1428.

Candel-Sanchez F. and J. C. Campoy-Minarro (2004), "Is the Walsh Contract Really Optimal?," *Public Choice* **120**: 29–39.

Canzoneri, M. (1985), "Monetary Policy Games and the Role of Private Information," *American Economic Review* **75**: 1056–1070.

Chappell, H. W., Jr., T. M. Havrilesky, and R. R. McGregor (1993), "Partisan Monetary Policies: Presidential Influence through the Power of Appointment," *Quarterly Journal of Economics* **108**: 185–218.

Chortareas, G. E. and S. M. Miller (2003a), "Central Banker Contracts, Incomplete Information, and Monetary Policy Surprises: In Search of a Selfish Central Banker?," *Public Choice* **116**: 271–296.

  (2003b), "Monetary Policy Delegation, Contract Costs, and Contract Targets," *Bulletin of Economic Research* **55**: 101–112.

(2004), "Optimal Central Banker Contracts and Common Agency," *Public Choice.* **121**: 131–155.

(2007), "The Walsh Contract for Central Bankers Proves Optimal After All," *Public Choice* **131**: 243–247.

Crosby, M. (1994), "Electing Monetary Policymakers According to Inflation Performance," *Economics Letters* **46**: 333–338.

Cukierman, A. (1992), *Central Bank Strategy, Credibility, and Independence: Theory and Evidence* (Cambridge, MA: The MIT Press).

Cukierman, A. and A. Meltzer (1986), "A Theory of Ambiguity Credibility and Inflation under Asymmetric Information," *Econometrica* **54**: 1099–1128.

Cukierman, A. and N. Liviatan (1991), "Optimal Accommodation by Strong Policymakers under Incomplete Information," *Journal of Monetary Economics* **27**: 99–127.

Cukierman, A., S. B. Webb, and B. Neyapti (1992), "Measuring the Independence of Central Banks and Its Effect on Policy Outcomes," *World Bank Economic Review* **6**: 353–398.

Dixit, A. (1996a), "Special-Interest Lobbying and Endogenous Commodity Taxation," *Eastern Economic Journal* **22**: 375–387.

(1996b), *The Making of Economic Policy: A Transaction-Cost Politics Perspective* (Cambridge, MA: The MIT Press).

(2000), "A Repeated Game Model of Monetary Union," *Economic Journal* **110**: 759–780.

Eijffinger, S. C. W. and J. de Haan (1996), *The Political Economy of Central Bank Independence.* Special Paper in International Economics (Princeton, NJ: Princeton University Press).

Federal Reserve Bank of Minneapolis (1999), "Donald Brash," *The Region,* Federal Reserve Bank of Minneapolis: 42–56.

Flood, R. and P. Isard (1989), "Monetary Policy Strategies," *International Monetary Fund Staff Papers* **36**: 612–632.

Fratianni, M., J. von Hagen, and C. J. Waller (1997), "Central Banking as a Political Principal–Agent Problem," *Economic Inquiry* **35**: 378–393.

Garcia del Paso, J. I. (1993), "Monetary Announcements and Monetary Policy Credibility," *Investigaciones Economicas* **27**: 551–567.

Garfinkel, M. R. and S. Oh (1993), "Strategic Discipline in Monetary Policy with Private Information," *American Economic Review* **83**: 99–117.

Grossman, G. M. and E. Helpman, (1994), "Protection for Sale," *American Economic Review* **84**: 833–850.

Herrendorf, B. and B. Lockwood (1997), "Rogoff's "Conservative" Central Banker Restored," *Journal of Money, Credit and Banking* **29**: 476–495.

Hughes Hallett, A. and D. N. Weymark (2005), "Independence before Conservatism: Transparency, Politics and Central Bank Design," *German Economic Review* **6**: 1–21.

Jensen, H. (1997), "Credibility of Optimal Monetary Delegation," *American Economic Review* **87**: 911–920.

Kreps, D. M. and R. Wilson (1982), "Reputation and Imperfect Information," *Journal of Economic Theory* **27**: 253–279.

Kydland, F. and E. Prescott (1977), "Rules Rather than Discretion: The Inconsistency of Optimal Plans," *Journal of Political Economy* **85**: 473–490.

Levy, P. I. (1997), "A Political-Economic Analysis of Free-Trade Agreements," *American Economic Review* **87**: 506–519.

Lohmann, S. (1992), "Optimal Commitment in Monetary Policy: Credibility versus Flexibility," *American Economic Review* **82**: 273–286.

Lomax, R. (2007), "The MPC Comes of Age. Bank of England", *Quarterly Bulletin* **47**: 106–111.

McCallum, B. T. (1995), "Two Fallacies Concerning Central-Bank Independence," *American Economic Review* **85**: 207–211.

(1997), "Crucial Issues Concerning Central Bank Independence," *Journal of Monetary Economics* **39**: 99–112.

Mishkin, F. S. and A. S. Posen (1997), "Inflation Targeting: Lessons from Four Countries. Federal Reserve Bank of New York," *Economic Policy Review* **3**: 9–110.

Muscatelli, A. (1998), "Optimal Inflation Contracts and Inflation Targets with Uncertain Central Bank Preferences: Accountability through Independence?," *Economic Journal* **108**: 529–542.

Obstfeld, M. and A. M. Taylor (2004), *Global Capital Markets: Integration Crisis and Growth* (Cambridge, UK: Cambridge University Press).

O'Flaherty, B. (1990), "The Care and Handling of Monetary Authorities," *Economics and Politics* **2**: 25–44.

Orphanides, A. (2001), "Monetary Policy Rules Based on Real-Time Data," *American Economic Review* **91**: 964–985.

Persson, T. and G. Tabellini, G. (1993), "Designing Institutions for Monetary Stability," *Carnegie-Rochester Conference Series on Public Policy* **39**: 53–84.

Persson, T., M. Persson, and L. E. O. Svensson (2006), "Time Consistency of Fiscal and Monetary Policy: A Solution," *Econometrica* **74**: 193–212.

Rogoff, K. (1985), "The Optimal Degree of Commitment to an Intermediate Monetary Target," *Quarterly Journal of Economics* **100**: 1169–1189.

Sargent, T. and N. Wallace (1981), "Some Unpleasant Monetarist Arithmetic," Federal Reserve Bank of Minneapolis *Quarterly Review* **5**: 1–17.

Schaling, E. (1995), *Credibility, Flexibility and Central Bank Independence* (Cheltenham, UK: Edward Elgar Publishing).

Siklos, P. L. (2002), *The Changing Face of Central Banking*. Studies in Macroeconomic History (Cambridge, UK: Cambridge University Press).

Simons, H. C. (1936), "Rules versus Authorities in Monetary Policy," *Journal of Political Economy* **44**: 1–30.

Sleet, C. (2001), "On Credible Monetary Policy and Private Government Information," *Journal of Economic Theory* **99**: 338–376.

Spiller, P. T. (1990), "Politicians, Interest Groups, and Regulators: A Multiple Principals Agency Theory of Regulation, or 'Let Them Be Bribed'," *Journal of Law and Economics* **33**: 65–101.

Stock, J. H. and M. W. Watson (2003), "Has the Business Cycle Changed? Evidence and Explanations," in *Monetary Policy and Uncertainty: Adapting to a Changing Economy*, Symposium Proceedings, Federal Reserve Bank of Kansas City, Jackson Hole, WY: 9–56.

Svensson, L. (1997), "Optimal Inflation Targets, Conservative Central Banks and Linear Inflation Contracts," *American Economic Review* 87: 98–111.

Svensson, L. O. and M. Woodford (2005), "Implementing Optimal Policy through Inflation-Forecast Targeting," in B. S. Bernanke and M. Woodford (Eds.), *The Inflation-Targeting Debate* (Chicago: The University of Chicago Press), pp. 19–92.

Tucker, P. (2007), "Central Banking and Political Economy: The Example of the UK's Monetary Policy Committee," Speech at Inflation Targeting, Central Bank Independence and Transparency Conference, Cambridge, UK. Available at http://www.bankofengland.co.uk/publications/speeches/2007/speech312.pdf

Vickers, J. (1986), "Signaling in a Model of Monetary Policy with Incomplete Information," *Oxford Economic Papers* 38: 443–455.

Waller, C. J. (1992), "A Bargaining Model of Partisan Appointments to the Central Bank," *Journal of Monetary Economics* 29: 411–428.

Waller, C. J. and C. E. Walsh (1996), "Central-Bank Independence, Economic Behavior, and Optimal Term Lengths," *American Economic Review* 86: 1139–1153.

Walsh, C. E. (1995a), "Optimal Contracts for Central Bankers," *American Economic Review* 85: 150–167.

(1995b), "Is New Zealand's Reserve Bank Act of 1989 an Optimal Central Bank Contract?," *Journal of Money, Credit and Banking* 27: 1179–1191.

(2002), "When Should Central Bankers Be Fired?," *Economics of Governance* 3: 1–21.

(2003), *Monetary Theory and Policy*, 2nd. ed. (Cambridge, MA: The MIT Press).

Yuan, H., S. M. Miller, and L. Chen (2006), "The Making of Optimal and Consistent Policy: An Analytical Framework for Monetary Models," RePEc, Working Paper 2006–5. Available at http://ideas.repec.org/p/uct/uconnp/2006–05.html

4

Implementing Monetary Policy in the 2000s: Operating Procedures in Asia and Beyond

Corrinne Ho

Abstract

Monetary policy at the strategic level has undergone significant changes over the years; so has its day-to-day implementation. This chapter presents a snapshot of 17 central banks' monetary operating frameworks as of early 2007, and discusses their major developments over the preceding decade. It finds that although some common themes and practices can be identified, there is no unique "best" way to implement monetary policy. Central banks everywhere have continued to refine their operating frameworks and procedures and to innovate where necessary, responding to changing needs in changing times.

4.1 Introduction

At the strategic level, monetary policy has undergone significant changes over the years. Exchange rate pegs or bands, monetary aggregate targets, and inflation targets have at different times gained favor as the mainstream intermediate objective of monetary policy. At the tactical (or operational) level, the day-to-day implementation of monetary policy has also evolved, driven in part by the changing views about the preferred intermediate targets, and in part by the changes in the broader banking and financial systems both at home and abroad.

This is an abridged version of BIS Working Papers no 253 (June 2008). The author thanks the participants at the BIS meetings on monetary policy operating procedures for providing information and inspiration on the subject matter. Gratitude is due to Eric Chan and Gert Schnabel for statistical assistance and to Claudio Borio, Dietrich Domanski, John Groom, Hirotaka Hideshima, Spence Hilton, Nazrul Hisyam bin Mohd Noh, Jonathan Kearns, Daniel Lau, Robert McCauley, Thammarak Moenjak, William Nelson, Priyanto B Nugroho, Eli Remolona, Chris Ryan, Ilhyock Shim and Pierre Siklos for comments on earlier drafts. The author takes responsibility of any remaining mistakes. Views expressed are those of the author and not necessarily those of the Bank for International Settlements.

This operational evolution has been less popular as a subject of academic research than its strategic counterpart, but has nonetheless been examined by specialists in the central banking community. Kneeshaw and Van den Bergh (1989) and Borio (1997) document the migration of industrial economy central banks in the 1980s and early 1990s, respectively, toward what we now consider mainstream operating frameworks. Van 't dack (1999) observes a similar process among emerging market economies in the 1990s. These and other related studies note that the evolution of monetary policy implementation has accompanied several major financial, institutional, and policy developments. These include domestic banking system deregulation, the rise of nonbank financial intermediation and new financial instruments, external accounts liberalization, increased central bank autonomy, reduced central bank responsibility in public debt management and policy lending, a reduced use of quantities (e.g., M2) as intermediate targets, a shift away from irregular interval signaling toward explicit announcement of the policy stance at predetermined dates, and a migration from end-of-day net settlement to real-time gross settlement (RTGS).

Against this backdrop, several stylized trends in the choices of operating frameworks and instruments can be identified. For instance, many central banks now express their official monetary policy stance in interest rate terms (e.g., a central bank facility/operation rate, or a target for a market rate). At the same time, the day-to-day operating objective of central banks has focused more on stabilizing some measure(s) of short-term interest rate, and less on targeting quantities (e.g., reserve money). As for the nature of instruments, there has been a reduced use of direct controls, and more use of indirect instruments based on market mechanisms and incentives. Where they apply, reserve requirements have tended to become more simplified and less onerous, serving less as a main monetary control instrument and more as a means to make reserve demand more predictable and to buffer short-term interest rate volatility. Standing facilities have also become simpler, serving less as a source of subsidized lending or a main policy signaling device, and more as a back-stop or safety valve for short-term liquidity needs to help contain interest rate volatility.

Buzeneca and Maino (2007) confirm these general trends with data from the International Monetary Fund (IMF's) Information System for Instruments of Monetary Policy (ISIMP). Implicit in their analysis is that the practices among "developed" economies represent a kind of "state-of-the-art," something to which "emerging" and "developing" economies should aspire.[1] However, a closer look at the choices in individual economies and

---

[1] The authors classified the ISIMP economies into "developed," "emerging," and "developing," which correspond to "high income," "upper middle income," and "lower middle and

their evolution reveals that operating frameworks and practices are not a simple function of the level of economic development. In fact, considerable differences prevail, even among the "developed" economies.

Behind the broad global trend of the past decades, how much diversity remains? And perhaps more interestingly, why does this diversity remain? This chapter seeks to shed some light on these questions by surveying a smaller group of 14 Asia-Pacific central banks, plus the European Central Bank (ECB), the Bank of England (BoE), and the Federal Reserve.[2] It presents a snapshot of these central banks' operating frameworks as of early 2007, and highlights the notable changes that took place in the late 1990s and early 2000s. Of the 17 economies covered, 11 are "developed" according to the classification in Buzeneca and Maino (2007), the other 6 are "emerging" or "developing."[3] This sample size and mix lends itself to a more tangible assessment of where the trend ends and the diversity begins.

Following the conceptual framework laid out by Borio (1997), the rest of the chapter is organized as follows. Section 4.2 overviews the *institutional aspects* of monetary policy decisions and operations among the 17 central banks. It discusses the frequency of monetary policy announcements, the choice of policy rates, and its connection, if any, to the strategic policy framework. Section 4.3 surveys the different choices of *operating targets*, their evolution and implications for interbank overnight interest rate volatility. Because day-to-day monetary policy implementation basically revolves around getting the quantity and price of bank reserves right so as to achieve the desired operating target, it is natural to present the "nuts and bolts" of monetary operations with reference to the demand for and supply of bank reserves.[4] Thus, Section 4.4 looks at the two main factors affecting the *demand for bank reserves*: settlements needs and reserve requirements. In particular, it reviews the features of reserve requirements and relates these features to the functions of such requirements. Section 4.5

---

low income" according to the World Bank analytical classification based on Gross National Income per capita (2004 data). International Monetary Fund (2004) discusses the difficulties developing and postconflict economies face in emulating the market-based operations of industrial economies.

[2] The 14 Asia-Pacific central banks are those in Australia, China, Hong Kong, India, Indonesia, Japan, South Korea, Macao, Malaysia, New Zealand, the Philippines, Singapore, Taiwan, and Thailand.

[3] This chapter partly overlaps with Buzeneca and Maino (2007) in coverage, but includes seven economies not covered by the other two authors: four "developed" ones (Hong Kong, Macao, Singapore, and Taiwan – all small and very open economies) and three "developing" ones (Indonesia, the Philippines, and Thailand).

[4] See section 1 in Borio (1997) for the conceptual underpinnings of how the various aspects of monetary operations can be analytically classified as supply and demand factors in the market for bank reserves.

then examines the two main channels through which a central bank regulates the *supply of reserves*: standing facilities and discretionary operations. It discusses the evolution of the two channels' relative roles, as well as the connection between the choice of monetary instruments and financial market development. Section 4.6 concludes.

This chapter finds that, while a number of common themes and practices can be identified, there is no unique "best" way to implement monetary policy. Even among just the four major industrial economy central banks, appreciable differences exist reflecting, inter alia, differences in the domestic financial environment, history, legal and regulatory constraints, and even political philosophy.[5] A more striking finding, perhaps, is the considerable number of innovations even just within the last couple of years in virtually all aspects of monetary policy implementation. It is clear that central banks in "developing," "emerging," and "developed" economies alike are constantly refining their operating frameworks and procedures, and innovating where necessary, responding to changing needs in changing times.

In fact, within just a few months after the early 2007 sample date, the snapshot presented in this chapter already required updating. In particular, the money market turmoil that broke out in August 2007 led many industrial economy central banks to adjust their operating frameworks and procedures. There were also changes that were not triggered by the turmoil (e.g., in Korea and Indonesia). By the time of the final revision of this chapter, the dust had yet to settle.[6] Some of the turmoil-induced measures will be phased out after the return of normality. Other measures may remain or evolve further to reflect any lasting changes in the financial system and lessons learned during the turbulent period. These latest developments reinforce the basic message of this chapter.

4.2 The Institutional Aspects of Monetary Policy Decisions

In order to understand the implementation of monetary policy at the operational level, it is helpful to begin with the institutional aspects of monetary policy decision making. This section overviews the different practices with regard to the frequency of policy announcements and the expression of policy stance. It also assesses whether there is any connection between the choice of policy rate and monetary policy strategy. Table 4.1 summarizes these

---

[5] Woodford (2000) discusses how the familiar, academically mainstream operating framework of the Federal Reserve is, in fact, not the mode among industrial economies.

[6] The main changes that had taken place up to early June 2008 are outlined in the annex of the full version of this chapter [Ho (2008), available at http://www.bis.org/publ/work253.pdf]

Table 4.1. *Institutional setup of monetary policy decision and operation* (*as of March 2007*)

	Basic frequency of policy announcement	Formal policy rate	Formal operating target	Memo
Australia	Monthly	Target cash rate (= O/N rate target)	O/N cash rate	Inflation targeting
China	As and when required	1-year deposit and loan reference rates	Excess reserves	Refers to M-growth targets
Eurosystem	Monthly	Minimum bid rate for the main refinancing operation (1-week maturity)	No formal target	
Hong Kong[1]	–	–	USD/HKD spot rate	Currency board
India	Quarterly	1-day repo and reverse repo rates	No formal target	
Indonesia	Monthly	BI rate (= target rate for 1-month SBI)	1-month SBI rate	Inflation targeting
Japan	Up to twice a month	Uncollateralized O/N call rate target	O/N call rate	
Korea	Monthly	O/N call rate target	O/N call rate	Inflation targeting
Macao[2]	–	–	HKD/MOP spot rate	Currency board

(*continued*)

Table 4.1. (*Continued*)

	Basic frequency of policy announcement	Formal policy rate	Formal operating target	Memo
Malaysia	8 times a year	Overnight policy rate (= O/N rate target)	Average O/N interbank rate	
New Zealand	8 times a year	Official cash rate (= O/N rate target)	O/N cash rate	Inflation targeting
Philippines	Every 6 weeks	O/N repo and reverse repo rates	No formal target	Inflation targeting
Singapore	Semiannually	Policy band for Singapore dollar NEER	Singapore dollar NEER	NEER-based regime[3]
Taiwan	Quarterly	Discount rate	Reserve money	Refers to M-growth targets
Thailand	Every 6 weeks	1-day repo rate	1-day repo rate	Inflation targeting
United Kingdom	Monthly	Official bank rate	Short-term money market rates	Inflation targeting
United States	8 times a year	Fed funds rate target (= O/N rate target)	O/N interbank rate	

[1] Currency board regime with a U.S. dollar anchor, thus no independent monetary policy. The central bank's lending facility rate (base rate) is linked to the U.S. Federal Reserve funds rate target by formula and changes whenever the U.S. policy rate is changed.

[2] Currency board regime with a Hong Kong dollar anchor. The central bank's lending facility rate (base rate) is linked to Hong Kong's base rate.

[3] The NEER band is set with reference to inflation and growth objectives.

Sources: Central banks.

various aspects for the central banks covered herein. Unless otherwise stated, the data in this and all other tables reflect the situation as of March 2007.

Frequency of Policy Decision Announcements

Almost all of the central banks make monetary policy decision announcements at predetermined dates (Table 4.1, column 1). A popular frequency of policy announcement is once every 4–6 weeks (about 8–12 times per year). A minority of central banks have quarterly, half-yearly, or even nonscheduled announcements. However, some central banks' decision-making bodies convene more frequently than the frequency of announcements suggests. For example, the ECB Governing Council meets twice a month but typically announces policy decisions only in the first meeting of each month. The Singaporean authorities hold regular monetary and investment policy meetings, even though it makes monetary policy statements only once every half a year. Central banks typically reserve the right to meet or to announce policy changes in between scheduled dates if deemed necessary.

What exactly do central banks announce?

The majority of the central banks express their monetary policy stance in terms of an interest rate – the *policy rate* (Table 4.1, column 2). Two main types of policy rates are represented. One type is an announced target for a market interest rate (e.g., overnight interbank market rate). As of early 2007, the central banks of Australia, Japan, Korea, Malaysia, New Zealand, and the United States have this type of policy rate. The other type is an official rate of a central bank operation or facility. The ECB, for example, indicates policy stance with the minimum bid rate of its main refinancing operation, which is a weekly tender for supplying liquidity to financial institutions at a 1-week maturity. The BoE used to use its repo rate as the policy rate between 1997 and mid-2006 and has since recast its policy rate as the official bank rate.[7] In part influenced by the BoE's former practice, the Bank of Thailand's policy rate is also an official repo rate. India and the Philippines signal policy with both the official repo and reverse repo rates.[8] Taiwan signals policy with the official discount rate, while Indonesia uses the BI rate, defined at the time of its inception in 2005 as the target auction rate for the 1-month certificates

---

[7] The bank rate is both the reference for the short end of the money market yield curve (the regular weekly open market operations are conducted at bank rate), and the remuneration rate for bank reserves contracted and held under the voluntary reserves averaging scheme introduced in May 2006 (more on this in Section 4.4). The history of the BoE's policy rate (definitions and levels) since 1970 can be found on the BoE's web site: http://www.bankofengland.co.uk/statistics/rates/baserate.pdf

[8] The Reserve Bank of India announces also a bank rate, which used to be the main policy rate but now serves only as a medium-term signal.

(SBIs) issued by the central bank. China represents a special case. Its formal policy rates are, unlike the others', not directly related to the money market but are instead the reference rates for 1-year bank lending and deposits – clearly a legacy of central planning and of a banking system that is still undergoing deregulation.[9]

However, not all central banks express their policy stance with an interest rate. Central banks running exchange rate-based regimes with no capital controls obviously cannot independently set policy interest rates. The currency board regimes of Hong Kong and Macao are typically identified by their respective spot exchange rate anchors. Their domestic money market interest rates are endogenously determined by the forces of capital flows.[10] Under its unique regime, the Monetary Authority of Singapore (MAS) expresses its policy stance with a qualitative statement about the center, width, and gradient of its target band for the Singapore dollar nominal effective exchange rate (NEER).[11] Although the Singaporean regime allows more flexibility than the single-anchor regimes of Hong Kong and Macao, the high degree of capital mobility means that the Singapore dollar interest rate level is still broadly endogenous.

Policy rate choice and monetary policy strategy: any relationship?

Judging by the central banks' choices, there is no obvious mapping between the expression of policy stance and the monetary policy framework (Table 4.1, columns 2 and 4). Among the seven inflation-targeting central banks, three signal policy with a target for the overnight rate (Australia, Korea, and New Zealand), while four do so with an official operation rate (Indonesia, Philippines, Thailand, and the United Kingdom). Conversely, while both India and the Philippines adopt the same choice of policy rates, they have different monetary policy frameworks.

---

[9] In fact, some practices in China today are illustrative of how things used to work in a larger number of economies in the earlier era of highly regulated banking systems.

[10] The Hong Kong dollar is anchored at HKD 7.80 per USD (with a ± HKD 0.05 tolerance band since May 2005), while the Macanese pataca is anchored at MOP 1.03 per HKD. Accordingly, the HKD and MOP short-term market interest rates are directly and indirectly influenced by USD interest rates.

[11] For example, the October 2006 monetary policy statement says that the MAS would "maintain the policy of a modest and gradual appreciation of the S$NEER policy band" and that there would be "no re-centering of the policy band, or any change to its slope or width." The NEER series is published occasionally, but the basket composition and the parameters of the policy band are not published. Over time, however, many Singapore-based market economists have, with some success, reverse-engineered plausible versions of the S$NEER policy band. See Monetary Authority of Singapore (2001) for details on Singapore's policy regime.

Moreover, there have been changes in the choice of policy rate without any change in the higher-level policy regime and vice versa. For example, the Bank of Thailand moved from the 14-day repo rate to the 1-day repo rate in January 2007, but left all the strategic aspects of its inflation-targeting framework unchanged. The BoE also migrated over the past decade from a 14-day repo rate to a 7-day repo rate to the current official bank rate, while retaining the inflation-targeting framework. Bank Negara Malaysia (BNM) switched from using the "3-month intervention rate" to using the overnight policy rate (OPR) to signal policy in April 2004, without altering its dollar peg-cum-capital controls regime. The OPR remains the policy rate after the exit from the dollar peg in July 2005. These examples support the view that there is no one-to-one link between the choice of policy rate and the monetary policy framework.[12]

What governs the choice of the policy rate?

The choice of policy rates often has much to do with legacy and even cross-country emulation. For instance, the ECB's choice of a 1-week (originally 2-week) tender rate is reminiscent of the choices of the German, French, Belgian, and Austrian central banks in the pre-EMU era. Elsewhere, the popularity of overnight rate targets may be an influence of the Federal Reserve. The prevalence of "bank rates" and repo rates as policy rates among other central banks may reflect the influence of the BoE.

History and peer emulation aside, functionality also matters. As a signal of the policy stance, the policy rate should ideally provide clarity and good controllability. This perhaps explains why so many central banks signal policy with their official operation or facility rates, which are naturally fully within their control. And to the extent that the policy rate, once properly implemented, is also the starting point of monetary transmission, it should ideally be something economically relevant. This may be the reason why some central banks prefer to target a market interest rate instead. Moreover, the relevant market rate to target may change over time with financial system development. The 2004 policy rate reform in Malaysia mentioned previously is a good illustration of this point. The former policy rate, adopted in 1998, had been highly relevant in principle given its link by formula to the base lending rate (BLR) ceiling. The BLR was then the benchmark for pricing retail and corporate interest rates. However, as more and

---

[12] Tucker (2004, 370) observes that even the evolution of the implementation framework (not just policy rate) bears no clear relationship with changes in the monetary regime at the BoE in the entire post–World War II era.

more banks moved toward cost-based pricing, the BLR lost significance. The policy rate's relevance also diminished. This development eventually led BNM to adopt a new framework, with the overnight rate target as its new policy rate.[13]

Regardless of the choice of policy rate, any *decision* to raise the overnight rate target or to cut the official repo rate is of little significance unless the decision is *implemented* properly. The next section takes the first step into the operational sphere of monetary policy implementation by taking a closer look at the relationship between the policy rate and the day-to-day objective of the central bank's market operations desk.

4.3 The Operational Objectives of Monetary Policy Implementation

Just as monetary policy making has its strategic-level goals, monetary policy implementation also has its operational-level objectives. Such objectives that central bank operations desks pursue in their everyday work are often set in terms of their *operating targets*, which can be of three main types: interest rate, exchange rate, and quantity (e.g., bank reserves).

Interest Rate Targets: The Current Mainstream

Referring again to Table 4.1 (columns 2 and 3), one can see that, apart from the three central banks with exchange rate-based regimes, most of the others tend to adopt some measure of short-term interest rate as their operating targets. Central banks that signal policy with an overnight rate target naturally give their operations desks instructions to keep the overnight *market* rate close to the targeted level. Central banks that signal their policy stance with other official interest rates, however, show some variation in operating objectives. But even there, overnight or short-term interest rates still constitute the majority. Some central banks do not adopt a *formal* operating target, but nonetheless keep an eye on the overnight and other short-term interest rates in their day-to-day operations. The euro area, Indian, and Philippine central banks are in this category. The BoE has traditionally watched short-term money market rates in general, but in 2006 reformulated its operating objective in more specific and innovative terms: "a flat money market yield

---

[13] Moreover, each banking institution would establish its own BLR based on cost and business considerations and would no longer be subject to any BLR ceiling (BNM Press Release dated April 23, 2004).

curve, consistent with the official bank rate, out to the next Monetary Policy Committee (MPC) decision date, with very limited day-to-day or intraday volatility in market interest rates at maturities out to that horizon" (Bank of England 2007, 3).

Quantitative operating targets, in contrast, are now in the minority. In an earlier era, the focus on quantities such as bank reserves or monetary base was, in part, related to the popularity of monetary aggregates as intermediate targets. The prevalence in that era of heavily regulated banking systems and underdeveloped nonbank financial intermediation also meant that monetary transmission via market interest rates – something now almost taken for granted – used to be less prominent. But as banking deregulation got underway and as other channels of financial intermediation opened up, the link between monetary aggregates and the ultimate objectives of policy weakened.[14] Bank reserves or monetary base targeting also came to be seen as less relevant, while market interest rates began to have more roles to play.[15]

Residual uses of quantity targets
Among the major industrial economy central banks, the reorientation from quantities back to interest rates was mostly complete by the early 1990s. Many emerging market central banks did the same from the 1990s onward.[16] Barring the exceptional case of the Bank of Japan (BOJ) during the quantitative easing era (March 2001 to March 2006), the Taiwanese and Chinese central banks are the only two in the sample that still consider bank reserves to be their formal operating targets.

In Taiwan, there is still official reference to the M2 growth target range as a guide to policy at the strategic level. The central bank therefore still accords some importance to the level and growth of reserve money at the operational level. However, judging by the other aspects of operation and the overall relative stability of short-term money market rates, the central

---

[14] Especially over the short to medium horizon and when the economy is not in extreme inflation or deflation.

[15] Bindseil (2004) discusses the rise and fall of the "reserve position doctrine" between the 1920s and 1980s, and how in his view this fallacious doctrine, which supported the focus on quantities in that era, especially in the United States, is still being perpetuated by some academic work even today.

[16] Korea made a gradual transition in 1998–99 (Bank of Korea, 2002). India began the transition in 2000 by deemphasizing the role of quantities with the introduction of the Liquidity Adjustment Facility. Indonesia formally exited from base money targeting (a legacy of the IMF program) in 2005 with the adoption of the one-month SBI auction rate as policy rate. Even before this formal adoption, market participants had already, for some time, perceived the auction rate as a de facto policy rate (Borio and McCauley 2001).

bank in practice pays considerable attention to interest rates in its everyday operations.

In China, too, the central bank's emphasis on bank reserves is in part related to its use of monetary aggregates as intermediate targets. In addition, Laurens and Maino (2007) point out that, despite much progress with financial and institutional reform, China's interest rate transmission channel is still not fully functioning, posing an obstacle to solely relying on interest rates as an operating target. Furthermore, China's chronic excess liquidity in recent years makes keeping quantities under control a high-priority objective. That being said, the fact that the Chinese central bank also has in place a de facto interest rate corridor suggests that it is also increasingly paying attention to short-term interest rates (more on this in Section 4.5).

Implications for overnight rate volatility

Regardless of whether the overnight interbank market rate *level* is of policy significance, central banks often have some interest in monitoring the overnight rate *volatility*. On the one hand, some volatility is healthy because it creates trading opportunities and thus promotes interbank market activity. On the other hand, too much volatility may indicate that the interbank market is not functioning smoothly. Moreover, large or persistent deviations from the policy target, if not explainable by purely technical factors, may risk being interpreted as either an unintended failure to achieve the announced policy stance or an intended deviation from it.

The volatility of the overnight rate is in part affected by the choice of policy rate and operating target. Figure 4.1 shows the key official central bank interest rates and the overnight interbank market rates for the economies in the sample. Where the central bank targets the overnight rate itself, overnight rate volatility, both in terms of its variability (e.g., standard deviation) and its deviation from the target, is likely to be low. In Australia in particular, where banks have over time developed a convention to deal with each other only at the target cash rate, the actual cash rate has virtually no variation around its target. This had also been the case in New Zealand until mid-2006, when a change in the liquidity management regime prompted market participants to start trading at a small margin above the official cash rate.[17]

---

[17] The changes included a reduction in the frequency of open market operations, the phasing out of the intraday liquidity facility and the resetting of the overnight standing facility rates from a symmetric ±25 basis points to an asymmetric +50/−0 basis points around the policy rate. See Reserve Bank of New Zealand (2006).

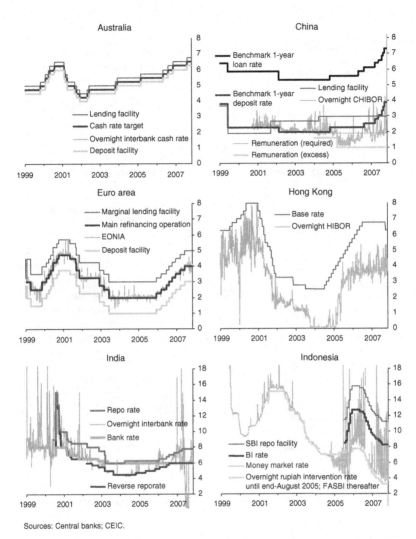

Figure 4.1. (Continued)

In economies where the central bank does not formally target the overnight interbank rate, there could be more room for overnight rate volatility. It is apparent from Figure 4.1 that nonovernight rate targeters such as China, the euro area, Hong Kong, India, Indonesia, Macao, the Philippines, Singapore, and the United Kingdom tend to have higher daily overnight rate volatilities than do the explicit overnight rate targeters. However, this characterization does not seem to apply to Taiwan and

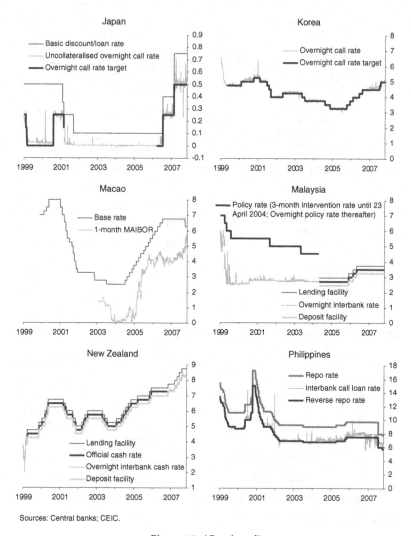

Sources: Central banks; CEIC.

Figure 4.1. (Continued)

Thailand, where the overnight rates seem to be no more volatile than those in Korea or the United States.

Indeed, the choice of policy rate and operating target is not the only determinant of overnight rate volatility. Other aspects of the operating framework arguably have just as much, if not more, influence.[18] A case in

---

[18] In a study of industrial economy central banks, Prati et al. (2003) find that operating procedures and operation styles play a crucial role in shaping empirical features of short-term interest rates.

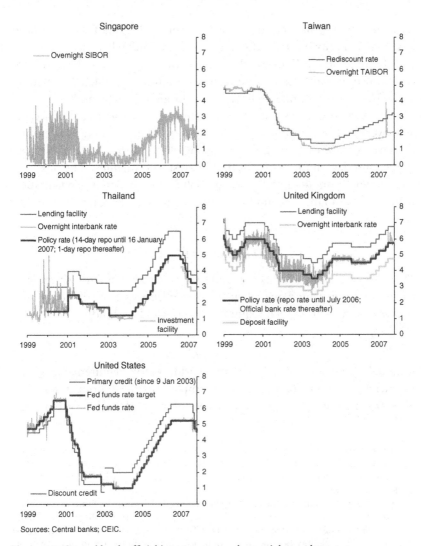

Figure 4.1. Central bank official interest rates and overnight market rate
Sources: Central banks; CEIC.

point is the traditionally more volatile overnight rate in the United Kingdom than in the euro area. This is attributable to some features of the BoE's operating framework, which had been until mid-2006 quite different from the ECB's. There was no reserve requirement in the United Kingdom and thus no averaging to smooth out banks' demand for reserves over time (more on this in Section 4.4). The width of the interest rate corridor was the same as in the euro area, but access to the BoE's standing facilities was limited to settlement banks, and the supply of funds at the lending facility was also limited in quantity (more on this in Section 4.5). These characteristics made for a more volatile U.K. overnight rate and were modified in the May 2006 operating framework reform.[19] As can be seen from Figure 4.1, the volatility of the U.K. overnight rate declined markedly after the reform.[20]

In sum, central banks can, to some extent, choose the degree of acceptable overnight rate volatility by choosing some combination of operating framework features, though there may be a limit to their control over the supply and demand factors affecting interest rate volatility. The next two sections will zoom in on the "nuts and bolts" of monetary implementation with reference to the demand for and the supply of reserves.

4.4 Demand for Reserves

There are two main reasons for banks to hold reserves. One reason is to facilitate everyday interbank *payments and settlements*. The other is to fulfill *reserve requirements*, if such requirements exist and are binding.

Settlement Balances

Although quite common around the world, reserve requirements are by no means universal. Banks in, for example, Australia, Hong Kong, and New Zealand are not subject to such requirements.[21] In these economies,

---

[19] Tucker (2004) outlines this and other problems under the previous framework, and previews the design principles for the new framework. Clews (2005) explains the new system and notes that while the individual elements are not new, this particular combination of elements is novel.

[20] Other examples abound. Hilton (2005) links the rise and fall in federal funds rate volatility since 1989 to the changes in the reserve requirement framework and the Fed's sensitivity to the patterns of reserve demand. Monetary Authority of Singapore (2007) shows how overnight rate volatility became more contained after the introduction of the end-of-day lending facilities in November 2000, and more so after the introduction of reserves averaging in September 2001. The overnight rate level is also known to play a role. The very low level of the U.S. Fed funds rate between 2001 and 2004 may have contributed to some "rate compression," reducing movements at least on the downside (Hilton 2005). A low interest rate environment also makes it less costly to hold reserves, thus reducing the likelihood of scrambles for liquidity and upward spikes in the overnight rate. Japan, during the quantitative easing era, provides an extreme illustration of this point.

[21] Freedman (2000) points out that nonbinding or eliminated reserve requirements are not uncommon in the global context (e.g., Canada and Sweden), and explains how a central bank can exert leverage over the policy rate even without binding reserve requirements. Woodford (2000) discusses how the central bank's influence need not depend on imposing requirements on banks to hold unremunerated reserves.

banks only need to hold settlement balances (or working balances). Because holding balances that are unremunerated (or remunerated at less than the prevailing market rate) incur an opportunity cost, banks would normally tend to keep their settlement balances to the minimum necessary. However, responding to this incentive to economize does carry some risks. In the event of unexpectedly large settlement needs, a bank would have to borrow funds from its peers at a market-determined rate or from the central bank's lending facility, which usually charges a penalty rate. Banks must, therefore, balance the opportunity cost of holding excess balances against the risk of having to borrow dear in case they fall short. All these also imply that the demand for settlement balances on any given day tends to be inelastic, depending mainly on settlement needs (both expected and precautionary), and responding relatively little to small changes in interest rate levels.[22]

Reserve requirements: design, usage, and functions

In the other economies, reserve requirements do apply, exerting an influence over the demand for reserves. Table 4.2 presents the main features of such requirements in early 2007. Several key observations are worth highlighting, as they provide an indication of the current functions of reserve requirements and their recent evolution.[23]

With regard to *how requirements are calculated and fulfilled,* a key feature that widely applies nowadays is the *averaging provision* (Table 4.2, column 1). By allowing financial institutions to fulfill their reserve requirements on an average basis over the maintenance period, averaging makes the demand for reserve more elastic, which in turn helps to buffer the impact of any instability in the supply of reserves on the interbank market interest rates.[24] This smoothing effect, in principle, works better with a higher level of requirements (a thicker cushion) and a longer maintenance

---

[22] Reserve Bank of Australia (2003) provides an account of how uncertainty over future settlement needs prior to the changeover to RTGS prompted banks to increase their reserve holdings in the late 1990s. As banks became accustomed to functioning under RTGS, their demand for balances declined. The article also notes that there is no relationship between the level of settlement balances and the interest rate level.

[23] Borio (1997) outlines four typical functions: (1) to influence reserve demand elasticity to buffer interest rate volatility; (2) to influence reserve demand level to offset autonomous changes in reserve supply; (3) to control monetary aggregates; and (4) to generate seigniorage revenue. All four are to some extent still served in practice, but the interest rate buffer function has notably gained prevalence over the past two decades.

[24] For averaging to perform the buffering function, reserve requirements must be a binding factor affecting the marginal demand for reserves (see Borio 1997, 17–19). The alternative of no averaging (e.g., in China and Indonesia) means that banks are required to hold a fixed amount every day throughout the maintenance period, with a demand elasticity

Table 4.2. *Reserve requirements – main features and key ratios (as of March 2007)*

	Averaging	Carry-over	Accounting	Maintenance period	Requirements on domestic currency	Requirements on foreign currency	Remuneration
Australia							
China	No	No	Lagged	10 days	10%	4%	Yes
Eurosystem	Yes	No	Lagged	28–35 days[1]	2%	2%	Yes
Hong Kong							
India	Yes	No	Lagged	2 weeks	6%	6%	Yes (on amounts > 3%)
Indonesia	No	No	Lagged	Daily	5% + additional[2]	3%	Yes (on amounts > 5%)
Japan	Yes	No	Half-lagged	1 month	0.05%–1.3%	0.15%–0.25%	No
Korea	Yes	No	Half-lagged	Half a month	0%–7%	0%–7%	No
Macao	Yes	No	Lagged	1 week	1%–3%	1%–3%	Yes
Malaysia	Yes[3]	No	Lagged	2 weeks	4%	4%	No
New Zealand							
Philippines	Yes	Yes	Lagged	1 week	10%[4]		Yes (up to a limit)
Singapore	Yes	No	Lagged	2 weeks	3%		No
Taiwan	Yes	Yes	Half-lagged	1 month	4%–10.75%	0.125%	Yes
Thailand	Yes	Yes	Lagged	2 weeks	6%[5]	6%[5]	No (on the 1% held at CB)
United Kingdom	Yes	No	Lagged	1 MPC month	Voluntary[6]		Yes[7]
United States	Yes	Yes	Lagged	2 weeks	0%–10%		No

1 Varies with the monetary policy meeting schedule.
2 Additional requirement is linked to size of domestic currency liabilities and loan-to-deposit ratio (LDR): higher requirement for banks with higher liabilities or lower LDR.
3 Daily shortfall or excess limited to 20% of required reserves.
4 Refers to statutory reserves only; excludes 11% liquidity reserve requirement.
5 Of which, 1% is held as nonremunerated reserves; 5% can be held in eligible public securities.
6 Each reserves scheme participant chooses a targeted level of reserves for maintenance period.
7 For reserves successfully maintained within a range (normally ± 1%) around the target.

Sources: Central banks.

period.[25] Among the economies in the sample, 2-week maintenance is a typical choice, although there are also a number of systems with 1-month maintenance periods (Table 4.2, column 4). An interesting innovation is the ECB's variable length maintenance period (adopted in March 2004), which is set to be aligned with the monetary policy meeting schedule to avoid having a policy rate change in the middle of a maintenance period. This setup reduces the incentive for banks to distort their reserve-holding pattern in anticipation of policy rate changes.[26]

Another notable feature is the widespread adoption of a *lagged reserve accounting* framework (Table 4.2, column 3). With the calculation period having ended before the maintenance period begins, the amount of reserves required is thus known with certainty. This certainty helps banks plan their reserve-holding pattern. It also helps the central bank anticipate reserve demand in the period ahead. That being said, some diversity remains: at early 2007, Japan and Korea had half-lagged reserve accounting frameworks, while Taiwan had an almost contemporaneous setup (with only 4-days lag for a 1-month maintenance period), which is reminiscent of the practice in the United States between 1984 and 1998.[27]

With regard to *how much reserves are required*, the broad trend over the past decade or so has been a general reduction in the reserve ratios and a consolidation of the various classes of requirements. In the earlier era with mainly bank intermediation, reserve requirements were an important lever of monetary control and served a prudential function as well. Reserve ratios were, as a normal course of policy implementation, raised or lowered to affect liquidity conditions, and in turn other variables such as monetary aggregates. Different ratios were often applied to different types of bank liabilities to influence their composition, among other things. But with

implication similar to that in the case of no reserve requirement: the demand for reserves is determined mainly by settlement needs and not by small changes in money market rates.

[25] The smoothing of reserve demand across time can be taken further if financial institutions are allowed to "carry over" at least some (excess) reserve holdings in one maintenance period to count toward fulfilling the requirement in the following maintenance period (see Table 4.2, column 2).

[26] See http://www.ecb.int/events/calendar/reserve/html/index.en.html and European Central Bank (2003). The BoE and the Bank of Thailand have also since aligned their maintenance periods with their respective Monetary Policy Committee meeting schedules.

[27] Contemporaneous reserve requirement was once seen as a way to keep banks on their toes so as to heighten the influence of the central bank [see, e.g., Patrawimolpon (2002)]. The decline of this arrangement suggests that central banks reckon that they do not really need such an arrangement to have an influence, and that they prefer to see a more predictable demand for reserves.

the evolution of the financial system and the reduced role of monetary aggregates as intermediate targets, high ratios, and differentiated ratios, and the active manipulation thereof, have also declined in significance.

That said, there is still a lot of diversity (Table 4.2, column 5). The reserve ratios range from the very low levels in Japan to the 10% or higher (applied to at least some categories of deposits) in a number of other economies. Differentiated ratios still exist. In Japan, the reserve ratios are highly differentiated by the type of institution and the type and size of deposits.[28] In Taiwan, requirements vary according to the type of deposits.[29] In Korea, there are three levels of requirement, based on whether the bank liabilities are short, medium, or long term. In the United States, the differentiation is based on the size of the liabilities.[30]

An interesting case in this area is the BoE's voluntary reserves-averaging scheme, introduced as part of the operating framework reform in May 2006. Scheme members choose their own reserves targets, to be fulfilled on average over the maintenance period. Scheme members that manage to meet their targets (within a specified tolerance range) will be remunerated at the official bank rate.[31] With the introduction of the scheme, the reserve balances held at the BoE rose from typically less than GBP 1 billion to over GBP 16 billion, providing a substantially larger cushion.[32]

Although the active manipulation of the reserve ratio is no longer a typical means to implement monetary policy for many central banks, one can nonetheless find some recent examples.[33] In the face of excess liquidity associated with persistent capital inflows, the Chinese central bank has raised the reserve ratio a dozen times starting in September 2003. Compared to issuing central bank bills to mop up the excess liquidity, hiking reserve requirements has the advantage of being more permanent in nature and lower in cost (remuneration rate is lower than bills rate). Facing a similar situation, the Indian central bank has raised the cash reserve ratio

---

[28] See http://www.boj.or.jp/en/type/stat/boj_stat/junbi.htm

[29] See http://www.cbc.gov.tw/EngHome/ebanking/Statistics/RESERVE_REQUIREMENTS _E.asp The general trend of declining reserve ratios over time is also apparent in the cited table.

[30] See http://www.federalreserve.gov/monetarypolicy/reservereq.htm

[31] A penalty applies in case of failure to meet the target. See BoE (2007) for details.

[32] A similar voluntary reserve scheme ("contractual clearing balances") exists also in the United States, alongside the regular reserve requirements, and contributes to stabilizing the overall demand for reserves [see Board of Governors (2005, chapter 3)].

[33] An illustration of the active use of reserve requirements in former times as a lever of monetary control can be found in Bank of Korea (2002), pp. 67–70 and pp. 141–148. A general description of how reserve requirements were used in the past in a number of southeast Asian economies can be found in Dasri (1990).

multiple times since September 2004, partly reversing the trend reduction in the reserve ratio over the past decade. Reserve requirements on short-term deposits in Korea were raised for the first time in 16 years in December 2006 to influence the mix of short-term versus long-term deposits and to check the rapid growth in bank lending.[34]

Also of note is that reserve requirements since 2000 have partially shed their reputation as a "tax" on banks or a source of seigniorage revenue. Over half of the sampled central banks that impose reserve requirements do explicitly remunerate reserves in part or in full (Table 4.2, last column). While some central banks offer remuneration at rates that are clearly below the prevailing market rates, thereby still implying a "tax," some others such as the ECB and the BoE have designed their remuneration scheme on purpose to avoid this tax burden.[35] In contrast, there is no explicit remuneration in Japan, Korea, Malaysia, and Singapore. However, these economies tend to have relatively low reserve requirements on average.[36] In the United States, where nonremuneration has long been a key feature, legislation was passed in October 2006 to amend section 19 of the Federal Reserve Act, which would eventually allow explicit remuneration of reserve balances and lower the statutory *minimum* reserve requirement to zero.[37] This change in legislation opens up an opportunity for the Federal Reserve to review and possibly update its reserve requirement framework.

[34] Reserve requirements have also been used for other purposes. In Taiwan, reserve requirements on foreign currency deposit were introduced in December 2000 to put foreign and domestic currency deposits on equal footing. The authorities have since, on occasion, used this tool to counter abrupt short-term capital movements and exchange rate pressures (Central Bank of China 2006, 33). In the Philippines, the authorities hiked both liquidity and statutory reserve requirements in 2004 and 2005 to help contain exchange rate pressures. In Indonesia, currency weakness in 2004 prompted the central bank to impose an additional requirement that increases with the size of short-term liabilities. In September 2005, the additional requirement was raised further according to the banks' loan-to-deposit ratios: the more actively lending banks were subject to less additional requirement. This latter move was meant to encourage the "lazier" banks to lend more.

[35] The ECB and the BoE remunerate reserves at their policy rates, which in practice represent the levels around which very short-term money market rates fluctuate. This means that banks are on average not "taxed" for holding reserves, and is consistent with reserve requirements serving mainly reserve demand smoothing and interest rate buffering functions in these economies.

[36] The Bank of Korea stopped remunerating reserves in 1987 on the grounds that, because banks could use reserves for settlement purposes and the central bank's settlement services is provided for free, the "tax" on reserves could be seen as a means to finance the service. Moreover, because the central bank has a loan facility from which banks could borrow at subsidized rates, banks are compensated (Bank of Korea 2002, 72).

[37] See http://www.federalreserve.gov/aboutthefed/section19.htm

Taken all together, the "how" and "how much" features of reserve requirements in the early 2000s suggest that, while the liquidity management and interest rate buffer functions have become more prominent, the use of reserve requirements as an active tool of monetary control has remained relevant in some instances. Moreover, in light of the considerable number of new developments, it is clear that the design and use of reserve requirements is still very much a live issue in central banking.

4.5 Supply of Reserves

There are many instruments with which a central bank can regulate the overall supply of bank reserves (liquidity) in the system. One can classify these into two categories: *standing facilities*, which are accessed at the initiative of eligible counterparties, and *discretionary operations*, which are conducted at the initiative of the central bank. Most central banks have both categories of instruments at their disposal.

4.5.1 Standing Facilities: Evolving Roles

Standing facilities, like reserve requirements, used to play a key role in monetary policy implementation. There was a time when it was quite common for a central bank to signal its policy stance and guide bank interest rates via standing facilities rates.[38] It was then also quite common to offer multiple types of lending facilities, some of which were meant to provide loans for strategic or developmental purposes. Lending at subsidized rates was also widespread. However, with the general trend toward banking deregulation and the reduction in (or even prohibition of) policy lending by central banks, the character of standing facilities has evolved. Overall, standing facilities have tended to become simpler. Facilities that have become irrelevant relative to the central bank's mandate have been abolished, suspended, consolidated, or taken over by the fiscal authorities.[39]

---

[38] Bindseil (2004) points out that in the pre-1914 world, monetary policy implementation meant controlling short-term interest rates, mainly via the use of standing lending facilities. Tucker (2004) describes the "classical system" (1890s–1970s) in which lending at the then-penal bank rate was the BoE's main weapon for controlling market interest rates. Open market operations at the time were merely a tool for adjusting the scale or probability of market borrowing at the bank rate and had no rate-setting functions per se.

[39] The past complexity and eventual consolidation of central bank lending facilities is illustrated in Bank of Korea (2002), pp. 45–48 and pp. 129–140. A liberalization of the rediscount window, implying the elimination of directed credit for selected sectors, also

Table 4.3 summarizes the types of standing facilities offered for short-term liquidity management purposes as of early 2007.[40] Essentially all central banks have facilities for providing liquidity (by lending) to banks, typically at penal interest rates (Table 4.3, column 1). Over half of the central banks also have facilities for absorbing liquidity (by borrowing or deposit taking) from banks, usually at below-market interest rates, thus forming an interest rate corridor (Table 4.3, column 2). Some of these corridors were put in place only in recent years. Malaysia's was set up in April 2004, when the OPR was introduced. Singapore's new corridor was put in place in June 2006, and Thailand's in January 2007. Both Singapore and Thailand used to have only lending facilities – as had the United Kingdom before a deposit facility was added in June 2001. By contrast, Bank Indonesia used to offer only a deposit facility (FASBI), but introduced a lending facility in 2005.

One notable development is that the provision of short-term liquidity at subsidized, below-market rates is no longer practiced among the central banks in the sample. The BOJ's discount rate used to be a below-market lending rate, but became de facto above market in 1998, as the market interest rate declined further. This new reality was formalized with the introduction of the Complementary Lending Facility in February 2001.[41] The Federal Reserve's Discount Window, the classic textbook example of below-market lending facilities, was also replaced in 2003 by the Primary and Secondary Credit Facilities, with lending rates set at policy rate plus a margin.[42] In Taiwan, the central bank's discount rate also went from below market to above market at around the same time.

Standing facility rates are of two main types (Table 4.3, columns 3 and 4), reflecting two functions of such facilities. One type is represented by India and the Philippines, where the key standing facility rates are, in fact, the formal policy rates and thus, by definition, still perform a policy signaling function. The other is adopted by most of the other central banks, where

---

occurred in the Philippines (Tuaño-Amador 2003, 226). A brief account of a similar evolution in Japan and how the former "official discount rate" was renamed to reflect its new role can be found at http://www.boj.or.jp/en/type/release/zuiji_new/nt_cr_new/ntdis01.htm

[40] These are the key facilities for mainly short-term liquidity management purposes. Many central banks offer other longer-term facilities as well.

[41] A number of facilities that had already lost significance with respect to monetary policy implementation were also abolished. See http://www.boj.or.jp/en/type/release/zuiji/kako02/k010228b.htm

[42] See http://www.ny.frb.org/aboutthefed/fedpoint/fed18.html for a description and a brief history of the Federal Reserve's lending facilities. See http://www.frbdiscountwindow.org for the current lending rates.

Table 4.3. *Standing facilities for short-term liquidity management (as of March 2007)*

	Lending facility type[1]	Borrowing/deposit facility type[1]	Ceiling	Floor	Intraday lending facility[2]
Australia	Repo	Deposit	Policy rate + 25 bp	Policy rate – 25 bp	Yes
China	Fixed rate loan[3]	Deposit	Rediscount rate	Remuneration rate	Yes
Eurosystem	Repo or collateralized credit	Deposit	Policy rate + 100 bp	Policy rate – 100 bp	Yes[4]
Hong Kong	Repo		Base rate[5]		Yes
India	Repo	Reverse repo	Repo rate	Reverse repo rate	Yes
Indonesia	Repo	Deposit	Policy rate + 300 bp	Policy rate – 500 bp	Yes
Japan	Fixed-term loan		Basic loan rate[6]		Yes[7]
Korea	Loan (not in use)		Policy rate + 200 bp		Yes[7]
Macao	Repo		Base rate		Yes
Malaysia	Repo, sometimes collateralized loans	Direct borrowing	Policy rate + 25 bp	Policy rate – 25bp	Yes[8]
New Zealand	Repo	Deposit	Policy rate + 50 bp	Policy rate	Discontinued[9]
Philippines	Repo[10]	Reverse repo[10]	Repo rate	Reverse repo rate	Yes

Singapore	Collateralized lending	Deposit	O/N cash rate + 50 bp	O/N cash rate − 50 bp	Yes
Taiwan	Fixed rate loan[11]		Discount rate + 37.5 bp		Yes
Thailand	Repo	Borrowing (collateralized)	Policy rate + 50 bp	Policy rate − 50bp	Yes
United Kingdom	Repo	Deposit	Policy rate + 100 bp (25 bp last day of maintenance)	Policy rate + 100 bp (25 bp last day of maintenance)	Yes
United States	Fixed rate loan[12]		Policy rate + 100 bp		Yes[7]

1 Overnight or 1-day maturity unless otherwise stated.
2 Repos unless otherwise stated.
3 Various maturities.
4 Repo or overdraft depending on country.
5 Defined as max (Fed funds rate target +150 bp, 5-day moving averages of the average of overnight Hibor and 1-month Hibor).
6 Back to 25 bp above the policy rate, since the February 21, 2007 monetary policy meeting.
7 Overdraft.
8 Collateralized loans.
9 Since the liquidity management regime change in mid-2006.
10 Overnight, 2-week and 1-month maturities.
11 Various maturities, up to 360 days.
12 Small institutions lacking access to wholesale funding markets may get somewhat longer-term loans.

Sources: Central banks.

standing facility rates are set at a margin relative to their policy rates. For these central banks, standing facilities are not a policy signal per se but are a supporting device to help keep short-term market interest rates in line with the formal signal of the policy stance.[43]

The width of the interest rate corridor also speaks to the standing facilities' role. As noted in Section 4.3, the width of the corridor and the terms of access to these facilities have implications for the overnight rate volatility. All else being equal, a narrow corridor defined around the policy rate (e.g., in Australia, Malaysia, and New Zealand) would serve to dampen short-term market rate volatility around the policy rate (a "rate setting" or "rate stabilizing" function). In contrast, a wider corridor (e.g., in the euro area, the Philippines, and Indonesia) would serve mainly to reduce the chance of market rates wandering too high or too low in the event of unusual market pressures (a "safety valve" or "back-stop" function).[44]

The BoE's variable-width corridor, introduced in May 2006 as part of its operating framework reform, attempts to balance these two functions. Instead of setting the ceiling and the floor at the same fixed margin at all times, the margin stays wide ($\pm$ 100 basis points) during most of the maintenance period, emphasizing the safety valve function, but narrows to $\pm$ 25 basis points on the last day of the maintenance period to enforce the rate stabilizing function. To further enhance these two functions, the access to the standing facilities was also broadened to include even financial institutions that are not members of the reserves-averaging scheme. The quantity of liquidity on offer is also no longer rationed by the central bank's forecast of liquidity shortage. The ability to borrow from the lending facility is now only limited by the availability of eligible collateral.

Finally, it should be noted that the discussion thus far has focused on the standing facilities for satisfying the day-to-day demand for liquidity. With the general migration toward RTGS over the last decade or so, liquidity needs

---

[43] There are also special cases. In China, the lending facility rate is not related to the formal policy rates (which, in turn, have little to do with money market interest rates), while the de facto market floor is defined by the remuneration rates on excess reserves. In Singapore, because the MAS is not an interest rate targeter, there is no formal policy rate to serve as a reference. Instead, the standing facilities are priced at a $\pm$50 basis point margin around a market-determined interest rate (weighted average of successful bids at the daily morning auction for uncollateralized overnight borrowing by the MAS from primary dealers), which changes daily.

[44] Whether overnight rate fluctuations would indeed take up the full width of the corridor depends on the other aspects of the operating framework, such as whether there is averaging (see Section 4.4) and whether the central bank regulates the overall supply of reserves proactively via discretionary operations (see below).

are no longer concentrated at the end of the trading day, but exist throughout the day. Most central banks in the sample offer some kind of intraday liquidity facility, in the form of either lending or overdraft (Table 4.3, last column).[45] A notable exception is New Zealand, which opted in 2006 to discontinue its intraday facility as part of its new liquidity management regime.[46]

4.5.2 Discretionary Operations

With standing facilities now playing mostly a supporting role, discretionary operations have become the main tool that central banks use to regulate the overall supply of bank reserves (liquidity). Discretionary operations can be of six main types: (1) outright purchases or sales of domestic currency assets in the secondary market, (2) issuance of central bank paper in the primary market, (3) reversed purchases or sales of domestic currency assets (repos and reverse repos), (4) reversed purchases or sales of foreign currency assets (e.g., FX swaps), (5) direct borrowing or lending in the interbank market, and (6) transfer of public entity deposits at the central bank to or from the banking system. Most central banks have more than one of these at their disposal. However, not all available instruments are necessarily in active use under normal circumstances.[47] Table 4.4 outlines the key and supporting discretionary operations that are typically in use as of early 2007. Three observations are in order.

First, operations based on marketable assets (types 1 to 4) are currently more widely used than is direct interbank borrowing/lending (type 5). This is the case even for central banks that target the overnight interbank market rate. In particular, reversed transactions (typically based on public sector securities) are quite popular, given the greater flexibility they offer and the smaller impact they have on the prices of the underlying securities compared to outright transactions. The transfer of public sector deposits (type 6), though still an available option for some central banks, is currently not a typical operation.

---

[45] Because intraday liquidity is mainly for the purpose of facilitating settlement, it is often provided interest-free against eligible collateral or at a service charge.

[46] The new regime basically seeks to supply the system with sufficient liquidity up front, so that there will be less need for banks to resort to central bank lending. See Reserve Bank of New Zealand (2006).

[47] An extreme example is Hong Kong, where the monetary authority is technically capable of conducting most types of operations, but chooses to eschew discretionary operations in order to comply with the ideal of a rule-based currency board regime.

Table 4.4. *Main and other discretionary operations (as of March 2007)*

	Main or keynote operation(s)			Other operation(s) in use	
	Type	Typical maturity	Typical frequency	Type	Typical maturity
Australia	RT	1 day to 3 months	Daily	OT, FXS	1 day to 3 months
China	CBP (PBC bills)	Up to 3 years	2 × week	RT	7–182 days
Eurosystem	RP or CL	1 week/ 3 months	Weekly/monthly	RP (Quick tenders)	Varies
Hong Kong					
India	RT	1 day	2 × day	OT (Market stabilization scheme)	From 91 days
Indonesia	CBP (SBIs)	28 days	Weekly		
Japan	CL, RT	O/N up to ~3 months	2–3 × day	OT	Up to 91 days, mainly 1 to 14 days
Korea	CBP (MSBs)	Up to 2 years	Weekly	RT	
Macao	CBP (MBs)	1 to 365 days	Daily	FXS, OT	1–365 days
Malaysia	DB	O/N to 3 months	Daily	RP, RS, securities-lending CBP	2–4 months / 3–12 months
New Zealand	FXS	1 week to 18 months	Varies (≤ daily)	Bond lending facilities	O/N to 1 week
Philippines			Discretionary	FXS	Varies
Singapore	RP, FXS, DB, DL	Up to 1 year	Daily		
Taiwan	CBP (CDs/NCDs)	Up to 3 years		FXS, RP, OT	Up to 3 months
Thailand	RP, FXS, OT, CBP		Varies by type	Securities lending, bilateral RP	
United Kingdom	RP	1 week/longer term	Weekly/monthly	Fine-tuning at end of maintenance	
United States	RP	O/N to 14 days	Daily/weekly	OT (purchase)	O/N

Key: CBP = issuance of central bank paper, CL = collateralized lending, DB = direct borrowing, DL = direct lending, RP = reversed purchases ("repo"), RS = RRP = reversed sales ("reverse repo"), RT = reversed transactions (= RP and/or RS), FXS = FX swaps, OT = outright transactions (purchases and/or sales).
Sources: Central banks.

Second, the baseline liquidity scenario faced by a central bank is an important determinant of the modal operation. Central banks that tend to face liquidity deficits in the system would typically need to inject liquidity by purchasing assets, either outright or under repo agreement. This is the case in Australia, the euro area, Japan, New Zealand (prior to June 2006), the United Kingdom, and the United States. In contrast, central banks that tend to face structural liquidity surpluses would typically need to absorb liquidity by selling assets. This is the case in most of non-Japan Asia.

On this second observation, it is worth noting that central banks facing *chronic* surpluses or deficits could eventually exhaust their typical instrument and need to look for alternatives. For example, if a central bank does not have a lot of readily sellable assets, its capacity to handle a chronic liquidity surplus could be constrained. There are several alternatives. One is to have the central bank issue its own securities in the primary market to absorb liquidity. This has been a typical solution in much of non-Japan Asia, where traditionally small fiscal deficits have meant small outstanding stocks of government securities in general, and even less at the disposal of central banks.[48] Regular auctions of central bank paper have long been the key operation in Indonesia, Korea, and Taiwan. China joined this group in 2003, when the central bank resumed issuing bills and bonds. In Malaysia, while daily tenders for uncollateralized, direct interbank borrowing have so far remained the key operation, central bank paper issuance has gained importance with the amendment of the central bank law in 2006.[49] Singapore and India represent two notable exceptions. In both cases, it was the government that took up the responsibility of issuing more eligible securities to facilitate liquidity absorption.[50] This approach amounts to fiscal overfunding (McCauley 2006).

---

[48] Even with the stepped-up efforts to develop the local bond market after the Asian crisis, the availability of government securities is still nowhere comparable to that in Japan or the United States, where operations based on government securities have been the standard fare.

[49] Before the amendment (effective October 2006), BNM had limited scope to use Bank Negara Bills as a key instrument, given the strict issuance limit (linked to BNM's capital). But since then, BNM could issue a new type of securities, Bank Negara Monetary Notes, which are usable in both conventional and Islamic financial markets and are subject to a more flexible issuance limit (linked to the level of international reserves). Adding another active instrument can diversify the cost of operations.

[50] When the proceeds of issuance are deposited with the central bank, private sector liquidity becomes "locked up" as government deposits. The additional government securities in private sector hands can potentially also serve as collateral for subsequent repurchase transactions.

The need to find alternatives is also a theme among some central banks that are chronic net injectors of liquidity. In Australia and New Zealand, fiscal surpluses since the late 1990s have not only tended to see a net drain of liquidity from the system but also a decline in the outstanding stock of government securities. Absent any initiative for the fiscal authorities to overfund and issue more debt securities, it would not be sustainable to continue to rely on purchasing central government securities as the main means to inject liquidity.[51] In response, the Australian central bank has chosen to accept other high-quality securities to extend its ability to conduct reversed purchases, and has supplemented reversed purchases of securities with more foreign exchange swap operations.[52] Less ready to expand the range of eligible securities, the New Zealand central bank has initially opted to use mainly foreign exchange swaps to supply the bulk of needed liquidity.

Third, there is a link between the choice of instruments and the state of financial market development. As mentioned above, an underdeveloped government securities market (or a developed but shrinking one) has impinged upon some central banks' ability to conduct operations with government securities, thus requiring them to seek alternatives. That being said, financial market sophistication does not always have to be a binding constraint on instrument choice.[53] Among the central banks surveyed, there are examples of innovations that were undertaken with the expressed intention of fostering financial market development.

Two cases in point are the introduction of exchange fund bills and notes in Hong Kong in the early 1990s, and the decision by the Singaporean government to overfund and issue government securities in the late 1990s. Both actions served to create new eligible paper for monetary operations and to kick-start the public sector securities market. Rather than changing the law to allow central bank paper issuance, India's approach of having more government issuance under the monetary stabilization scheme adds size and

---

[51] The United States faced a similar concern at the turn of this century. The concern eventually faded with the return of fiscal deficits. Nonetheless, the efforts made at the time to identify alternative instruments and study their implications helped the Fed prepare for subsequent initiatives to modify its operating procedures. See Federal Reserve System Study Group on Alternative Instruments for System Operations (2002).

[52] The list of eligible paper was first expanded in March 2004 to include state government securities, Australian dollar securities issued by certain foreign entities, bank bills, and certificate of deposits. Broadbent (2008) provides a discussion of this development.

[53] McCauley (2008) explores the reciprocal relationship between financial market development and monetary operations. Archer (2006) makes a similar point about banking system development and monetary operations.

potentially liquidity to the government bond market. In Thailand, the initiative to shift operations away from "BOT repos" to "bilateral repos," and ultimately phase out the "BOT repo market" in 2003–2007, was intended to pave the way for a genuine private repo market.[54] A facility to allow primary dealers to borrow specific bonds on a temporary basis was also introduced in 2004 to help support market-making activity and market liquidity. Other central banks (e.g., in Australia, Japan, Malaysia, New Zealand, and the United States) also operate securities-lending facilities to recycle in-demand issues back to market participants. The Malaysian central bank even introduced a program to borrow securities from the typically buy-and-hold institutional investors. It could then conduct liquidity absorption operations by reversed sales of these freed-up securities.

4.5.3 Putting the Pieces Together

While it is instructive to compare individual features across central banks, it is also important to make sense of how the features fit together within a framework. If a central bank prefers to manage liquidity actively with discretionary operations (e.g., operating daily), it will have relatively less need to rely on standing facilities as a safety valve, or on reserve requirement as an interest rate buffer. This approach characterizes the Federal Reserve- or BOJ-style framework. However, if a less frequent operation schedule (e.g., weekly) is preferred, then it would make sense to have user-friendly standing facilities and a robust reserves-averaging scheme to help smooth out imbalances between operation dates. This approach characterizes the BoE- or ECB-style framework. Both framework styles could, in principle, achieve the same operating objectives equally well.

Different approaches also apply with respect to the range of discretionary operations, counterparties, and collateral. A "narrow" set of operations (e.g., repos on government securities with primary dealers only) may be quite sufficient if the relevant collateral is always available and the counterparties are effective agents for propagating the impact of operations to the broader market. Otherwise, using a wider set of operations with diversified collateral and counterparty types may be more practical. As seen in Table 4.4 (column 1), a number of Asian central banks have relied on issuing paper

---

[54] In the BOT repo market, the central bank acted as the central counterparty in every transaction. The pricing thus did not reflect the true credit risks of the ultimate lenders and borrowers. It also left market participants with little incentive to deal directly with each other, as in a genuine private repo market.

as their main discretionary operation. This approach is in part a solution to the lack of other eligible collateral, but has at times raised questions about the snowballing interest cost and the possible impact on market liquidity of having more than one public sector issuer. By contrast, some other central banks (e.g., in Malaysia, Singapore, and Thailand) have opted for a mix of operations. This diversified approach may have its origins also in market underdevelopment or legal constraints, but could in principle reduce the risk of putting any one operation or collateral type under excessive strain.

All in all, each of the possible approaches represented by the central banks discussed in this chapter has both benefits and costs. The suitability of any given approach is always a function of factors such as the state of financial development, institutional characteristics, legal and regulatory constraints, and the objectives and even preferences of the central bank. It is difficult, or even inappropriate, to talk of "best practices" in monetary policy implementation without giving reference to these factors.

4.6 Concluding Remarks: And the Evolution Continues

This survey of 17 central banks' operating frameworks highlights the notable changes that took place in the late 1990s and early 2000s. It confirms a number of common themes: a focus on short-term money market rates as operating objectives, a widespread adoption of reserves averaging, use of interest rate corridors with penalty rates, and a search for alternative instruments. The variety of circumstances represented in the sample also clearly demonstrates that there is still a lot of diversity with respect to how the different operational elements fit together. The differences are not just between industrial and emerging economies, but exist even among the four major central banks. In short, there is no unique "best" way that suits all central banks, even if they happen to pursue similar operating objectives.

A perhaps more striking finding is that even within just the last couple of years, there have been innovations in virtually all aspects of monetary policy implementation – from redefinition of policy rates and operating targets, to adoption of new instruments, to complete overhaul of reserve requirement frameworks. It is therefore also clear that no operating framework can be the "right" one for all times.

Just a few months after the early 2007 sample date, there were already some notable updates. The Bank of Korea announced in July 2007 plans to reform its operating framework in 2008, migrating from a Federal Reserve-/BOJ-style framework to a BoE-/ECB-style one.[55] Bank Indonesia formally changed its operating target to the overnight interbank rate in June 2008.[56] Many industrial economy central banks had to adjust their operating frameworks and procedures to different degrees in response to the protected money market turmoil that broke out in August 2007.[57] Some of these turmoil-induced adjustments will be phased out after the return of normality. Others may remain or evolve further to reflect any lasting changes in the financial system and lessons learned during the turmoil. All these latest developments only reinforce the basic message of this chapter: that central banks everywhere will continue to refine their frameworks and procedures and to innovate where necessary, responding to changing needs in both normal and turbulent times.

References

Archer, D. (2006), "Implications of recent changes in banking for the conduct of monetary policy," in *BIS Papers* **28**: 123–151.

Bank of England (2007), *The Framework for the Bank of England's Operations in the Sterling Money Markets* (the 'Red Book'), February.

Bank of Korea (2002), *Monetary Policy in Korea*. Available at http://www.bok.or.kr/content/old/attach/00000888/200301161403380.pdf

Bindseil, U. (2004), "The operational target of monetary policy and the rise and fall of reserve position doctrine," *ECB Working Paper Series* **372**, June.

Board of Governors of the Federal Reserve System (2005), *Purposes & Functions*. Available at http://www.federalreserve.gov/pf/pf.htm

Borio, C. E. V. (1997), "Implementation of monetary policy in industrial countries: a survey," *BIS Economic Papers* **47**, August.

Borio, C. E. V. and R. N. McCauley (2001), "Comparing monetary policy operating procedures in Indonesia, Korea, Malaysia and Thailand," in G. De Brouwer (Ed.), *Financial Markets and Policies in East Asia* (London: Routledge), pp. 253–285.

Broadbent, J. (2008), "Financial market innovation in Australia: implications for the conduct of monetary policy," in *BIS Papers* **39**.

Buzeneca, I. and R. Maino (2007), "Monetary policy implementation: Results from a survey," *IMF Working Paper* 07/7.

Central Bank of China (2006), *CBC Purposes and Functions*, December. Available at http://www.cbc.gov.tw/EngHome/Eeconomic/Publications/CBC_Purposes_Function.asp

[55] See http://www.bok.or.kr/template/eng/html/index.jsp?tbl=tbl_FM0000000066_CA0000009927

[56] See http://www.bi.go.id/web/en/Ruang+Media/Siaran+Pers/sp_102608.htm

[57] Committee on the Global Financial System (2008) has a chronology of actions up until mid-June 2008.

Clews, R (2005), "Implementing monetary policy: reforms to the Bank of England's operations in the money market," *Bank of England Quarterly Bulletin*, Summer: 211–220.

Committee on the Global Financial System (2008), "Central bank operations in response to the financial turmoil," *CGFS Papers* **31**, July.

Dasri, T. (1990), *The Reserve Requirement as a Monetary Instrument in the SEACEN Countries*, The South East Asian Central Banks Research and Training Centre, Kuala Lumpur, Malaysia.

European Central Bank (2003) "Changes to the Eurosystem's operational framework for monetary policy," *ECB Monthly Bulletin*, August: 41–54.

Federal Reserve System Study Group on Alternative Instruments for System Operations (2002), *Alternative instruments for open market and Discount Window operations*, Board of Governors of the Federal Reserve System, December.

Freedman, C. (2000), "Monetary policy implementation: Past present and future – will electronic money lead to the eventual demise of central banking?," *International Finance* **3**:2: 211–227.

Hilton, S. (2005), "Trends in federal funds rate volatility," in *Current Issues in Economics and Finance*, Federal Reserve Bank of New York, July.

Ho, C. (2008), "Implementing monetary policy in the 2000s: Operating procedures in Asia and beyond," *BIS Working Papers* **253**, June.

International Monetary Fund (2004), "Monetary policy implementation at different stages of market development," paper prepared by staff of the Monetary and Financial Systems Department, 26 October 2004. (Also as *IMF Occasional Paper* **244**, December 2005)

Kneeshaw, J. T. and P. Van den Bergh (1989), "Changes in central bank money market operating procedures in the 1980s," *BIS Economic Papers* **23**, January.

Laurens, B. J. and R. Maino (2007), "China: Strengthening monetary policy implementation," *IMF Working Paper* **07/14**.

McCauley, R. N. (2006), "Consolidating the public bond markets of Asia," in *BIS Papers* **30**: 82–98.

    (2008), "Developing financial markets and operating monetary policy in East Asia," in *BIS Papers* **39**.

Monetary Authority of Singapore (2001), *Singapore's Exchange Rate Policy*, monograph. Available at http://www.mas.gov.sg/publications/

    (2007), *Monetary Policy Operations in Singapore*, monograph. Available at http://www.mas.gov.sg/publications/

Patrawimolpon, P. (2002), "Open market operations and effectiveness of monetary policy," *Occasional Papers* **34**, The South East Asian Central Banks Research and Training Centre, Kuala Lumpur, Malaysia.

Prati, A., L. Bartolini, and G. Bertola (2003), "The overnight interbank market: Evidence from the G-7 and the Euro zone," *Journal of Banking & Finance* **27**, 10: 2045–2083.

Reserve Bank of Australia (2003), "The Reserve Bank's open market operations," *Reserve Bank of Australia Bulletin*, June.

Reserve Bank of New Zealand (2006), *Reform of the Reserve Bank of New Zealand's Liquidity Management Operations*, June.

Tuaño-Amador, M. C. N. (2003), "Central banking in the Philippines since 1993," in *Money & Banking in the Philippines*, Bangko Sentral ng Pilipinas.

Tucker, P. (2004), "Managing the central bank's balance sheet: where monetary policy meets financial stability," *Bank of England Quarterly Bulletin*, Autumn: 359–382.

Van't dack, J. (1999), "Implementing monetary policy in emerging market economies: an overview of issues," *BIS Policy Papers* 5: 3–72.

Woodford, M. (2000), "Monetary policy in a world without money," *International Finance* 3:2: 229–260.

PART II

THE SCOPE OF CENTRAL BANKING OPERATIONS AND CENTRAL BANK INDEPENDENCE

5

Analysis of Financial Stability

Charles A. E. Goodhart and Dimitri P. Tsomocos

Abstract

There is a remarkable consensus about the framework whereby a central bank should fulfill its macromonetary functions. In sharp contrast, there is no consensus about the framework for achieving its financial stability objective, either on the appropriate theory or practice. In this chapter we record how and why it has been so difficult to achieve consensus in this field. We start with a historical outline of central banks' financial stability role, describe their current functions in this respect, and then discuss the reasons why there has been, in recent years, such a diversity of views on the best way to organize the management of financial stability. In the second part of the chapter we ask how a satisfactory theoretical basis to address financial stability issues might be obtained. The first essential is that any such theory and model must be firmly based on a proper analysis of the probability of bank default (PD). We outline how such a model can be developed.

5.1 Introduction: The Financial Stability Role of Central Banks

On the macroeconomic policy side of central banking, a remarkable consensus has been emerging over the last two decades. This covers both the applicable theoretical framework for analyzing the transmission mechanism of monetary policy and also the appropriate institutional structure for the central bank to deploy its macroeconomic policies. The consensus about the latter structure generally involves a high degree of operational independence from government; the de facto selection of price stability as the primary objective (except in those countries on a pegged or fixed exchange

Our thanks are due to Forrest Capie, Rosa Lastra, Pierre Siklos, and two anonymous referees for helpful comments and suggestions. All errors are, however, our own.

rate, or in a currency union); and the choice of a short-term interest rate, selected on preannounced dates within the context of a forward-looking forecasting structure as the main instrument. When a country strays from this consensus – for example, when Poland or Venezuela seeks to curtail its central bank's operational independence, or when a French politician casts doubt on the primacy of the price stability objective – one can almost hear the sharp intake of breath among the world-wide "club" of central banks and at its focal point, the Bank for International Settlements (BIS) in Basel.

There is no such consensus on the appropriate theoretical framework for the analysis of financial stability. Indeed, some would claim that there is no proper theoretical framework for this function at all. We shall turn to this issue later, in Section 5.2, but first let us turn to the great diversity of institutional structures that exist for central banks on the stability/prudential/systemic stability wing. On this, see in particular, Mayes and Wood (2007), especially their introduction, Mayes and Wood (Chapter 6, this volume), also Masciandaro and Quintyn (2007), and Masciandaro, Quintyn, and Taylor (Chapter 8, this volume).

5.2 Historical Development of the Financial Stability Role of Central Banks

The earliest banks that eventually became transformed into central banks, such as the Riksbank, the Bank of England, and the Banque de France, were initially established to provide certain banking and financial services to the government, notably including the provision of funding during war time. In return they received certain competitive and governance advantages that quickly enabled them to become the largest *commercial* bank in their own country. As a result of their central role, they had both a complementary relationship, especially with the smaller country banks, and also a competitive relationship, especially with the larger joint-stock banks (Cameron 1967, 1972; Goodhart 1988).

It then became more efficient to centralize reserve holdings of specie with the governments' (central) bank with the other commercial banks using claims on the central bank, notes, and deposits, as reserves. By the same token, it was far simpler to settle payment imbalances between banks by an exchange of claims on the central bank than by carting gold bullion around the country. Moreover, a commercial banker that held balances with a central bank and had a long-standing customer relationship with it would be more likely to obtain loans from the central bank when there were temporary liquidity problems.

Nevertheless, the central bank was also a direct rival for the other main commercial banks during the nineteenth century, especially for the large, diversified joint stock banks that developed in the second half of the century. There are many examples of quite bitter rivalry. It was only slowly, and quite reluctantly, that the central bank shed its commercial role toward the end of the nineteenth century. Given this commercial rivalry, the idea that the central bank should have direct supervisory oversight of the commercial banks and be able to inspect their books and review their management practices, would have been unacceptable to commercial bankers at the turn of the last century.[1]

The way that central banks tried to keep oversight over the stability of the banking system was to keep watch over the *quality* of the commercial bills in money markets, as it was such bills that the central bank would be requested to discount in a crisis. Indeed many central banks have strict limits on the nature and quality of assets that they can buy, rediscount, or use as collateral for their lender of last resort (LOLR) functions; this was a major reason why the Bundesbank arranged for the establishment of the Likobank in 1974, since their own capacity to undertake LOLR operations was so constrained by legal limitations. The aim of central banks was to ensure that the quality of available money market assets was good enough to enable them to inject liquidity into the banking system in case of need, without running into unacceptable danger of loss themselves. This was one of the foundations of the "real bills" doctrine. This doctrine provided a unifying basis both for the prudential/systemic and the macroeconomic policy aspects of central bank policy.[2] If the self-liquefying characteristics of the commercial bills were good enough, being based on real trade activities whereby the final sale of products would raise more than enough funds to repay the debt, then both the quality and, it was assumed, the volume of such debt was sustainable, and could safely be the basis for central bank market actions, including LOLR (Bagehot 1873).

So much of the early central bank prudential oversight focused on the nature and quality of bank assets, primarily in commercial bill markets, and *not* on a direct examination of the books or the management practices of other commercial banks. For example, in the United Kingdom, prior to

---

[1] Also see Grossman (2006).
[2] Though, as well-known now, the "real bills" doctrine is a misleading guide for macropolicy purposes, and has been blamed for leading the Fed astray in the Great Depression in the United States, 1929–33, see Meltzer (2003), Friedman and Schwartz (1963), and Timberlake (2007).

the Fringe Bank crisis in 1973–1974, prudential oversight in the Bank of England was the province of the Discount Office, a small section within the Cashier's Department, run by a principal with a couple of deputies. They focused their attention on the Accepting Houses, whose role then included the acceptance of commercial bills, turning them into two-name bills, and on the Discount Houses, which acted as a buffer between the commercial banks on the one hand, and the central bank on the other. The discount houses were initially fostered by the Bank of England, and used by the commercial banks, precisely because the historical rivalry between the two made direct dealings between them problematic. When that faded into the dim, historical past in the 1990s, so did the discount houses.

The Bank of England's Discount Office was meant to gather general *market intelligence*, that is, the standing and reputation of banking and credit institutions, but had no right of onsite inspection of the commercial banks. In so far as there was any authority in the United Kingdom that could examine banks' books, it lay in the hands of the Department (Board) of Trade, but was rarely utilized. The Chairmen of the big London clearing banks did come into the Bank of England to discuss their accounts and general position with the Governor, but only on an informal, nonstatutory basis.

In the United States, prudential oversight of the national banks, as contrasted with state-chartered banks, had been allocated to the Office of the Comptroller of the Currency, a part of the Treasury Department in 1864 as part of the National Banking Act. Before the foundation of the Federal Reserve System in 1913, state banks were regulated and supervised by the respective state banking authorities.

The Glass–Steagall Act [of 1933] also created the FDIC with the authority to resolve failed banks, but left the authority to close banks with their respective regulators – state, Federal Reserve, OCC – or the bank's directors. This had the effect of creating a resolution process for banks that was entirely separate from the bankruptcy process that applied to other corporations (and individuals) (Bliss 2007, 135).[3]

The structure of U.S. financial supervision is, as a consequence of successive acts creating separate regulatory bodies, quite a muddle, involving problems of coordination and interagency rivalry. But attempts to rationalize it have failed; each of the agencies involved has defended its own turf with some passion.

World War I not only destroyed much of the prewar international financial system, centered on the international, commercial bill on London, but

---

[3] Also see Bliss and Kaufman (2006).

also left the European combatant countries with a huge overhang of government debt. Because such government debt, denominated in domestic currency, is supposedly default free, the banks in such countries had more than a sufficiency of "high quality" assets that the central bank could rediscount without loss. The problems that arose in the "Great Depression" were of insolvency, arising out of credit risk, rather than of illiquidity. This had to be handled by governments rather than by central banks; central banks can create liquidity, they cannot create capital.

The banking crises in Europe in the interwar period were handled in different ways in the different countries involved. In many cases this adverse experience with bank insolvencies led to the establishment of separate institutions entrusted with responsibility for bank examination and oversight. In some countries this body, and the responsibility, was allocated to and embedded within the central bank, for example, Italy,[4] Spain, Ireland, and, in so far as it was done at all, in the Netherlands (Mooij and Prast 2003). In several other countries, the responsible prudential institution was, or became, totally separate, for example, Canada, Germany,[5] Denmark,[6] Norway, Sweden, and Switzerland.[7] In yet other countries, there was a formally

---

[4] See Cope (1938). A financial inspectorate was created by the Law of 1926 and reaffirmed by the Laws of 1936 and 1937. This was housed in the Banca d'Italia and its head was the Governor. But especially after the laws of 1936 and 1937, overriding control of key decisions rested with Fascist ministers.

[5] "When the stability of the banking system was at stake during the Great Depression of the 1930s, the power of the Reichsbank to intervene in the management of this crisis was constrained by high levels of foreign debt and a system of fixed exchange rates. Consequently, the government had to intervene, acquiring substantial shareholdings in the problem banks. In 1961, the government founded the Federal Banking Supervisory Office as an independent institution responsible to the Minister of Finance, establishing the separation of monetary and banking supervision functions" (Kahn and Santos 2007, 190). Also see Dark (1938).

Dark notes that the Banking Act of 1934 led to a system of regulatory/supervisory control, "through a Supervisory Board (Aufsichtsamt für das Kreditwesen) and a Banking Commissioner (Reichskommisar für das Kreditwesen)" (p. 199). Initially this was "established at the Reichsbank" (p. 218), and headed by the President of the Reichsbank Directorate, but in 1938 this role reverted to the Ministry of Finance (see Grossman 2006).

[6] See Cope (1938). In the Nordic countries of Denmark, Norway, and Sweden, an Inspectorate of Banks was set up, quite early in the twentieth century, separate from the central bank.

[7] See Allen (1938, 369–370). He wrote, "The Banking Commission itself, while a state-created organisation, is not a government department, and is claimed to be free of 'red tape' and to constitute a supple instrument of control. The state itself, and incidentally the central bank (although this latter point is not emphasized in the official literature), avoid responsibility. This, at least, is the published opinion of the legislators, but one cannot see how the state can avoid responsibility in a sphere in which it has undertaken to legislate."

separate institution, but the relevant commission or supervisory body had such strong links with the central bank, notably in management, personnel, and location, that the separation was more formal than real (e.g., Belgium[8] and France).

In so far as there was any common denominator to the choice between having a completely separate banking inspectorate and one housed in the central bank, it may have depended on the degree of distrust of the centralization of power. In countries with a tradition of a separation of powers (e.g., Switzerland, the Nordic countries, and Canada), the inspectorate was separate. In more unitary, centralized, and bigger countries, the prudential authority became part of the central bank; indeed, in fascist countries it became eventually transferred into the Ministry of Finance (see also Grossman 2006).

So there was no common historical tradition of the central bank acting as banking supervisor. Moreover, in the next 35 years, from about 1935 until about 1970, the need for the exercise of bank supervision fell into abeyance. A key feature of these decades was the absence of banking crises, as evidenced by Figure 5.1, taken from Bordo et al. (2001). In the aftermath of the Great Depression, interest rates became low and stable, and bankers more cautious. The onset of World War II led to a further

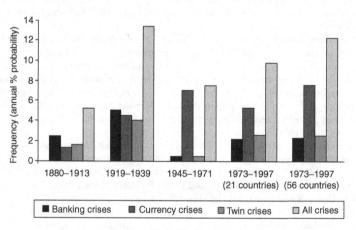

Figure 5.1. Crisis frequency

---

[8] See Witheridge (1938). The key reform of the Law of September 1935 establishing the Commission Bancaire: "It is intended that the Commission shall work in close co-operation with the National Bank..." (p. 102), and "their remuneration is... paid in the first instance by the National Bank" (p. 197).

expansion of government debt, much of which was held in the banking sector. The need to make room for such debt, and the rise of socialist command and control ideology, led to the imposition of direct credit controls. Such controls, in the context of postwar rebuilding and balance of payments problems, generally directed such limited credits to the private sector to the largest, long-established manufacturing and export sectors. This was not, in general, an efficient way to allocate scarce capital, but it did have the merit that banks subject to such direct controls bore little credit risk, and were predominantly safe, somewhat akin to nationalized utilities.

This somewhat artificial stability came to an end in the late 1960s and 1970s. A restoration of faith in the operation of free markets, the liberalization of direct controls, and the continuing improvement of international communications, all led to conditions in which banks were able to choose differing strategies, some of them riskier. In international finance, the eurodollar market emerged, and the ability of financial institutions to use this as a vehicle for avoiding exchange controls helped to lead to the breakdown of the Bretton Woods pegged exchange rate system. In national financial systems, fringe banks (and nonbank financial institutions) emerged to exploit business opportunities that the main commercial banks were prevented from entering by direct credit controls. This disintermediation into uncontrolled, and sometimes less reputable, institutions led to inherent weakness, for example, the British fringe bank crisis (1973–1974). In turn, this generated pressures to dismantle the prior direct controls, freeing banks to decide on the disposition of their portfolios. But for the prior 35 to 40 years bankers had had relatively little experience or training in risk assessment. And with the macroeconomic conjuncture becoming more volatile in the late 1960s and 1970s, it is no surprise that banks, and banking systems, similarly became more unstable.

5.3 The Functions of a Central Bank in the Provision of Financial Stability

As already noted, the institutional structure of banking supervision at this juncture was extremely diverse, with central banks sometimes playing no supervisory role and sometimes having full responsibility for bank supervision. But whatever their supervisory role, central banks must have a functional concern and an operational role in the maintenance of systemic stability of the banking and payments system, and for the resolution of financial crisis should such stability be threatened. So central banks will want, and need, to play a continuing role in designing the *regulations* (rules) under which the banks operate, even if the *supervision* of banks (i.e., checking that the rules are actually observed and imposing sanctions when they are not), is conducted by a separate institution. The importance and relevance of distinguishing between regulation and supervision is emphasized in Lastra (2001; Chapter 2; Chapter 3).

The fact that payments are finally settled in transfers of a central bank's own liabilities gives it a necessary role in overseeing a country's payments and settlements systems, both internally and externally (e.g., in FX markets, CLS, Target, Swift, etc.). Somewhat more arguably, this may also extend to a concern with the risk management and payment and settlement systems of the other major financial markets, for example, for bonds, equities, and, perhaps, commodities, within its purview. After all, a central bank usually seeks to maintain price stability by money market operations and to sustain some chosen level of interest rates, and such market operations will be impeded and less effective if such markets have become disturbed and subject to panics. Neither its money market operations nor its macroeconomy policy objectives (price stability) will be achieved smoothly if financial institutions and markets are in a state of crisis.

Moreover there is no other institution besides the central bank that can create liquidity quickly in a crisis, and injections of liquidity are frequently a prerequisite for crisis management. Alternatives have been tried. One such example is a consortium of commercial banks, acting together in their role as managers of a clearing house (see Timberlake 1984). But historical experience, notably in the United States, showed that their ability to stem a crisis was limited and subject to commercial conflicts of interest. Another possibility is for the government to act on its own, and some such government action may indeed become necessary when some of the banks involved are probably insolvent. But such government action has its own disadvantages of delay, potential corruption, and favoritism, and the intermediation in the process of a disinterested and professional central bank is comparatively preferable.[9]

---

[9] Indeed, direct government intervention in banking has complicated the operation of regulation and supervision in numerous ways, whether such supervision is carried out by the central bank or by a separate body. In many countries, for example, India, the government is the owner of a large segment of the commercial banking system. In such cases the supervision of such banks may not be allocated to the bank supervisor, as was the case until recently in Brazil, or constrained in various other ways. For this and other reasons, government ownership of banks has been statistically significantly related to contagious failure (see Barth, Caprio, and Levine 2005).

Buiter (2006) suggested that, not only should the responsibility for banking supervision be hived off to a separate supervisory body, but also that that body be given sufficiently large overdraft facilities with the central bank to undertake liquidity injections attendant on crisis management on its own. Our response to that is that the supervisory body would then become the de facto central bank, and the other body setting nominal interest rates would just be a macroeconomic committee, and not a bank of any kind. It is, perhaps, arguable that the macroeconomic function of a central bank should be separated from the banking and stability functions of a central bank, and transferred to a committee of "wise men" of professional economists; this does seem to be the direction of current trends, but we doubt whether it is really possible, or desirable, to try to separate macroeconomic stability issues from financial market and institutional stability matters, as Buiter (2008) now seems to agree.

Be that as it may, it is surely possible to separate operational oversight over banking *supervision* from responsibility for overall market and systemic stability, if only because this is what has happened in many countries. But when concern about banking and financial stability came to the fore again in the late 1960s and early 1970s, it often did so in an *international* context, for example, with the failure of Bankhaus Herstatt in 1974. There was no world-wide forum then established for bank supervisors to meet and discuss common problems, though within the European Economic Commission (EEC) an autonomous initiative of supervisory officials had set up the Groupe de Contact in 1972. By contrast, the central banks did have an international forum in being, in the guise of the G-10 Governors' Committee at the BIS in Basel. In 1974–1975 they co-opted the banking supervisors, whether central bank based or not, into the new Basel Committee on Banking Supervision, but under overall central bank direction.

With the international aspect of crisis management having become more important, the central banks became the dominant players in this international field. The 1970s and 1980s became decades during which central bank responsibility for setting financial regulation, for example, the Concordat and Basel I, and for operational control of crisis management became institutionalized and extended.

Furthermore, government guaranties (explicit or implicit) of banks have been an important characteristic of banking in Germany and some other European countries. Thus the state guarantees that public sector banks in Germany have enjoyed – Sparkassen and Landesbanken – have only been phased out recently. Such guarantees distort banking markets, and their effect on relative competitiveness may weaken the rest of the banking system.

5.4　Recent Challenges to the Financial Stability Role of Central Banks

The high point, or apogee, of this shift of regulatory/prudential functions toward central banks was reached about the end of the 1980s. This was marked by four events: the successful passage of the Basel I capital Accord in 1987–1988; the adoption of a new regime of inflation targetry, together with operational independence, in New Zealand in 1988–1989; the gradual blurring of the commercial dividing lines between commercial and investment banking and insurance, with the rise of universal banking; and, finally, the growing importance of financial/pension arrangements for a wealthier and longer-lived population.

Let us take these four developments in reverse order. First, the growing importance of finance/pensions to a growing swathe of the population enhanced its political salience. This meant that conduct of business/consumer protection issues would tend to loom even larger in retail regulatory/supervisory matters (Westrup 2007). Central banks, with a primarily economic rather than legal/accounting tradition, and a comparatively small staff, were not well placed to do this kind of work and did not wish to take it on. Second, the blurring of commercial divisions again implied that central banks would have to extend their field of professional competence, and perhaps the safety net, to a wider range of institutions and markets than those with which they had been historically involved. Only in a few, mostly small, countries such as Ireland and Singapore was responsibility for supervision of the full range of financial institutions vested in the central bank.

Third, inflation targetry involved not only making price stability the primary objective, but also giving the central bank operational independence from government to vary interest rates so as to achieve that end. For most central banks, which had become increasingly subservient to governments under the requirements of World War II and postwar socialism, this was a marked recovery of power. Moreover, the successful pursuit of price stability is much facilitated by the credibility of the central bank, so that expectations of future inflation should remain anchored. But financial intermediation is a risky business, and there will always be shady and fraudulent fringes of the financial system. Any regulatory/supervisory system that attempts to prevent *all* risk and any fraud will stifle enterprise and be impossibly heavy-handed. But the supervisor will take the blame for any crises/frauds that do occur. Frequently supervisory authorities will be simultaneously accused of being both too restrictive and also too lax to prevent failures. Being a supervisor, therefore, entails considerable reputational risk. A central bank that is trying to maintain credibility in order to assist its primary role of hitting an inflation target, might regard being also allocated a supervisory function as a poisoned chalice.

Moreover, the combination of operational independence, to achieve price stability, together with supervisory oversight over the whole financial system, might seem to concentrate excessive power in the hands of unelected central bank officials. Would that be entirely consistent with democratic government? There is, perhaps, some tendency for governments to combine the award of operational independence to a central bank with the removal of peripheral roles, such as banking supervision, debt management, and so on, as occurred in the United Kingdom in 1997. This, it may be claimed, enhances the central bank's focus on its main responsibility, and lessens potential conflicts of interest, and incidentally will please the Ministry of Finance, which normally has an underlying rivalry with the central bank. Putting the same issue another way, a central bank that loses its macroeconomic monetary policy role, as the National Central Banks (NCBs) did within the European System of Central Banks (ESCB), will struggle much harder to retain its remaining supervisory functions; there are many current examples of this among the NCBs.

Finally, Basel I represented a high-water mark for the application of traditional central bank methods for achieving international convergence on fairly simple, best-practice capital adequacy requirements (CARs). Thereafter, additional bodies, both specialist supervisory authorities and governmental bodies, international such as the EC and IMF as well as national, wanted to become involved in the process; moreover, the procedures for assessing and estimating risks and regulatory requirements became much more complex. In effect, a whole new technical profession of risk assessment and risk management has developed. The micro-, financial skill base of this profession is quite different from the macroeconomic monetary policy skill base of those undertaking the central function of a monetary policy committee.

For all these various reasons, the tide that had been pushing additional regulatory/supervisory functions and responsibilities toward central banks in the 1970s and 1980s reversed and ebbed away in the 1990s. The direction was now clearly toward the establishment of specialist, universal, separate (from the central bank), financial supervisory authorities (FSAs), as has occurred in Germany, Japan, Korea, and the United Kingdom, following from the Scandinavian countries where this had already taken place.

Yet this tide is not universal or overwhelming. There are a variety of countervailing considerations. First, for the reasons already adduced, a central bank has to be involved in crisis management in its own bailiwick. If so, it must cooperate, and coordinate, with its FSA.[10] But will not such cooperation and coordination work best, and crisis management be done most efficiently, if the two institutions are jointly run, with some degree of common management, possibly common location, and frequent exchange of personnel? Put another way, most central banks are still treated as being responsible for systemic stability. But exactly what can, and should, this mean if all responsibility for financial supervision is hived off to a separate institution? In our view the appropriate institutional functions of a central bank charged with maintaining systemic stability in a country with a separate, fully fledged FSA, are not yet clearly and firmly delineated. As noted earlier, this whole question has come to the fore again with the financial crisis of 2007–2008.

Moreover, financial regulation does not have one single purpose, or objective, to be attained with one set of instruments. While the divisions of business line, for example, between commercial banks, securities houses, and (life) insurance companies, have become utterly blurred, the separation between the objectives of *consumer protection* and conduct-of-business concerns, mostly in retail markets, on the one hand and *systemic stability*, crisis management, issues on the other hand remains. Inevitably, conduct-of-business issues will be much more frequent in occurrence and require many more staff than for systemic stability. Also the skills of the staff dealing with such issues will diverge, involving lawyers and accountants for conduct of business, and financial economists for systemic stability. It is also arguable that conduct-of-business concerns will occur primarily in retail markets, and will tend to require more detailed rules and regulations than systemic issues, which may occur more often in wholesale markets, and may be handled more expeditiously by the application of principles-based rules.

Bundling these two main functions together in a single, universal FSA could, perhaps, lead to the systemic function being swamped by the sheer number of those involved in the conduct-of-business function. Essentially economic issues pertaining to systemic stability could be decided by committees dominated by those with legal and accountancy training (see Goodhart et al. 2002). Yet the social welfare benefits of preventing, and

---

[10] In the United Kingdom, after the transfer of supervisory responsibilities to the FSA, the coordination of crisis management is undertaken via a standing Tripartite Committee consisting of the Treasury, the Bank of England, and the FSA. Both FSA and the Bank are represented on the Basel Committee on Banking Regulation. General coordination is further enhanced by cross-membership on the governing boards of the two institutions.

successfully resolving, financial crises greatly outweigh the gains from better customer protection by all accounts. There is, therefore, a prima facie case at least for a "twin peaks" approach, whereby the conduct-of-business regulatory/supervisory function is separated from the systemic stability role (see Taylor 1995, 1996; Taylor and Fleming 1999).

So, the question of the appropriate institutional structure of financial regulation and supervision remains in flux. Unlike the general consensus about the way in which monetary macroeconomic policy should be run, with an operationally independent central bank aiming primarily for price stability, there is no such consensus, either in theory or in practice, for the appropriate institutional setting for maintaining financial stability. There was a tide toward establishing separate, universal FSAs in the 1990s, but that tide was not all encompassing; the FRS successfully beat off its encroachment in the United States. Moreover, the financial crisis in late summer/autumn of 2007 has led to questions about the division of financial stability responsibilities both in Germany, as between Bafin and Bundesbank, and in the United Kingdom, as between FSA and the Bank. There is considerable discussion of the prior determinants of the various alternative institutional structures, and of what might work best [see Masciandaro and Quintyn 2007; Masciandaro, Quintyn, and Taylor (Chapter 8, this volume), and the bibliographic references therein], but little in the way of general conclusions. This is a field in which there remains much to play for.

5.5 Is There a Theoretical Basis for the Conduct of Financial Stability?

In the ECB *Financial Stability Review* (December, 2005, 131), it is stated bluntly that "financial stability assessment as currently practiced by central banks and international organizations probably compares with the way monetary policy assessment was practiced by central banks three or four decades ago – before there was a widely accepted, rigorous framework."[11] It should be no surprise that the analysis of financial stability issues lags behind that of monetary policy. The former is just that much more difficult to model. In particular, financial (in)stability is generated by the PD and bankruptcy. In contrast, most mainstream macro- and monetary analysis makes the assumption that no economic agent ever defaults. This

---

[11] Also see Kahn and Santos (2007), and the literature review therein.

latter assumption enormously simplifies modeling and allows for the use of representative agents, whereas a considered treatment of PD *must* face heterogeneity, that is, some agents follow a riskier strategy with a higher PD than others.

Given the inherent implausibility of a world without default, it is quite remarkable how much such current mainstream models can achieve in monetary and macroeconomic analysis and policy prescription; Woodford (2003) is an icon in this respect. Whether or not such monetary policy analysis would retain all its validity in a more realistic setting, it is just not possible to approach an analysis of financial stability without addressing bankruptcy, PD, and the heterogeneity of agents, both banks and their clients, head on.

There are two main approaches to a theoretical assessment of the probability of default in the literature. The first was initiated by Diamond and Dybvig (1983), and has been extended most notably by Allen and Gale (2007, and the references therein). In this model the uncertainty is generated by lack of knowledge about when depositors may need to withdraw their money from the bank. This risk is exacerbated by the illiquidity of some of the banks' assets. Although the ultimate return from such illiquid assets is, in most of these exercises, assumed to be known and certain, there is a friction in these models whereby early redemption of such illiquid assets can only be done at a cost, so much so that the commercial bank may then not be able to honor its pledge to redeem all its deposits, plus stated interest, at par. Because of the sequential repayment convention, that is, first come/first served, when the probability of failure to repay rises above some small probability, a run ensues and the bank(s) default.

In this approach, insolvency derives from illiquidity. It is certainly true that at a time when financial institutions are under strain and need to raise extra cash, there can be severe stress in asset markets, and asset prices can fall sharply (Cifuentes et al. 2005; Shin 2005a, b). This is an externality whereby pressure to realize assets in one segment of the financial system can impact on every other agent by lowering asset prices and thereby weakening their balance sheet strength.

However, it is exactly such fluctuations in the demand for money (liquidity) that central banks are meant to offset and to meet. Recall that the FRS was founded in 1913 to provide an "elastic currency," as noted in Lastra (2006, 34–35). A central bank has two core purposes, to maintain not only price stability but also the systemic stability of the banking and payments systems. In a separate paper (Goodhart et al. 2008), we demonstrate that, when the central bank pegs interest rates in the short run rather than the monetary base, thereby allowing the money stock to fluctuate endogenously in response to such shocks in the demand for money, their damaging effect on the system, in terms of interest rates, profits, and default rates, falls to a small fraction of the effect when the monetary base is fixed.

Indeed, in most examples of this genre of literature there is no central bank in the model. It is conspicuous by its absence. We would argue that, in most normal circumstances, an efficiently managed central bank should be able to counteract this kind of crisis. There is, however, one set of conditions, when the domestic agents need foreign currency liquidity, when the central bank's ability to help may be strictly limited by the extent of its foreign currency reserves. Thus, we would agree that the Diamond/Dybvig and Allen/Gale analysis is applicable to the problems of those developing countries whose borrowing and financial system is largely denominated in foreign currencies (e.g., U.S. dollars).

There is, however, one particular advantage that this genre of crisis literature possesses. This is that, in such models, generally either all depositors run and then default becomes certain, or nobody runs and the bank(s) remain solvent. Thus, there is little need to model the PD. This contrasts with the main other branch of the literature, and most practical concerns, where default arises from declines in the value of bank assets, for example, arising from credit or market risk. The main uncertainty in this latter genre is about the value of bank assets, insolvency rather than illiquidity. Of course these two, insolvency and illiquidity, go hand in hand, because depositors will flee and potential lenders will refrain from a bank perceived as potentially in trouble. So the first sign of potential insolvency is often actual illiquidity, a syndrome which causes problems for central banks.

A problem for modeling such causes of systemic crisis is that incorporating PD (and loss given default, LGD) into a theoretical model is hard to do because default is, by definition, a discontinuity. In our own view, as expressed in Goodhart et al. (2006a) the best way to do so that has yet been devised was developed by Dubey et al. (2005) and Shubik and Wilson (1977). Shubik sees every agent as choosing a strategy, depending on his/her risk aversion, which will generate differing PDs and LGDs, depending on the state of the world. There have to be penalties for bankruptcy, which penalties may be nonpecuniary; otherwise no one would ever repay and no one would lend. The penalties cannot be extreme, or no one would borrow.

Indeed, the PD is a key concept in any analysis of financial fragility. It is, of course, central to the Basel II exercise. At the more formal level, modeling of default, following on from the approach pioneered by Martin Shubik and his co-authors, is the crucial element for the analysis of financial fragility that we have been developing. (See Tsomocos 2003a, b; Goodhart et al. 2004, 2005, 2006a, 2006b; Tsomocos and Zicchino 2005; Aspachs et al. 2007a, b.)

Our model incorporates heterogeneous banks and capital requirements in a general equilibrium model[12] with incomplete markets, money, and default. It extends over two periods and all uncertainty is resolved in the second period. Trade takes place in both periods in the goods market. In the first period, agents also borrow from, or deposit money with, banks, mainly to achieve a preferred time path for consumption. Banks also trade among themselves, to smooth out their individual portfolio positions. The central bank intervenes in the interbank market to change the money supply and thereby set the interest rate. CARs on banks are set by a regulator, who may or may not also be the central bank. Penalties on violations of CARs, and on the default of any borrower, are in force in both periods. In order to achieve formal completeness for the model, banks are liquidated at the end of the second period and their profits and assets distributed to shareholders. Figure 5.2 makes the time line of the model explicit.

In the first period, trades by all agents take place against a background of uncertainty about the economic conditions (the state of nature) that will prevail in the second period. Agents are, however, assumed to have rational expectations and to know the likelihood of good or bad states

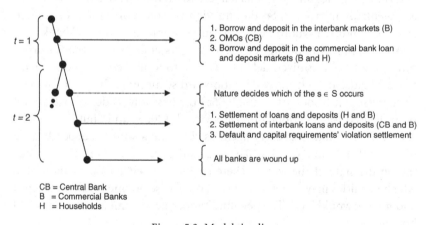

Figure 5.2. Model timeline

---

[12] For an extensive description of this variant of the model see Goodhart et al. (2005).

occurring when they make their choices in period one. In period two the actual economic conjuncture is revealed and all uncertainty is resolved.

The model incorporates a number of distinct, that is, heterogeneous, commercial banks, each characterized by a unique risk/return preference and different initial capital. Because each bank is, and is perceived as being, different, it follows that there is not a single market for either bank loans or bank deposits. In addition, we introduce limited access to consumer credit markets, with each household assigned (by history and custom) to borrow from a predetermined bank. This feature allows for different interest rates across the commercial banking sector. In sum, multiple credit and deposit markets lead to different loan rates among various banks and to endogenous credit spreads between loan and deposit rates.

Individual nonbank agents are also assumed to differ in their risk attitudes and hence in their preferences for default. We model the incentive for avoiding default by penalizing agents and banks proportionately to the size of default. Banks that violate their capital adequacy constraint are also penalized in proportion to the shortfall of capital. Both banks and households are allowed to default on their financial obligations, but not on commodity deliveries.

Our specification of the banking sector involves three banks and can, in principle, be applied to the banking system of any country or region. Banks γ and δ can represent any two of these individual banks or groups of banks, whereas bank τ represents the aggregation of the remaining banks. We have done calibration exercises in which banks γ and δ were chosen specifically to represent two actual U.K. banks (Goodhart et al. 2005).

All banks in the model, $b\varepsilon B = \{\gamma, \delta, \tau\}$, are assumed to operate under a perfectly competitive environment (i.e., they take all interest rates as exogenously given when making their optimal portfolio decisions) and satisfy their capital requirements. The structure of their balance sheets is given in the following table.

Assets	Liabilities
Loans to agents	Deposits from Mr. Φ
Interbank deposits	Interbank borrowing
Market book	Equity
	Others

We assume that all banks endogenize their decisions in the loan, deposit, and interbank markets.[13] The remaining variables are treated as exogenous.[14] We further assume that banks can default on their financial obligations, subject to default penalties set by the regulator. Thus, by varying the penalties imposed on default from zero to infinity, we can model 100% default, no default, or an equilibrium level of default between 0% and 100%.[15] At first glance, this "continuous" default rate approach may seem problematic because, in reality, banks either repay in full at the due date or are forced to close down. However, we interpret a bank's default rate in our model as a *probability* that such bank *chooses* to shut down, and hence in the short run to default *completely* on its financial obligations. Therefore, a bank's decision to increase its default rates is isomorphic to its decision to adopt a riskier position in pursuit of higher expected profitability.[16] With a large number of agents, as in a competitive equilibrium, conditions where everyone defaults on, say, 5% of their liabilities are equivalent to those where 5% of agents default on all their debts. This, however, is not the case when there are only a few agents in a concentrated field. If there are, say, only two agents in the field, and their failures are independent of each other, then in 0.25% of all cases there will be 100% default, in 9.75% of cases 50% default, and in 90% of cases, no default, which is clearly vastly different from a 5% default rate among a large number of agents.

In most countries banking is a concentrated service industry. Moreover, reputational effects and cross-default clauses, among other things, mean that banks cannot default partially and remain open. If they cannot meet their payment obligations, (except under force majeure as for September 11, 2001), they have to close their doors. Except when such closed banks are tiny, such closure does not, in almost all cases, then turn into permanent liquidation. Effectively almost all banks are restructured, in some countries via a "bridge bank" arrangement,[17] in others by what is effectively

---

[13] The modeling of the banking sector follows Shubik and Tsomocos (1992) and Tsomocos (2003a, b).

[14] As explained in Goodhart et al. (2005), we cannot endogenize banks' decisions on market book or equity. Since the model has two states in the second period and one unconstrained asset (i.e., the interbank market investment), adding another unconstrained asset would make the markets complete.

[15] This modeling of default follows Shubik and Wilson (1977).

[16] For more on this issue, see Tsomocos and Zicchino (2005).

[17] This is only legally possible in a few countries, such as the United States. In many others, liquidation is the only option foreseen in the bankruptcy laws. Given the social costs involved in the latter, governments (and supervisory "authorities") may be tempted to exhibit undue forbearance.

nationalization, and shortly reopen, with the extent of shortfall of assets distributed among the various creditors (the "haircut" in the American phrase), the shareholders and taxpayers, depending on the deposit insurance arrangements, bank bankruptcy laws, and political pressures. In this latter sense, even though the banking system is concentrated, and banks have to close when they cannot meet due payments, it is perfectly valid to assess strategies as bringing about possible conditions in which a bank defaults by, say, 5% to all depositors because that would be the effective loss of funds, or haircut, in the event of a bad state of the world.

Each household borrower, $h^b = \{\alpha^\gamma, \beta^\delta, \theta^\tau\}$, demands consumer loans from the nature-selected bank and chooses whether to default on loans in state $s \in S$.[18] The remaining agent, ϕ, supplies deposits to each bank b.[19] We do not explicitly model the optimization problems of households but assume reduced-form equations. Because of the limited participation assumption in every consumer loan market, each household's demand for loans is a negative function of the lending rate offered by the nature-selected bank. In addition, the demand for loans also depends positively on the expected GDP in the subsequent period.[20] Unlike the loan markets, we do not assume limited participation in the deposit markets. Finally, we assume that each household's repayment rate on the loan obligation

---

[18] In particular, household h^b's loan demand from the nature-selected bank b, $\forall h^b \in H^b$, and $b \in B$ is as follows:

$$\ln(\mu^{h^b}) = a_{h^b,1} + a_{h^b,2} \ln[p(GDP_i) + (1-p)GDP_{ii}] + a_{h^b,3} r^b$$

where, $\mu^{h^b} \equiv$ amount of money that agent $h^b \in H^b$ chooses to owe in the loan market of bank $b \in B$, and $GDP_s \equiv$ Gross Domestic Product in state $s \in S$ of the second period.

[19] In symbols,

$$\ln(d_b^\phi) = z_{b,1} + z_{b,2} \ln[p(GDP_i) + (1-p)GDP_{ii}]$$
$$+ z_{b,3}[r_d^b(pv_i^b + (1-p)v_{ii}^b)]$$
$$+ z_{b,4} \sum_{b \neq b \in B} [r_d^b(pv_i^b + (1-p)v_{ii}^b)]$$

where, $d_b^\phi \equiv$ amount of money that agent ϕ chooses to deposit with bank $b \in B$.

[20] In particular, the following functional form for GDP in state $s \in S$ of the second period (GDP_s) holds:

$$\ln(GDP_s) = u_{s,1} + u_{s,2}[\ln(\bar{m}^\gamma) + \ln(\bar{m}^\delta) + \ln(\bar{m}^\tau)]$$
$$+ u_{s,3}[\ln(e_s^\gamma) + \ln(e_s^\delta) + \ln(e_s^\tau)].$$

to the nature-selected bank in state $s \in S$ is a positive function of the corresponding GDP level, as well as the *aggregate* credit supply in the economy.[21]

Finally, as in Bhattacharya et al. (2007), we make the simplifying assumption that banks' default rates in the deposit and interbank markets are the same, that is, that banks are restricted to repay all their creditors in the same proportion.

Banks can also violate their CAR, subject to capital requirement violation penalties set by the regulator. In principle, each bank's *effective* capital-to-asset ratios may not be binding (i.e., their values may be above the regulator's requirement), in which case they are not subject to any capital requirement penalty. However, in our calibration exercises, we assume that each bank wants to keep a buffer above the required minimum, so that there is a nonpecuniary loss of reputation as capital declines; in this sense, the ratios are *always* binding. Put differently, we assume that banks' self-imposed ideal capital holdings are always above the actual values of all banks' capital-to-asset ratios. Given this assumption, we can rule out corner equilibria and therefore focus our analysis entirely on well-defined interior solutions whereby banks violate their enhanced capital requirements. We assume that penalties are linear as capital declines from its ideal level.[22]

In addition, we assume that GDP in each state is a positive function of the aggregate credit supply available in the *previous* period. Because the Modigliani–Miller proposition does not hold in our model,[23] higher credit extension as a result of loosening monetary policy, or any other shocks, generates a positive, real balance effect that raises consumption demand and ultimately GDP.

We have used this model for simulation (Goodhart et al. 2004), calibration (Goodhart et al. 2005), and to develop a quantified metric of financial stability (Aspachs et al. 2007a, b). We certainly would not claim that financial stability, and PD, *must* be modeled in this manner; indeed, like any

---

[21] Specifically, the functional form of the repayment rate of household h^b, $\forall h^b \in H^b$, to the nature-selected bank $b \in B$, in state $s \in S$ is as follows:

$$\ln(v_{sb}^{h^b}) = g_{h^b, s, 1} + g_{h^b, s, 2} \ln(GDP_s) + g_{h^b, s, 3}[\ln(\bar{m}^\gamma)$$
$$+ \ln(\bar{m}^\delta) + \ln(\bar{m}^\tau)].$$

[22] In practice, there will be some nonlinearity as capital falls below its required minimum, but this is just too complex to model at this stage.

[23] See Goodhart et al. (2006a) for an extensive discussion.

model, it has numerous deficiencies, on some of which we are continuing to work, particularly on the attempt to model liquidity within this framework. But we do believe that any serious model of financial fragility *has* to include and be centered around measures of PD, and that our own approach makes a start in that direction, a start which we hope others will soon overtake.

One reason for developing models of this kind is that they could be used to overcome one of the main weaknesses of the current methodologies for assessing systemic stability. Such methodologies are often based on stress, or scenario, tests. In such tests, a scenario is assumed wherein some bad state occurs, and the banks are then asked what that might do to their profitability and capital adequacy. But this usually measures only a first-round effect. If such bad outcomes did happen, the banks would often respond to these first-round effects by reducing their loan extension and becoming themselves more conservative. This would have second round effects on asset prices, risk premia, and real economic activity, usually then amplifying the original first-round effect. While it is possible, in principle, to iterate through various rounds of effect in collaboration with the (main) commercial banks, in practice this is virtually never done. Instead, using a (centralized) model, such as ours, does enable one to estimate the *equilibrium* outcome; that is one of its main purposes. Of course, our model depends on several variables that are difficult to observe, such as the degree of risk aversion and the risk strategies being adopted by both banks and their borrowers. But these are key fundamental elements in the determination of systemic stability. As all sensible central bank officials know, it is just when (over) confidence during periods of boom and expansion leads banks and their borrowers to accept (or ignore) more risk in pursuit of higher returns that the seeds of the next crisis are sown. It happens all the time.

5.6 Conclusions

It is rare to recognize that one is living in a golden age. It is usually only by contrast to a miserable present that the past seems, often mistakenly, golden. Yet much of the world, including Europe, North America, and most of Asia, has been living in such a golden age in the last 15 years with low and stable inflation and steady growth. Much of this, though how much remains debatable, is due to improved macromonetary policies, themselves a function of the new consensus of how such policies should be conducted. As the other chapters in this volume demonstrate, the consensus is not total, and there remains much to debate. But the range of agreement on the macromonetary side is far greater than the remaining areas of disagreement.

The same cannot be said about the second core purpose of central banks, which is maintaining systemic stability. The practical record remains patchy. There have been many more banking crises than in the quiet years of 1935–1965. Many cases of potential bank failures, for example, in China and Japan, have been pushed under the rug by throwing taxpayers' money at the problem. Difficulties in achieving good outcomes have been partly responsible for experimentation in the organization and structure of the regulatory/supervisory system. As discussed in Section 5.2, such experimentation has not, at any rate so far, resulted in any consensus on the best approach for this purpose. The procedures for doing so are further complicated by the fact that banking and finance are becoming increasingly international in structure, whereas regulation/supervision has to be based on a specific legal structure, which is inherently national in coverage (as emphasized in Lastra 2006); likewise, crisis management depends primarily on *national* fiscal purses.

The agreement on the appropriate macromonetary policies is based on an underlying consensus on the basic theoretical framework. There is no such consensus and no such framework (and little enough basic theory) that relates to systemic stability. This is partly because such theoretical analysis is more difficult and complex than that underlying macromonetary policies. We have argued here that any serious theory of systemic (in)stability has to focus on PD, yet PD is assumed away entirely (by the transversality condition) in the macro consensus model.[24] We end by presenting a (somewhat potted) version of our own attempt to take default seriously. It is at best a start, *mais c'est le premier pas qui coûte.*

References

Allen, A. M. (1938), "Switzerland," in A. M. Allen et al. (Eds.), *Commercial Banking Legislation and Control* (London: Macmillan), Chapter 13, pp. 351–374.
Allen, F. and D. Gale (2007), *Understanding Financial Crises* (Oxford, UK: Oxford University Press).
Aspachs, O., C. A. E. Goodhart, D. P. Tsomocos, and L. Zicchino (2007a), "Towards a Measure of Financial Fragility," *Annals of Finance* 3(1), January: 37–74.
  (2007b), "Searching for a Metric for Financial Stability," Paper presented at JMCB/FDIC Conference at Arlington Va, September.
Bagehot, W. (1873/1999), *Lombard Street* (originally published 1873, New York: Scribner, Amstrong; republished 1999, Chichester, UK: John Wiley & Sons).

---

[24] Thus, several critical macroeconomists regard this consensus model as suitable only for "fair weather" policy making.

Barth, J. R., G. Caprio, and R. Levine (2005), *Rethinking Bank Regulation: Till Angels Govern* (Cambridge, UK: Cambridge University Press).

Bhattacharya, S., C. A. E. Goodhart, P. Sunirand, and D. P. Tsomocos (2007), "Banks, relative performance, and sequential contagion," *Economic Theory* 32(2): 381–397.

Bliss, R. R. (2007), "Multiple Regulators and Insolvency Regimes: Obstacles to Efficient Supervision and Resolution" in D. G. Mayes and G. E. Wood (Eds.), *The Structure of Financial Regulation* (Abingdon, UK: Routledge), Chapter 6.

Bliss, R. R. and G. G. Kaufman (2006), "A Comparison of U.S. Corporate and Bank Insolvency Resolution," Federal Reserve Bank of Chicago Economic Perspectives, Second Quarter.

Bordo, M., B. Eichengreen, D. Klingebiel, and M. S. Martinez-Peria (2001), "Is the Crisis Problem Growing more Severe?," *Economic Policy* 32: 51–82.

Buiter, W. (2006), "Rethinking Inflation Targeting and Central Bank Independence," Background paper for inaugural lecture at LSE, October 26th, mimeo.

(2008), "Central Banks and Financial Crises," Paper presented at FRB of Kansas City Conference at Jackson Hole, WY, August 21–3.

Cameron, R. (1967), *Banking in the Early Stages of Industrialization* (New York: Oxford University Press).

Cameron, R. (Ed.) (1972), *Banking and Economic Development* (New York: Oxford University Press).

Cifuentes, R., C. Ferrucci, and H. S. Shin (2005), "Liquidity Risk and Contagion," *Journal of the European Economic Association* 3(2): 556–566.

Cope, S. R. (1938), "Denmark"; "Italy"; "Norway"; "Sweden", Separate Chapters in A. M. Allen et al. (Eds.), *Commercial Banking Legislation and Control* (London: Macmillan).

Dark, L. J. H. (1938), "Germany," in A. M. Allen et al. (Eds.), *Commercial Banking Legislation and Control* (London: Macmillan), Chapter 7, pp. 183–225.

Diamond, D. and P. Dybvig (1983), "Bank Runs, Deposit Insurance and Liquidity," *Journal of Political Economy* 91(3), June: 401–419.

Dubey, P., J. Geanakoplos, and M. Shubik (2005), "Default and Punishment in a General Equilibruim," *Econometrica* 73(1), January: 1–37.

Friedman, M. and A. J. Schwartz (1963), *A Monetary History of the United States, 1867–1960* (Princeton, NJ: Princeton University Press).

Goodhart, C. A. E. (1988), *The Evolution of Central Banks* (Cambridge, MA: MIT Press).

Goodhart, C. A. E., D. Schoenmaker, and P. Dasgupta (2002), "The Skill Profile of Central Bankers and Supervisors," *European Finance Review* 6: 397–427.

Goodhart, C. A. E., P. Sunirand, and D. P. Tsomocos (2004), "A Model to Analyse Financial Fragility: Applications," *Journal of Financial Stability* 1: 1–30.

(2005), "A Risk Assessment Model for Banks," *Annals of Finance* 1: 197–224.

(2006a), "A Model to Analyse Financial Fragility," *Economic Theory* 27: 107–142.

(2006b), "A Time Series Analysis of Financial Fragility in the UK Banking System," *Annals of Finance* 2: 1–21.

(2008), "The Optimal Monetary Instrument for Prudential Purposes," Financial Markets Group, London School of Economics, Discussion Paper No. 617, (June).

Grossman, R. S. (2006), "The Emergence of Central Banks and Banking Regulation in Comparative Perspective," Wesleyan Economics Working Paper, # 2006–021, June.

Kahn, C. M. and J. Santos (2007), "Institutional Allocation of Bank Regulation: a Review," in D. G. Mayes and G. E. Wood (Eds.), *The Structure of Financial Regulation* (Abingdon, UK: Routledge), Chapter 7.

Lastra, R. (2001), *Central Banking and Banking Regulation* (London, UK: Financial Markets Group, London School of Economics).

(2006), *Legal Foundations of International Monetary Stability* (Oxford, UK: Oxford University Press).

Masciandaro, D. and M. Quintyn (Eds.) (2007), *Independence, Accountability and Designing Financial Supervision Institutions* (Cheltenham, UK: Edward Elgar), forthcoming.

Mayes, D. G. and G. E. Wood (Eds.) (2007), *The Structure of Financial Regulation* (Abingdon, UK: Routledge).

Meltzer, A. H. (2003), *A History of the Federal Reserve, Volume 1, 1913–1951* (Chicago: University of Chicago Press).

Mooij, J. and H. Prast (2003), "A Brief History of the Institutional Design of Banking Supervision in the Netherlands" in T. Kuppens, H. Prast, and S. Wesseling (Eds.), *Banking Supervision at the Crossroads* (Cheltenham, UK: Edward Elgar), Chapter 2.

Shin, H. S. (2005a), "Financial System Liquidity, Asset Prices and Monetary Policy," Paper prepared for the 2005 Reserve Bank of Australia Conference on 'The Changing Nature of the Business Cycle'. Sydney, July 11/12.

(2005b), "Liquidity and Twin Crises," *Economic Notes* by Banca Monte dei Paschi di Siena, 34(3): 257–277.

Shubik, M. and D. P. Tsomocos (1992), "A Strategic Market Game with a Mutual Bank with Fractional Reserves and Redemption in Gold," *Journal of Economics* 55(2): 123–150.

Shubik, M. and C. Wilson (1977), "The Optimal Bankruptcy Rule in a Trading Economy Using Fiat Money," *Journal of Economics* 37: 337–354.

Taylor, M. (1995), *Twin Peaks: A Regulatory Structure for the New Century* (London: Centre for the Study of Financial Innovation).

(1996), *Peak Practice* (London: Centre for the Study of Financial Innovation).

Taylor, M. and A. Fleming (1999), "Integrated Financial Supervision: Lessons from Northern European Experience," World Bank Policy Research Working Paper, no. 2223.

Timberlake, R. H. Jr. (1984), "The Central Banking Role of Clearinghouse Associations," *Journal of Money, Credit and Banking* 16(1): 1–15.

Timberlake, R. H. (2007), "Gold Standards and the Real Bills Doctrine in U.S. Monetary Policy," *The Independent Review* 11(3), Winter: 325–354.

Tsomocos, D. P. (2003a), "Equilibrium Analysis, Banking and Financial Instability," *Journal of Mathematical Economics* 39: 619–655.

(2003b), "Equilibrium Analysis, Banking, Contagion and Financial Fragility," *Bank of England Working Paper* 175.

Tsomocos, D. P. and L. Zicchino (2005), "On Modelling Endogenous Default," Financial Markets Group discussion paper no. 548.

Westrup, J. (2007), "Independence and Accountability: Why Politics Matters," in D. Masciandaro and M. Quintyn (Eds.), *Designing Financial Supervision Institutions* (Cheltenham, UK Edward Elgar) Chapter 9.

Witheridge, H. J. (1938), "Belgium," in A. M. Allen et al. (Eds.), *Commercial Banking Legislation and Control* (London: Macmillan), Chapter 3, pp. 79–102.

Woodford, M. (2003), *Interest & Prices* (Princeton, NJ: Princeton University Press).

6

National Central Banks in a Multinational System

David G. Mayes and Geoffrey E. Wood

Abstract

The two core functions of central banks are monetary stability and financial stability. We explore in turn what is meant by each of these concepts, and consider the effects of internationalization on them. The internationalization of commercial banking, although in many ways capable of being handled by national central banks, does create for them a problem which by its nature is one they cannot, and never will, solve. In the European Union we can expect that this experience might ultimately lead to the development of a new transnational body or the assigning of powers to an existing institution such as the European System of Central Banks (ESCB). Outside the European Union, the solution is less obvious.

6.1 Introduction

Central banks, with one important exception, remain national, but commercial banking has become increasingly international. The aim of this chapter is to explore the problems this creates for central banks. To do so we first consider the functions of central banks to better understand which of their functions may be impeded by the internationalization of commercial banking. In summary, their two core functions are monetary stability and financial stability. We explore in turn what is meant by each of these concepts, and consider the effects on them of internationalization. That discussion prepares the way for examination of what can be done, and, perhaps, what should be done, to deal with how internationalization of commercial banking affects or impedes the carrying out of these central bank tasks. These matters cover the first six sections of this chapter. We then turn to how the internationalization of financial markets may impinge on central banks. That examined, we move on to the historical precedents that may help in judging the conclusions so far reached, for, as we shall argue, the current objectives of central banks are, in fact, well-established objectives going under new names. That historical discussion prepares the way for the concluding section of the chapter.

6.2 Monetary Stability

Monetary stability, where that is an explicit central bank function, is currently defined as a low rate of change, invariably zero or above, of some specified measure of the price level. Not all central banks have such a clearly specified objective – the U.S. Federal Reserve for example has its objectives specified in very general terms. But even when there is no such explicit mandate, there is the expectation that something regarded as price stability or a reasonable approximation to it will be sought. Whatever is specified, what invariably seems to be in mind is Alan Greenspan's much-quoted definition of price stability – a rate of change of prices so low that no one bothers about it in their day-to-day transactions.

Now if a central bank is not in charge of the monetary policy of its country – as the central banks of the euro system are not – then that central bank lacks the traditional central bank tool to control inflation. Such a central bank cannot set monetary policy for its country. It can, as banks in the euro system do, participate in setting policy for the currency area as a whole, but that can at best produce the desired outcome for the area as a whole. Only by chance does it produce the desired outcome for an individual country within the area.[1]

But that is not a difficulty caused by the internationalization of commercial banking. Can we identify any problems caused by that? The answer is that, fundamentally, there are no such problems. A national central bank is by definition the only supplier of base money in its nation, and, therefore, ultimately has control of monetary policy and, therefore, still more ultimately, control of inflation. There may be operational difficulties caused by internationalization, but these are as much likely the result of the internationalization of financial markets as of commercial banking. These problems are the ones created by the rapid movement of large amounts of funds from one currency to another. If the exchange rate is floating, there can be substantial transitional effects on the exchange rate, which can make the control of inflation difficult both by affecting inflationary expectations and

---

[1] To an extent, this is like the situation of a national central bank, in that there can be quite substantial inflation divergences within a country.

by making the actual interpretation of price changes more difficult. (There are also financial stability implications; these are considered in the following discussion.) Meanwhile, if the exchange rate is pegged, the central bank has to respond to these flows to ensure that their effect on domestic monetary conditions, if permanent, is trivial and preferably is only transitory. This raises issues about central bank operating procedures, and about how to define and then measure the minimum sensible domain for a currency, but these are beyond the scope of this chapter.[2]

Accordingly, our conclusion on the interaction of the task of maintaining monetary stability with the internationalization of commercial banking can be brief. Internationalization causes no fundamental problems for central banks in seeking to carry out that responsibility. Where currencies have a considerable role outside the country of origin, as is the case with the U.S. dollar and the euro, this can complicate monetary policy, especially when their relative importance is changing. But the problems are significant only if the monetary aggregates are used either as a target or as a significantly important, perhaps the sole, indicator of the stance of policy.[3]

6.3 Financial Stability

What of financial stability? As is revealed by the numerous views quoted in Allen and Wood (2006), there is no universally accepted, precise, and rigorous definition of financial stability (also see Goodhart and Tsomocos, this volume). Happily, for our purposes, we do not need a precise and rigorous definition but can make use of the general version of the concept outlined in that paper.

To quote:
We begin by proposing a definition of financial instability.... Thus we define episodes of financial instability as episodes in which a large number of parties, whether they are households, companies, or (individual) governments, experience financial crises which are not warranted by their previous behaviour, and where these crises collectively have seriously adverse macro-economic effects.... This is our preferred definition of financial instability. As indicated above, we would define financial stability as a state of affairs in which financial instability is unlikely to

---

[2] Recent advances in the optimum currency area literature, Frankel and Rose (1998), for example, set out some conditions after allowing for the fact that economies adjust to new regimes and, hence, reactions by both the private sector and the authorities change with the regime and in the light of experience with it.

[3] The issues are closely akin to those in the literature of the influence of the euro dollar market on U.S. monetary conditions. See, for example, Wood and Mudd (1978).

occur, so that the fear of financial instability is not a material factor in economic decisions taken by individuals or businesses. (Allen and Wood 2006, 159–160)

It is worth emphasizing at this point that the above definition deals with prevention as much as with cure; central banks should not only be able to respond to a crisis, but most of the time prevent them from happening, so that "...the *fear of instability* is not a material factor...." The emphasis on making clear that crises will be nipped in the bud, not just have their consequences ameliorated after they have occurred, is both important and long standing in this area.

Banks can fail because of loss of liquidity or loss of capital. In this chapter these are dealt with in that order, as that is the order in which policy toward banking problems evolved. Failure is itself a somewhat ill-defined concept. Banks can fail in the sense that they have to close their doors because they cannot meet their obligations and they, their creditors, or the authorities file for insolvency. They can also fail in the sense that they no longer meet the regulatory requirements laid down, and the authorities decide to terminate their licence. Two features of bank failure are worth highlighting at this point. The first is that a bank can be unable to meet its obligations not because the value of its assets does not cover its liabilities, but because it cannot gain access to sufficient liquidity, at a viable price, to make its payments. The second is that, in the event of failure in the regulatory sense, it may prove possible to keep the banking business alive by transferring the assets and liabilities to another bank that is regulatorily compliant. These two features of bank failures lie, in turn, at the heart of the next two sections.

6.4 Failure Through Loss of Liquidity

Concern with the role of the central bank in maintaining financial stability developed first in the particular context of a shortage of liquidity caused by the outbreak of a war – a clear-cut example of financial instability in the sense of Allen and Wood (2006). The problem arose in 1793. In that year, war broke out between France and Britain. This caused immediate problems in the British banking system. These problems were described, and the solution hinted at, only 4 years later by Francis Baring:

The foreign market was either shut, or rendered more difficult of access to the merchant. Of course he would not purchase from the manufacturers;... the manufacturers in their distress applied to the Bankers in the country for relief; but as the want of money became general, and that want increased gradually by a general alarm, the country Banks required the payment of old debts... In this predicament the country at large could have no other resource but London; and having exhausted the bankers, that resource finally terminated in the Bank of England. In such cases the Bank are not an intermediary body, or power; there is no resource on their refusal, for they are the *dernier resort.*[4]

Only the Bank of England could provide the necessary cash, as it was, for all practical purposes, the monopoly note issuer.[5] When it supplied cash in such circumstances of general shortage when no one else could, it was acting as the "lender of last resort" (LOLR). The reliability of such action for preventing a crisis was demonstrated in Britain in 1825 and again in 1866. By 1878, when the City of Glasgow Bank failed, confidence that the Bank of England would act if necessary appears to have been sufficient to prevent a panic.[6] This conclusion is reinforced by what happened when Barings failed in 1890.[7]

So in Britain, classic LOLR action, that is, flooding the banking system with cash so as to alleviate both shortage and fear of shortage, was sufficient to prevent banking crises. The same lesson can be drawn outside Britain; experience in both France and Italy confirms that such action prevents crisis and maintains banking stability.

Does this matter today? Surely it does. Consider first the recent Argentinean and east Asian experiences. In April 1991, Argentina fixed its peso against the U.S. dollar. Inflation fell, fiscal discipline was restored, and private capital flowed in. But the banking system remained undercapitalized, and the central bank could not, because of the currency board system in conjunction with own modest reserves, act as a liberal LOLR. And to be successful, a LOLR must be capable of being liberal. The banking system

---

[4] A few words on the nature of the British banking system of the time are useful. There were numerous banks. Country banks operated outside London, settling among themselves but having London banks with whom they dealt and from whom they could borrow, and the London banks meanwhile had access to the Bank of England. The Bank of England itself was still not a central bank, but it was the government's bank as well as conducting normal banking business with the private sector, both banks and nonbanks.

[5] Other banks had the right of note issue, but those which had that right fell in number through the century, and, more important and indeed crucial, only the Bank of England could be freed from the constraints of the gold standard and issue without stint should a crisis necessitate that.

[6] The City of Glasgow Bank case is particularly interesting as it emphasizes the difference between liquidity and credit losses. As there was unlimited liability and the shareholders were able to cover the losses to creditors and depositors under the insolvency procedures, the contagion related mainly to liquidity losses although Caledonian Bank had to close its doors until the position was clear as it was a shareholder.

[7] Barings is important in another regard, and we return to the 1890 Barings failure subsequently.

was, therefore, both fragile and without access to a LOLR. The fall of the Mexican peso in 1995 triggered a run on Argentinean banks; there was, inevitably in the absence of a LOLR, a sharp monetary contraction followed by a sharp fall in gross domestic product (GDP) and rise of unemployment. Similar problems emerged by a different route, but again allowed by the absence of LOLR, in east Asia. The collapse of the Thai baht turned attention to Indonesia, Malaysia, and the Philippines. It was observed – perhaps it should have been observed earlier – that banks had been lending extensively in domestic currency and funding this by borrowing in foreign currency that they then converted to domestic. Demands for foreign currency could not, of course, be met by any lenLOLR, so severe banking and economic problems followed.[8] The Argentinean case, however, plainly reveals the continued usefulness of a traditional LOLR.

Does such usefulness remain in developed economies? Some maintain that classic LOLR is no longer necessary in such economies, because capital markets are so developed that solvent but illiquid institutions can always get funds. There are, it seems to us, two slight difficulties with this claim. First, in some circumstances that are admittedly rare but certainly not impossible, it is not true. Recollect when the computers at the Bank of New York failed in 1985. That bank was central in the market in U.S. government securities. The problem was that it could not identify and receive payments for government securities, so it was being debited by the Fed for the securities but getting no inflow from the purchasers, so it had to start borrowing on a huge scale, creating a hole of nearly $24 billion in the space of an hour and a half before it managed to halt further transactions. This was rapidly draining the U.S. banking system of liquidity, so the Federal Reserve Bank of New York essentially "opened the discount window" and supplied whatever was demanded. This was a classic LOLR operation, albeit not for a classic reason. The other problem with the claim that LOLR in the classic sense will never be needed is the belief that solvent institutions can always get funds. Solvency is not always easy to discern. An excellent example of consequences of this is the drying up of interbank markets in 2007–2008. There was scarcely any discrimination among institutions; rates rose to all, and quantities were sharply restricted for all. Why this happened is clear. Determining solvency takes time, and further, whether or not a firm is solvent depends on assumptions about the future. For example, if it gets the loan it may be solvent, and if it does not get the loan, it may not be solvent, as it may be forced to

---

[8] Whether this episode makes a case for an international LOLR we discuss subsequently.

liquidate assets at distress prices to meet some of its liabilities.[9] That is why classic LOLR lending takes place on security, rather than on unsecured lending granted on a calculation of the borrower's solvency. To quote from a classic text,

> It is not ordinarily possible to examine in detail the entire assets of an applicant for a loan. Demonstration of solvency therefore cannot be made an express condition of the loan, at any rate at a time when the need for cash has become urgent. (Hawtrey 1932, 126–127)

In the year since September 2007, the authorities in the United States, the euro area, and the United Kingdom have found it necessary to make extensive use of the classic LOLR, providing liquidity to the market, not simply for the very short term but for more extended periods. The problem in the market has been not so much the fear that counterparties cannot honor their immediate claims, but that they may fail to do so in the future when suspected losses are realized. As a result, the central banks have been prepared to accept collateral for longer periods. In the case of the United Kingdom, it has been necessary to extend the list of acceptable collateral. However, in the euro area, which was already prepared to take an extensive list of collateral, a tightening of the terms has been announced.

To summarize so far on threats to financial stability arising from loss of liquidity, we have argued that is a problem that can be dealt with by classic LOLR action – by the relevant national central bank lending freely on security to the affected banking system. We must, therefore, next consider whether that desirable solution is a feasible one in a system of international banks.

6.5 Internationalization and Classic LOLR

So long as the country concerned has a floating exchange rate, there is almost nothing to discuss. In the face of a sudden crisis – a driven, surge in the demand for liquidity – the national central bank supplies it. Whatever the nature of the banking system, as long as the exchange rate is floating, the funds stay in the country.[10] The argument is exactly the same as that which demonstrates monetary autonomy in the presence of a floating

---

[9] This is why it is important to be clear what is meant by the advice that a LOLR should lend freely *at a high rate*. The rate should be above that prevailing before the crisis [for a brief discussion of reasons for this, see Rockoff (1986)], but *not* at the rate that would prevail in the absence of lending – not least because that latter rate could well be infinite.

[10] For a reserve currency, liquidity that has been exported is likely to be brought back in during a crisis.

exchange rate, an argument dating back to David Hume in 1752 and never yet challenged. In essence, any attempt to ship the funds overseas may affect the exchange rate but, in the absence of official intervention by the central bank (in effect offsetting its own monetary policy action), cannot affect the money stock. Any effect on the exchange rate may complicate the monetary stability task of the central bank, but it does not, in this context, impinge on financial stability unless that is threatened by unhedged corporate borrowers damaging the banking system. Any response to that, however, even if desirable, would require the provision of capital, a task which on any scale other than a trivial one is beyond the capacities of any central bank.

Does that conclusion change when the exchange rate is pegged, as it has been in, for example, some less-developed countries? It is evident that it need not, for classic LOLR evolved in the days of the gold standard, but why it need not should be explored, for doing so may reveal some crucial differences between then and now.

Normally, if the exchange rate is pegged, one might expect a monetary expansion simply to flow out across the exchanges, as described in the classic Hume reference mentioned previously. But if there is a crisis-driven monetary expansion, what is happening is that there is an increase in the supply of money matching more or less exactly the increase in demand for it. In principle, that is to say, there is no *excess* supply of money at all. Hence is the paradox of being able to change the supply of money while not possessing monetary autonomy resolved: Stabilizing the interest rate in response to a shock to the demand for central bank money creates neither excess supply nor excess demand for that money, but adjusts supply to demand. Does the presence of international banks affect or complicate the matter? That may be a change from the gold standard period, albeit a change in degree not kind, for as observed below there were international banks then, too.

Suppose there is a panic in country A. The central bank responds by supplying cash. Might international banks ship the cash overseas, thus not allowing the cash injection to alleviate the shortage? The answer is that they might, and if *the exchange rate were pegged*, they could. But why should they? If a particular bank were not experiencing a cash drain, it could and surely would lend domestically, so long as it had confidence in the security of the system as a whole and in the collateral it was taking, for the interest rate would be higher relative to abroad than before. And if a bank were caught up in the panic, it would be concerned with survival, and so would not seek to ship funds abroad to another part of the bank.[11]

---

[11] At this point, bank structure requires consideration. An international bank can have branches, subsidiaries, or other forms of representation spread across the world, and these

A currency union may be regarded as a special case of a pegged rate system, and a currency board another. Further, currency unions can be divided into two types.[12] There is one such as the euro system, where the national central banks survive and contribute to policymaking at the newly created system central bank, and then there is the one where the national central banks vanish, and are replaced by one "union" central bank. All three varieties of pegged exchange rate systems require discussion. As before, we first analyze the situation without regard to the internationalization of commercial banking, and then see what difference that can make.

If we have what may be regarded as a traditional currency union, there is only one central bank, with no other bank retaining any central bank responsibilities. In that case, the situation is either capable of being regarded as one country with no international banks – if there are no banks with significant business both inside and outside the union – or as one country with international banks, if there are banks working both inside and outside the union. Either way, as argued above, there are no fundamental problems for traditional LOLR actions.

That case does not match the most important monetary union of modern times, the euro area. Here the national central banks remain and participate in decision making. In principle this is no different from the case just discussed – if, that is, one maintains that the various nation states of the euro area are no longer countries from the monetary point of view. That is certainly defensible, but it may overstate the degree of financial integration among them. A better way to view the situation might be to think of the euro area as a country with a single central bank whose branches have substantial autonomy. Each of the areas (countries) served by one of these branches manifestly has financial links to every other such area, but these links are less close than those within the area (country). If this is accepted, then again there are no fundamental problems in carrying out traditional LOLR policy. There would, of course, have to be cooperation between the ECB and the national central bank whose area was most affected, if there were such a bank, but that could surely be taken for granted, as could

can be capitalized independently or not. This raises the possibility that in some cases, a part of the bank might be allowed to fail so as to save the rest. The reputational effects of doing so could well be such as to make the action pointless, but this matter is better discussed when we examine failure through loss of capital, in which context the issues are more obvious.

[12] There is a third form of currency union that is unilateral, resulting from adopting another currency as in Montenegro with the euro. In such a case, a LOLR role can be played by the central bank to the extent that it has access to funds in the same foreign currency.

the speed of that cooperation; rapid action is essential in an incipient crisis.[13]

Last in this section we turn to currency boards. It has frequently been claimed that a currency board, because it simply imports its monetary policy and has no independent control over domestic monetary conditions, cannot conduct LOLR operations. First, it is important to reiterate that LOLR is not intended to change monetary conditions, but rather to maintain them close to unchanged in the face of a surge in demand for cash (or for its equivalent, deposits at the central bank). Hence if a currency board can inject liquidity, there is no reason to expect it simply to drain overseas as excess liquidity would do – for it would not be excess. But can a currency board inject liquidity? If it is holding excess reserves, as prudence suggests it should, then it can inject liquidity to the extent of these reserves. Currency boards have done so in the past. Another possibility is the kind of situation that prevailed in some British-dependent currency boards. The banks in these were simply branches or subsidiaries of British banks, and therefore had ready access to the London money markets, and, if necessary, the Bank of England, so sterling could be obtained whenever necessary to bolster the issue of currency in the currency board's area.

We can thus divide currency boards into two categories – those that, for one of the reasons described above, can inject emergency liquidity when needed and those that cannot. Boards that cannot are plainly at risk, unless like Estonia, their banking systems are foreign owned and liquidity problems would be solved through the parent.

So, in summary, it would appear that internationalization of commercial banking does not impede a national central bank seeking to carry out a classic LOLR operation so as to stabilize the banking system in (not of) its country. Bank internationalization does not expose countries to financial crises arising from sudden increases in the demand for liquidity. It may, however, produce problems of *implementing* LOLR policy. These are discussed below, under the heading "Preventing Problems." A bank with

---

[13] The problem of "forum shopping" may arise in the euro zone, however. Interest rates are the same throughout the zone, but it is possible that national central banks' willingness to lend in emergency could differ. National central bank cooperation could prevent this should it be necessary to do so. The euro system central banks operate with a single list of eligible collateral and pricing arrangements. The risks involved are shared across the system not simply concentrated in the national central banks. "Forum shopping" across pegged or floating exchange rates to take advantage of lower collateral standards or lower interest rates, would expose the bank doing the shopping to exchange rate risk. "Forum shopping" is discussed further, in the context of failure through loss of capital.

subsidiaries in different jurisdictions may be able to repackage its assets so that it can gain more liquidity if central banks' rules for collateral and interest rate penalties are not the same in each location.

6.6 An International LOLR?

The east Asian crisis prompted some calls for an international LOLR. As the above discussion makes clear, such an organization as defined in the classic sense cannot exist. It would need to be a body that could issue any currency in the world, on demand and without stint, whenever there was a surge in demand for it. There can be little doubt that few countries would permit their currencies to be thus dispensed.

A run on a country can also be a liquidity rather than a solvency issue, as the problem may simply be the realization of eligible assets in a hurry at an acceptable price. However, what is usually meant by the term is an extension of the LOLR concept to include the provision of bail-out capital. That proposal has come in for substantial criticism. A leading proponent of the idea is Stanley Fischer; leading critics are Charles Calomiris (1998) and Anna Schwartz (1999).

It is unnecessary for us to become involved in that debate at this point, beyond noting that there might well be substantial problems in finding agreement over who would provide the capital. As will emerge below, it seems likely that ensuring the rapid provision of sufficient capital, even on a scale sufficient to support a bank rather than a country or group of countries, is not an easy task. Those interested to pursue the international LOLR discussion further will find the above cited papers a stimulating introduction to the subject.

6.7 Failure Through Loss of Capital

Banks can fail because of loss of capital. Governments have to decide what to do about this – how much effort they wish to spend on reducing the chances of such failures, how drastically they wish to intervene to head off incipient failures, how they wish to structure the financial system to limit the costs and exposures, and how they wish to insulate those directly affected (as creditors and debtors) through deposit insurance and specific resolution methods and those who are indirectly affected through contagion and the need to recontract failed transactions. All failures may affect public confidence in the financial system, but concern tends to focus on the larger institutions whose functions are central to the system and where a sudden cessation in trading would have a serious impact.

Many of the problems associated with failure through loss of capital require government action. Laws may need to be passed if sufficient powers have not already been granted to the central bank. If capital is required to deal with the problem, then in the absence of a private sector provision the government must use taxpayers' funds to provide that capital; central banks are invariably too small to provide capital sufficient to deal with banking sector problems of any significance. But central banks have responsibility for financial stability. Any problems caused by internationalization are, therefore, central bank problems, although the bank may well require government assistance to deal with them.

Advice on how to structure a national system is highly developed and practice, in the United States in particular where failures have been relatively common, has responded to try to construct a system where the incentives to restrict losses are compatible across the parties involved.[14] However, as soon as we look across borders, the various countries' national systems are ill matched. Indeed, in many cases, they are explicitly contradictory. If each country attempts to minimize the losses in the event of a cross-border bank within its own jurisdictional powers, it will almost certainly be doing so at the expense of losses in another jurisdiction.[15] While the European Union has been alert to these problems and has tried to construct the arrangements for handling failures so that the cross-border bank is treated as a single entity under the Winding Up Directive,[16] and all creditors and debtors within its jurisdiction are treated equally according to priority, irrespective of their nationality or residence, there are major gaps in the system (Hadjiemmanuil 2003).

Outside the European Union the problems are greater because there is no explicit drive to create an effective single financial market. Even in Australia and New Zealand, between which countries *economic* integration is more

---

[14] The phraseology used is loss "minimization" but clearly this is in practice with respect to an acceptable level of risk taking. Risk taking and hence loss making is an essential part of a successful banking system; the key is good risk management rather than risk avoidance per se.

[15] This principle, known as "territoriality" is discussed at length in Baxter et al. (2004). The contrasting alternative is universality – treating the banking group in a single composite proceeding in one country (or at least with the local proceedings attached to the main proceedings). In practice many large banks will be subject to some uneven combination of the two.

[16] Directive 2001/24/EC of 4 April on the reorganization and winding up of credit institutions OJ 2001 L 125/15.

developed than in the European Union, each country is currently trying to make sure that it can apply as near a national approach as is possible so that it can control the impacts on its own country. This, to some extent, destroys the point of cross-border banking if regulatory requirements restrict it to being essentially the linking of a set of largely independent national banks within an international group. The economies of scope, scale, and knowledge transfer could be inhibited to the disadvantage of the customers and shareholders alike. While it has been argued that in practice the banks have found that there is relatively limited benefit in running their Australian and New Zealand operations together (see Tripe 2004, for an analysis), this has not been the finding in Europe; banks such as Nordea in the Nordic region and Raiffeisen in central Europe and the Balkans have been running increasingly integrated operations.

The central bank is placed in a difficult position when there are cross-border banks – it has the responsibility for financial stability within its jurisdiction without necessarily having the means of achieving it. The position is particularly acute for a small country. If much of its banking system is foreign-owned, then it may effectively be dependent upon the decisions of the authorities in other countries both for the avoidance of problems and for their resolution. If on the other hand, like Switzerland, it is home to large multinational banks whose main operations are abroad, it may not have the resources to handle a major failure on its own.[17] (Sweden is facing the prospect of having both problems with being the home country for Nordea, which has the large majority of its operations abroad and host to Danske Bank, which is growing to systemic proportions.)

The problem is least acute when organizing the effective *supervision* of a cross-border bank by the various authorities involved. The United States has already shown that it is possible to coordinate the activities of different supervisors (Bliss 2007), and the supervisory committees that are required under the new Basel II arrangements help ensure that supervisors set up structures for sharing information and cooperating. These arrangements under Basel II probably do not go far enough to achieve adequate cooperation even in the European Union and Vesala (2005), Mayes (2006), and Mayes et al. (2007) advocate the formation of a college of supervisors and the construction of a single database on the group to which all have

---

[17] In Switzerland, for example, the authorities have announced that there will be a cap of 4bnCHF on the payout associated with any single institution, thus limiting the liability of the insurance fund but leaving open the prospect of some residual disturbance to the financial system at home and abroad.

access. Then at least the national authorities can be reasonably informed. We explore possible structures in the next section.

However, cross-border cooperation becomes much more difficult once positive action is required by the authorities, either to head off a failure, which we consider next, or to handle one, to which subject the present discussion is devoted.[18]

Clearly the better the system is at ensuring prudent behavior and the earlier it manages to handle emerging problems, then the fewer will be the failures that do have to be handled and the smaller their size. This will make problems of burden sharing and decision making easier.

6.8 Dealing with Failure

While the Basel Committee created a set of criteria for determining the minimum adequate capital, whether under Basel II or the original proposal, it does not except in very general terms lay down rules for behavior for when banks become undercapitalized. This has been addressed most clearly in the United States by the requirements of prompt corrective action (PCA) (Table 6.1) by which successive falls in capital below the required level trigger an increasingly harsh list of required and discretionary actions. These actions are designed to bring the bank back to adequate capitalization within a time period whose length is laid down in the Act, and to prevent management from worsening the position or extracting value from the company for their benefit or that of their shareholders at the expense of the creditors. While the strict time limit is intended to galvanize response, these actions must of course be measured, allowing time for and ideally promoting recovery (see Goodhart 2007).

A key ingredient of the U.S. system is that, although the Federal Reserve System supervises many banks and bank-holding companies, it is not the institution that handles bank failures. That is the responsibility of the Federal Deposit Insurance Corporation (FDIC). The central bank manages its own exposures through the terms of its liquidity assistance. As a collateralized creditor, it will be well placed in any resolution but will not direct it. It must, therefore, be confident that the regulatory structure will deliver financial stability. Furthermore, it is the FDIC and not the Federal

---

[18] This is similar to John Pinder's (1968) observation that it is much easier to arrange negative aspects of integration among countries, for example, removing barriers and agreeing not to act against each other, than positive aspects, where harmonized legislation and new behavior patterns need to be agreed.

Table 6.1. *Summary of prompt corrective action provisions (PLA) of the Federal Deposit Insurance Corporation Improvement Act of 1991*

Description	Mandatory	Discretionary	Capital ratios risk based		Leverage (%)
			Total	Tier 1	Tier 1
Well capitalised			>10	>6	>5
Adequately capitalised	No brokered deposits, except with FDIC approval		>8	>4	>4
Undercapitalised	Suspend dividends and management fees Require capital restoration plan Restrict asset growth Approval required for acquisitions, branching, and new activities No brokered deposits	Order recapitalisation Restrict interaffiliate transactions Restrict deposit interest rates Restrict certain other activities Any other action that would better carry out prompt corrective action	<8	<4	<4
Significantly undercapitalised	Same as for undercapitalised Order recapitalisation* Restrict interaffiliate transactions* Restrict deposit interest rates* Pay of officers restricted	Conservatorship or receivership if fails to submit or implement plan or recapitalise pursuant to order Any other provision below, if such action is necessary to carry out prompt corrective action	<6	<3	<3
Critically undercapitalised	Same as above Receiver/conservator within 90 days* Receiver if still critically undercapitalised after four quarters Suspend payments on subordinated debt* Restrict certain other activities				<2

* Not required if primary supervisor determines action would not serve purpose of prompt corrective action or if certain other conditions are met.

Source: Board of Governors of the Federal Reserve System adapted from Eisenbeis and Kaufman (2006)

Reserve that makes the recommendation that a bank may present a systemic problem if it is resolved under the normal procedures – the "systemic risk exemption."[19] While the Federal Reserve, the Treasury, and the Comptroller of the Currency have to agree for this exemption to be invoked, the central bank is not the leading player. However, the systemic risk exemption has not (yet) been invoked, so its operation remains somewhat hypothetical.

In other countries, the central bank plays a larger role, but it is clear that any national arrangement that relies on confidence by one party in the mandate and likely actions of another independent agency is going to be difficult to replicate at the international level.

In the course of 2008 the United States has found that it has needed to expand the framework for handling failure. The two largest mortgage institutions, Fannie Mae and Freddie Mac, have both reached the point where they were probably insolvent. These two institutions, supervised by the Office of Federal Housing Enterprise Oversight (OFHEO) and outside the ambit of the FDIC, have been placed in conservatorship as a result of legislation enacted on July 30, 2008 to extend the provisions for conservatorship and receivership that applied to banks to these organizations.[20] Fortunately, large organizations tend to slide into failure sufficiently slowly so that there is some time to put adequate provisions in place.

There have also been problems with investment banks that lie outside the arrangements for "depository institutions." Financial instability can be caused by the failure of nonbanks as well as banks. As a first example, the authorities found it necessary to assist a merger of Bear Stearns in March of 2008 with JP Morgan–Chase, largely on the grounds that they were apprehensive about the spillover from a failure into the rest of the sector. A second example involves Lehman Brothers; in September of 2008, the authorities were prepared to let the holding company file for bankruptcy under Chapter 11, As a third example, Merrill Lynch was the subject of an unassisted takeover by Bank of America. While this may have represented more confidence on the part of the authorities as to how the sector would continue, it is as yet too early to give an opinion on the spillover.

In part, this inability to judge comes from a third problem over how far out to draw the boundary of central bank responsibility for financial

---

[19] Stern and Feldman (2006) argue that the Federal Reserve should try to ensure that banks are never allowed to become sufficiently large or dominant in markets that they are deemed systemically important and hence "too big to fail."

[20] The new legislation, the Housing and Economic Recovery Act, has created a new Federal Housing Finance Agency (FHFA) combining the OFHEO and the Federal Housing Finance Board with wider powers including the appointment of conservators or receivers.

stability, as at the same time AIG, the country's largest insurer reached the point of insolvency. Here again the Federal Reserve has stepped in by establishing a $85 billion credit line at 8.5% over London Inter Bank Offer Rate (LIBOR) in return for warrants that effectively give it 80% of equity in the company and a dividend moratorium for ordinary shareholders. The fear was that as the insurer of a large part of bank securities the failure of AIG would have drastic consequences for banks in the United States and overseas where many of the securities were held.

These three examples among them show that, in practical terms, the boundary of where the central bank may have to act is drawn more widely than was thought to be the case beforehand. In the first two cases, the fall out for other countries outside the United States would be principally for counterparties and other creditors. A U.S. focus on its own problems, therefore, has probably resulted in outcomes that those exposed abroad would have been able to withstand, irrespective of the particular decision. In the AIG case, the answer is not so clear, as the concentration of exposure of counterparties, particularly in Europe, is not known with any accuracy.

The international contagion in the short run from these problems has been considerable and despite heavy liquidity injections in the United States, the United Kingdom, and the euro area, it is still not clear what the outcome is going to be.

6.9 Cross-Border Institutional Structures that Renationalize the Problem

There is a clear distinction between the sorts of arrangement that can be made within the European Union or other groups of countries that are actively engaged in economic integration, and more general international coordination. Neither the IMF nor the Basel arrangements under the auspices of the BIS show any particular inclination to try to create supranational organizations to deal with cross-border banks. Indeed, the advice from the Basel Committee (1996) is straightforward. Countries need to work together and the presumption is that they would do so under the leadership of the lead regulator in the home country. This means that different countries and authorities would need to cooperate and work together across different jurisdictions rather than within a single one.

This is a recipe for difficulty and it is really only the arrangements being set in place by the New Zealand authorities, or something similar, that make sense in this regard.[21] New Zealand effectively requires that the cross-border nature of banks should not be such as to cause a problem – effectively trying to outlaw the difficulty. They have two simple requirements:

- Any bank that has functions that the authorities deem systemically important must structure itself in such a way that there is a viable local organization that can operate separately and ultimately be taken over and run by the authorities without a break in business in the event of its failure.
- There must be specific legislation in place that allows the authorities to step in if a bank becomes inadequately capitalized and to impose a resolution of the problem if the bank cannot do so voluntarily.

The first of these is described largely as an "outsourcing policy" (RBNZ 2006) as it relates to the bank's ability to keep operating in the event of the failure any of its "suppliers" to deliver their services. Clearly this covers computer systems, ability to access the payment system, access to collateral, and other essential services, but it also covers decision making. Because all the banks with systemic functions in New Zealand are foreign (Australian) owned, their parents are, of course, major suppliers in this sense and the New Zealand operation must be able to continue even in the event of the failure of the parent. It is, therefore, also a requirement of the New Zealand system that these banks be locally incorporated and have a local management team who can actually run the business and directors who are liable for the prudential operation and disclosure statements.

This immediately distinguishes the New Zealand situation from that in the European Union/EEA as one of the features of the single financial market is that a bank licensed in one member state can operate as a branch in another member state without any local prudential hurdles and subject to the supervisory control of the authorities in the home, not the host, country.[22] This same responsibility of the home country extends to

---

21 The New Zealand arrangements have a fortunate neatness as the central bank, the Reserve Bank of New Zealand, is responsible for banking supervision and the administration of failed banks. However, such arrangements could also be put in place where there are multiple authorities in a country, but they would need an explicit, legally enforceable agreement to do so.

22 Branches are required to adhere to the host country's conduct of business rules and also to legislation covering employment, health and safety, and so on, like any other local firm.

undercapitalization and failure, and hence to deposit insurance.[23] The New Zealand system is thus a means of making separate jurisdictions work. It is particularly necessary in this case as Australia applies domestic depositor preference and New Zealand depositors would be lower ranked – thus possibly receiving very little, even nothing, in the event of a substantial failure. The position is exacerbated as neither country has deposit insurance, although Australia is exploring that option.

However, such an outsourcing policy alone is not sufficient. If a bank becomes insolvent (or its net worth becomes negative), the authorities need to be able to step in and take over the bank without delay. They need to be able to make a satisfactory estimate of the losses, assign those losses, and without a break open for business again under a public guarantee against any further loss. In intervening the authorities do not take on any of the losses themselves. It is only in subsequent operation that there is any exposure for the taxpayer. The New Zealand system is also unique in this regard although other systems, including the bridge bank arrangements in the United States, have equivalent effects (Mayes et al. 2001; Mayes 2006).[24] Under the New Zealand system, a statutory manager is appointed by the courts. This manager determines which aspects of the bank need to be kept running, and after the loss assessment, applies it to the creditors of the bank in reverse order of priority until the bank is returned to solvency/positive net worth. This "bank creditor recapitalization" gives the creditors a claim on the bank equivalent to a debt-equity swap. These claims may well prove tradable, especially when a capital injection is obtained to get the bank out of statutory management and back into normal operation. The shares of the previous shareholders will become worthless if the bank fails, although eventually, if the creditors can be paid off and there is any residual after costs, they could receive a compensating payment. They would not, however, be able to get the ownership of the bank returned to them.

The bridge bank concept in the United States has similar characteristics but there the principal creditor, the FDIC becomes responsible. The legal personality of the existing bank is terminated, and the insured deposits and such other parts of the bank are transferred to a new bank chartered by the Comptroller of the Currency, according to the principle of what the FDIC

---

[23] There is a provision for a branch to top up its deposit insurance to the host country level through the host country's deposit insurer (reduction to the local level could only be achieved by local incorporation).

[24] The difference lies in the existence of deposit insurance where the authorities agree to compensate insured depositors for their losses.

thinks will minimize its losses. Because banks are often parts of groups in the United States, the FDIC has sometimes turned each subsidiary into a separate bridge bank rather than forming a single bank for the whole group.

6.10 Cross-Border Institutional Structures with Joint Responsibility

It is clearly difficult to translate this arrangement into something that can be operated for cross-border banks unless each of the operating units can be carved off the group in the manner required in New Zealand. Ironically, if the cross-border bank chose to operate entirely through branches [as has been proposed for Nordea (2003) under the European Company Statute], then such a scheme could be administered by the home country authorities. As in the United States, they would be the insurer of the deposits across the whole group. Where the arrangement is more mixed, some national authorities may be prepared to see subsidiaries close because they are not of systemic importance, while others would wish to apply the bridge bank or an equivalent technique. This can apply equally to some host countries and to the home. For example, if none of the subsidiaries in a particular host country were of systemic importance to it, the host would be unlikely to have any direct interest in participating in the financial support of a subsidiary (or of the parent) in another country, even though that subsidiary (or parent) may be of systemic importance there. It would only have regard to the spillover from such a systemic problem to its own jurisdiction, or to the need to obtain matching support from the other countries for some other international bank whose operations it does regard as systemic. Clearly if a branch of a bank that the home country did not regard as systemic were deemed systemic by the host country, there would be a serious conflict of interest. The host authorities would have no means of keeping the whole banking group going and the home authorities might be unwilling to do so on another country's behalf unless doing so minimized their own losses.

This implies that some joint arrangement needs to be established, and one that can operate swiftly according to some predetermined guidelines. Protracted committee discussions where unanimity among the countries is required at the time are not appropriate for a crisis. Some body has to have responsibility, adequate access to funds, technical expertise, and the power to act, in many cases under the aegis of a court. This implies that if there is no supranational executive body and no international court to refer to, then it will be under some national jurisdiction, even if the consequences run over a group of countries. The predetermined guidelines, while they cannot address every detail, need to have principles as to how systemic concerns will be addressed in any of the jurisdictions. If the parent organization is taken into a bridge bank, then clearly this effective change of ownership needs to apply to the subsidiaries even though they are subject to different jurisdictions and authorities. Similarly, if the parent is allowed to fail but systemic subsidiaries become bridge banks, again there needs to be a clear arrangement between the host authority that is effectively assuming ownership and the receivership estate in the home country. The pricing of such deals is likely to be controversial. If a new organization is to be carved out of branches, then the agreement will need to be even more complex, but this latter route seems unlikely unless the branch were close to freestanding.

Goodhart and Schoenmaker (2006) emphasize that burden sharing among the countries involved needs to be established in advance according to some simple rule such as the distribution of assets or deposits. It is inevitable that the cause of a problem is likely to be relatively concentrated, the actual losses unevenly distributed, and the systemic need for action asymmetric. Not only would an argument at the time, particularly over who is to blame and therefore over who should pay, render prompt solution impossible but it contravenes the whole idea of insurance where those who are lucky enough not to be affected provide the compensation to those who are.

6.11 Adequate Powers

However, in most European countries, it is pointless to pursue this discussion at present, as they do not have the power to step in and take over the bank from the shareholders in this manner. They have the bank declared insolvent, and hence almost certainly see its operations stop, or they have to provide some sort of bailout, whether a loan or a guarantee or a combination thereof. Because the first route is unlikely to solve the problem of keeping systemic operations going, the latter route seems more likely. The drawback is that then there is a burden to be shared among the countries.

In the United States, the authorities can step in when a bank is still solvent but critically undercapitalized if the leverage ratio falls below 2% and the bank does not take action that solves the problem to the satisfaction of the FDIC within a predetermined period (90 days). Although stepping in while the bank still has positive value entirely gets round the problem of burden sharing, it seems unlikely that such an intervention would be permitted under European law (Hadjiemmanuil 2003). The problem, therefore, is to intervene as soon as losses appear and to take strong action to turn the bank round as soon as capitalization falls below regulatory requirements – PCA. This we deal within the next section. However, it is worth noting at this point that Eisenbeis and Kaufman (2006) have an ingenious suggestion for enabling PCA in cross-border banks. They argue that applying the European Company Statue should be sufficiently attractive that systemically important cross-border banks will want to opt for it. Then they suggest that, because the bank will have a new legal personality, it will need to reapply for banking status and hence the authorities in the home country can insist that being subject to coordinated PCA is a condition for granting this new license. They argue that the risks will be reduced so that the deposit insurance charge for these banks can also be lower, which will act as an inducement. This gives a single cross-border system and adequate powers of intervention all in one step. The drawback is that no bank has yet found the statute sufficiently attractive, even without the powers of intervention, to adopt it, which makes the idea that they would adopt it with such powers unlikely.

Even within the European Union there is considerable variety over how the responsibility for the functioning of the financial system is allocated, both with respect to sectors – banks, insurance companies, financial markets, payment and settlement, pensions, and other institutions[25] – and functions – prudential regulation, crisis prevention, and management, conduct of business. As a result there is a wide variety of authorities with overlapping mandates that must get together to work out how to handle the problems. The European Union, with the ESCB, CEBS, CESR, and CEIOPS,[26] has decided to cut the cake four ways but the authorities in the member states do not map neatly into this (Eisenbeis and Kaufmann 2006; Masciandaro et al. 2006). To this is added considerable variety in powers and approach, despite the unifying framework of EU legislation. Elsewhere, without that unifying framework, the variety is even larger and the major institutions that have to be handled run right across many of the boundaries (as set out in the various chapters on large complex financial institutions in Evanoff and Kaufman 2005).

---

[25] Indeed there is continuing discussion about the range of nonbank institutions to be covered: building societies, investment funds, finance companies, sharebrokers, custodians, hedge funds.

[26] The EU system is littered with acronyms: ESCB, European System of Central Banks; CEBS Committee of European Banking Supervisors; CESR, Committee of European Securities Regulators; CEIOPS, Committee of European Insurance and Occupational Pension Supervisors.

While it is always tempting to want to cut through this complexity and advocate the setting up of the central bank as the sole prudential authority for all financial institutions[27] as in Ireland, the Netherlands, and New Zealand, in practice central banks have to deal with the complexity and accept that they will have to handle their responsibilities in cooperation with other usually independent entities whose mandates may well be somewhat contradictory. This inevitably means that a network of explicit and implicit agreements and arrangements has developed. While within individual countries these can have full legal force, although they have frequently taken the form of softer "Memoranda of Understanding," internationally they tend to rely on soft law and hence will be difficult to enforce, and the difficulty of obtaining recompense even greater. The Maastricht Treaty setting up the ESCB and the ECB is very much the exception; there the law is clear.

As we have noted, a supranational organization becomes most important when it comes to either PCA or intervention on insolvency. It is probably possible to organize cooperative arrangements for satisfactory supervision and exchange of information even if these are not the theoretically optimal arrangements (Schoenmaker and Oosterloo 2007). Provided that the ordinary insolvency procedures are thought adequate, then current arrangements could work. As soon as intervention for systemic reasons is required, then there is a prima facie case for new institutions. They could take the form of a designated resolution agency to handle the problem. Because the number of banks across the world that have systemic implications outside their domestic markets is relatively limited, it might be possible to handle this on a case-by-case basis.[28] The resolution agency would presumably be based in the home country, but with the ability to draw on resources in the host countries.[29] Since such failures are likely to be rare and perhaps even nonexistent, there seems little justification for setting up much in the

---

[27] Such an authority could also include conduct of business as well as prudential oversight.

[28] Schoenmaker and Oosterloo argue that there are only around 30 such banks in the European Union. Further, if Britain's Midland Bank is a precedent, there would be plenty of time to act. That bank was the biggest in the world in 1934, and then went into a slow decline, eventually being taken over by HSBC in 1992, changing its name to HSBC Bank plc in 1999. (A few years earlier, in 1987, it did experience the ignominy of receiving a take over approach from its advertising agency, Saatchi and Saatchi.)

[29] Provided that banks can be caught early, which one hopes is likely for large cross-border banks, the question of how such an institution would be funded becomes more manageable. Goodhart and Schoenmaker (2006) argue that any contributions should be in proportion to assets in the respective countries. The principal need, if the organization is not funded up front, will be to borrow from the respective governments until it can be recapitalized from the banking system. In the United States, the need to provide such

way of an enduring organization. It would probably form part of the home country's existing resolution arrangements. The FDIC model is probably not the right way to envisage this unless all banks are to be treated in a manner similar to that in the United States. Most insolvencies will be primarily national affairs to be sorted out by national authorities.

The position in the European Union is somewhat easier to envisage, as a new European-level organization to handle resolutions in these 30 or so banks identified by Schoenmaker and Oosterloo (2007) might make sense. It could be labeled EDIC (European Deposit Insurance Corporation) or European Resolution Agency. Various ideas have been advanced as to whether it should be independent or linked to the ECB (Di Giorgio and Di Noia 2003; Masciandaro 2004; Schoenmaker and Wierts 2004; Masciandaro, Quintyn, and Taylor, Chapter 8, this volume), but there is no need for a grand organization, merely a framework that can leap into action when problems appear. The trigger for action would come from the supervisory process. However, it will need to have a noticeable permanent staff if, like the FDIC, it is to be actively involved in the supervision of these 30 or so large banks. For this system to work, either the bank needs to be headquartered in the European Union or its EU operations need to be a viable unit (or group of units) separate from the parent. Outside the European Union the role of host countries will inevitably be smaller and require great confidence in the home country authorities. If that confidence does not exist, then the likely response will probably be the inhibition of cross-border arrangements at least to the New Zealand extent.

6.12 Preventing Problems

Key to avoiding problems with cross-border banks lies in the actions to reduce the potential causes of problems, both macroeconomic ones and those specific to the bank, and in those actions that are taken to reduce the impact when problems are imminent. The macroeconomic actions will normally be purely national in character and not represent any deviation from the concerns of monetary and exchange rate policy that we have already dealt with. Concerted, preemptive action across countries, taken to preserve macroeconomic stability, are the exception rather than the rule, except of course in the case of the euro area and other multicountry currency zones.[30]

---

extra funding has not occurred since the enactment of FDICIA (Federal Deposit Insurance Corporation Improvement Act) and the setting up of PCA in 1991.

[30] The other multicountry currency areas, such as the franc zones, are not similar in character to the euro area.

Even so there is a danger of the bank trying to shop among regimes seeking to find the best terms that it can. It would then benefit from the terms, and the borrowing these terms allowed, across the whole range (geographic as well as economic) of its operations. The major weakness that triggers the need for emergency assistance may be in another market from that of the central bank being approached for funds. In the absence of coordination among the central banks, one central bank that thinks that the solvency problems are worse and hence that collateral values are impaired may hope that the others will make advances against collateral so its own risks are reduced. It therefore seems inevitable that requests for emergency lending require consultation and information sharing across the range of central banks involved – even if, as in the euro system, the responsible national central bank steps in, takes the risk upon itself, and informs the others of what it has done after the event. It is in this sense that the internationalization of banking can complicate the implementation of classic LPLR action. National central banks can still carry out such operations, but coordination among central banks is required to prevent socially inefficient forum shopping and inappropriate risk transfer.

In recent years, as part of maintaining financial stability, central banks have developed a concept of macroprudential risk management; this forms part of the preempting of problems. It is not immediately clear what the term macroprudential risk management embodies, except that it refers to risks that are not related to individual financial institutions. To some extent it is simply delineated by the content of published "financial stability reviews." Thus, it clearly involves the assessment of macroeconomic risks, including market risk and exchange rate risk. It includes the assessment of risks from the structure of the financial system and how it is regulated. It includes risk from concentration of activity by financial institutions and the development of new products, that is, risks only apparent from the aggregation of actions each of which appears individually prudent to those taking them. However, information and associated cautioning form only a part of the response. Central banks take direct action to reduce and manage risks through monetary policy, provision of payment services and insurance, and altering the structure of as well as indirect pressure on other agencies and government to address the risks. Further, skilled as they are, central banks can not foresee everything – some events may be intrinsically unforeseeable, and other problems involve uncertainty rather than risk. Not every failure is preventable.

Nevertheless, prevention is important. The key ingredients to preventing problems are the following:

- Having a clear and credibly workable exit strategy for failing banks that does not involve a bail out of the existing owners or creditors – this way there is a strong incentive to owners and creditors to avoid failure.
- Having a framework for ensuring prudential capital and risk management standards such as those recommended by the Basel committee.
- Ensuring that the structure of financial markets limits the risks – such as avoiding excess concentration, ensuring that the regulatory authorities have clear mandates and compatible incentives, ensuring that there are properly functioning routes to market discipline.
- Ensuring that macrorisks are addressed and markets and institutions properly informed.
- Ensuring that crisis management tools are in place and thought to be effective.
- Ensuring that prompt action is taken to resolve any problems that do emerge in individual banks.

We have already noted that the requirements for PCA in the United States provide strong incentives for banks to recapitalize voluntarily as problems worsen, for the alternatives, of increasingly harsh mandatory requirements from the FDIC and ultimately takeover and possibly liquidation, are clearly less attractive. The same applies in Mexico where, in some respects, the mandatory requirements are harsher (LaBrosse and Mayes 2007). Most countries have requirements for action and powers of intervention, but on the whole, they are neither mandated in the United States' manner nor so clearly time limited. If the treatment of cross-border banks is to be effective, it is clear that it has to go beyond coordinated supervision and include coordinated intervention according to rules agreed beforehand without the pressure of an incipient crisis. While it would help agreement if these rules were widely promoted, say by the Basel Committee, it is nevertheless possible for the colleges of supervisors to agree to them and set them out as a written agreement.

Clearly someone needs to be in charge in just the same way that there is a lead supervisor for the coordinated monitoring of the banking group. However, here there can be an institutional mismatch. In the United States there is a resolution agency, the FDIC, that seeks to minimize its losses by its actions while the bank is in trouble but not yet facing insolvency or takeover. This separation of the responsibility for efficient resolution from the responsibility for monitoring to ensure compliance means that there is much less danger from forbearance. Intervention can be thought to imply supervisory failure and hence induce some reluctance for a supervisor to take public action. If some countries have a deposit insurer with strong powers charged with minimizing its losses, while others have deposit insurers that simply pay out on the say so of the supervisory authority, the pressure for action and the nature of it will vary from country to country and make agreement more difficult. Where there is either implicit insurance or even no insurance the position is even more complex.

LaBrosse and Mayes (2007) argue that in many countries the structure of the deposit insurance system is such that the countries either implicitly intend or will find themselves forced to issue a blanket guarantee if a large institution gets into difficulty. As Kaufman (2006) points out, if depositors are going to be protected adequately enough for them not to run on the bank, they need to know that they will have continuing access to their insured funds with only a small break if any. The prospect of substantial delays is not plausible, yet in the European Union, the Deposit Insurance Directive only requires a payout within 90 days of establishing the existence of the liability and even then the 90 days is extendable twice if there are problems in identifying the extent of the insured deposits and the beneficial owners. It thus seems likely that, as was found in the Nordic crises, some other means of offering people continuing access to their accounts will be required, whether through blanket guarantees as in Finland and Sweden, or through takeover of the banks as in Norway. If the authorities cannot swiftly form a bridge bank or pass the deposits over to another bank to provide continuing services, then the alternative is liquidation and a payout by the insurer. Unless there is an interim dividend, the insurer will have to cover the full value of the payout for some time, requiring either the ability to borrow or very extensive funding until the rest of the banking system can refinance it.[31]

This likelihood of serious difficulties in intervention on reaching zero net worth, or whatever other intervention point is used, and the moral hazard from the expectation of a bailout being forced in these circumstances to avoid an interruption in business emphasizes the importance of PCA. The rules for such PCA need to be at least as specific as in the United States, there need to be designated authorities in each jurisdiction who will carry them out, and there must be a clear leader to organize and coordinate the action. While a "collegial" approach may be the best way to agree on the plans and discuss progress, it must be possible for the lead organization to act even

---

[31] If the insurer is publicly financed, then the problem is rather different but it still leaves the government to make a choice over whether it wishes to offer some sort of bailout or guarantee that involves less expenditure up front or a repayment of depositors, which is itself expensive to administer.

in the event of disagreement. As a consequence the PCA, rules need to be set out in the form of a legal agreement among the designated authorities. Furthermore, the participating authorities may have to change their own national regulations if they lack the powers to do what PCA requires or if cross-border and national banks will be treated unequally.

6.13 Cross-Border Financial Markets

Central banks have been playing an increasing role in international financial markets and in the payment and settlement system. Inside the European Union, this is understandable as they have a positive duty to encourage a Single European Payments Area and the development of efficient European securities markets. It is by no means clear that the central banks need to act as the provider but in the case of intercountry payments in euros, this was taken as a given, with the setting up of TARGET and its more recent development into TARGET2 with a wider range of services and more restricted range of platforms.

However, getting progress through the private sector in securities settlement has proved difficult for two main reasons. First of all, it is a network industry and there needs to be a single system in which all can participate. No one wants to be a first mover, make a large investment, and then find the industry goes in a different and incompatible direction. Agreement is needed and central banks can be catalytic in getting the parties together. But the second reason limits the efficacy of this. There are relatively few major players in the industry and an expectation that there may eventually be only one main securities market in the European Union or at least just one or two dominant systems as in the United States, with the NYSE, Nasdaq, and DTCC. Clearly each incumbent would like to be the survivor and strategic positioning in the interim will lead each of them to try to get an advantage over the others.

The response has been for the euro system to suggest that it will itself set up the system, based on the TARGET platform and labeled TARGET2 Securities. While this in part may be an incentive for the market to come up with its own solution, it is largely a response to a problem that is specific to Europe with its single currency running across a number of jurisdictions. There is a clear tension between the role of the central bank in ensuring the existence of an efficient financial infrastructure with open entry and adequate resilience, and actually being the provider of some or all of the system.

Much of the rest of the world does not face the same difficulties although it is generally the case that it is much more difficult to conduct transactions across borders than within them. Nevertheless, it is still necessary to have some means of ensuring that the national authorities provide adequate supervision of institutions that are providing key cross-border services. SWIFT is an obvious case in point, as is CLS in the foreign exchange market. Here it seems to have been possible to get a team of regulators led by the home country to put together a satisfactory approach so that there can be confidence that the cross-border system works to a satisfactory standard and provides against operational and other risks to an extent that engenders general confidence.

In cross-border financial markets, the role of the central bank is small and largely limited to the concerns of financial stability. Major failures in the cross-border system would have important domestic consequences. The problems international financial markets present for national central banks depend on how central banks see their responsibility to these markets. If they see themselves as obliged to stabilize them (the "Greenspan put"), then for most countries the cause is lost. They do not have the resources. We do not, therefore, have to consider whether central banks should so view their role. However, if they feel, rightly or wrongly, that they have a national role to stabilize financial prices, whether in securities markets or real estate, this will have implications for international markets if only because of their interconnection. To some extent, this stabilization will come not just from the operation of monetary policy but from the rules that govern lending and securities market operations. To some extent it is possible for investors to get around national constraints by operating in more than one country.

This does not mean there can be total neglect of financial market and of financial market linkages between countries. As is traditional, should a market collapse trigger problems within a banking sector, the central bank should stand ready to supply liquidity or to take other actions as appropriate – by, for example, disseminating information about the state of some financial institution, or acting to coordinate creditors in the presence of a weakness in a country's bankruptcy code. We see the behavior of the Fed in response to the collapse of LTCM, central bank actions after September 11, 2001, and, indeed, the behavior of the Bank of England in the 1914 panic in London as examples of such traditional central bank behavior. (For additional discussion and detail, see Wood 1999.) Further, financial markets can transmit problems. See, for example, the east Asian crisis. Note, though, that they transmitted problems only to countries with unsound banking systems. It would therefore appear fair to say that those international markets do not create problems for central banks, but that they increase the incentives to ensure that the domestic banking system is prudently run. Ensuring that has been seen as a central banking responsibility as long as – indeed, by some arguments presented long before – the concept of a central bank was fully articulated. Observe Thornton's (1802) insistence that unsound banks should be allowed to fail in a crisis. When that is known to be central bank policy, most banks will seek to be prudent.

6.14 Some Historical Evidence

The gold standard was in many ways a monetary system like that of today. Central banks had two obligations – maintaining convertibility and maintaining financial stability. The system can, indeed, be interpreted as a monetary rule. (See Bordo and Kydland 1995.)

As Capie (2002) argued, accepting the two obligations of the standard were what defined a central bank. Further, there were international banks. Of course the importance of these varied from country to country and from time to time, but they were an important part of the British banking system by the last quarter of the nineteenth century – British banks had an extensive presence overseas. Much of this presence was in British colonies, and these were, as noted earlier, on currency board systems based on sterling. But not all the overseas presence was of that form. Britain also had fairly important banking connections with South America, and it is from there that an illuminating episode comes. This episode is the Baring crisis of 1890.

In April of 1890, the Argentinean government found difficulty in repaying its debt, and the national bank suspended interest payments on *its* debt. This precipitated a run on the Argentinean banking system, a run which was in July followed by a revolution. Barings had lent very substantially to Argentina, and faced what seemed likely to be heavy losses. It revealed its difficulties to the Bank of England on November 8th.

The Bank was horrified, as it feared a run on London should Barings default. A hurried inspection of Barings suggested that the situation could be saved, provided that current and immediate obligations were met. A consortium was organized, and capital, initially £17 million, was injected.

Various features of this are of interest, not least the absence of panic in the London money market. But of particular relevance at this point is the demonstration that injection of capital to an international bank can be readily engineered, even in a fixed exchange-rate system, if the providers of capital are willing. Willingness in this case was produced not by any set of rules or indeed by coercion, but by an awareness that cooperation would produce mutual benefits. In this case, the benefits were believed to be the continued importance of London as an international financial center. This strongly suggests that in designing rules for the preservation of financial stability across national boundaries, heed must be paid to national self interest, both political and financial.

6.15 Conclusion

The internationalization of banking does not prevent national central banks taking classic LOLR action when it is necessary to do so. Hence, liquidity problems can be handled in the traditional manner. But where capital is required, problems are much less tractable, and pessimism is hard to resist. Complete separation, or the ready possibility of it, as New Zealand requires, produces an environment where stability can be maintained. But the price may well be high in terms of efficiency gains foregone. Clear mutuality of interest, as was displayed in London when Barings failed in 1890, can ensure provision of capital. But what can ensure clear mutuality of interest across national boundaries? Much can be done to help prevent problems, and indeed was done in the development of Basel II, but problems requiring provision of capital are inevitable. These are likely to require the provision of capital by taxpayers in one country in response to problems originating in and perhaps if not confined mainly to another country. We are not convinced there would be great willingness to do this. Our conclusion is, therefore, a pessimistic one. The internationalization of commercial banking, although in many ways capable of being handled by national central banks, does create for them a problem which by its nature is one they cannot, and never will, solve. Thus far in the difficulties stemming from the problems with the United States subprime mortgage market, national solutions have proved acceptable to the large exposure of foreign institutions, despite considerable difficulties, including the failure of other banks, such as Northern Rock in the United Kingdom.[32] In the European Union we can expect that this experience might ultimately lead to the development of a new transnational body or the assigning of powers to an existing institution such as the ESCB. Outside the European Union, the solution is less obvious.

---

[32] The failure of Northern Rock was a major event in the United Kingdom, but it was an entirely national bank so it does not have direct implications for our analysis here. The only cross-border element is that without the U.S. problems, Northern Rock would still be going today but with low profitability and as a strong takeover target.

References

Allen, W. A. and G. E. Wood (2006), "Defining and Achieving Financial Stability," *Journal of Financial Stability* 2(2): 152–172.

Basel Committee on Banking Supervision (1996), *The Supervision of Cross-Border Banking,* Basel, October.

Baxter, T. C., J. Hansen, and J. H. Sommer (2004), "Two Cheers for Territoriality: an essay on international bank insolvency law," *American Bankruptcy Law Journal* 78(1): 57–91.

Bliss, R. R. (2007), "Multiple Regulators and Insolvency Regimes," in D. G. Mayes and G. E. Wood (Eds.), *The Structure of Financial Regulation* (Abingdon and New York: Routledge), pp. 132–154.

Bordo, M. and F. Kydland (1995), "The Gold Standard as a Rule," *Explorations in Economic History* 32(4): 423–464.

Calomiris, C. W. (1998), "The IMF'S Imprudent Role as Lender of Last Resort," *Cato Journal* 17(1): 275–294

Capie, F. (2002), "The Emergence of the Bank of England as a Mature Central Bank," in D. Winch and P. K. O'Brien (Eds.), *The Political Economy of British Historical Experience 1688–1914* (New York: Oxford University Press).

Di Giorgio G. and C. Di Noia (2003), "Financial Market Regulation and Supervision: How Many Peaks for the Euro Area?," *Brooklyn Journal of International Law* 28: 463–493.

Eisenbeis, R. A. and G. G. Kaufman (2006), "Cross-Border Banking: Challenges for Deposit Insurance and Financial Stability in the European Union," Federal Reserve Bank of Atlanta Working Paper 2006–15.

Evanoff, D. and G. Kaufman (Eds.) (2005), *Systemic Financial Crises: Resolving Large Bank Insolvencies* (Singapore: World Scientific).

Frankel, J. A. and A. K. Rose (1998), "The Endogeneity of the Optimum Currency Area Criteria," *Economic Journal* 108, July 449: 1009–1025.

Goodhart, C. A. E. (2007), "Why Prevention is Better than Cure," *Central Banking* 17(3), February: 19–24.

Goodhart, C. A. E. and Schoenmaker, D. (2006), "Burden Sharing in a Banking Crisis in Europe," *Sveriges Riksbank Economic Review* 2: 34–57.

Hadjiemmanuil, C. (2003), "Bank Resolution Policy and the Organization of Bank Insolvemcy Proceedings: Critical Dilemmas," in D. G. Mayes and A. Liuksila (Ed.), *Who Pays for Bank Insolvency?* (Basingstoke: Palgrave-Macmillan), pp. 272–330.

Hawtrey, R. (1932), *The Art of Central Banking* (London: Longmans, Green, and Co).

Kaufman, G. (2006), "Using Efficient Bank Insolvency Resolution to Solve the Deposit Insurance Problem," *Journal of Banking Regulation* 8(1): 40–50.

LaBrosse, R. and D. G. Mayes (2007), "Promoting Financial Stability Through Effective Depositor Protection: The Case for Explicit Limited Deposit Insurance," in A. Campbell, R. LaBrosse, D. G. Mayes, and D. Singh (Eds.), *Deposit Insurance* (Basingstoke: Palgrave-Macmillan), pp. 1–39.

Masciandaro, D. (Ed.) (2004), *Central Banks and Single Financial Authorities in Europe* (Cheltenham: Edward Elgar).

Masciandaro, D., M. Nieto, and H. Prast (2006), "Who Pays for Banking Supervision? Principles, Practices, and Determinants," University of Bocconi Monetary and Financial Economics Working Paper No. 169 (April).

Mayes, D. G. (2006), "Cross-border Financial Supervision in Europe: Goals and Transition Paths," *Sveriges Riksbank Economic Review* **2**: 58–89.

Mayes, D. G., L. Halme, and A. Liuksila (2001), *Improving Banking Supervision* (Basingstoke: Palgrave).

Mayes, D. G., N. Nieto, and L. A. Wall (2007), "Multiple Safety Net Regulations and Agency Problems in the EU: Is Prompt Corrective Action Partly the Solution," Bank of Finland Discussion Paper 7/2007.

Nordea (2003), "Nordea Reduces Complexity in its Legal Structure by Forming one European Company," Press release, 19 June. Available at http://www.seeurope-network.org/homepages/seeurope/file_uploads/nordeasepressrelease19.6.2003.pdf.

Pinder, J. (1968), "Positive Integration and Negative Integration: Some Problems of Economic Union in the EEC," *The World Today* **24** (3): 89–110.

Reserve Bank of New Zealand (2006), "Outsourcing Policy," BS11. Wellington, January.

Rockoff, H. (1986), "Walter Bagehot and the Theory of Central Banking," in F. H. Capie and G. E. Wood (Eds.), *Financial Crises and the World Banking System* (London: Macmillan), pp. 160–180.

Schoenmaker, D. and S. Oosterloo (2007), "Cross-border Issues in European Financial Supervision," in D. G. Mayes and G. E. Wood (Eds.), *The Structure of Financial Regulation* (Abingdon and New York: Routledge), pp. 265–285.

Schoenmaker, D. and P. Wierts (2004), "Survival of the Fittest: Competing Models for Financial Supervision in Europe," *Current Politics and Economics of Europe* **13**: 31–46.

Schwartz, A. (1999), "Is There a Need for an International Lender of Last Resort?," *Cato Journal* **19**(1): 1–6.

Stern, G. H. and R. J. Feldman (2006), "Managing TBTF by Reducing Systemic Risk," *The Region*, June, 18–21: 46–49

Thornton, H. (1802), *An Enquiry into the Nature and Effects of the Paper Credit of Great Britain*, Reprinted 1939 (London: Allen and Unwin).

Tripe, D. (2004), "Efficiency in Integrated Banking Markets – Australia and New Zealand," mimeo, Massey University.

Vesala, J. (2005), "Prudential Supervision and Deposit Insurance Issues Raised by the European Company Statute," Colloquium on the European Company Statute, ECB, Frankfurt, 23 February.

Wood, G. E. (1999), "Great Crashes in History: Have They Lessons for Today?," *Oxford Review of Economic Policy* **15**(3): 98–109.

Wood, G. E. and D. Mudd (1978), "Do Foreigners Control the US Money Supply?," *Federal Reserve Bank of St. Louis Review*, March.

7

The Complex Relationship between
Central Bank Independence and Inflation

Bernd Hayo and Carsten Hefeker

Abstract

In this survey, we present a number of arguments that question some aspects of the conventional view of central bank independence (CBI). We argue that CBI is neither necessary nor sufficient for reaching monetary stability. First, CBI is just one potentially useful monetary policy design instrument among several. Second, while the relevant economic theories focus on the aspect of goal independence, in practice most central banks tend to be only instrument independent. Third, CBI should not be treated as an exogenous variable, but attention should be devoted to the question of why central banks are made independent. CBI is chosen by countries under specific circumstances, which are related to their legal, political, and economic systems. Fourth, in a number of empirical studies, researchers found CBI to be correlated with low inflation rates. By taking the endogeneity of CBI into account, however, there remains little reason to believe the correlation between CBI and low inflation tells us anything about causality.

7.1 Introduction

Central bank independence has become one of the central concepts in monetary theory and policy. Most economists agree that CBI is desirable because it helps to reach the long-term goal of price stability. Although one might think about alternative mechanisms to reach low rates of inflation, CBI is the one most-often recommended. The idea has also found confirmation in the fact that an increasing number of countries in all regions of the world made their central banks independent in the last 20 years (Arnone et al.

We thank Alex Cukierman, Sylvester Eijffinger, the editors, the referees, and participants of the Budapest conference for helpful comments.

2007; Cukierman 2007).[1] The culmination of this trend was perhaps the creation of the European Central Bank (ECB), which is the most independent central bank of all (Buiter 2006). The ECB is not only independent concerning the use of instruments, but defines its target inflation rate itself.

In this survey chapter, we revisit the argument for CBI. Compared to other surveys (Eijffinger and de Haan 1996; Berger et al. 2001; Arnone et al. 2007), which confirm conventional wisdom, we focus on a selection of critical papers. Building upon Hayo and Hefeker (2002), we argue that CBI is neither necessary nor sufficient for reaching monetary stability. Concerning the claim that CBI is not a necessary condition to achieve price stability, we point out that CBI is just one monetary policy design instrument among several that can be employed for achieving this objective, and conclude that no one monetary policy design instrument is optimal under all conditions. Concerning sufficiency we argue that CBI should not be treated as an exogenous variable. In particular, we think too little attention is devoted to the question of why central banks are actually made independent. It would be wrong to regard CBI as the underlying cause for low inflation.

We begin by reviewing the theoretical foundations of CBI. First, we briefly summarize the fundamental models underlying the case for CBI. Then we demonstrate that there are serious theoretical problems with the standard argument that CBI is the optimal choice of a monetary policy design instrument. Although these problems are stated in the literature, the typical conclusion is that CBI seems to work in practice, and it should be seen as the best workable way to achieve low rates of inflation (see, e.g., Arnone et al. 2007). We do not find this inference convincing, and it certainly does not follow from any of the empirical tests of the CBI hypothesis.

Second, we show there are alternative monetary policy design instruments available that can be employed to achieve low inflation rates. In particular, we focus on fixed exchange rate and currency boards, inflation targets, and inflation contracts. It is important to note that these approaches have equally or more favorable theoretical properties than CBI, and have also been successfully implemented in practice. At the same time, there is no doubt that every one of these approaches also comes with disadvantages, which leads us to the conclusion there is no design instrument available that is optimal under all conditions. Thus, CBI is not a necessary condition for achieving monetary stability.

---

[1] Interestingly, Arnone et al. (2007) find that independent central banks in developing countries are often more independent than the central banks in OECD countries were in the 1980s.

Third, in a number of empirical studies, researchers found that CBI is correlated with low inflation rates. A typical policy conclusion based on this finding is that the creation of an independent central bank will bring about price stability. We argue that this conclusion is not warranted for a number of reasons. Our focus is on the issue of endogeneity of CBI. Even assuming we measure the right thing and that there is strong evidence of a relationship between CBI and inflation, there is no reason to expect that this finding will be policy robust. In other words, this correlation does not tell us anything about causality. Instead, we argue that at least two decisions determine the choice of CBI by a society. First, a decision must be made regarding the importance of price stability as a major economic policy objective. If price stability is viewed as relatively significant, then the second question is about the appropriate choice of a monetary policy design instrument. Thus, the "true" cause underlying the empirical relationship between CBI and low inflation rates is the social choice in favor of a stability-oriented monetary policy.

Taking these aspects into account, we lay out existing theories and empirical evidence regarding the decision to make price stability an important aim for economic policy. The two main explanations rest on either the idea of an "inflation culture" in societies that opt for a stable monetary regime, or, alternatively, that specific interest groups are able to influence the government so that such a monetary policy objective is implemented. We proceed to show under which conditions societies are likely to choose CBI as the monetary policy design instrument. Using political economy arguments, we consider a country's legal and political systems.[2] Dependent upon the existence of specific circumstances in these societal subsystems, countries will either choose CBI or other available instruments.

7.2 The Conventional View of Central Bank Independence

The seminal article on CBI is by Barro and Gordon (1983). It builds upon earlier work by Kydland and Prescott (1977), who introduced the idea of time-inconsistent behavior. In its attempt to maximize social welfare, the central bank will try to use monetary surprises to stimulate employment after private contracts have been fixed. However, the forward-looking behavior of rational private agents will lead them to expect higher prices and to act accordingly. Thus, there will not be any employment gain but

---

[2] Gärtner (2008) provides a survey on monetary policy and central bank design from the point of view of public choice theory.

instead a positive rate of inflation.[3] Promises not to inflate are not credible, because the welfare-maximizing government has an incentive to renege on its promise once wages are set. Hence, an inflationary bias exists.

To avoid positive rates of inflation that carry only costs but no benefits, a mechanism is sought to commit the monetary authority to a noninflationary monetary policy. The mechanism suggested by Rogoff (1985) is to appoint someone whose preferences are known to diverge from those of the welfare-maximizing authority. If someone who puts more relative weight on avoiding inflation than unemployment were to set monetary policy, the rate of inflation would be lower, because marginal costs and benefits from inflation are different for that person. Given that these preferences are known, expected and actual inflation would fall. Thus, appointing a "conservative" central banker, as Rogoff called these preferences, can help to reduce the inflation bias.

However, as he also pointed out, this solution is not costless in a world with stochastic shocks, where there is a stabilizing role for monetary policy. With a conservative central banker, stabilization policy would be relatively weak. Hence, on the one hand, lower average inflation may come at the potential price of higher output variability, and, as Crosby (1998) argues, on the other hand, only countries characterized by shocks that are relatively unimportant will grant independence to central banks.

Another aspect pointed out by Rogoff (1985) is that conservatism is only a second-best solution to the inflation bias problem. The first-best would be to eliminate existing rigidities in labor and product markets. Rigidities in labor and product markets must be present to generate an inflation bias, because if all factors of production are employed, there is no incentive to increase production and employment.[4]

7.3 Problems with the Conventional View

7.3.1 Independence and Conservatism

The Rogoff solution has become the major justification for CBI. Implicitly in this argument is the equalization of independence and conservatism.

---

[3] An unexpectedly low rate of inflation would create unemployment and thus not be pursued in a one-period model. If the central bank aims to build a reputation, this might change. This incentive to build reputation is significantly reduced, however, if unemployment is persistent.

[4] As Posen (1998) points out, there might be circularity between rigidities and conservatism of the central bank. If a central bank is very conservative, it might cause nominal wage rigidities to increase, making disinflation more costly (Debelle and Fischer 1994). See Gros and Hefeker (2002) for a model with endogenous degrees of rigidities.

Rogoff (1985, 1177) wrote: "Society can make itself better off by selecting an agent to head the independent central bank who is known to place greater weight on inflation stabilization (relative to unemployment stabilization) than is embodied in the social loss function." There are a number of serious problems with setting these two concepts equal, as it is often done in the literature, which undermine the case for CBI.

Almost all independent central banks are free to choose the instruments with which they want to pursue their ultimate goal(s). But almost no central bank is allowed to autonomously set its targets. Central banks are usually charged with pursuing price stability (or more practically a low rate of inflation) and given freedom to pursue this goal as they consider best. There is, therefore, no goal independence but only instrument independence (Debelle and Fischer 1994). For instance, the Bank of England, even after being made independent from the Ministry of Finance, is still given its inflation target from the Minister (and must publicly explain why it failed to reach that goal).[5] Even the ECB, which can define its own target rate of inflation, is mandated to pursue price stability above other goals. This is hardly comparable to appointing someone with different preferences and letting that person decide what policy it would set. This leads to a related question, namely, to what extent the widely used concept of instrument independence in practice corresponds to the theoretically relevant concept of goal independence. There may be a substantial gap between the two concepts, potentially undermining any conclusions derived from observing the behavior of instrument-independent central banks for the underlying theory. We feel that this is a serious problem that has not received sufficient attention in the literature, and that further research in this area might turn out to be fruitful.

Note that the above discussion does not imply that we subscribe to the view that it is highly desirable to implement Rogoff's solution. In fact, there are good reasons for assigning specific goals to the central bank in a democratic society (Blinder 1998, 2004; Tootell 1999; Siklos 2002). Fuhrer (1997) even challenges the unconditional primacy of price stability over other goals, such as employment and growth. If the ultimate goal of public policy is economic welfare, presumably closely connected to unemployment and growth, and if there is a trade-off between inflation and growth, there may be little reason to rank price stability above growth.[6]

---

[5] For instance, in March 2007, in an open letter to the government the Governor of the Bank of England had to explain why inflation exceeded the target rate of 2% over the last 12 months.

[6] Most empirical studies, however, tend to find that there is long-run neutrality of money with regard to output (see, e.g. in the case of the United States, King and Watson 1997).

Empirically, moreover, the negative empirical relationship between legal indicators of CBI and inflation typically breaks down in a sample consisting of developing countries (Cukierman 1992).[7] In the case of transition economies, Hillman (1999) argues that the higher the degree of CBI, the higher the rate of inflation becomes, thus turning the evidence that appears to hold for OECD countries on its head. A striking example is the central bank of Belarus, which possessed a high degree of de jure independence. Nevertheless, the president of the central bank was jailed and replaced by the finance minister when his policy fell in disgrace with the government. Other examples are Russia or Zimbabwe, where nominally independent central banks presided over rampant or even hyperinflation (Banian et al. 1998; Acemoglu et al. 2008). Hillman draws the conclusion that what is necessary is how CBI is actually applied, which he sees as a question of political culture (see also Forder 1996).

However, Loungani and Sheets (1997) come to a different conclusion. They find for a single point in time (1993) that in a cross-section of 12 countries' CBIs is negatively correlated with inflation.[8] The major drawback of their study is that it does not take an average of inflation rates over time into account. Supporting the case for CBI, Cukierman et al. (2002) argue that, after controlling for a number of influences related to the process of transformation, legal CBI and inflation are negatively correlated.

It is also possible to find examples that might question the equality of CBI and low rates of inflation even among OECD countries. For instance, Banian et al. (1998) report that focusing on particular subindices of legal CBI leads to the conclusion that more independent central banks might even increase inflation. An interesting example is Japan before the introduction of formal independence in 1998, where inflation rates were low and the central bank was directly influenced by the Ministry of Finance. Thus, in spite of the temptations coming from the government revenue side, there was a consensus that monetary policy should not be used to finance deficits.

Regarding the United States, it is arguably the case that the Federal Reserve Bank (Fed) exhibits a higher degree of factual than legal independence. The Humphrey–Hawkins Act imposes a specific unemployment

---

[7] The conventional results can be restablished when using the turnover rate of central bank governors as an indicator of de facto CBI instead of the legal CBI indices. As pointed out by de Haan and Kooi (2000), this outcome is conditional on the high-inflation countries in the sample.

[8] Apparently, the construction of the indicator plays a role, as they do not get significant results based on an index which does not take into account political independence.

target on the Fed that appears to be consistently relegated behind the inflation target, at least after the Volcker era (Hakes et al. 1998). Finally, German economic history provides another example where the Reichsbank was designed as politically independent after World War I but nevertheless accommodated the policy of the government in the 1920s (Vaubel 1997a).

More generally, Fuhrer (1997) and Siklos (2002) find that the connection between independence and inflation has been reversed in the 1990s, and that there is actually a *negative* correlation between low inflation and independence. However, Carlstrom and Fuerst (2006) claim that the linear relationship between inflation and independence as identified, for example, by Alesina and Summers (1993), is still valid. While some authors (Arnone et al. 2007) claim that the general trend in the 1990s toward lower rates of inflation across almost all countries can be explained by more legal independence, we are somewhat more skeptical. Given that this reduction in average inflation rates coincides with a reduction in the variability of income – the great moderation – it is difficult to explain this development within a Rogoff-type model.

A high level of credibility is often seen as one of the most important conditions for a successful monetary policy (see, for instance, Blinder 1998), and the success of specific central banks, such as the Bundesbank, is often linked to the reputation that they have built up.[9] We do not discount reputation and credibility as an important ingredient to the success of monetary policy. However, we point out that simply granting independence will not necessarily yield immediate and prompt credibility. In fact, Fuhrer (1997) and Blinder (1998) find that the costs of disinflation in countries with greater CBI have not generally been smaller than in countries with lesser independence. This suggests that a simple change in the laws does not yield immediate credibility, which would then translate into lower costs of disinflation. One reason for this might be that countries with a track record of several years (or decades) of very expansive and loose monetary policy will not be able to convince the public of a change in its monetary strategy by simply changing the legal status of the central bank. However, a change in monetary policy may precede CBI, and a low inflation record may have been already established before formal independence is introduced. A good example is France, where the break in the inflation time series occurred sometime in the mid-1980s, while the law on CBI was passed in 1993 in the run-up to European Economic and Monetary Union (EMU). Muscatelli

---

[9] Forder (2001) puts forward a number of critical points regarding the usefulness of the concepts of credibility and reputation in the discussion of monetary policy.

et al. (2002) and Acemoglu et al. (2008) show that the breakpoint in monetary policy in a number of countries that have formally adopted inflation targeting, predates the institutional change. Siklos (2002) as well finds that central banks that were made more independent in the 1990s produced lower rates of inflation already in the 1980s.

Therefore, a change in the effective exchange rate regime or a change in the thinking by the Ministry of Finance on debt financing might be more credible and effective in changing the public's expectation of future monetary policy. This conclusion is supported by Blinder (1999), who surveyed central bankers around the world, concluding that monetary history is probably the most important ingredient of a credible monetary policy.

One further argument for having legally independent central banks is to avoid political business cycles generated by governments trying to improve their reelection chances. It might be argued that the simplest solution to this problem is to delegate monetary policy away from the government. If governments are unable to set monetary policy, they cannot pursue political business cycles using this instrument. There is conflicting evidence with regard to the existence of systematic monetary policy-induced political business cycles in OECD countries. While the literature following the original contributions gives little evidence of political business cycles in monetary policy (see Drazen 2000 for a survey), there is some evidence of manipulation in fiscal policy that might ultimately have an impact on monetary policy (Brender and Drazen 2005; Mink and de Haan 2006; Shi and Svensson 2006). The more dependent the central bank, the greater is the likelihood that fiscal policy ultimately dominates monetary policy.

However, as Vaubel (1997a) points out, delegating monetary policy may not always work as a solution to the political business cycle. He argues that independent central bank councils could be politically "captured" by the government to perform a monetary policy that corresponds closely to its interests. Governments will make political decisions when appointing central bankers, which will then support the respective party's economic policy. He shows the German Bundesbank has, in several cases, engineered an active monetary policy to help the ruling party and, in other cases, set a tighter monetary policy than necessary to deteriorate the chances of the government of reelection. Thus, although central banks are formally independent, they could be politically influenced via the appointment procedure. Waller (2000) shows formally that political appointments are less likely in a repeated game setting but cannot be ruled out, and Lohmann (1998) and von Hagen (1998) argue that federal political systems might help to prevent the occurrence of political business cycles because of diverging interests, political leanings of state governments, and staggered election dates. In any case, legal CBI seems to be a rather poor instrument to measure monetary policy independence, and actual independence depends, among other things, on the behavior of governments in the appointment procedure and the behavior of independent central bankers after they have been appointed.

Berger and Woitek (1997) use time series modeling to investigate the validity of Vaubel's claim in the context of political business cycles. If central bank councils were captured, they would support economic growth by loosening monetary policy. They neither find evidence of such a behavior in the time series data nor in an analysis of the Bundesbank minutes (see also Vaubel's reply 1997b). At least one criticism of the Berger and Woitek study is that it presupposes that output or employment is always valued higher than low inflation by the population. Empirically, a number of analyses using representative survey data indicate that, at least in certain periods, inflation is seen as more important than unemployment (see Fischer and Huizinga 1982; Rose 1998; Hayo 2004). Whatever the evidence in this particular case, the general point should be taken into account. Because most central bank boards have terms of office going beyond the government's, nothing rules out that an independent central bank has and pursues a political agenda on its own that may or may not coincide with that of any particular party in power.

A related point is made by Tootell (1999) in his analysis of the Fed's monetary policy. He finds that central bankers systematically respond to changes in the attitude of the American population toward monetary policy. At times when unemployment is, according to Gallup polls, of more concern for American voters, the Fed's policy becomes looser. He also finds that the response of the Fed's policy to changing perceptions in the population is stronger before election dates. This seems to reflect not only a (presumably democratically justified) response of monetary policy to society's interests, but a political business cycle element as well.[10]

A further point is that the independence of the central bank and the conservativeness of the central bank's preferences are not complements, as the discussion along the lines of Rogoff suggests, but rather substitutes. Eijffinger and Hoeberichts (1998) show that if the actual monetary policy stance is negotiated between the government and the central bank (something one

---

[10] He argues that the central bank has to adjust to the changing preferences of the population if it wants to defend its independence. In this view, the Fed is not goal independent and thus does not conform to the Rogoff model (Tootell 1999, 219).

might reasonably assume if the central bank is not goal independent), any desired outcome can be achieved by making the central bank more conservative, and thus lowering the rate of inflation that the central bank prefers, or by giving it more decision power at a lower degree of conservativeness. In both cases, the same iso-inflation line can be obtained. This would again caution against setting independence and conservativeness equal. Moreover, as shown empirically by de Haan and Kooi (1997), it is less conservativeness as embedded in the law than instrument independence that correlates with price stability.

Finally, almost all of the models assume the degree of conservativeness could be observed, something that is at least questionable in reality. If indeed it is assumed that maximizing social welfare is the core policy problem then it might easily happen that a central banker is appointed whose decisions do not yield the optimal trade-off between inflation and unemployment for society. Appointing someone who is "too" conservative would produce excessive output and employment losses at a rate of inflation that might be suboptimally low. This line of reasoning leads directly to the recently much-discussed issue of independence and accountability.

7.3.2 Independence and Accountability

In recent years, there is a growing consensus that CBI should be accompanied by a high degree of accountability and transparency, and there is a general trend for central banks to be more open and transparent (Blinder et al. 2001; Dincer and Eichengreen 2007; van der Cruijsen and Eijffinger, Chapter 9, this volume). As Blinder (1998) stresses, accountability is a "moral corollary" of CBI because independent agents should be held accountable and be transparent with respect to their goals, the methods they use to reach them, and the process of decision making. They must be willing to "take the heat" for their decisions, and be able and willing to explain to society their actions and how and why they select certain goals and instruments. For this to work well, transparency needs to be established. Thus, central banks should not only hold press conferences but they should also publish projections and forecasts, which are the background to their decisions, and go even so far as to publish the minutes of their meetings (Buiter 2006). In addition, it might help if the central bank puts forward a monetary policy strategy that allows an easy interpretation of its actions by the public, which is something the ECB has arguably failed to do (see, e.g., Hayo 2003).

However, one could devise other, more personal controls of the behavior of central bankers, for instance, related to their salary or job position.

Nevertheless, it is contested how far accountability and transparency should go. In some countries, for example, New Zealand, central bankers might lose their jobs if they fail to reach their targets. In other countries, for instance, the United Kingdom, the governor has to publicly explain in a letter why the bank failed to reach its target. In most cases, however, there is no formal mechanism, and central bankers only communicate with the public via speeches, publications, and press statements. There is considerable variation in the actual degree of openness and transparency even among central banks in the OECD countries (Blinder et al. 2004; Dincer and Eichengreen 2007; van der Cruijsen and Eijffinger, Chapter 9, this volume). Moreover, it is interesting to note that there is no consensus among central bankers themselves about how transparent they should be.[11] Perhaps, the most independent central bank in the world, the ECB, is usually considered to be one of the less transparent.[12] While there might be good reasons for this, it at least raises the question of democratic accountability. Not only is the ECB relatively opaque with regard to how and why it reaches its decisions, there is, in addition, almost no mechanism by which it can be held formally accountable for its action and failures to reach its overall goal.[13]

If it is not possible to observe a central banker's characteristics, one can argue that society (or its representative government) should have the means to overrule or correct actions taken by the central bank. However, this would not be possible with a truly independent central bank, as Buiter (2006) has argued.[14] CBI could also be viewed as a very undemocratic solution, and raises the question of whether a society would like to put itself into the hands of bureaucrats who may or may not have the "right" preferences.[15]

Without entering into the debate about the optimal degree of transparency and accountability (see Geraats 2002; Grüner et al. 2005; Eijffinger

---

[11] An interesting applied aspect of this general discussion is the exchange between Buiter (1999) and Issing (1999) concerning the way the ECB should communicate with the public. Buiter is in favor of maximum openness in the process leading to monetary policy decision, while Issing thinks that this will just shift secret negotiations to a different level.

[12] Consistent with this, Siklos (2002, 222) finds that more CBI is related to *less* transparency.

[13] The central bank president has to testify before the European Parliament biannually but there is no mechanism that he or the board can be forced to resign. All members have a single fixed period of 8 years of appointment, and are thus "personally" independent.

[14] While not rejecting CBI, he argues that the central bank should be strictly confined to monetary policy (and not allowed comment on other policy areas), and not be charged with other functions (such as financial market oversight or lender-of-last-resort responsibility) in addition to its main task.

[15] Moreover, it is possible that the preferences of society change (see Lippi 2000; Lindner 2000).

and Geraats 2006; van der Cruijsen and Eijffinger, Chapter 9, this volume), it is clear that a larger degree of accountability undermines CBI in the sense of Rogoff (1985), where a conservative central banker implements his or her preferences. Even instrument independence might be incompatible with maximum accountability. In any case, the consensus that accountability is desirable only makes sense if society (presumably represented by the government) can remove central bankers that are not following society's preferences. The issue of removals is what we turn to next.

7.3.3 Credibility and Removal of Independence

Another argument that sheds doubt on the general applicability of independence is the question of how credible independence is. As McCallum (1995) has argued, just granting CBI does not solve the credibility problem but simply shifts it to another level. Even if the objective function of the central bank had the "right" weights, what ensures that the government does not take away independence if it deems it necessary? As long as governments can revoke the status of independence, not much is gained in terms of credibility of monetary policy. One can even argue that the incentive to remove independence increases with the gain in credibility due to CBI (see Forder 2001).[16]

Again the theoretical argument may be stronger than its practical implications. In most cases, independence is granted via a central bank law that could, maybe with simple or qualified majority, be revoked and changed. Given that such a process would probably take some time, the likelihood of generating a "monetary surprise" is quite small. Nevertheless, such considerations have prompted some observers to demand constitutional status for CBI. Hence, at least part of the credibility of CBI is related to the strength of the government's incentive to revoke independence. The possibility of a trade-off between removing the inflation bias by delegating monetary policy to a conservative central banker and the corresponding loss in discretion to perform stabilization policy is at the center of this literature.

In an early contribution, Lohmann (1992) argues that governments may want to be able to override independent central banks in case of particularly large, negative shocks to the economy. This restricts the independence

---

[16] The argument is simple: The more conservative the central bank, the more its policy will differ from what the government prefers and the higher the incentive to revoke CBI. Thus, the "tougher" the policy, the less credible a commitment might be (Drazen and Masson 1994; Neut and Velasco 2003).

of the conservative central bank to situations where shocks are relatively small. At the same time, the incentive of the government depends on the costs it incurs when overriding. However, in equilibrium, the government will never actually override, as the monetary authority will react according to the interests of the government in situations of large output shocks. In this framework, although central banks are independent, they nevertheless take the government's preferences into account. The empirical implication of this model is that, although two central banks are similar in terms of their statutes, they may differ dramatically in practice depending on the costs governments incur when overriding monetary decisions. Lohmann assumes that the costs to override monetary decisions depend on political institutions in society, or, alternatively, that the policymaker is a heterogeneous institution that has to overcome a number of procedural rules to change central bank decisions.[17] Thus, CBI, as measured by legal indices, has to be adjusted for the costs of policymakers to override decisions and is, therefore, endogenous relative to the political and social framework.

Cukierman (1994) puts forward a related argument. He points out there could be economic and political variables influencing the degree of legal independence granted to central banks. The incumbent party faces a trade-off between flexibility of monetary policy, necessary to use according to its interests, and credibility, which results in a lower inflation premium on its debt. To compensate for these effects, CBI should be higher when there is greater political uncertainty, larger government debt, and a stronger preference for low unemployment.

Jensen (1997) analyzes a deterministic intertemporal game, theoretic framework with the exogenous costs of replacing the (conservative) central banker that enter the loss function of the government. He finds "the more important such costs are, the better are economic outcomes in absence of precommitment in comparison with the case without delegation" (pp. 918–919). At the same time, monetary policy delegation cannot remove the dynamic inconsistency as long as those costs are not infinite, the reason being the government will always have an incentive to implement surprise inflation after the private sector has fixed labor-market contracts. Moreover, because the desirable goal for society should be to obtain the optimal solution to the dynamic monetary policy game, he shows that reappointment

---

[17] Giordani and Spagnolo (2001) analyze theoretically how political institutions affect how easy central bank laws can be changed. They argue that some institutions generate sufficient inertia to undermine McCallum's argument.

costs in the case of delegation can make it more difficult to reach such a solution.

On the empirical side, de Haan and van' t Hag (1995) test two hypotheses relating to a possible inflationary bias coming from the choice of flexibility of monetary policy, versus credibility for the incumbent government. They look at the relation between CBI as a dependent variable and proxies for the inflationary bias as regressors. Further, they try to find out whether governments that are planning to incur higher debt are attempting to increase their credibility to reduce the interest rate premium resulting from the Fisher effect. Using data for 19 countries, they do not find evidence for either of the two hypotheses. Cukierman and Webb (1995) reach a similar conclusion. Thus, it is unclear how much weight these theoretical considerations have for practical central banking.

To summarize this section, there are a large number of theoretical problems connected with the CBI argument. One needs to distinguish carefully between CBI in the sense of autonomous actions and conservative, that is, particularly inflation-averse behaviors. There is an inherent conflict between CBI and central bank accountability that does not receive sufficient attention in the current debates. Finally, because CBI is usually granted by politicians, they can always change their minds and remove the special status of a central bank. This implicit threat is like a limit on the autonomy of monetary policymakers. While theoretical in nature, we believe that at least some of these issues have practical relevance.

7.4 Alternatives to Central Bank Independence

7.4.1 Fixed Exchange Rates, Currency Boards, and Monetary Union

One can doubt the necessity of CBI if one compares it to alternative instruments to achieve low and stable rates of inflation. One of these alternative instruments, often used in transition, emerging, and developing countries, is the choice of a fixed exchange rate as a monetary policy strategy.[18] By delegating monetary policy to a proven inflation fighter, such as the U.S. Fed or the ECB, countries import the credibility of this particular central

---

[18] The use of this instrument is not restricted to the mentioned class of countries. The EMS peg of many countries to the deutsche mark has been interpreted as an attempt to import the Bundesbank's monetary credibility (Giavazzi and Pagano 1988), and the EMU can be seen in the same light as well (Wyplosz 2006).

bank. This is basically the same as appointing a conservative central banker because an independent monetary policy is not compatible with a fixed exchange rate at full capital mobility. Even more important, governments, having the exchange rate authority, can make this decision with or without approval of the central bank.

It must be acknowledged, however, that such a monetary strategy is subject to the arguments made in the preceding discussion regarding a sudden change in the monetary regime undermining credibility. There are many examples where countries have given up their fixed exchange rates overnight, either willingly or because they were forced to. It has been even suggested that "simple" pegs are not operative any longer, simply because they could be brought down too easily in a world of almost unrestricted capital mobility (Fischer 2001), although this argument has been challenged (Frankel 1999). For instance, Obstfeld and Rogoff (1995) claim that most fixed exchange rate regimes tend to fail within a time period of about 5 years. Credible exchange-based monetary policy must then come in the form of a full monetary union or as a currency board. The choice by several smaller countries of currency boards or even full dollarization (or euroization) demonstrates such an arrangement is preferred to an independent central bank in some cases.[19] One reason for this movement away from fixed exchange rates, besides the increasing openness of capital accounts, is that alternative instruments, such as inflation targeting, are promoted by economist and official institutions like the International Monetary Fund (IMF 2006). In spite of this trend away from openly declared fixed exchange rates, there is nevertheless still a lot of de facto pegging (Reinhart and Rogoff 2004; Levi-Yeyati and Sturzenegger 2005).

7.4.2 Inflation Contracts and Targets

While the idea of fixing the exchange rate is quite old, there are newer concepts in the academic discussion of monetary policy, which can be seen as viable alternatives to CBI. They might even come at a lower cost to society because there is no suboptimal degree of stabilization of shocks, like in the case of the conservative central banker (Persson and Tabellini 1993; Walsh 1995a; Chortareas and Miller, Chapter 3, this volume). Instead of appointing someone with different preferences than society, one could influence the incentives of the monetary policymaker. The inflation bias

---

[19] Currency boards can be found in Hong Kong, Estonia, Bulgaria, and Lithuania; dollarization and euroization is observed in Ecuador and Montenegro, respectively.

could be corrected by imposing a contract on the central banker that forces him or her to pay a pecuniary penalty if monetary policy is employed to combat unemployment over and above its use for stabilization. While monetary policy could still fully account for economic shocks, systematic inflation would disappear. Of course, in reality it would be rather difficult to write such a central bank contract, as Obstfeld and Rogoff (1996) point out. It would require full information about the preferences of the central banker to be able to correct for his or her marginal incentives to create surprise inflation. It would also be difficult to define those shocks that are within the scope of stabilization policy. Hence, such a contract might lead to conflicts about what degree of monetary expansion is still in accordance with the central bank's area of competence.

A more practical solution is to assign an inflation target to the central bank. This solution, adopted by countries such as the United Kingdom, New Zealand, Sweden, Australia, Israel, and Canada, and often found in connection with a nominally independent central bank, can be understood as the opposite of (goal) independence.[20] However, while it may not be a necessary condition for the implementation of an inflation targeting regime, instrument independence will facilitate the conduct of monetary policy and is often found in actual inflation targeting arrangements.

Here the government either assigns a target for the inflation rate, say 2% over the short to medium run, to the central bank, or the government and the central bank "negotiate" such a target. If the central bank fails to meet this target, it not only has to justify its failure, but in some cases it is then foreseen that the central bank president loses his or her job as a penalty (in New Zealand). In this way, one hopes to achieve a low and stable rate of inflation by holding the central bank, like in the contract solution, responsible for too high a rate of inflation. However, the New Zealand example also indicates that there is a large degree of discretion involved in the interpretation of a violation of such a contract. The governor of the Reserve Bank of New Zealand was not sacked in spite of having missed the target.

Abstracting from the actual solutions adopted in some countries, the important point is that the monetary credibility problem and the inflation bias can be overcome without resorting to CBI. Further, at least theoretically, it might be possible to achieve a better trade-off between credibility and the ability to stabilize exogenous shocks by adopting an inflation target

---

[20] For a thorough discussion of countries' experiences, see Bernanke et al. (1999). Walsh (1995b) reflects on the case of New Zealand as an application of an optimal contract.

(Svensson 1997). Thus, in principle, the inflation bias problem can be solved without compromising the central bank's ability to stabilize.

A related aspect is that the empirical importance of time inconsistency as a source of an inflation bias has never been empirically scrutinized, and one may have doubts that it is indeed a major concern (McCallum 1995). Another argument of why central banks should be independent is based on the political objectives of governments that are economic leviathans, that is, all-powerful states controlling their economies (Harashima 2007). In practice, it is typically argued that the monetary policy will be removed from the *direct* control of governments, and thereby from everyday political pressures. This interpretation is fostered by theoretical work within the context of dynamic general equilibrium macroeconomic models, which indicates that time inconsistency effects play only a limited role within a wide range of parameter values (Albanesi et al. 2003). However, for our question of interest, it does not really matter what the specific reasons for inflationary tendencies are. We would also like to point out that the literature in this field has concentrated on basically static models. It may be possible that the time needed to reach the optimal position in the inflation and output gap space varies systematically between the alternative monetary policy regimes discussed here. This would be a fruitful area for further research.

7.4.3 Labor Market Institutions

The underlying analysis stressing the desirability of CBI is usually based on the U.S. experience with many weak labor unions where there is no strategic interaction between labor and central banks. If labor instead is not atomistic, as is the case in many European countries, one should expect that labor unions internalize, to a certain degree, the negative effects of high wages on employment and inflation (Calmfors and Driffill 1988).[21]

Using the same idea, it has been argued that labor unions should discipline their wage demands if they have an interest in low rates of inflation. If this is the case, a large union will show wage discipline to an extent that reflects their interest in avoiding high inflation. Guzzo and Velasco (1999) have pointed out that an ultraliberal central banker will produce low rates of inflation because labor unions themselves will discipline their

---

[21] If there are many labor unions, or if the central bank is able to commit to its monetary policy, the underlying game structure is changed. If instead of the Stackelberg approach a Nash approach is chosen, labor unions would not discipline their wage demands and, therefore, a conservative central bank would be more adequate (Jerger 2002).

wage demands, thus ensuring high employment and making an overexpansive monetary policy no longer necessary. This line of reasoning turns the conservativeness argument on its head (see also Skott 1997).

This theory has to be qualified if labor unions are not monopolistic, as Cukierman and Lippi (1999) have shown. Lippi (2002, 2003) has further qualified the case for the liberal central bank by showing in the intermediate case of several large labor unions that the effect of inflation on the relative real wage set by a trade union could produce a so-called competition effect. Given the other unions' nominal wage demands, the individual union will demand higher nominal wages, which will lead to a lower level of labor demand in the economy from the perspective of the individual union. The moderating effect of this mechanism will be larger the more conservative the central bank is, because in this case, a nominal wage translates into a higher real wage, thus disciplining any single labor union.[22]

Moreover, Berger et al. (2004) analyze the question of why labor unions should be inflation averse. While it makes sense to assume labor unions – like the rest of society – care about inflation (Cubitt 1992), this is nevertheless an ad-hoc assumption. They provide a microfoundation for this inflation aversion of monopolistic labor unions by distinguishing between outside options (such as unemployment benefits) for the labor union defined in nominal versus real terms. Only if the outside option of the union is in nominal terms can the case for a liberal central banker be made. In this case, a wage-induced price increase will leave nonemployed labor union members worse off (as their real unemployment benefits are reduced), which moderates the union's wage demands.[23] In the case of a real outside option, however, the union's wage-setting behavior and monetary policy are no longer connected. Hence, when taking strategic behavior of labor market participants into account, the case for the conservative central bank could be once again undermined. Reflecting the sensitivity of these theoretical results to changes in the assumptions, the decision to implement CBI should be made conditional on the actual labor market arrangements in a country.

Finally, Dolmas et al. (2000) put forward a dynamic general equilibrium model where the income or wealth inequality in a country in conjunction with a specific political progress (median voter) affects the inflation rate

---

[22] See also Soskice and Iversen (2000) and Coricelli et al. (2006). Lawler (2000), in addition, argues that central banks should not be ultra-liberal in a stochastic environment because they would produce high inflation variance.

[23] They assume a monopoly labor union and do not allow for multiple large unions. If, however, the case for the conservative central banker can be made for a monopoly union, the argument must be even stronger with multiple unions.

via the setting of the money supply. In particular, it is shown that greater inequality can lead to higher inflation rates than optimal to maximize seigniorage due to lower income groups preferring the government to run higher budget deficits to finance transfers. They argue, based on their theoretical model and the finding of a significant relationship between inequality and inflation in democracies, that the causality runs from inequality to inflation. Moreover, in a regression covering democracies with an indicator for income inequality, the Cukierman et al. (1992) CBI index is not statistically significant. It is not quite clear, however, whether this result is due to the interaction between the inequality proxy and the CBI index or just reflects the usual problem of CBI indices in a sample also containing non-OECD countries.

In this section we discussed a number of alternatives to CBI of achieving monetary policy credibility. Fixed exchange rates, currency boards, and monetary union are widely used mechanisms to raise the reputation of central banks. More recent developments are the introduction of inflation contracts with the central bankers and the implementation of inflation targets. Finally, we presented arguments why labor market institutions may have a substantial impact on the usefulness of independent central banks. So far, we have argued that the creation of CBI is not a necessary condition for price stability. In the next section we attempt to show why CBI is not a sufficient condition for price stability.

7.5 Alternative Explanations of Low Inflation

7.5.1 Central Bank Independence Is an Endogenous Variable

A number of studies find that CBI and low inflation rates are correlated (early studies are Alesina 1988; Grilli et al. 1991; Cukierman 1992; and are defended, e.g., by Brumm 2002). In Figure 7.1, we display the CBI indicator by Alesina and Summers (1993) for core EU member countries and average inflation rates. There is a clear negative relationship, that is, those countries with more independent central banks have experienced relatively lower inflation rates.[24]

In conjunction with the theoretical CBI literature, the conclusion drawn from these results is that CBI causes low inflation rates. This is exemplified by the conclusion in the extensive survey by Arnone et al. (2007): "In

---

[24] The negative relationship is less fragile then it may appear. Deleting the obvious outlier Germany from the sample lowers the correlation to -0.50. Excluding other countries does not affect the correlation in a noteworthy way.

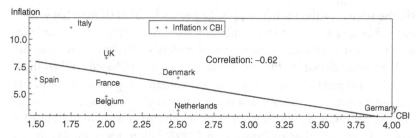

Figure 7.1. CBI index for EU countries and average inflation rates (in percent)
Note: The CBI index is taken from Alesina and Summers (1993). Average inflation rates are computed over the period 1967–1993.

conclusion, the evidence on the beneficial effects of CB autonomy is more than substantial, but some technical issues remain for further research" (p. 55). This all but ignores research done by Forder (1996, 1998a, 1998b), who raises a number of methodological concerns (see also Banian et al. 1998 or Mangano 1998) that go much beyond technical issues. For instance, Forder points out that legal and factual CBI may differ and, thus, measuring legal CBI and finding a correlation with inflation rates may not tell us a lot about the influence of factual CBI. It is more than indicative that the relationship between legal independence and inflation rates completely breaks down in a sample consisting of a large number of third-world countries (e.g., de Haan and Kooi 2000). Moreover, even for the widely used proxy of de facto CBI in third-world countries, the turnover rate of the central bank governor, there is conflicting evidence in the literature (see King and Ma 2001; Brumm 2002).

There are also studies indicating that the relationship is not totally robust with regard to control variables and the choice of countries (Cukierman 1992; Posen 1995; Campillo and Miron 1997; Forder 1998b). In our view, the question of causality cannot be solved by these studies, as running a single-equation regression imposes the causality relationship from the outset. Too often the following important question is ignored: Why is it the case that some countries have implemented independent central banks and others did not? Apart from assuming some kind of historical random mechanism, it is unlikely that CBI itself is the start of the story.[25] Thus, for some reason some societies have chosen to implement institutional reforms

---

[25] Acemoglu et al. (2008) as well make a strong argument that institutions are endogenous and should not be taken as given. Thus, whether CBI is granted and taken seriously depends on political interests and political institutions.

while others did not. Arguably, instead of devoting additional resources to the study of the CBI-inflation nexus, more research input should be devoted to this fundamental question.

In our view, there exists a two-stage problem in understanding the existence of CBI. In the first stage, societies have to decide on their policy priorities, for example, whether price stability should be regarded as an important policy objective. In the literature, basically two explanations for cross-country variation have been put forward. The first one emphasizes that societies differ with regard to their inflation aversion because they have different "inflation cultures." Consequently, the nature of the inflation culture will, directly or indirectly, determine the choice of the monetary policy objective. The second approach focuses on the political decision process and looks at the interests of economic actors and their ability to influence monetary policy objectives.

If a society has decided to pursue price stability, then, in the second stage, a decision has to be made about the monetary policy arrangements that can help to bring about such an outcome. One of the alternatives is CBI, but above we discussed other approaches that also qualify as potential candidates. Under what conditions are societies going to choose CBI? The literature points to the characteristics of the legal and political systems of countries. In the rest of this section, we analyze the conditions for the choices made in this two-stage framework in more detail.

7.5.2 National Inflation Cultures

The first approach to answer the question why countries differ in their inflation record is related to the idea that societies differ with respect to the importance of pursuing a monetary policy directed toward low inflation, which one could call inflation culture.[26] A simple view, called the "preference-instrument view" in Hayo (1998), argues that societies, for whatever reason, have differing preferences for inflation rates, and this is reflected in the setup of monetary institutions and in the conduct of monetary policy. Here causality runs from society's preferences to the establishment of specific monetary institutions, such as central bank laws granting independence. It is not the degree of CBI that is responsible for differing inflation records of countries, but rather the existing variations

---

[26] Attempts to track and measure the existence of inflation culture, as well as to provide a definition, are made in Bofinger et al. (1998). See also the discussion of the historical context by Hetzel (1990).

in national inflation preferences, which ultimately determine, for instance, whether independent central banks will be set up. In our view, societies decide first about the goal of monetary policy, and then grant instrument independence to their central banks to achieve that goal in an efficient way.

This view is somewhat naïve, however, in the sense that it presumes preferences for inflation are fixed over time. More realistically, we would expect that the actual performance of the central bank influences people's attitudes toward price stability. If, on the one hand, an independent monetary authority does not bring about price stability, people's trust in this organization will be undermined and its ability to perform a tough monetary stance against conflicting interests may be severely damaged. On the other hand, if people believe that the central bank handles monetary policy competently, they will support it in a power struggle against, for instance, the government (see Berger and de Haan 1999 for a case study of the Bundesbank and the German government). One might call this the "historical-feedback interpretation." In the case of Germany it is often argued that the apparent inflation aversion can be directly traced back to the hyperinflation after World War I, and perhaps to the introduction of the Deutsche Mark after World War II. In our view, this account is oversimplified, and it is important to point out that the concept of an "inflation culture" does not necessarily rely on personal experiences. Rather, a multitude of personal experiences leads to a situation where a shared and collective memory is created that encapsulates the lessons from such an extraordinary period. Thus, while inflation aversion has its roots in individual experiences, it becomes a social perception, which can be described as a form of "culture." Although many people do not recall much from this historic episode on a conscious level, they still react strongly to rising prices based on the diffuse "inflation culture" they absorbed during their socialization in Germany. Moreover, this is not a deterministic relationship, as other societies were exposed to one or more hyperinflations without developing a similar aversion toward rising prices.

In any case, a major problem with historical-feedback mechanisms of the kind outlined in the preceding discussion is that the path dependence of such an explanation makes it very difficult to test it empirically. Using Eurobarometer survey data on core EU countries, Hayo (1998) derives an indicator for a country's inflation aversion.[27] Figure 7.2 shows the relationship between this indicator of national inflation cultures and inflation rates.

---

[27] In an earlier study by Collins and Giavazzi (1993), attitudes toward inflation and unemployment are estimated using consumer expectations derived from surveys.

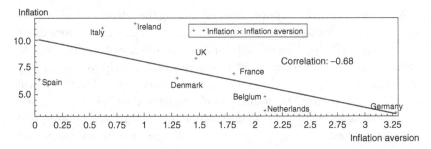

Figure 7.2. Inflation aversion for EU countries and average inflation rates (in percent)
Note: The inflation aversion data are taken from Hayo (1998). Average inflation rates are computed over the period 1967–1993.

There is a clear negative relationship between these variables, that is, those countries with a stronger inflation aversion are characterized by relatively low inflation rates. This correlation is at least as strong as that of CBI and inflation given in Figure 7.1.[28] Moreover, both CBI and inflation aversion proxy are positively correlated. This finding supports the idea that inflation cultures matter, although it does not help very much in discriminating between a preference-instrument and historical-feedback view.

Hayo's study is based on a macrolevel approach, and it cannot tell us much about who within a society may be particularly interested in obtaining price stability. van Lelyveld (1999a) focuses on a cross-section of countries at one particular point in time (see also Prast 1996). He uses Eurobarometer 5 from 1976 to analyze two hypotheses put forward in the literature: First, higher income leads to more inflation aversion relative to unemployment. Second, having a more left-wing political opinion implies less concern for inflation. In his results, van Lelyveld finds little support for the importance of income, while there is more evidence that a higher preference for income inequality will lead to less inflation aversion. An update of this analysis using a survey from 1997 (Eurobarometer 48) shows that these general results appear to hold, although individual models turn out to be rather unstable (van Lelyveld 1999b).

---

[28] As in the previous figure, the result does not hinge upon one crucial outlier. The observation for Germany shows the strongest influence in terms of weakening the relationship. The deletion of this country from the sample reduces the correlation to −0.63. However, excluding Spain very much tightens the association (−0.84). Because there are fewer observations (1986–93 only) to estimate the inflation sensitivity in the case of Spain, this rather strengthens the argument.

A somewhat different approach to explaining the relative inflation aversion of societies is used by de Jong (2002). Here the idea is that nations differ in cultural attributes. Certain cultural characteristics, such as the extent to which an unequal distribution of power is accepted, help to explain why some countries experience low inflation and others do not. The theoretical argument is supported by country-level empirical data based on cultural constructs developed by Hofstede (1980). One should note, however, that the empirical estimates are plagued by small sample sizes and nonrobust estimates. Apparently, some effects of cultural values on inflation take on a more direct route without affecting CBI. The indicator for uncertainty avoidance appears to be the most important of the cultural variables in the explanation of inflation. Regarding CBI as a dependent variable, de Jong (2002) finds that an unequal distribution of power is the most important cultural concept.

Thus, from the point of view of an endogenous choice of monetary institutions, we would argue that cultural differences across countries affect the choice of CBI as an instrument to achieve low inflation rates. However, the question of how exactly cultural variables affect CBI and inflation, that is, the transmission channel(s) from culture via social preferences to economic institutions, remains largely unsolved.

7.5.3 Political Interest Groups

One of the first contributions to take the idea of CBI endogeneity seriously is that by Posen (1993). In his view, economic policy reflects the struggle of interest groups attempting to influence policy in a way they consider favorable. It is inappropriate to concentrate on questions of design of organizations only, such as central banks, and to ignore political interest groups. In particular, he argues monetary policy is affected by the lobbying effort of the financial sector, which is assumed to be highly inflation averse.

There are at least two reasons why commercial banks might fear inflation and thus prefer a conservative monetary policy. As banks usually borrow short and lend long, they are particularly vulnerable to changes in the spread of interest rates. Times of high inflation are, sooner or later, followed by attempts of disinflation or even deflation. Under these circumstances, banks may come under severe pressures: First, the interest rate they have to pay to get liquidity could be higher than the yield generated on their lending side. Second, the resulting high real-interest rates lead to the problem of recovering outstanding loans due to an increase in the likelihood of creditor bankruptcies.

Under these circumstances, introducing CBI may make it easier for the financial-sector interest groups to lobby for their interests directly to the policymaker itself, the central bank, rather than having to go through the checks and balances of the political system. Further, since there are flows of staff members between the central banks and private banks, it might be relatively easy for the financial sector to make its interests heard by the monetary authorities and vice versa. In view of this complementarity of interests, both financial sector and central bankers form a coalition supporting each others' demands, with the result that inflation will be kept low. This is supported by recent evidence in Göhlmann and Vaubel (2007), who find for 11 European Monetary Union (EMU) countries (using data from 1973 to 2003), that the professional background of central bankers is strongly correlated to their policy. In particular, they find that professional economists run more expansive monetary policy (which they attribute to Keynesian attitudes), but that professional bankers implement a more restrictive monetary policy if they are appointed to central bank boards. This is at least consistent with Posen's argument.

Thus, in this framework, it is not CBI that causes monetary policy to strive for low inflation rates. Rather, central bankers simply reflect the interests of a specific group, namely the private financial sector, which is ultimately the source of low inflation. The stronger the financial sector in its ability to lobby for low inflation, the more weight will be given to price stability by the monetary authority.

There are a number of problems related to Posen's approach. First, it is not obvious that low inflation rates are always in the interest of the financial sector. For instance, the increase in nominal interest rates as a result of higher inflation may mask a larger spread applied by banks. However, in an empirical study on the performance of the financial sector, an empirical study by Boyd et al. (2001) shows that monetary regimes allowing for high inflation rates have a negative impact on the economic outcome of financial institutions. In particular, an inflation rate of 15% appears to be a threshold; the financial sectors in countries with a higher inflation rate experience a significantly lower performance compared to those in lower inflation countries.

Second, the empirical evidence that the financial sector is inherently inflation averse is not compelling. Although Posen (1995) presents supportive evidence, other studies find little support if at all (de Haan and van't Hag 1995; Campillo and Miron 1997; Temple 1998). This need not necessarily be seen as a rejection of Posen's theory. The construction of the empirical indicator for financial-sector inflation aversion involves a number of strong assumptions, and therefore may not capture the underlying theoretical concept very well. Maier et al. (2002) show that the Bundesbank's monetary policy was influenced by financial-sector pressure. Although they do not make this claim, their finding can be interpreted as indirectly supporting Posen's theory, based on the following argument: First, there is empirical evidence that the financial sector affected monetary policy in Germany. Second, Germany had one of the lowest inflation rates in the world over their sample period. Third, this can be interpreted as indirect, albeit weak, support for Posen's claim of an inflation-averse financial sector influencing monetary policy. However, as we have just discussed, there are other explanations for the low inflation rate in Germany and, hence, we face a situation of observational equivalence between different theoretical explanations.

Finally, if it truly were the influence of the financial sector that determines CBI, then we should observe fluctuations in inflation rates over time to correspond with variations in financial-sector lobbying power. Casual evidence does not suggest a close correspondence, but this may be an issue deserving more attention. Here one could try to test, in a multivariate context using (smoothed) time series data, whether an indicator of financial-sector lobbying is able to significantly explain some parts of the variation in inflation rates.

Taking for granted that some countries care a lot about keeping inflation down, what makes them choose CBI and not one of the alternatives?

7.5.4 Legal System, Political System, and Factual CBI

We start off our discussion by returning to McCallum's (1995) point that delegation cannot solve a possible dynamic inconsistency problem, but only relocates it to a different level. The crucial issue is the question of why delegation should be more credible than leaving monetary policy in the hands of the government. As argued above, credibility might be improved if changing delegation decisions is costly. A related point is based on the idea of a constitutional arrangement as an insurance against short-run deviations from the longer-run interests of society (Elster 2000). Society binds itself in the same way that Ulysses had himself tied to the mast of his ship before approaching the sirens. Hence, it may be useful to look at legislation, jurisdiction, and the political system in more detail. Indeed, there is theoretical and empirical evidence that certain aspects of institutional characteristics correlate with inflation rates.

Maxfield (1997) emphasizes that CBI could be used as an international signaling device. It can be employed by politicians as a credible signal to international investors of their country's high degree of creditworthiness. Whether countries will use this signal depends on several national characteristics: the actual effectiveness of the signal, the need for foreign capital, the strength of the politicians' power position, and the degree of capital mobility. Thus, because countries will differ across these characteristics, they have a varying degree of incentives to actually implement CBI.

Moser (1999) develops a model that contains two conditions for delegation to be credible. First, there must be two decision-making bodies that share the legislation and have veto powers over one another. Second, these two legislative bodies differ with regard to their inflation-output preferences.[29] The hypothesis he derives from this setup is that those countries characterized by these conditions will have more independent central banks. In the empirical analysis, he distinguishes among three groups of countries: those with strong checks and balances in their legislation, those with weak checks and balances, and those with no checks and balances. He finds that countries with strong checks and balances have more independent central banks compared to those with weak or no checks and balances, a point that is confirmed by Keefer and Stasavage (2002, 2003). In a second step, he regresses group dummies for checks and balances, plus these dummies interacted with CBI on average inflation rates. The outcome of this regression is less straightforward. In particular, the shift term of the country group with no checks and balances is smaller than that of the other groups. This implies that countries with dependent central banks do not necessarily have higher inflation rates. In our framework, this can be interpreted as evidence that some countries have found other means to achieve low inflation rates. It is worth pointing out that the proxy used by Moser to measure the legislative framework is limited in scope, and he might miss distinctive features of the legal framework of some countries.

A related study makes the point that certain characteristics of political systems may help us understand why countries have implemented CBI and other countries did not is Farvaque (2002). Countries that have a bicameral system may not have much need to delegate monetary policy, and thus feature less-independent central banks. This result somewhat contradicts Moser's finding, as Farvaque uses a very similar proxy variable. An argument to consolidate both results would be to point out that the presence of two chambers does not by itself guarantee strong checks and balances and vice

---

[29] Crowe (2008) makes a related point. He argues that countries with strong distributional conflicts will grant independence to central banks in order to take monetary policy "from the table," thus making coalitions more likely.

versa. More federal countries also exhibit a higher degree of CBI. An indicator for the proximity of politicians to voters shows that the further away politicians are, the higher CBI is. This is interpreted as a precommitment device by the society. Finally, the longer governments stay in power (average duration to longest duration in percent), the higher CBI is. This result is interpreted as evidence that CBI is more prominent in countries exhibiting greater political stability. However, this argument does not facilitate the interpretation of CBI as a precommitment device in the above sense. In this hypothesis, we would rather expect that societies showing greater short-term volatility will bind themselves via formal institutional arrangements.

An empirical paper by Bagheri and Habibi (1998) analyzes the relationship between CBI and political liberty and instability. They find both political liberty and stability are positively linked to CBI, which means countries that allow more political freedom and are characterized by less regime and political party instability show higher degrees of CBI. It is conjectured that CBI changes while countries move from nondemocratic to highly democratic political systems. Within our framework, this implies that CBI becomes directly dependent upon the nature of the political system in a country, and the law of motion with respect to political change and CBI is also clearly defined.

However, the empirical analysis shows a number of weaknesses. For instance, there are almost no control variables in the models, while, at the same time, the authors introduce a country group dummy for Austria, Germany, and Switzerland, claiming the "... index of legal central bank for these three countries was much higher than others and introduction of this dummy variable significantly increased the quality of regressions" (p. 197). This sounds very much like data mining and does not enhance trust in the stability of the results.

There is a similar problem with Moser's results, as he finds no supporting evidence using the CBI indicator by Eijffinger and van Keulen (1995). He states this is not surprising, as this index includes changes in central bank law in preparation of entering the EMU. His defense is "...independent of their political system, member countries of the European Union are forced by the Treaty of the European Community to install independent central banks" (p. 1584, footnote 12). This is not a convincing argument because the "old" member countries entered into EMU by their free will, so if there had not been a sufficient political commitment (as in the case of the United Kingdom and Denmark), then they would not have joined. Survey data (Eurobarometer) reveal that in each member country, except the United Kingdom, Denmark, and Germany, that there was a majority of people in favor of entering the EMU (Hayo 1999). This also suggests that checks and balances are only part of the story. In particular, if there were a consensus in society on this issue, it is unlikely the two legislative bodies would differ to such an extent that we would see noteworthy differences in the setup of the central bank. In other words, the existence of an agreement to delegate monetary policy to an institution with a higher degree of independence than any national central bank, can be seen as a sign of a strong political consensus rather than disagreement, and Moser's argument becomes void.

A related argument with respect to checks and balances is put forward by Keefer and Stasavage (2002, 2003). They show that checks and balances are likely going to reduce expected inflation, and that delegation of monetary policy to a central bank will only have the desired effect if checks and balances are a characteristic of the country's political system. Moreover, checks and balances should matter most when there is a high level of polarization between veto players. In their empirical analysis they are able to show that inflation tends to be lower in the presence of checks and balances. But the existence of checks and balances makes little difference in situations of low levels of polarizations and low levels of CBI. In other words, the usefulness of checks and balances is conditional on the state of the other variables.

Finally, Hayo and Voigt (2008) argue that there is an interaction between independence of the judiciary and CBI. In their view, judicial independence affects inflation in – at least – two distinct ways: directly by lowering transactions costs and thereby increasing growth and output, thus reducing the incentive to use monetary policy, and indirectly by supporting and possibly defending CBI against the interests of the executive or legislative in a country. A culture of rule of law may very much strengthen the position of an independent central bank. If the government tried to undermine legal CBI through the backdoor, the central bank could defend its rights as codified in the respective laws by appealing to the relevant independent constitutional court. In a cross-section of countries, they find evidence of both types of transmission channels from the legal system to CBI and inflation rates.

In addition, government and central bank may create some sort of mutual agreement or accord on the use of monetary policy. For instance, Goodfriend (1994) states that the 1951 Accord between the Treasury and the Federal Reserve was a major step forward with regard to increasing the de facto independence of monetary policy. He argues that a similar Accord would help to protect central bank credit policies from misuse. In particular, he proposes rules regarding liquidity assistance to private financial institutions, sterilized foreign exchange rate interventions, and the transfer of Fed surplus to the Treasury.

Furthermore, in a lawful society, public support for the central bank may increase if it turns out that the government tries to bend the rules. A related argument is based on the interpretation of the task of a central bank as being similar to that of the legal system in terms of the protection of property rights. Through their influence on seigniorage and the price level, central banks can directly affect the taking and disposition of wealth from the public and the distribution of wealth by government among individuals (Hetzel 1997).

In a similar vein, Goodhart and Meade (2004) argue that countries' choices for the independence of the judicial system and the independence of their central banks are related. They discuss in particular the United States, the United Kingdom, and the European Union, finding that the United States and the United Kingdom have more individualistic monetary and judicial systems than the European Union. Related to this, the accountability of these two systems is larger than in the European Union. These findings indicate that societies quite deliberately choose institutions in a consistent manner.

Thus, the propulsion to create institutions for the protection of property rights, including those that relate to the effects of money in the economy, may be related to the rule of law in a society. As briefly discussed above, Hayo and Voigt (2008) show empirically that the legal system affects inflation through both a direct and an indirect channel. Hence, a culture of rule of law may be some sort of substitute for a stability-oriented inflation culture. However, a prerequisite for this argument to work is that CBI already exists, and this again raises the question of why it came about in the first place.

Another issue is related to the problems created for written, formal central banks rules in the context of changing economic circumstances. For example, in the preamble of the Bank of Canada, Act Two objectives are stated, stabilizing the external value of the currency and smoothing the business cycle (Laidler 1997). At the time when it was written, it was expected that the gold standard would be revived; nowadays, it reads like an anachronism. This indicates that one needs to be prepared to adjust to changes in relevant economic environment and economic knowledge, and over time. Hence, even highly formalized central bank rules should be drafted allowing for a possible adjustment in the future, even if this implies a weakening of the legal foundation today. While the literature has started to isolate specific characteristics of the legal and political system that help to explain the introduction of CBI, there remain a number of unresolved issues.

To summarize, in this section we argued that CBI is not even a sufficient condition for achieving low inflation rates. CBI is an endogenous variable and, thus, the theoretical assumption of a causal link between CBI and inflation is flawed. As underlying causal factors, we discussed national inflation cultures, political interest groups, and particular features of the legal and political systems in a country. It can be shown that empirical proxies for these theoretical concepts explain inflation rates at least as well as indicators for formal CBI.

7.6 Conclusion

In this chapter, we have argued that the conventional view that CBI is a necessary and/or sufficient instrument for achieving low inflation rates is not convincing. We present an alternative way of thinking about CBI that we consider as theoretically and empirically more plausible. The underlying idea is that societies have to make two decisions about monetary policy. First, they decide on the importance they attach to fighting inflation as an objective. Then, the second decision has to be made on what is the best institutional arrangement to achieve the objective of price stability, given the existing political, legal, and economic framework. The first decision indicates CBI is not a sufficient condition for price stability, as it is not the ultimate cause but just one instrument among others to achieve this objective. The second decision makes clear that CBI is not a necessary condition for price stability in general, although it may be the right solution for some countries. Using this two-step procedure, we can encompass a wide variety of findings on monetary policy and CBI in the literature, while this is arguably not possible within the conventional framework.

In the first part of the chapter, we use theoretical arguments to ask how strong and convincing the case for CBI really is. We argue that other solutions to the time-consistency problem exist, such as inflation targets, fixed exchange rates, and inflation contracts, and that some may be preferable to independence and conservativeness because they involve lower costs of achieving low inflation. It is usually impossible to write complete inflation contracts, but inflation targets or exchange rate–based monetary policies are practical and frequently chosen alternatives to CBI. These alternatives are often combined with "independence" of the central bank, but as we have argued, this cannot really be understood as proper independence because goal independence is usually not granted. Hence, CBI is a relevant concept in practice but it is not at all the only choice. Providing a clear list of condition under which one or the other monetary policy solution is superior should receive high marks on a list of further research topics.

In the second part of the chapter, we present the existing literature on CBI endogeneity. In particular, we identify two approaches that help to explain why some societies choose to give fighting inflation a high policy priority and others do not. First, there are cultural differences, which help to classify societies according to inflation aversion. Second, political interest groups may have a specific interest in keeping inflation low, and if they are strong enough, they may be able to affect the political outcome in their favor. In regard to the choice of CBI versus the other potential instruments, we discuss the literature looking at political, legal, and economic determinants of this choice. For instance, the higher costs of changing the legal status of central banks in terms of political difficulties may lead to an adoption of CBI. Political freedom may be a condition conducive to implementing CBI. So while countries move toward greater political freedom, we would expect CBI to be chosen more often. If, for whatever reason, CBI has already been established, then an independent judiciary and a "culture of law" may help to prevent any disguised attempts of a government to undermine legal CBI. Under these circumstances, any change in the de facto degree of CBI would only be possible through the normal legislative process, which would be publicly debated and would raise the danger for politicians that the public might turn against them.

Although our framework for analyzing monetary policy arrangements is more refined than the usual CBI argument, it is still quite crude. For instance, it does not allow for much flexibility in terms of informal arrangements. In an interesting case study of France, Italy, and the United Kingdom, Cobham et al. (1999) emphasize the importance of informal CBI in the conduct of monetary policy. They show that changes in average inflation were not always accompanied by changes in the degree of CBI, and that changes in the formal degree of CBI did not always lead to the expected changes in inflation rates, a finding that is also supported by later literature (see Siklos 2002). Another point noted by several authors is public support for the central bank needs to be strong enough to make the implementation of (sometimes harsh) monetary policy measures successful (Posen 1995; Bofinger et al. 1998; Hayo 1998).

There are several areas where further research would be necessary. First, there is more to be learned about the causes for choosing antiinflationary policy institutions by analyzing survey data. In particular, one could combine macro- and microlevel information in a panel data set to address a multitude of interesting questions. An interesting first step is the paper by Di Tella et al. (2001), who look at the trade-off between inflation and unemployment using a large cross-section of survey data, and combine micro- and macroseries in a two-step process. Second, the empirical evidence for the interest group argument is still ambiguous. In addition, one could fruitfully look at other interest groups apart from the financial sector. Even more can be learned about why societies choose CBI and not one of the other possible design instruments. Here the empirical results are quite weak, and more energy should be spent on constructing appropriate indicators to capture relevant characteristics of a country's legal, political, and economic framework.

References

Acemoglu, D., S. Johnson, P. Querubin, and J. Robinson (2008), "When Does Policy Reform Work? The Case of Central Bank Independence," *NBER Working Paper 14033*.

Albanesi, S., V. V. Chari, and L. J. Cristiano (2003), "How Severe is the Time Inconsistency Problem in Monetary Policy?," *Federal Reserve Bank of Minneapolis Quarterly Review* 27: 17–33.

Alesina, A. (1988), "Macroeconomics and Politics," *NBER Macroeconomic Annual* 3: 13–52.

Alesina, A. and L. Summers (1993), "Central Bank Independence and Macroecomic Performance: Some Comparative Evidence," *Journal of Money, Credit, and Banking* 25: 151–162.

Arnone, M., B. Laurens, J. Segalotto, and M. Sommer (2007), "Central Bank Autonomy: Lessons from Global Trends," *IMF Working Paper 07/88*.

Bagheri, F. M. and N. Habibi (1998). "Political Institutions and Central Bank Independence: A Cross-country Analysis," *Public Choice* 96: 187–204.

Banian, K., R. Burdekin, and T. Willett (1998). "Reconsidering the Principal Components of Central Bank Independence: The More the Merrier?," *Public Choice* 97: 1–12.

Barro, R. J. and D. Gordon (1983), "Rules, Discretion, and Reputation in a Positive Model of Monetary Policy," *Journal of Monetary Economics* 12: 101–121.

Berger, H. and J. de Haan (1999), "A State Within a State? An Event Study on the Bundesbank," *Scottish Journal of Political Economy* 46: 17–39.

Berger, H. and U. Woitek (1997), "How Opportunistic Are Partisan German Central Bankers: Evidence on the Vaubel Hypothesis," *European Journal of Political Economy* 13: 807–21.

Berger, H., C. Hefeker, and R. Schöb (2004), "Optimal Central Bank Conservativeness and Monopoly Labor Unions," *IMF Staff Papers* 51: 585–605.

Berger, H., J. de Haan, and S. C. W. Eijffinger (2001), "Central Bank Independence: An Update of Theory and Evidence," *Journal of Economic Surveys* 15: 3–40.

Bernanke, B., T. Laubach, F. Mishkin, and A. Posen (1999), *Inflation Targeting* (Princeton, NJ: Princeton University Press).

Blinder, A. (1998), *Central Banking in Theory and Practice* (Cambridge: MIT Press).
    (1999), "Central Bank Credibility: Why Do We Care? How Do We Build It?," *American Economic Review* 90: 1421–1431.

Blinder, A., C. Goodhart, P. Hildebrand, D. Lipton, and C. Wyplosz (2004), *How Do Central Bank Talk?*, Geneva Reports on the World Economy 3 (London: CEPR).

Bofinger, P., C. Hefeker, and K. Pfleger (1998), *Stabilitätskultur in Europa* (Stuttgart: Deutscher Sparkassen-Verlag).

Boyd, J. H., R. Levine, and B. S. Smith (2001), "The Impact of Inflation on Financial Sector Performance," *Journal of Monetary Economics* 47: 221–248.

Brender, A. and A. Drazen (2005), "Political Budget cycles in New versus Established Democracies," *Journal of Monetary Economics* 52: 1271–1295.

Brumm, H. J. (2002), "Inflation and Central Bank Independence Revisited," *Economics Letters* 77: 205–209.

Buiter, W. (1999), "Alice in Euroland," *Journal of Common Market Studies* 37: 181–209.
    (2006), "Monetary Economics and the Political Economy of Central Banking: The Twin Threats of Sloppy Analysis and Institutional Hubris," mimeo, London School of Economics.

Calmfors, L. and J. Driffill (1988), "Bargaining Structure, Corporatism and Macroeconomic Performance," *Economic Policy* 6: 13–62.

Campillo, M. and J. A. Miron (1997), "Why Does Inflation Differ Across Countries?," in C. D. Romer and D. H. Romer (Eds.) *Reducing Inflation: Motivation and Strategy* (Chicago: University of Chicago Press), pp. 335–357.

Carlstrom, C. T. and T. S. Fuerst (2006), "Central Bank Independence and Inflation: A Note," *Federal Reserve Bank of Cleveland Working Paper* 06/21.

Cobham, D., S. Cosci, F. Mattesini, and J.-M. Serre (1999), "The Nature and Relevance of Central Bank Independence: An Analysis of Three European Countries," mimeo, University of St. Andrews.

Collins, S. M. and F. Giavazzi (1993), "Attitudes Towards Inflation and the Viability of Fixed Exchange Rates: Evidence From the EMS," in M. Bordo and B. Eichengreen (Eds.), *A Retrospective on the Bretton Woods System: Lessons for International Monetary Reform* (Chicago: University of Chicago Press), pp. 547–577.

Coricelli, F., A. Cukierman, and A. Dalmazzo (2006), "Monetary Institutions, Monopolistic Competition, Unionized Labour Markets and Economic Performance," *Scandinavian Journal of Economics* 108: 39–63.

Crosby, M. (1998), "Central Bank Independence and Output Variability," *Economics Letters* 60: 67–75.

Crowe, C. (2008), "Goal-Independent Central Banks: Why Politicians Decide to Delegate," *European Journal of Political Economy* 24(4): 748–762.

Cubitt, R. P. (1992), "Monetary Policy Games and Private Sector Precommitment," *Oxford Economic Papers* 44: 513–530.

Cukierman, A. (1992), *Central Bank Strategy, Credibility, and Independence* (Cambridge: MIT Press).
    (1994), "Commitment through Delegation, Political Influence and Central Bank Independence," in J. O. De Beaufort Wijnholds, S. C. W. Eijffinger, and L. H. Hoogduin (Eds.), *A Framework for Monetary Stability* (Dordrecht: Kluwer), pp. 55–74.
    (2007), "Central Bank Independence and Monetary Policymaking Institutions: Past, Present and Future," *CEPR Discussion Paper* 6441.

Cukierman, A. and F. Lippi (1999), "Central Bank Independence, Centralization of Wage Bargaining, Inflation and Unemployment – Theory and Some Evidence," *European Economic Review* 43: 1395–1434.

Cukierman, A. and S. B. Webb (1995), "Political Influence on the Central Bank: International Evidence," *World Bank Economic Review* 9: 397–423.

Cukierman, A., S. B. Webb, and B. Neyapti (1992), "Measuring the Independence of Central Banks and Its Effect on Policy Outcomes," *World Bank Economic Review* 6: 353–398.

Cukierman, A., G. Miller, and B. Neyapti (2002), "Central Bank Reform, Liberalization and Inflation in Transition Economies: An International Perspective," *Journal of Monetary Economics* 49: 237–264.

Debelle, G. and S. Fischer (1994), "How Independent Should a Central Bank Be?," in J. C. Fuhrer (Ed.), *Goals, Guidelines and Constraints Facing Monetary Policymakers* (Boston, MA: Federal Reserve Bank of Boston), pp. 195–221.

de Haan, J. and G. J. van't Hag (1995), "Variation in Central Bank Independence Across Countries: Some Provisional Empirical Evidence," *Public Choice* 85: 335–351.

de Haan, J. and W. Kooi (1997), "What Really Matters? 'Conservativeness or Independence?'," *Banca Nazionale del Lavorno Quarterly Review* 200: 23–28.

(2000), "Does Central Bank Independence Really Matter? New Evidence for Developing Countries Using a New Indicator," *Journal of Banking and Finance* 24: 643–664.

de Jong, E. (2002), "Why are Price Stability and Statutory Independence of Central Banks Negatively Correlated? The Role of Culture," *European Journal of Political Economy* 18: 675–694.

Di Tella, R., R. MacCulloch, and A. Oswald (2001), "Preferences Over Inflation and Unemployment: Evidence from Surveys of Happiness," *American Economic Review* 91: 335–341.

Dincer, N. and B. Eichengreen (2007), "Central Bank Transparency: Where, Why and to What Effect?," *NBER Working Paper* 13003.

Dolmas, J., G. W. Huffman, and M. A. Wynne (2000), "Inequality, Inflation, and Central Bank Independence," *Canadian Journal of Economics* 33: 271–287.

Drazen, A. (2000), "The Political Business Cycle after 25 Years," *NBER-Macroeconomics Annual* 15: 75–117.

Drazen, A. and P. Masson (1994), "Credibility of Policies Versus Credibility of Policy Makers," *Quarterly Journal of Economics* 109: 735–754.

Eijffinger, S. and J. de Haan (1996), "The Political Economy of Central-Bank Independence," *Princeton Special Papers in International Economics* 19.

Eijffinger, S. and M. Hoeberichts (1998), "The Trade Off Between Central Bank Independence and Conservativeness," *Oxford Economic Papers* 50: 397–411.

Eijffinger, S. and M. van Keulen (1995), "Central Bank Independence in Another Eleven Countries," *Banca Nazionale del Lavoro Quarterly Review* 192: 39–83.

Eijffinger, S. and P. Geraats (2006), "How Transparent Are Central Banks?," *European Journal of Political Economy* 22: 1–21.

Elster, J. (2000), *Ulysses Unbound – Studies in Rationality, Precommitment and Constraints* (Cambridge: Cambridge University Press).

Farvaque, E. (2002), "Political System and Central Bank Independence," *Economics Letters* 77: 131–135.

Fischer, S. (2001), "Exchange Rate Regimes: Is the Bipolar View Correct?," *Journal of Economic Perspectives* 15/2: 3–24.

Fischer, S. and J. Huizinga (1982), "Inflation, Unemployment and Public Opinion Polls," *Journal of Money, Credit and Banking* 14: 39–51.

Forder, J. (1996), "On the Measurement and Assessment of 'Institutional' Remedies," *Oxford Economic Papers* 48: 39–51.

(1998a), "Central Bank Independence – Conceptual Clarifications and Interim Assessment," *Oxford Economic Papers* 51: 307–334.

(1998b), "The Case for an Independent Central Bank: A Reassessment of Evidence and Sources," *European Journal of Political Economy* 14: 53–71.

(2001), "The Theory of Credibility and the Reputation-bias of Policy," *Review of Political Economy* 13: 5–25.

Frankel, J. (1999), "No Currency Regime is Right for all Countries or at all Times," *Princeton Essays in International Finance* 215.

Fuhrer, J. (1997), "Central Bank Independence and Inflation Targeting: Monetary Policy Paradigms for the Next Millennium?," *New England Economic Review* (January/February): 19–36.

Gärtner, M. (2008), "The Political Economy of Monetary Policy Conduct and Central Bank Design," in C. K. Rowley and F. Schneider (Eds.), *Readings in Public Choice and Constitutional Political Economy* (Amsterdam: Springer), pp. 423–446.

Geraats, P. (2002), "Central Bank Transparency," *Economic Journal* 112: F 532–565.

Giavazzi, F. and M. Pagano (1988), "The Advantage of Tying One's Hands: EMS Discipline and Central Bank Credibility," *European Economic Review* 32: 1055–1082.

Giordani, P. and G. Spagnolo (2001), "Constitutions and Central-Bank Independence: An Objection to "McCallum's Second Fallacy," *Stockholm School of Econ./EFI Working Paper* 426.

Göhlmann, S. and R. Vaubel (2007), "The Educational and Professional Background of Central Bankers and Its Effect on Inflation: An Empirical Analysis," *European Economic Review* 51: 925–941.

Goodfriend, M. (1994), "Why We Need an 'Accord' for Federal Reserve Credit Policy," *Journal of Money, Credit, and Banking* 26: 572–584.

Goodhart, C. and E. Meade (2004), "Central Banks and Supreme Courts," *Moneda y Credito* 218: 11–42.

Grilli, V., D. Masciandaro, and G. Tabellini (1991), "Institutions and Policies," *Economic Policy* 6: 341–392.

Gros, D. and C. Hefeker (2002), "One Size Must Fit All. National Divergences in a Monetary Union," *German Economic Review* 3: 247–262.

Grüner, H. P., B. Hayo, and C. Hefeker (2005), "Unions, Wage Setting and Monetary Policy Uncertainty," *ECB Working Paper* 490.

Guzzo, V. and A. Velasco (1999), "The Case for a Populist Central Banker," *European Economic Review* 43: 1317–1344.

Hakes, D. R., E. Gamber, and C.-H. Shen (1998), "Does the Federal Reserve Lexicographically Order Its Policy Objectives?," *Eastern Economic Journal* 24: 195–206.

Harashima, T. (2007), "Why Should Central Banks be Independent?," *MPRA Paper* 1838.

Hayo, B. (1998), "Inflation Culture, Central Bank Independence and Price Stability," *European Journal of Political Economy* 14: 241–263.

(1999), "Knowledge and Attitude Towards European Monetary Union," *Journal of Policy Modeling* 21: 641–651.

(2003), "European Monetary Policy: Institutional Design and Policy Experience," *Intereconomics* **38**: 209–218.

(2004), "Public Support for Market Reforms in Eastern Europe," *Journal of Comparative Economics* **32**: 720–744.

Hayo, B. and C. Hefeker (2002), "Reconsidering Central Bank Independence," *European Journal of Political Economy* **18**: 653–674

Hayo, B. and S. Voigt (2008), "Inflation, Central Bank Independence, and the Legal System," *Journal of Institutional and Theoretical Economics* **164**(4): 751–777.

Hetzel, R. L. (1990), "Central Banks' Independence in Historical Perspective," *Journal of Monetary Economics* **25**: 165–176.

(1997), "The Case for a Monetary Rule in a Constitutional Democracy. Federal Reserve Bank of Richmond," *Economic Quarterly* **83**: 45–65.

Hillman, A. L. (1999), "Political Culture and the Political Economy of Central Bank Independence," in M. Blejer and M. Streb (Eds.), *Major Issues in Central Banking, Monetary Policy, and Implications for Transition Economies* (Amsterdam: Kluwer), pp. 73–86.

Hofstede, G. H. (1980), *Cultures Consequences: International Differences in Work-related Values* (Beverly Hills: Sage Publications).

International Monetary Fund (2006), *Inflation Targeting and the IMF* (Washington: IMF).

Issing, O. (1999), "The Eurosystem: Transparent and Accountable or 'Willem in Euroland'," *Journal of Common Market Studies* **37**: 503–519.

Jensen, H. (1997), "Credibility of Optimal Monetary Delegation," *American Economic Review* **87**: 911–920.

Jerger, J. (2002), "How Strong Is the Case For a Populist Central Banker? A Note," *European Economic Review* **46**: 623–632.

Keefer, P. and D. Stasavage (2002), "Checks and Balances, Private Information and the Credibility of Monetary Commitments," *International Organization* **56**: 751–774.

(2003), "The Limits of Delegation: Veto Players, Central Bank Independence and the Credibility of Monetary Policy," *American Political Science Review* **97**: 407–423.

King, D. and Y. Ma (2001), "Fiscal Decentralization, Central Bank Independence and Inflation," *Economics Letters* **72**: 95–98.

King, R. G. and M. W. Watson (1997), "Testing Long-Run Neutrality," *Economics Quarterly*, Federal Reserve Bank of Richmond **83**: 69–101.

Kydland, F. W. and E. C. Prescott (1977), "Rules Rather than Discretion: The Inconsistency of the Optimal Plans," *Journal of Political Economy* **85**: 473–491.

Laidler, D. (1997), *Where We Go From Here: Inflation Targets in Canada's Monetary Policy Regime,* Policy Study 29 (Toronto: C.D. Howe Institute).

Lawler, P. (2000), "Centralised Wage Setting, Inflation Contracts, and the Optimal Choice of Central Banker," *Economic Journal* **110**: 559–575.

Levi-Yeyati, E. and F. Sturzenegger (2005), "Classifying Exchange Rate Regimes: Deeds vs. Words," *European Economic Review* **49**: 1603–1635.

Lindner, A. (2000), "Long Term Appointment of Central Bankers: Costs and Benefits," *European Journal of Political Economy* **16**: 639–654.

Lippi, F. (2000), "Median Voter Preferences, Central Bank Independence and Conservatism," *Public Choice* **105**: 323–338.

(2002), "Revisiting the Case for a Populist Central Banker," *European Economic Review* **46**: 601–612.

(2003), "Strategic Monetary Policy with Non-Atomistic Wage Setters: A Case for Non-Neutrality," *Review of Economic Studies* **70**: 909–919.

Lohmann, S. (1992), "Optimal Commitment in Monetary Policy: Credibility versus Flexibility," *American Economic Review* **32**: 273–286.

(1998), "Federalism and Central Bank Independence: The Politics of German Monetary Policy. 1957–92," *World Politics* **50**: 401–446.

Loungani, P. and N. Sheets (1997), "Central Bank Independence, Inflation, and Growth in Transition Economies," *Journal of Money, Credit, and Banking* **29**: 381–399.

Maier, P., J.-E. Sturm, and J. de Haan (2002), "Political Pressure on the Bundesbank: An Empirical Investigation Using the Havrilesky Approach," *Journal of Macroeconomics* **24**: 103–123.

Mangano, G. (1998), "Measuring Central Bank Independence: A Tale of Subjectivity and of its Consequences," *Oxford Economic Papers* **50**: 468–492.

Maxfield, S. (1997), *Gatekeepers of Growth. The International Political Economy of Central Banking in Developing Countries* (Princeton, NJ: Princeton University Press).

McCallum, B. (1995), "Two Fallacies Concerning Central-bank Independence," *American Economic Review* **82**: 273–286.

Mink, M. and J. de Haan (2006), "Are There Political Budget Cycles in the Euro-Area?," *European Union Politics* **7**: 191–211.

Moser, P. (1999), "Checks and Balances, and the Supply of Central Bank Independence." *European Economic Review* **43**: 1569–1593.

Muscatelli, A., P. Tirelli, and C. Trecroci (2002), "Does Institutional Change Really Matter? Inflation Targets, Central Bank Reform and Interest Rate Policy in the OECD Countries," *Manchester School* **70**: 487–527.

Neut, A. and A. Velasco (2003), "Tough Policies, Incredible Policies?," *NBER Working Paper 9932*.

Obstfeld, M. and K. Rogoff (1995), "The Mirage of Fixed Exchange Rates," *Journal of Economic Perspectives* **9**: 73–96.

(1996), *Foundations of International Macroeconomics* (Cambridge: MIT-Press).

Persson, T. and G. Tabellini (1993), "Designing Institutions for Monetary Stability," *Carnegie Rochester Conference Series on Public Policy* **39**: 53–84.

Posen, A. (1993), "Why Central Bank Independence Does Not Cause Low Inflation," in R. O'Brian (Ed.) *Finance and the International Economy* 7, (Oxford: Oxford University Press), pp. 40–65.

(1995), "Declarations Are Not Enough: Financial Sector Sources of Central Bank Independence," *NBER Macroeconomic Annual*: 253–274.

(1998), "Central Bank Independence and Disinflationary Credibility. A Missing Link?," *Oxford Economic Papers* **50**: 335–359.

Prast, H. (1996), "Inflation, Unemployment and the Position of the Central Bank: The Opinion of the Public. *Banca Nazionale del Lavoro Quarterly Review* **49**: 415–454.

Reinhart, C. and K. Rogoff (2004), "The Modern History of Exchange Rate Regimes: A Reinterpretation," *Quarterly Journal of Economics* **119**: 1–48.

Rogoff, K. (1985), "The Optimal Degree of Commitment to an Intermediate Monetary Target," *Quarterly Journal of Economics* **100**: 1169–1190.

Rose, R. (1998), "What is the Demand for Price Stability in Post-Communist Countries?," *Problems of Post-Communism* 45: 43–50.

Shi, M. and J. Svensson (2006), "Political Business Cycles: Do They Differ across Countries and Why?," *Journal of Public Economics* 90: 1367–1389.

Siklos, P. (2002), *The Changing Face of Central Banking* (Cambridge: Cambridge University Press).

Skott, P. (1997), "Stagflationary Consequences of Prudent Monetary Policy in a Unionized Economy," *Oxford Economic Papers* 49: 609–622.

Soskice, D. and T. Iversen (2000), "The Non Neutrality of Monetary Policy with Large Price or Wage Setters," *Quarterly Journal of Economics* 115: 265–284.

Svensson, L. E. O. (1997), "Optimal Inflation Targets, 'Conservative' Central Banks and Linear Inflation Contracts," *American Economic Review* 87: 98–114.

Temple, J. (1998), "Central Bank Independence and Inflation: Good News and Bad News," *Economics Letters* 61: 215–219.

Tootell, G. (1999), "Whose Monetary Policy Is It Anyway?," *Journal of Monetary Economics* 43: 217–235.

van Lelyveld, I. (1999a), "Inflation or Unemployment? Who Cares?," *European Journal of Political Economy* 15: 463–484.

(1999b), "Inflation Aversion in Europe," paper presented at the EEA conference in Santiago de Compostela, September.

Vaubel, R. (1997a), "The Bureaucratic and Partisan Behavior of Independent Central Banks: German and International Evidence," *European Journal of Political Economy* 13: 201–224.

(1997b), "Reply to Berger and Woitek [How Opportunistic Are Partisan German Central Bankers: Evidence on the Vaubel Hypothesis]," *European Journal of Political Economy* 13: 823–827.

von Hagen, J. (1998), "Reciprocity and Political Business Cycles in Federal Monetary Unions," in S. Eijffinger and H. Huizinga (Eds.), *Positive Political Economy* (Cambridge: Cambridge University Press) pp. 29–46.

Waller, C. J. (2000), "Policy Boards and Policy Smoothing," *Quarterly Journal of Economics* 115: 305–339.

Walsh, C. E. (1995a), "Optimal Contracts for Central Bankers," *American Economic Review* 85: 150–167.

(1995b), "Is New Zealand's Reserve Bank Act of 1989 an Optimal Central Bank Contract?," *Journal of Money, Credit, and Banking* 27: 1179–1191.

Wyplosz, C. (2006), "European Monetary Union: The Dark Sides of a Major Success," *Economic Policy* 46, 207–261.

8

Independence and Accountability in Supervision Comparing Central Banks and Financial Authorities

Donato Masciandaro, Marc Quintyn, and Michael W. Taylor

Abstract

Unlike the monetary policy function – nowadays, invariably the core function of a central bank – the financial supervisory function is being performed by a variety of institutions for whom there is less consensus about the governance model than for central banks. This chapter sheds light on recent trends in, and determinants of, financial supervisory governance, with special attention to the position of the central bank. We first identify similarities and differences in the theoretical approaches to the two key features of governance for central banks and supervisors – independence and accountability. We then disentangle empirically the institutional differences between supervisory regimes governed by central banks and other institutional arrangements. The analysis of the determinants of independence and accountability arrangements for supervisors indicates that (1) the quality of public sector governance plays a decisive role in establishing accountability arrangements, more than independence arrangements; (2) politicians' decisions regarding the degree of independence and accountability seem to be driven by different sets of considerations; and (3) the likelihood for establishing governance arrangements suitable for the supervisory task seems to be higher when the supervisor is located outside the central bank.

8.1 Introduction

During the past 30 years, the monetary policy mandate of central banks has been narrowing significantly. In a large number of countries, the central bank mandate is now exclusively geared toward the goal of price stability. All other goals that were explicit at some point in history, such as achieving broader economic goals, gradually shed their importance. This narrowing of the mandate has been accompanied by modifications to their external and internal governance arrangements.[1] On the external side, a fair degree of independence has been proclaimed a necessity to pursue its mandate. During the initial push for independence, accountability arrangements were almost an afterthought (see Amtenbrink 1999; Eijffinger and Geraats 2006 for overviews). Lately, accountability has started to receive more attention, mainly among central banks that adopted an inflation targeting framework (Siklos 2002, and for a critical review, see Buiter 2007).

All this time in the history of central banking, many central banks were also the supervisors of the banking system. In some countries, such as the United Kingdom, this function has historically been attached to the central bank (Goodhart and Tsomocos, Chapter 5, this volume), while in other countries, such as the younger nations in Africa and those emerging from the former Soviet Union, capacity constraints, combined with the fact that the central bank was one of the few reputable institutions in these countries, made the central bank the natural institution to become the supervisor.

The fact that many central banks thus took upon them – or were given – a second mandate, instigated an intense debate among scholars on the pros and cons of having monetary policy and bank supervision under one roof.[2] The debate has not seen a clear winner: arguments pro and con were always fairly balanced, with perhaps for developing countries the capacity constraints argument tilting the balance in favor of having both functions under one roof.

The "emancipation" of financial sector supervision at the end of the era of "financial repression" has added a new dimension to this debate. As argued in Quintyn (2007a), in today's liberalized financial systems, the quality of corporate governance in financial institutions plays a pivotal role in achieving financial system soundness and good corporate governance in the economy more generally. Hence, in this environment, supervisors are increasingly "governance supervisors" and, to pursue their mandate, they need to be endowed with strong governance arrangements as well.

---

[1] External governance arrangements define how the central bank relates to its principles (independence, accountability, and transparency). Internal governance arrangements are those arrangements needed to support the external arrangements, such as arrangements to preserve the integrity of staff and its work (Das and Quintyn 2002; Quintyn 2007a), as well as institutional arrangements regarding composition and operation of the various boards inside the bank (Berger et al. 2008; Frisell et al. 2004).

[2] Goodhart and Schoenmaker (1992, 1995), Haubrich (1996), Di Giorgio and Di Noia (1999), Peek et al. (1999), and Abrams and Taylor (2000) for relevant contributions to the debate.

Faced with rapid changes in the financial systems worldwide, supervisory architectures have been undergoing significant changes. The restructuring wave of the past 10–15 years has made the supervisory landscape less uniform than before. In several countries, the architecture still reflects the classic model, with separate agencies for banking, securities, and insurance supervision. However, an increasing number of countries show a trend toward consolidation of supervisory powers, which in some cases has culminated in the establishment of a unified regulator, either inside or outside the central bank. In Europe this trend has seemed rather strong in recent years.[3] So, unlike the monetary policy function, which is typically performed by central banks, the supervisory function is implemented by an array of different types of institutions.

This reshaping of the supervisory architecture has set off a debate about governance arrangements for these new agencies. In the U.K. case, Goodhart (2002) and Westrup (2007) stressed that, among all the arguments that led the Government in 1997 to establish the Financial Services Authority (FSA), removing supervision from the Bank of England could have been a *quid pro quo* for giving the latter monetary policy independence. The link between the reform of the supervisory setting and the redefinition of its governance can also be found in the views expressed by market actors. Westrup (2007) reports, for instance, that in Germany, at least one part of the financial sector representatives (represented in the Bunderverband Deutscher Banken, BdB) were in favor of a unified model outside the Bundesbank, and with a weaker degree of independence from the government than the latter.

The growing attention for the quality of the governance of those agencies is no coincidence. Indeed, the restructuring of supervisory agencies is a manifestation of the importance that policymakers, academia, and practitioners, are giving to having in place a supervisory structure that matches the needs of the markets and customers in the current, fast-evolving financial landscape. In addition, the new regulatory emphasis on the quality of

---

[3] In addition to Norway, the first small country to establish a single supervisor in 1986, and Iceland (1988), six "old" European Union member states – Austria (2002), Belgium (2004), Denmark (1988), Germany (2002), Sweden (1991), and the United Kingdom (1997) – have established a single supervisory authority outside the central bank. In Ireland (2003), the supervisory responsibilities were concentrated in the hands of the central bank; the central bank increased its responsibilities in the Netherlands (2005) too. Four countries involved in the 2004 European Union enlargement process – Estonia (1999), Latvia (1998), Malta (2002), and Hungary (2000) – have also moved to concentrate all powers in a single authority. Outside Europe, a unified agency has been established in Kazakhstan (2004), Korea (1997), Japan (2001), and Nicaragua (1999).

the governance of the supervised institutions leaves no other option for the supervisors but to have good governance practices as well.

Against this background, the premise of this chapter is that changing tasks require appropriate institutional and governance arrangements. While a multitude of institutional solutions are thinkable, each of these solutions needs to be endowed with appropriate governance arrangements so that these institutions can meet their objectives.

This chapter analyzes the emerging frameworks for supervisory governance, with a focus on independence and accountability, and with special attention to the question of what the determinant of these emerging frameworks are—that is, what the driving forces behind policymakers' decisions on independence and accountability frameworks are – and how they mesh with existing frameworks for monetary policy governance. The chapter is structured as follows. Section 8.2 sets the stage by reminding us of the highlights of the central bank governance debate relevant for the topic of this chapter – supervisory governance. Section 8.3 draws parallels and contrasts between central bank independence (CBI) and the case for independence and accountability for supervisors. Sections 8.4 and 8.5 discuss the empirical work. First, we analyze the independence and accountability arrangements in 55 countries and compare those countries where central banks are in charge of supervision with those that have a separate authority. Section 8.5 provides a first empirical analysis of the determinants of independence and accountability in the sample. Section 8.6 summarizes the conclusions.

8.2 Designing Supervisory Governance: Hints from the Central Banking Literature on Monetary Policy

We consider the design of the governance of the financial supervision agencies as the solution to a delegation problem. The literature on CBI has been the trendsetter in the broader discipline of studying the relationship between regulatory agencies and their principal, the government. So, it is tempting to draw methodological analogies with the abundant and still growing literature on CBI.[4] This section will indeed take this strand in the literature as the starting point and subsequently (next section) highlight the parallels and differences between the theories behind central bank and supervisory governance. In comparing the two types of agencies, we will point out that the *nature of the mandate* that is delegated should be reflected in the way

---

[4] For a complete survey, see Berger et al. (2000). See also Cukierman (2007).

the governance arrangements are shaped. Before we embark on this, it is useful to highlight that, when we talk about CBI, we essentially mean independence with respect to the *monetary policy function*. We will contrast this with the *financial supervision function*.

For central banks, the discussion about external governance arrangements centered for a long time on independence alone, and even that topic is of a recent date. As has been pointed out by Cukierman (2007), up to 20 years ago economic theory did not attach any importance to the concept of CBI. The institutional arrangements became important when the theory started to stress their role in controlling inflation. The theoretical foundation for CBI is the so-called KPBGR inflation bias story, where KPBGR stands for the three seminal contributions, that is, Kydland and Prescott (1977), Barro and Gordon (1983), and Rogoff (1985).

The starting point is Kydland and Prescott's (1977) time-inconsistency argument – when a government's optimal long-run policy differs from its optimal short-run policy, it has an incentive to renege on its long-term commitments. The problem is that, if economic agents anticipate such a policy change, they will behave in ways that prevent policymakers from achieving their original objectives (Barro and Gordon's 1983 inflation bias) and can therefore never build up policy credibility. Delegation to an independent agency with different time preferences, or a different incentive structure, than the government's is considered the solution to this problem (Rogoff's 1985 conservative central banker) as this will establish policy credibility.

These theoretical foundations, supported by empirical evidence from countries with low inflation records, gave a strong push to the emergence of independent central banks in many parts of the world in the late 1980s and the 1990s. However, while the CBI model sometimes took on some mythical proportions,[5] some doubts and criticisms emerged from two sides. On the one hand, several scholars raised the issue of the endogeneity of CBI and the CBI-inflation nexus. On the other hand, objections were raised against the near-total emphasis on the independence of central banks, and the almost complete neglect of other aspects of governance in the debate, most notably accountability – the so-called democratic deficit.

The democratic-deficit debate has a direct bearing on the discussion in this chapter because it deals with the appropriate external governance arrangements of central banks. The discussion on the endogeneity of the

---

[5] See, for instance, references in Shiller (1997) and Tognato (2004). For an overview see Quintyn (2007b).

CBI-inflation nexus remains a very topical debate, but because it is less relevant for the remainder of this chapter, we will not deal with it.[6]

The CBI model has also come under criticism for being too focused on "independence," as opposed to a more complete and balanced governance model. The first angle emphasizes the risk for a "democratic deficit" inherent in the operation of an independent central bank (Fischer 1995), and Stiglitz (1998) followed by others in the run-up to the creation of the European Central Bank). Their message is that an institution as important as the central bank cannot and should not escape or stand outside the process of democratic accountability. There should be means to hold the central bank accountable to the government, who bears the final responsibility for the conduct of economic policy and who is accountable to the electorate.

It is indeed fair to state that in the initial stages of the CBI literature, accountability was treated as a mere afterthought. Some authors mentioned the need for it, but not much attention was being paid. Accountability was seen by many (not least by some of the central banks themselves) as a requirement (nuisance) that undermined independence – the "trade-off" view between independence and accountability.[7,8] Progressively, the concept of accountability started to receive theoretical attention.[9] It became clear that a credibility commitment is a medal with two sides.

On the one side, the central banker has to be independent, that is, the bank enjoys the ability to implement monetary policy without external (e.g., political) interference. On the other side, the central banker has to be conservative, where conservativeness refers to the importance that he or she assigns to price stability in its relation to other macroeconomic objectives. Society trusts the central bank's conservativeness if accountability rules hold. In fact, the delegation of the monetary powers to a nonelected

---

[6] For a systematic and detailed review, as well as reference to the original contributions, see Hayo and Hefeker (2001 and in this volume), and the many papers referred to in those contributions.

[7] See, for instance, references to survey results of central bankers' views on accountability in Oosterloo and de Haan (2003).

[8] Buiter (2007) argues that the democratic deficit is aggravated by the fact that most central banks have only formal but no substantive accountability arrangements (in other words, weak accountability). The lack of substantive accountability prevents a real dialogue between the central bank and other stakeholders, notably the government.

[9] Hughes and Libich (2006) analyze a monetary policy game considering at the same time three institutional features: independence, accountability, and transparency, highlighting synergies and trade-offs. Mihailov and Ullrich (2007) analyze both independence and accountability in a model with monetary and fiscal policies.

institution should be accompanied by accountability to be trusted and be effective (Siklos 2002).

This is the point where the second angle comes in. With inflation targeting becoming a very popular monetary policy framework, the relationship between independence and accountability – and transparency as well[10] – is likely to have an important place in the future research agenda (see also Hayo and Hefeker, Chapter 7, this volume). The three institutional features mentioned in the preceding represent the core of so-called central bank governance. The virtuous effects of their interaction for the quality of central bank governance has been neglected for too long. The growing attention they receive now is a manifestation of the importance that policymakers, academia, and practitioners are giving to have in place an institutional structure that matches the needs of citizens.[11]

8.3 Defining Independence and Accountability in Financial Supervision

The debate on an appropriate financial supervision governance model is of recent origin and, hence, a "mainstream" view is only slowly emerging. In recent years, several papers have argued that the responsibility for financial supervision should be delegated to an independent agency, that is, an authority with clear objectives and political independence, having adequate supervisory instruments at its disposal to achieve these objectives, and held accountable in the exercise of its responsibilities to ensure adequate checks and balances.[12]

These contributions have been informed from two sides. First of all, by the discussion on CBI, as presented in the preceding. Second, by the emerging broader debate on the role, and position within government, of independent regulatory agencies as an inherent part of the spread of the "regulatory state" model. Contrary to the CBI debate, the discussion on financial supervisors has focused more rapidly on *all* aspects of their governance—independence

---

[10] An up-to-date overview of the literature on central bank transparency is van der Cruijsen and Eijffinger (Chapter 9, this volume).

[11] So far, few studies have actually examined the governance of the central banks in all its aspects. See Frisell et al. (2004), Crowe and Meade (2007), and Siklos (Chapter 11, this volume).

[12] Quintyn and Taylor (2003, 2007), Das et al. (2004), and Hüpkes et al. (2005). The Basel Committee on Banking Supervision recognized the importance of both independence and accountability in the revised "Core Principles for Effective Bank Supervision" (Basel Committee on Banking Supervision 2006).

was not seen as an end in itself, but as a means to achieve a solid governance model, in its interactions with accountability, transparency, and integrity (Das and Quintyn 2002; Quintyn 2007a,b).

The ongoing theoretical discussion has yielded the following insights: (1) the foundations for independence are broadly the same for monetary policy as for financial supervision, but (2) in the latter case, accountability needs much more attention, and (3) transparency needs to have a somewhat different emphasis, given the commercially sensitive issues with which supervisors deal with.

On independence, it has been argued that the case for supervisory agency independence is analogous to that for CBI, in the sense that the time-inconsistency problem, and the related issue of policy credibility, is a universal problem for policymakers, irrespective of the field of competence. Quintyn and Taylor (2007) argued in favor of the "robust regulator" in parallel with the "conservative central banker." Politicians have an incentive to interfere in the supervisory process, for example, by putting pressure on the supervisor not to close a bank, as bank closure comes at a short-term political cost, with depositors being harmed, even though forbearance produces higher long-term resolution costs.[13] In this analysis, the primary aim of politicians is to extract short-term political rent from the supervisory process, a phenomenon that can be explained within the framework of the grabbing hand theory of government.[14] To avoid this form of political capture, the supervisors have to be able to resist undue influence from government (what we term *upward independence*).

An additional argument in the supervisory independence discussion – which has less relevance for CBI – is the danger for industry capture, which derives from Stigler (1971). The argument stresses that regulation is likely to be captured by private interests in the sense that a regulatory agency, which is supposed to be acting in the public interest, becomes dominated by the vested interests of the existing incumbents in the industry that it oversees. In public choice theory, regulatory capture arises from the fact that vested interests have a concentrated stake in the outcomes of policy decisions, thus ensuring that they will find means – direct or indirect—to capture decision makers. In the case of banking supervision and regulation, such "industry capture" can take a number of different forms: using licensing requirements to set high barriers to entry to favor incumbents rather than new entrants to the industry; setting prudential regulations which

---

[13] See Quintyn and Taylor (2003).
[14] See Shleifer and Vishy (1998).

are more lax than social welfare would require; and exercising forbearance in the interests of the shareholders of specific institutions. Forbearance exercised by the supervisor as the result of industry capture will have the same long-run effects as forbearance exercised as the result of political capture, that is, long-run resolution costs will be higher and social welfare will be reduced. Hence, not only must supervisors be insulated from political interference, but they must also be insulated from pressures exerted by regulated intermediaries. Thus, independence from *financial industry capture* (*downward independence*) can also be evaluated a good practice.

Furthermore, supervisory independence can also be justified on the grounds of cognitive factors: politicians have neither the expertise to design policies in detail, nor the capacity to adapt them to changing conditions or to particular circumstances. Important though this argument is, it is certainly not as convincing as the time-inconsistency argument, because politicians can rely on experts in all sorts of specialized areas if and when needed.

The greater difference with the CBI debate is in the area of accountability arrangements. Financial supervision function differs in many critical areas from the monetary policy function, with a direct bearing on accountability.[15] First, their mandate is broader than in the case of monetary policy; very often they have multiple mandates; and these mandates are harder to measure than in the case of monetary policy. Second, they operate in a multiple-principals environment, which has an impact on the types of accountability arrangement. Third, but not the least, their supervisory and enforcement powers can have a far-reaching impact, for instance, on the property rights of bank owners. Finally, supervisory agencies – more than monetary policy agencies – can fall victim to "self-interest capture." This refers to a situation in which the powers of the agency are captured by individual supervisors pursuing their own self-interests, which may not be consistent with social welfare. Regulatory self-interest can take a variety of different forms including, in highly corrupt societies, the abuse of regulatory powers to extract rents that accrue directly to individual regulatory staff. Less blatant, but potentially just as damaging, is the motivation of "not on my watch," that is, the desire of regulators to delay the emergence of problems until after they have left office. Kane (1990) has stressed the role that the protection of reputations and pensions played in the avoidance by U.S. regulators of the recognition of problems in the savings and loan

---

[15] For a detailed overview of these differences, see Hüpkes et al. (2005).

industry at an earlier (and, thus, less costly to society) stage.[16] Self-interest capture can therefore lend itself as readily to forbearance and thus higher long-run resolution costs as either political capture or industry capture are likely to do. Unlike political or industry capture, the solution to self-interest capture must instead take the form of agency *accountability* to provide society with assurances that supervision is not being manipulated or subverted by private interests.[17] For example, there must be transparent reporting procedures on supervisory activities to provide evidence that the regulator's powers are being used in accordance with the social contract between depositors/taxpayers and the supervisory agency.[18,19]

Taken together, these features require a distinct approach to supervisory governance. Their importance does not justify limiting independence per se (as is sometimes argued) because there are many good reasons for supervisory independence, but rather strengthening the accountability structure. The design of accountability arrangements is in that regard all the more important because well-designed accountability arrangements can help to buttress agency independence. In other words, to arrive at solid governance arrangement for financial supervision, one needs to exploit the fact that independence and accountability are complementary and, thus, potentially reinforce each other (Quintyn 2007a,b).

In sum, this section comes to the conclusion that (1) on agency independence, the time-inconsistency argument justifies upward and downward independence of the supervisor, and (2) accountability arrangements need to be more elaborate for supervisors than for monetary policy to arrive at a system of effective financial supervision. The next sections will explore if politicians design the right institutional setting for financial supervision, along the lines defined in this section. We will also explore what the

---

[16] Kane (1990). See also Boot and Thakor (1993).

[17] Hüpkes et al. (2005).

[18] Accountability as an external governance mechanism must be supplemented by internal governance measures to enhance staff integrity in order to avoid self-interest capture. See Das and Quintyn (2002) and Quintyn (2007a), who identify integrity as a fourth pillar for regulatory governance.

[19] It is worth noting that the three forms of agency capture discussed here are closely intertwined. Supervisory self-interest obviously plays an important role in assisting politicians or the regulated industry to capture a regulatory agency. Alternatively, political capture could be merely a form of financial industry capture if the politicians involved receive campaign contributions or other forms of support from the industry. In other words, the grabbing hand theory, the capture theory, and the self-interest theory can be deeply intertwined in practice. The potential interaction among these three different principal-agent relationships and the agent self-interest incentives can create complications that add to – and interact with – the standard incentive alignment problems.

determinant are of the prevailing governance arrangements, and whether we see differences in the determinants and the actual arrangements between supervisors housed inside or outside the central bank.

The analysis of the "governance nexus" developed in Das and Quintyn (2002) and Quintyn (2007a) leads us to expect that governments that promote good public sector governance will also be supportive of good governance arrangements for supervisors (and other regulators). These governments understand that good supervisory governance is important for financial sector governance, and will therefore endow the supervisor with an appropriate degree of independence and matching accountability arrangements so that the agency can fulfill its mandate.

8.4 Governance of Supervisory Function: Main Findings

This and the next sections report on the empirical findings with respect to actual governance of the supervisory function. This section presents the main findings with regard to the computation of governance indices, and also compares them to some of the findings from CBI literature. The next section empirically analyzes determinants of supervisory governance with special attention to independence and accountability.

8.4.1 Sample and Methodology

This section builds on earlier work presented in Quintyn et al. (2007) (hereafter called QRT) on the computation of independence and accountability ratings for supervisory agencies. While QRT compared independence and accountability ratings before and after reforms in a sample of 32 countries, this section only analyzes the current state of affairs, but broadens the sample to 55 countries. While our interest goes to the quality of supervisory governance in its totality, we limit ourselves to independence and accountability because, in our opinion, arrangements with respect to these two elements of the governance framework need most input from the politicians and are therefore in most countries part of a process of political negotiations. The other two building blocks, transparency and integrity (as identified in Das and Quintyn 2002, and Quintyn 2007a), are just as important but seem easier to implement once the agency is endowed with appropriate independence and accountability attributes. However, future research should devote more attention to the relative importance of the four building blocks.

Furthermore, the focus of our research is on banking supervision. While the importance of supervision of other segments of the financial system is constantly growing, banking supervision still remains the most important supervisory activity in most countries, not the least because the banking system remains the core part of the financial system in a great number of countries. The sample contains 27 countries where bank supervision is part of the central bank's responsibilities and 28 countries where an agency, separate from the central bank, is in charge of banking supervision (see Appendix I for details). Among those separate agencies, 12 are unified (or integrated) supervisors (i.e., they supervise all segments of the financial system). In addition, two agencies located within the central bank are also unified supervisors.

The methodology is the same as in QRT (2007). A total of 19 criteria are identified to assess the degree of supervisory independence and 21 for accountability. These criteria are derived from the work on supervisory independence and accountability in Quintyn and Taylor (2003, 2007) and Hüpkes et al. (2005), respectively.[20] A rating of "2" is given if the law satisfies the criteria, a "1" is given for partial compliance, and a "0" for noncompliance. In some cases a "−1" is given for what are considered practices that undermine both independence and accountability (such as, for instance, a minister chairing the policy board, or legal provisions giving the minister the right to intervene in the supervisory process). The individual ratings are summed and normalized between 0 and 1. The rating process is based on a review of the individual countries' legal documents, supplemented by assessments of the "Basel Core Principles for Effective Banking Supervision" and of the "IMF code on Transparency of Monetary and Financial Policies" published in the International Monetary Fund's Financial Sector Stability Assessments (FSSA). In some cases, additional information was acquired from interviews with country officials. So, this is a de jure approach to the quality of supervisory governance, and the authors are aware of the fact that de facto situations may differ from de jure findings.[21]

8.4.2 Main Findings

Overview

Table 8.1 reports the total ratings (independence and accountability), together with the individual independence and accountability ratings. The total rating gives an indication of the overall quality of the arrangements, but

---

[20] For the list of criteria, see QRT (2007) as well as a separate Appendix II available on request.

[21] The difference between legal and actual indicators in the institutional analysis was introduced in Cukierman et al. (1992).

Table 8.1. *Overview of ratings on supervisory independence, accountability on independence in monetary policy*

| Country | Total rating | Governance features of supervisory function | | Governance features of monetary policy function |
		Independence	Accountability	Independence GMT
Armenia	0.74	0.84	0.64	0.81
Australia	0.71	0.76	0.67	0.63
Austria	0.64	0.79	0.50	0.94
Bahamas, The	0.60	0.84	0.57	0.31
Belgium	0.76	0.92	0.62	0.94
Brazil	0.53	0.55	0.50	0.63
Bulgaria	0.86	1.00	0.74	0.88
Canada	0.63	0.55	0.69	0.63
Chile	0.66	0.66	0.67	0.69
China	0.36	0.34	0.38	0.56
Colombia	0.60	0.68	0.71	0.50
Cyprus	0.56	0.74	0.40	0.56
Czech Republic	0.71	0.86	0.57	0.88
Denmark	0.63	0.63	0.62	0.75
Ecuador	0.66	0.87	0.48	0.94
Egypt, Arab Rep.	0.63	0.63	0.62	0.38
El Salvador	0.55	0.61	0.50	0.81
Estonia	0.66	0.69	0.55	0.81
Finland	0.69	0.61	0.67	0.94
France	0.65	0.63	0.67	0.94
Germany	0.63	0.47	0.76	0.88
Greece	0.63	0.79	0.48	0.81
Guatemala	0.35	0.21	0.48	0.63
Hungary	0.63	0.63	0.62	0.94
India	0.55	0.63	0.48	0.50
Indonesia	0.78	0.95	0.62	0.69
Ireland	0.86	0.92	0.81	0.81
Israel	0.50	0.53	0.48	0.38
Italy	0.66	0.82	0.52	0.81
Japan	0.55	0.47	0.62	0.44
Korea, Rep. of	0.53	0.47	0.57	0.56
Latvia	0.76	0.87	0.67	1.00
Mauritius	0.56	0.71	0.43	0.50
Mexico	0.71	0.82	0.62	0.69
Morocco	0.38	0.42	0.33	0.50
Netherlands	0.65	0.84	0.67	0.88

(*continued*)

Table 8.1. *(Continued)*

| Country | Governance features of supervisory function | | | Governance features of monetary policy function |
	Total rating	Independence	Accountability	Independence GMT
New Zealand	0.73	0.74	0.71	0.44
Nicaragua	0.65	0.79	0.52	0.56
Nigeria	0.56	0.61	0.52	0.44
Norway	0.58	0.53	0.62	0.75
Peru	0.68	0.89	0.48	0.69
Philippines	0.56	0.61	0.43	0.63
Poland	0.59	0.55	0.62	0.88
Portugal	0.74	0.89	0.60	0.81
South Africa	0.54	0.55	0.52	0.25
Spain	0.74	0.63	0.83	0.88
Sri Lanka	0.54	0.55	0.52	0.56
Sweden	0.63	0.47	0.76	0.94
Switzerland	0.64	0.76	0.52	0.94
Trinidad and Tobago	0.63	0.74	0.52	0.44
Tunisia	0.46	0.61	0.33	0.69
Turkey	0.71	0.82	0.62	0.81
Uganda	0.59	0.66	0.52	0.56
United Kingdom	0.76	0.82	0.71	0.69
Zambia	0.59	0.45	0.71	0.44
Average	0.63	0.69	0.58	0.69
Standard deviation	0.11	0.17	0.11	0.19

From QRT (2007) and the authors' own calculations for supervisory independence and accountability. See Arnone et al. (2007) for update of GMT index on monetary policy independence.

could mask possible discrepancies between independence and accountability arrangements, hence our interest in both separately as well.[22] Table 8.1 also reports the rating for independence in monetary policy. For that we used the updated results of the Grilli et al. (1991)-index (hereafter GMT), computed in Arnone et al. (2007). GMT uses 15 criteria to define monetary

---

[22] On the basis of the work on accountability in Hüpkes et al. (2005) and Quintyn and Taylor (2007), which argue that there is no trade-off between independence and accountability, but that accountability reinforces independence by making it effective, one would in theory and ideally expect that both ratings would be in each other's vicinity, that is, in a scatter plot centered around the 45 degree line.

policy independence. Some of these criteria overlap with the ones used to identify supervisory independence, while others are different. Unfortunately, no comparable data are available for central bank accountability in monetary policy. The only authors who investigated this area are de Haan et al. (1999) and Siklos (2002), but their sample is more limited than ours.[23]

The findings on the governments' revealed preferences with respect to the granting of independence and the accountability arrangements for supervisors broadly confirm the trends identified in QRT (2007). The average total rating is 0.63, with a low of 0.35 (Guatemala) and a high of 0.86 (Bulgaria and Ireland). However, these total ratings mask relatively significant differences between the way policymakers separately look at independence and accountability. There is, indeed, an impression that, in several cases, these two are not considered as representing two sides of the same coin. The average for independence (0.69) is higher than for accountability (0.58). Independence ratings range between 0.34 (China) and 1 (Bulgaria), while accountability ranges from a low of 0.33 (Morocco and Tunisia) to a high of 0.83 (Spain). Incidentally, the average of monetary policy independence is the same as for the supervisory function, but with a slightly greater standard deviation.

Overview by criteria

Turning to the individual criterion, the ratings per individual criterion across the sample lead to a number of interesting observations. On independence, starting with the highest satisfaction ratios, all agencies have an enabling law (this used to be not the case when several agencies were government departments), and nearly all of them have the legal powers to impose and enforce sanctions. Most of them have autonomy with respect to their internal organization (including staffing and salary structures). Around the 0.75 mark, we note a number of interesting observations. First, the number of agencies that have the autonomy to issue regulations is at 0.75 and also funding by, mainly, fees from the supervised entities is met at 0.77. On the other hand, the right to issue and withdraw licenses is also at the same level of compliance. While the right to issue regulations often is not allowed on constitutional grounds, the power to license and revoke licenses seems an inherent power of the supervisory process, yet many governments want to retain some say in it.

---

[23] Amtenbrink (1999) undertook an in-depth analysis of central bank accountability but did not produce an index.

Going further down the list of criteria, the critical issue of agency staff having legal immunity generates a rating of only 0.69. The rating for having in the law clear dismissal criteria for the chair of the agency is at 0.62. The rating for having a clear article in the law that the agency is independent stands at 0.45. Finally, a large number of agencies have government officials on their policy boards (compliance of 0.46) and an even larger number of laws provides for the possibility for the minister (of finance) to intervene in the supervisory process (compliance is at 0.20). As was also found in QRT (2007), we run into the contradiction in a number of cases that the law states that the agency is independent, while at the same time a government official is put in a decision-making function or the minister is given the right to intervene.

On accountability, some of the criteria are broadly satisfied across the sample of countries. These include the requirement to publish an annual report on the activities of the supervisor and developments in the supervised sectors, the requirement to have internal and external audit processes in place, and the procedures to disclose policies and decisions (typically through web sites) (all above 0.90). Ex post budgetary accountability scores at 0.85, and the same rating applies to the possibility of appeal for supervised entities. Interestingly, the traditional forms of accountability such as submission of the report to the legislative branch and the executive branch do not score extremely high (respectively, 0.80 and 0.67). Direct accountability to the legislative branch is not a practice in countries with a Westminster-type of government, where it is typically the minister who represents the agencies (irrespective of the degree of autonomy of the agency). Obligations for accountability to the executive branch are often missing in the laws of those countries where a government official sits on the agency's policy board. Indeed, this line of accountability must seem redundant in the eyes of those lawmakers if they opt for direct control.

Lower scores on accountability apply to the issuance of a mission statement (0.64) and the requirement to consult the supervised industry in shaping the regulatory framework (0.54). Many "newer" forms of accountability (as opposed to the traditional forms of accountability toward the legislative and executive branches) still need to gain ground: while the possibility of appeal by the supervised entities to the judiciary is fairly common, few countries have special courts or procedures in place. Also, involving the public at large in the regulatory process is still in its infant stages. Finally, the rating on the requirement that laws provide for penalties for faulty supervision is at a low 0.09.

Overview by country groupings

The following tables present a breakdown by groups of countries. Table 8.2 shows, by region, that the European countries score the highest in all respects. The discrepancies between supervisory independence and accountability are the highest in the Americas and the Middle Eastern countries. We also note that monetary policy independence (GMT) is higher in Europe than supervisory independence, while the reverse holds in all other regions.

Table 8.3 is organized by income levels. High-income countries score highest on the total and on accountability, while the middle-income countries score marginally higher on independence. The middle-income group contains a number of countries where CBI is constitutionally guaranteed. In some of them, supervision is housed in the central bank, while in others, there is perhaps a positive spillover of this guarantee for the central bank to the supervisory agency as well. We also see that monetary policy independence is marginally higher than supervisory independence in high-income countries, at the same level in middle-income countries and lower in low-income countries.

A classification according to the political system, as measured by the University of Maryland's (2006) Polity IV project, is presented in Table 8.4.

Table 8.2. *Governance ratings by region*

	Africa (sub-Saharan) (5)	Europe (25)	Western Hemisphere (12)	Asia and Pacific (9)	Middle East and northern Africa (4)
Total rating	0.57	0.68	0.62	0.59	0.55
Independence	0.59	0.74	0.68	0.63	0.63
Accountability	0.54	0.62	0.56	0.56	0.48
GMT	0.44	0.83	0.63	0.56	0.60

Table 8.3. *Governance ratings by country income levels*

	High income (25)	Middle income (21)	Low income (9)
Total rating	0.66	0.62	0.57
Independence	0.70	0.71	0.59
Accountability	0.62	0.55	0.55
GMT	0.72	0.71	0.54

Table 8.4. *Governance ratings according to polity**

	Mature democracies (26)	New democracies (24)	Autocratic regimes (5)
Total rating	0.67	0.62	0.48
Independence	0.72	0.68	0.53
Accountability	0.62	0.57	0.44
GMT	0.75	0.66	0.54

*See University of Maryland (2006) for source and explanation.

Mature democracies score highest in all respects. They grant greater degrees of independence to their supervisors and have more developed accountability arrangements than new democracies. However, the scores for mature and new democracies are not that far apart, but are far above those for autocratic regimes, as could be expected. We note again that monetary policy independence is higher than supervisory independence, but not in new democracies.

8.4.3 Impact of the Location and Comparison with Monetary Policy

This section compares the results from the point of view the central bank's involvement in the supervisory process. Table 8.5 presents the results according to the location of the supervisors, and Table 8.6 provides the standard deviations of the ratings. From Table 8.5 we see that the total ratings are nearly identical, irrespective of the location of the supervisor. However, as we have seen before, these total ratings may mask differences between independence and accountability. We note that supervisors that are located inside the central bank have been granted the highest degree of autonomy, but also have the least elaborate accountability arrangements. Supervisors located outside the central bank have lower degrees of independence, with more-developed accountability arrangements. Moreover, unified supervisors located outside the central bank are the lowest in degree of independence and the highest in accountability. As discussed in QRT (2007), accountability arrangements in central banks are typically geared toward the monetary policy function, and miss several of the "360 degree" features (accountability to *all* stakeholders, i.e., not just the government but also the judicial branch, the supervised entities, customers of financial institutions, and the public at large) that accountability in supervisory matters should possess.

Table 8.5. *Governance ratings by location of supervisor*

	Inside central bank	Outside central bank	
		All agencies	Of which unified supervisors
Total rating	0.63	0.63	0.65
Independence	0.71	0.67	0.64
Accountability	0.57	0.60	0.65
GMT	0.62	0.75	0.78

Table 8.6. *Standard deviations of total rating, independence and accountability and CBI (GMT) according to location*

	Inside central bank	Outside central bank		Pm. total sample
		All agencies	Of which unified supervisors	
Total rating	0.12	0.10	0.11	0.11
Independence	0.16	0.18	0.20	0.17
Accountability	0.13	0.10	0.09	0.11
GMT	0.20	0.17	0.18	0.19

Noteworthy, too, is that the degree of supervisory autonomy is higher than the degree of monetary policy autonomy for supervisors housed in the central bank, and lower in the other categories. To a great extent, this is due to the fact that GMT assigns a negative rating on monetary policy independence if the central bank is also the bank supervisor. The reason is that, in their view, supervision adds another objective to the central bank and may distract the central bank's attention from pursuing its primary objective. Let us take Bulgaria as an example of the impact of this. The country scores a "1" satisfaction ratio for supervisory independence. It complies with all criteria for monetary independence in the GMT index, with the exception of the bank supervision criterion. Hence, it has 0.88 for monetary policy independence. Other reasons may be that, for example, several central banks in low-income countries (still) have no prohibition to grant credit to the government, while they do have some (or most) of the features of institutional independence that count for supervisory independence.

The standard deviations for supervisory independence, reported in Table 8.6, are greater than for accountability. So countries, irrespective of the location of the supervisor, seem to agree less on the acceptable degree of independence than accountability. Interesting is also that standard deviations are the greatest for the unified supervisors when it comes to independence and the smallest for accountability. So there seems to be more consensus on a desirable accountability model than an independence model. For supervisors inside the central bank, this is exactly the opposite. The other finding is that the GMT index has a larger standard deviation than the supervisory independence measure for the total sample and for central banks that house supervisors.

It is worthwhile to briefly discuss areas where the discrepancies in independence and accountability arise, according to the location.[24] The most striking differences are in the relations with the political class: supervisory agencies outside the central bank often have politicians on their policy board (parliamentarians or ministers) and, in many cases, the law includes a clause allowing the minister to intervene in the supervisory process. These agencies also have less autonomy than the central banks in hiring staff, setting salaries, and defining their internal organization. A number of these agencies have been established, or been reformed recently, so one hypothesis could be that these forms of curbing independence are a reaction against something, perhaps the fact that politicians fear that central banks have received too much independence.[25] It should be noted too that supervisors outside central banks score better in terms of legal immunity for their staff, and the autonomy to issue regulations.

The picture that we get on the accountability side shows that supervisors outside the central banks have higher satisfaction ratios in areas of "newer" accountability.[26] They score significantly higher on accountability toward stakeholders (the regulated industry, consumers, and public at large), and marginally higher on accountability toward the judicial branch. We can interpret this as inertia on the part of central banks: several of these laws have not been reformed for a long time, while supervisors located outside central banks have relatively newer legal frameworks. Interestingly, accountability toward the executive branch is more developed for central banks. A plausible

---

[24] The detailed data are relegated to an appendix (not shown).

[25] The account offered by Westrup (2007) shows that such factors may have played a role in Germany, when it was decided to put supervision in a separate agency outside the Bundesbank. More generally, the famous "grabbing hand" of the government could be at work: reorganizing supervision to get more influence in the process.

[26] As indicated earlier, agency accountability was traditionally defined as giving account to the three branches of government. As discussed in Hüpkes et al. (2005) and Quintyn (2007a), accountability, in conjunction with transparency is now defined more broadly as giving account to *all* stakeholders, in order to build agency legitimacy.

explanation for this could be that supervisors outside central banks have comparatively more politicians in decision-making positions, and hence do not see the need for additional reporting lines to this branch of government.

8.5 The Determinants of Supervisory Governance

While the previous section reveals some aspects of the policymakers' preferences with respect to the governance arrangements for supervisors, it seems useful to dig deeper into the matter in an effort to identify some patterns. Thus, this section undertakes an econometric analysis of the determinants of the governance arrangements for supervisors.

8.5.1 The Econometric Approach

The governance arrangements for supervisors can be viewed as resulting from an unobserved variable: the optimal combination of the degrees of independence and accountability, consistent with the policymaker's utility. Each regime corresponds to a specific range of the optimal governance arrangements, with higher discrete values for the total, independence and accountability corresponding to a higher range of supervisory governance. Because the governance indices are qualitative variables, the estimation of a model for such a dependent variable requires the use of a specific technique.

Our qualitative dependent variable can be classified into more than two categories, given that the governance indices are multinomial variables. But the indices are also ordinal variables, given that they reflect a ranking. For this, the ordered Logit model is an appropriate estimator, given the ordered nature of the alternatives open to the policymaker.

Let y be the policymaker's ordered choices, taking the values $(0, \ldots, 1)$. The ordered model for y, conditional on a set of K explanatory variables x, can be derived from a latent variable model [equation (1)]. In order to test this relationship, let us assume that the unobserved variable vector, the optimal degree of supervisory governance y^*, is determined by

$$y^* = \beta'x + \varepsilon \qquad (1)$$

where ε is a random disturbance uncorrelated with the regressors, and β is a $1 \times K$ vector of regressors.

The latent variable y^* is unobserved. What is observed is the choice of each national policymaker to endow the supervisor with a degree of independence and accountability: this choice is summarized in the value of the total, independence and accountability indices, which represent the threshold values. For our dependent variable there are 100 threshold values. Estimation is carried out by means of maximum likelihood techniques, assuming that ε is normally distributed across country observations, and its mean and variance are normalized.

Which economic model will be tested? In Section 8.3 we highlighted the importance of the "governance nexus" developed in Das and Quintyn (2002) and Quintyn (2007a). So, public sector governance will be the key variable to be tested, together with a number of control variables to detect other influences and to test the robustness of our hypothesis. We expect a positive relationship between the quality of public sector governance and the three dependent variables to be tested, that is, the indices for the total, independence and accountability.

As usual, the potential endogeneity among institutional variables will allow us to draw only prudent statements in terms of causal relationships. One important point in a future research agenda will be to identify instrumental variables that minimize the risks entailed from the endogeneity of the relationship being estimated.

As a first control variable, we introduce *GDP* per capita as a scale variable to test for the effect of the economic size of the country and its level of economic development (the economic factor). Given the descriptive results presented earlier, the sign of this variable is a priori unknown.

Next, we test for the impact of the *structure of the financial markets* (bank-vs. market-dominated systems). In the literature on the determinants of the emerging supervisory architectures, the structure of the markets plays a role. Masciandaro (2006) and Freytag and Masciandaro (2007) find that countries with market-dominated systems tend to favor more the integrated supervisory model. However, with a larger and updated sample, Masciandaro (2007) and Masciandaro and Quintyn (2008) find that the financial market structure does not matter. So far, this control variable seems to be a sample-sensitive variable. In our analysis of the drivers of governance arrangements, it is a priori not clear whether the composition of the markets will have a decisive impact and, if so, whether its impact will be positive or negative.

The next variable, the *concentration ratio of the banking system*, measures regulatory capture risk. The hypothesis is that more concentrated banking systems can more easily bundle their lobbying powers and influence the government's decisions with respect to the desirable degree of independence and accountability. This is an example of the grabbing hand hypothesis in which the government serves the interests of special groups.[27] However, the sign of the impact on governance arrangements is not clear a priori. A negative sign would mean that the banking lobby has pushed for low independence and weak accountability in the hope of being able to influence the supervisor. A positive sign is also possible. Hardy (2006) shows that regulatory capture is not always negative. Bankers can push supervisors to have strong policies so that their banks are not affected by contagion from weak banks in the system. In that case, these lobbying bankers would probably prefer supervisors with high independence and good accountability.

Our control variables also include the *legal factor*. Variables in this category reflect one branch of the institutional approach that is suggested in the literature, that is, the "legal origin" (La Porta et al. 1998) We test the impact of possible common law effect, usually a proxy of a market-friendly environment, as well as a specific legal factor, the German-Scandinavian law effect to estimate a possible legal neighbor effect, highlighted in Masciandaro (2006, 2007) in the analysis of the determinants of the financial supervision architectures. Accordingly, the sign of the legal factor(s) is a priori undetermined.

The number of countries that are revisiting their supervisory structures and at the same time the governance arrangements has been increasing year after year. The Scandinavian countries were the forerunners at the end of the 1980s and early 1990s, but it was in fact the establishment of the FSA in the United Kingdom that stirred the wave of reforms that we have been witnessing since then. So the question that we ask here is whether there is a kind of *fashion effect* (or bandwagon effect) at work: are more recent reformers inspired by the type of changes in governance arrangements that were introduced by earlier reformers? A positive and significant coefficient would imply that there is some bandwagon effect, while an insignificant coefficient would mean that countries are not influenced by what others decided with respect to governance arrangements.

It is often stated that "it takes a crisis to reform." Hence, the model we estimate also tests for the *impact of a crisis experience* on governance arrangements. The expected sign is not clear because governments could react in various ways to a crisis. Supervisors could be blamed for the crisis and their level of independence could thereby be reduced, or for a given

---

[27] Masciandaro and Quintyn (2008) only found weak evidence of the impact of the concentration ratio on the government's decision regarding the degree of integration of the supervisory architecture.

level of independence, they could be subjected to greater accountability. Other reactions are also imaginable. For instance, the government could, in the wake of a crisis, grant more independence to the supervisor because the government does not want to be blamed again in the future if another crisis erupts.

We also test for the political factor, by introducing a variable for *the political system*. It is expected that mature democracies are more comfortable in granting independence to the supervisor and introducing accountability arrangements because the system has the necessary level of checks and balances.[28] New democracies may be inclined to go the same way, while notions of independence and accountability are fairly alien to autocratic regimes. So the expected sign is positive with the political system variable.

Finally, if we assume that the decision about the supervisory architecture and its governance arrangements is a two-stage process, we can separately test for the impact of two additional variables. In the first place, we control for the impact of the policymaker's decision to have, or keep, *the supervisor in the central bank*. The sign is a priori undetermined. The overall impact on supervisory governance of housing the supervisor in the central bank is somewhat ambiguous: QRT (2007) and Table 8.5 indicate that supervisors housed in central banks typically have a higher degree of independence and a lower degree of accountability than their colleagues housed outside the central bank.

The other part of the decision concerns the *degree of integration of the supervisor* – the choice between sector-specific supervisors on the one extreme and fully unified (or integrated) supervisors on the other. So we also control for the impact of this decision on supervisory governance. QRT (2007) and Table 8.5 show that governments tend to grant lower degrees of independence and more complex accountability arrangements to supervisors outside the central bank, and even more so to unified supervisors. The effect on total governance is a priori unknown.

The general specification is represented by equations (2) and (3):

$$
\begin{aligned}
(supgov)_i = {} & \beta_1(gov)_i + \beta_2(gdp/cap)_i + \beta_3(mcap)_i + \beta_4(conc)_i \\
& + \beta_5(anglosaxonL)_i + \beta_6(germscandL)_i + \beta_7(bandwagon)_i \\
& + \beta_8(crisis)_i + \beta_9(polity)_i + \beta_{10}(cb)_i + \varepsilon
\end{aligned}
\tag{2}
$$

[28] See, for example, Keefer and Stasavage (2001) and Moser (1999) on CBI.

$$(supgov)_i = \beta_1 (gov)_i + \beta_2 (gdp/cap)_i + \beta_3 (mcap)_i + \beta_4 (conc)_i$$

$$+ \beta_5 (anglosaxonL)_i + \beta_6 (germscandL)_i + \beta_7 (bandwagon)_i$$

$$+ \beta_8 (crisis)_i + \beta_9 (polity)_i + \beta_{11} (sfa)_i + \varepsilon \qquad (3)$$

with country $i = 1 \ldots 50$.[29]

The dependent variables (represented here by "*supgov*") are the total rating, the independence rating and the accountability rating.

The independent variables are the following:

gov = Public sector governance: a quantitative variable for the public sector governance factor. It shows the structural capacity of the government to formulate and implement sound policies[30];

gdp/cap = Gross domestic product per head of population: a quantitative variable for the economic size factor[31];

mcap = Market capitalization/GDP: a quantitative variable for the structure of the financial market and the private governance factor. It shows a measure of the securities market size, relative to GDP[32];

conc = degree of concentration in the banking system: percentage of the total deposits held by the five major banks of the country[33];

---

[29] Due to data limitations, only 50 countries were included in the econometric analysis.

[30] The index is built using all the indicators proposed by Kaufmann et al. (2003). They define (public) governance as the exercise of authority through formal and informal traditions and institutions for the common good, thus encompassing: (1) the process of selecting, monitoring, and replacing governments; (2) the capacity to formulate and implement sound policies and deliver public services; (3) the respect of citizens and the state for the institutions that govern economic and social interactions among them. Furthermore, for measurement and analysis purposes, these three dimensions of governance can be further unbundled to comprise two measurable concepts for each of the dimensions above for a total of six components: (1) voice and external accountability; (2) political stability and lack of violence; (3) government effectiveness; (4) lack of regulatory burden; (5) rule of law; and (6) control of corruption. The authors present a set of estimates of these six dimensions of governance for four time periods: 1996, 1998, 2000, and 2002. For every country, therefore, we first calculate the mean of the four time values for each dimension of governance; then we build up an index of global good governance in the period 1996–2004, calculating the mean of the six different dimensions.

[31] See World Bank (2003), *World Development Indicators*. For each variable we calculate the mean of five time values: 1996, 1998, 2000, 2002, and 2004.

[32] World Bank (2003), *World Development Indicators*, Stock Markets 5.3. For each variable we calculate the mean of five time values: 1996, 1998, 2000, 2002, and 2004.

[33] Barth et al. (2003).

anglosaxonL, GermanScandL = binary variables for the law factor. They are dummies that indicate the legal roots of a given country, representing the control variables for the law and finance view[34];

bandwagon = the year of the most recent reforms in the law(s) governing the country's bank supervisor. It is used to identify if reforms in later years are triggered by demonstration effect of reforms earlier on in other countries;

crisis = year of a banking crisis in the country, to identify if reforms in governance arrangements are triggered by a financial sector crisis; and

polity = is a measure of the political system of a country (see University of Maryland (2006) for further details).[35]

Equation (2) tests for impact of central bank as the supervisor (*cb*). This is a 0–1 dummy with 0 when central bank is not the supervisor, 1 otherwise.

Equation (3) tests the impact of the presence of a single financial authority (*sfa*), or the degree of concentration of supervisory activities. This index is calculated in Masciandaro (2007), and distinguishes 7 degrees of integration (0 being separate agencies, 7 fully integrated).

8.5.2 The Results

In multinomial ordered models the impact of a change in an explanatory variable on the estimated probabilities of the highest and lowest of the order classifications – in our case the governance ratings – is unequivocal: if β_j is positive, for example, an increase in the value of x_j increases the probability of having higher governance ratings.

Tables 8.7, 8.8, and 8.9 present the results for the total rating, independence, and accountability. They reveal highly interesting results. First of all, analyzing the overall ratings in Table 8.7, we find that supervisory governance arrangements are strongly driven by the quality of the country's public sector governance. The significance of this variable is highly robust in all specifications. In addition, we note that a bandwagon effect is at play, and fairly significantly. Polity also plays a significant role, meaning that the

---

[34] The legal roots are five: Anglo-Saxon Law (= Common Law); French, German, and Scandinavian Laws (= Civil Laws); and Socialist Law (Others). In this analysis, for theoretical reasons, we limited ourselves to the common law and the German-Scandinavian law.

[35] The correlation between public sector governance and polity is 0.53, indicating that these two variables measure different things.

Table 8.7. *Ordered logit estimates with total governance as the dependent variable (50 observations)*

Variables	(1)	(2)	(3)	(4)	(5)	(6)	(7)	(8)	(9)
Governance	1.01	1.04	1.04	1.93	1.48	1.74	1.24	1.30	1.08
St. error	(0.39)	(0.40)	(0.40)	(0.49)	(0.53)	(0.56)	(0.60)	(0.60)	
P > z	0.011***	0.009***	0.01***	0.00***	0.005***	0.002***	0.039**	0.029**	0.072*
GDP/capita	0.004	0.004	0.004	0.006	0.006	0.004	0.003	0.003	0.003
St. error	(0.003)	(0.003)	(0.003)	(0.003)	(0.003)	(0.003)	(0.003)	(0.003)	(0.003)
P > z	0.17	0.17	0.17	0.08*	0.06**	0.27	0.33	0.40	0.29
Market structure	−0.004	−0.002	−0.002	−0.018	−0.013	−0.025	−0.026	−0.035	−0.023
St. error	(0.025)	(0.026)	(0.026)	(0.026)	(0.027)	(0.027)	(0.027)	(0.028)	(0.026)
P > z	0.88	0.92	0.95	0.50	0.61	0.35	0.34	0.22	0.38
Market concentration		−0.011	−0.011	−0.017	−0.017	−0.021	−0.019	−0.015	−0.019
St. error		(0.012)	(0.013)	(0.013)	(0.013)	(0.013)	(0.014)	(0.013)	(0.013)
P > z		0.35	0.38	0.17	0.19	0.01*	0.17*	0.24	0.13
Common law			−0.12	−0.74	−0.48	−0.27	−0.53	−0.40	−0.60
St. error			(0.59)	(0.63)	(0.65)	(0.67)	(0.70)	(0.71)	(0.68)
P > z			0.21	0.23	0.46	0.69	0.44	0.57	0.37
Ger/Scand law				−2.63	−2.65	−3.59	−3.59	−4.22	−5.12
St. error				(0.82)	(0.84)	(1.01)	(1.02)	(1.09)	(1.23)
P > z				0.001***	0.002**	0.0000***	0.0000***	0.0000***	0.0000***

	(1)	(2)	(3)	(4)	(5)	(6)	(7)	(8)	(9)
Bandwagon effect					0.11	0.10	0.12	0.13	0.13
St. error					(0.04)	(0.04)	(0.04)	(0.04)	(0.04)
P > z					0.003***	0.004***	0.001***	0.001***	0.001***
Financial crisis						1.56	1.46	1.10	1.80
St. error						(0.85)	(0.84)	(0.85)	(0.87)
P > z						0.066***	0.082*	0.194	0.038**
Polity							0.23	0.25	0.23
St. error							(0.1)	(0.11)	(0.1)
P > z							0.021**	0.017***	0.025**
Central bank effect								−1.21	
St. error								(0.66)	
P > z								0.067*	
Integrated supervisor									1.83
St. error									(0.72)
P > z									0.011***
LR chi2	8.91	9.77	9.81	20.48	29.74	33.15	38.50	41.95	45.12
Prob > chi2	0.0305	0.0405	0.0808	0.0023	0.0001	0.0001	0.0000	0.0000	0.0000
Log likelihood	−143.31	−142.87	−142.85	−137.52	−132.89	−131.2	−128.50	−126.78	−125.19
Pseudo R^2	0.03	0.03	0.03	0.07	0.10	0.11	0.13	0.14	0.15

Table 8.8. *Ordered logit estimates with independence as the dependent variable (50 observations)*

Variables	(1)	(2)	(3)	(4)	(5)	(6)	(7)
Governance St. error P > z	1.25	0.65	0.78	0.33	1.13	0.33	0.21
	(0.45)	(0.49)	(0.51)	(0.54)	(0.51)	(0.54)	(0.54)
	0.006***	0.185	0.12	0.54	0.027**	0.54	0.69
GDP/capita St. error P > z	0.007	0.007	0.006	0.006	0.011	0.006	0.006
	(0.003)	(0.003)	(0.003)	(0.003)	(0.004)	(0.003)	(0.003)
	0.037**	0.02**	0.062*	0.084*	0.008***	0.097*	0.071*
Market structure St. error P > z	−0.034	−0.028	−0.033	−0.038	−0.007	−0.041	−0.033
	(0.26)	(0.26)	(0.27)	(0.27)	(0.31)	(0.28)	(0.27)
	0.19	0.29	0.22	0.17	0.82	0.14	0.22
Market concentration St. error P > z	−0.002	−0.001	−0.003	−0.002	−0.01	−0.004	−0.004
	(0.01)	(0.012)	(0.013)	(0.013)	(0.013)	(0.013)	(0.013)
	0.87	0.89	0.98	0.86	0.41	0.75	0.77
Common law St. error P > z	−0.53	−0.23	−0.13	−0.47	−3.79	−0.36	−0.50
	(0.59)	(0.6)	(0.61)	(0.64)	(0.81)	(0.65)	(0.63)
	0.37	0.70	0.83	0.46	0.000***	0.58	0.43
Ger/Scand law St. error P > z	−3.43	−3.91	−4.49	−4.77		−5.03	−5.43
	(0.88)	(0.96)	(1.15)	(1.19)		(1.25)	(1.34)
	0.000***	0.000***	0.000***	0.000***		0.000***	0.000***

Bandwagon effect	0.14	0.13	0.14	0.03	0.14	0.14
St. error	(0.038)	(0.038)	(0.036)	(0.036)	(0.037)	(0.037)
$P > z$	0.000***	0.000***	0.000***	0.21	0.000***	0.000***
Financial crisis		0.79	0.69	−0.99	0.50	0.79
St. error		(0.82)	(0.82)	(0.81)	(0.85)	(0.83)
$P > z$		0.33	0.40	0.22	0.55	0.34
Polity			0.23	0.14	0.23	0.23
St. error			(0.09)	(0.07)	(0.10)	(0.09)
$P > z$			0.013***	0.054**	0.014***	0.014***
Central bank effect					−0.53	
St. error					(0.66)	
$P > z$					0.42	
Integrated supervisor						0.77
St. error						(0.69)
$P > z$						0.26
LR chi2	18,74	34.63	41.20	41.46	41.85	42.46
Prob > chi2	0.0046	0.0000	0.0000	0.0000	0.000	0.0000
Log likelihood	−135.36	−127.42	−124.13	−98.11	−123.81	−123.5
Pseudo R^2	0.06	0.12	0.14	0.17	0.14	0.15

Table 8.9. Ordered logit estimates with accountability as the dependent variable

Variables	(1)	(2)	(3)	(4)	(5)	(6)
Governance	1.64	1.59	1.91	1.46	1.47	1.35
St. error	(0.48)	(0.51)	(0.54)	(0.60)	(0.61)	(0.61)
P > z	0.001***	0.002****	0.000***	0.015***	0.015***	0.026**
GDP/capita	−0.0003	−0.0004	−0.003	−0.004	−0.004	−0.004
St. error	(0.003)	(0.003)	(0.003)	(0.003)	(0.003)	(0.003)
P > z	0.91	0.89	0.35	0.29	0.23	0.27
Market structure	−0.006	−0.006	−0.016	−0.014	−0.019	−0.014
St. error	(0.02)	(0.02)	(0.026)	(0.026)	(0.027)	(0.025)
P > z	0.80	0.80	0.54	0.57	0.46	0.57
Market concentration	−0.029	−0.029	−0.03	−0.03	−0.03	−0.03
St. error	(0.013)	(0.013)	(0.014)	(0.014)	(0.014)	(0.014)
P > z	0.032**	0.032**	0.026**	0.042**	0.054***	0.061**
Common law	0.12	0.15	0.34	0.21	0.44	0.32
St. error	(0.63)	(0.64)	(0.65)	(0.67)	(0.69)	(0.67)
P > z	0.85	0.82	0.59	0.75	0.52	0.63
Ger/Scand law	−0.19	−0.18	−1.23	−1.13	−1.39	−1.92
St. error	(0.78)	(0.78)	(0.96)	(0.96)	(0.98)	(1.08)
P > z	0.81	0.82	0.20	0.24	0.15	0.076*

	(1)	(2)	(3)	(4)	(5)	(6)
Bandwagon effect		0.008	0.005	0.014	0.020	0.024
St. error		(0.026)	(0.22)	(0.27)	(0.27)	(0.27)
P > z		0.74	0.83	0.60	0.45	0.38
Financial crisis			1.67	1.56	1.33	1.89
St. error			(0.83)	(0.83)	(0.84)	(0.86)
P > z			0.043**	0.058**	0.11	0.028**
Polity				0.16	0.19	0.16
St. error				(0.10)	(0.10)	(0.10)
P > z				0.104*	0.064**	0.12
Central bank effect					−0.92	
St. error					(0.61)	
P > z					0.131	
Integrated supervisor						1.11
St. error						(0.63)
P > z						0.079*
LR chi2	20.98	21.08	25.21	27.94	30.23	31.03
Prob > chi2	0.0019	0.0037	0.0014	0.001	0.0008	0.0006
Log likelihood	−119.04	−118.98	−116.92	−115.56	−114.41	−114.01
Pseudo R²	0.08	0.08	0.10	0.11	0.12	0.12

more mature a democracy is, the more the government is willing to grant independence, with accompanying accountability. The impact of past crises is significant but less so than for the other relevant variables. The only other variable with significance is the German-Scandinavian law factor, but with a negative sign. We return to this (puzzling) finding later in our discussion. All other variables, including GDP per capita, do not have a significant impact on the probability of having high quality governance arrangements.

From equations (8) and (9) in Table 8.7, we also learn that the presence of supervisors in the central bank has a significant and negative impact on governance arrangements, while more integrated supervisors outside the central bank increase the probability of higher governance ratings.

When we dissect the results and look at the determinants of independence and accountability separately in Tables 8.8 and 8.9, respectively, we see that the results for the overall ratings mask a number of interesting findings. First of all, public sector governance does not seem to have a significant impact on the independence ratings. So the probability that supervisors have a high degree of independence does not seem to depend on the quality of a country's public sector governance, but instead depends positively on its economic size and political system, as well as a bandwagon effect. The latter implies that, as the idea of independent regulatory agencies continues to spread around the world, more countries are willing to embrace it. Another finding from the independence equations in Table 8.8 is that neither the role of the central bank as a supervisor, nor the degree of unification of supervision outside the central bank, seems to have an impact on the degree of independence.

The probability of having elaborate accountability arrangements, on the other hand, is very strongly driven by the quality of the country's public sector governance. This variable is highly significant, and robust across specifications. Other important determinants are the crisis experience and, again, polity. We also find that the presence of the central bank has a negative though insignificant impact on accountability, but for those supervisors located outside the central bank, the more unified they are, the more likely they will have elaborate accountability arrangements in place.

In sum, the empirical analysis of the drivers of supervisory governance arrangements brings the following evidence:

- Good public sector governance has a decisive impact, but nearly exclusively on accountability. Independence seems to be driven by other factors.

- Moreover, the results give the strong impression that policymakers do not see independence and accountability as two sides of the same coin. This impression was already raised in QRT (2007) and surfaced again from the analysis of the tables and charts in this chapter. It is fairly strongly confirmed by our econometric analysis. Politicians' decisions on the degree of independence and accountability of their supervisors seem to be driven by a different set of considerations. Only polity is present in both, meaning that the more mature a democracy is, the more likely it is that higher degrees of independence and accountability will be granted. Accountability is additionally driven by crisis experiences, while independence is influenced by a type of fashion or bandwagon effect.
- The location of the supervisor has an influence. We modeled a two-stage decision-making process by the policymaker (inside or outside central bank, unified or not). Location and unification do not seem to have a great impact on the probability of high independence, but they do have an impact on the degree of accountability. Indeed the likelihood for more elaborate accountability increases when the central bank is not the supervisor. This is obviously related to the fact that central bank accountability arrangements are and remain predominantly geared toward monetary policy, which are less demanding than supervision.[36]
- Finally, we are confronted with the puzzling strong negative impact of the German-Scandinavian law factor. This finding needs further analysis. A likely explanation is that this variable captures some other effect as it is very unlikely that the German legal tradition has a bias against independence – witness the high degree of independence that the Bundesbank enjoys. Inspection of the data shows that all the countries that fall under this law tradition have fairly low rates of supervisory independence for a variety of unrelated reasons.[37] If this is the case, it means that law traditions have no impact on governance arrangements, and that we need to look for another variable to capture the effects that we see in the German-Scandinavian variable.

---

[36] See Hüpkes et al. (2005) on this topic.

[37] The Scandinavian countries were the first ones to unify their supervisors in the late 1980s and early 1990s, and in those days, there was no talk about supervisory governance, let alone independence. They have relatively modest independence ratings. QRT (2007) discussed the reasons why Austria, Germany, and Korea also have below-average independence ratings.

8.6 Conclusions

Unlike the monetary policy function that is typically the core function of a central bank, the supervisory function is being performed by a variety of institutions for whom there is less consensus about the governance model than for central banks as monetary policy agents. This chapter analyzes empirically recent trends in, and determinants of, financial supervisory governance, with special attention to the role of the central bank as supervisor. The chapter starts from an identification of similarities and differences between the approaches to central bank governance as a monetary policy authority and financial supervisory governance. While the arguments for independence are found to be broadly similar, we demonstrate that the supervisory function requires more elaborate accountability arrangements to make supervision effective. Next we test whether, on the basis of a sample of 55 countries, this need for solid accountability arrangements is reflected in the reality. We first calculate the levels of supervisory independence and accountability and disentangle the institutional differences between supervisory regimes governed by central banks from those in which a different authority is in charge of supervision. Finally, we analyze empirically the determinants of independence and accountability arrangements and come to a number of interesting conclusions: (a) the quality of public sector governance plays a decisive role in establishing accountability arrangements, more than independence arrangements; (b) governments tend to lean toward a combination of independence and accountability arrangements for their supervisors that is different from the mainstream model of monetary policy governance, with more emphasis on accountability; (c) however, based on the revealed preferences, the model is not yet well defined. As a matter of fact, the econometric analysis of the determinants of governance arrangements reveals that independence and accountability are not seen as two sides of the same coin but that different considerations determine their degrees; and (d) that policymakers are better able to implement these preferences in separate financial authorities (i.e., outside central banks), whereas signs of inertia seem to surround the governance arrangements in central banks that are also supervisors, that is, their arrangements tend to remain geared toward the monetary policy function with accountability receiving less attention.

Findings (c) and (d) lead us to the main conclusion of this chapter: policymakers should approach accountability as a problem of institutional design. First, policymakers who now tend to lean mostly toward strong accountability for their financial sector supervisors – which is justified in light of their broad mandate – should appreciate independence and accountability more as two sides of the same coin and elaborate balanced arrangements. And second, central banks that are also supervisors may wish to accommodate this trend by revisiting their accountability arrangements and diversify them to meet the requirements posed by the need for financial sector supervision.

The second point deserves attention from another angle as well: current trends – reinforced by the 2007–2008 crisis – indicate that we have entered a new era with central banks again reaching beyond their current frontiers, as they are including the goal of financial stability into their mandate. Adding financial stability as an explicit objective requires revisiting accountability arrangements because this objective is not as clearly defined and definable as price stability. The survey by Oosterloo and de Haan (2004) indicates indeed that central bank accountability arrangements are, in general, not meeting the needs of this new objective. So pushing the frontiers requires an adaptation in the governance arrangements.

Appendix A. *Countries selected for the survey*

Country	Year of last reform (legislative or institutional)	Banking crisis (year)	Location bank supervision
Armenia			CB
Australia	1998		OCB, U[1]
Austria	2002		OCB, U
Bahamas (The)	2000		CB
Belgium	2004		OCB, U
Brazil			CB
Bulgaria			CB
Canada	2006		OCB, U
Chile	1997		OCB
China, PR	2004	Distress throughout 1990s	OCB
Colombia	2003/2005[2]		OCB, U
Cyprus			CB
Czech Republic			CB, U
Denmark	1988	Distress in early 1990s	OCB, U
Ecuador	2001	2000	OCB
Egypt			CB
El Salvador			OCB
Estonia	1998		OCB
Finland	1993/2003[2]	1991	OCB, U[3]
France			OCB[3]

(*continued*)

Appendix A. *(Continued)*

Country	Year of last reform (legislative or institutional)	Banking crisis (year)	Location bank supervision
Germany	2002		OCB/CB, U[4]
Greece			CB
Guatemala	2002		OCB, U
Hungary	2000/2004[2]		OCB, U
India			CB
Indonesia	2004	1997	CB[5]
Ireland	2003		CB, U
Israel			CB
Italy			CB
Japan	2000	Distress throughout 1990s	OCB/CB[4]
Korea	1997	1997	OCB
Latvia	2001		OCB, U
Mauritius	2004		CB
Mexico	1995	1994	OCB
Morocco			CB
Netherlands	2004		CB[1]
New Zealand			CB
Nicaragua	2004	2000	OCB, U
Nigeria			CB
Norway	1988/2003[2]	1991	OCB, U
Peru			OCB
Philippines (The)			CB
Poland	1997		CB[6]
Portugal			CB
South Africa	1991		CB
Spain			CB
Sri lanka			CB
Sweden	1991/2003[2]	1991	OCB, U
Switzerland			OCB
Trinidad and Tobago	2005		CB
Tunisia			CB
Turkey	2001	2000	OCB
Uganda	2004		CB
United Kingdom	1997		OCB, U
Zambia			CB

Note: CB = in the central bank; OCB = outside the central bank; U = unified.
[1] Part of a "twin peak" arrangement.
[2] Two reforms – last one is taking into account.
[3] Affiliated with the central bank.
[4] Central bank in charge of on-site inspections.
[5] Bank supervision will be transferred to unified supervisor in 2010.
[6] Bank supervision will be transferred to unified supervisor in 2010.

References

Abrams, R. and M. Taylor (2000), "Issues in the Unification of Financial Sector Supervision," *IMF Working Paper WP/00/213*.

Amtenbrink, F. (1999), *The Democratic Accountability of Central Banks: A Comparative Study of the European Central Bank* (Oxford and Portland: Hart Publishing).

Arnone, M., B. J. Laurens, J.-F. Segalotto, and M. Sommer (2007), "Central Bank Autonomy: Lessons from Global Trends," *IMF Working Papers* 88, International Monetary Fund, Washington, D.C.

Barro, R. J. and D. B. Gordon (1983), "A Positive Theory of Monetary Policy in a Natural Rate Model," *Journal of Political Economy* 91: 589–610.

Barth, J., G. Caprio, and R. Levine (2003), "The Regulation and Supervision of Banks around the World: A New Database," in R. Litan and R. Herring (Ed.), *Brookings-Wharton Papers on Financial Services* (Washington, DC: Brookings Institution Press).

Basel Committee on Banking Supervision (2006), "Core Principles for Effective Banking Supervision," Bank for International Settlements, Basel.

Berger, H., J. de Haan, and S. C. W. Eijffinger (2000), "Central Bank Independence: an Update of Theory and Evidence," *CESifo Working Papers* 255.

Berger, H., V. Nitsche, and T. Lybek (2008), "Central Bank Boards Around the World: Why Does Membership Size Differ?," *European Journal of Political Economy* 24(4): 817–832.

Boot, A. W. A. and A. V. Thakor (1993), "Self-Interested Bank Regulation," *American Economic Review* 83 (2): 206–212.

Buiter, W. (2007), "How Robust is the New Conventional Wisdom in Monetary Policy? The Surprising Fragility of the Theoretical Foundations of Inflation Targeting and Central Bank Independence," Paper presented at various conferences and seminars.

Crowe, C. and E. E. Meade (2007), "Central Bank Governance: What Is It and Does It Matter?," *Journal of Economic Perspectives*, Fall.

Cukierman, A. (1992), *Central Bank Strategy, Credibility, and Autonomy* (Cambridge, MA: MIT Press).

(2007), *Central Bank Independence and Monetary Policymaking Institutions–past, present and future*, CEPS Discussion Paper Series, No. 6441:1, September.

Das, U. and M. Quintyn (2002), "Financial Crisis Prevention and Crisis Management—The Role of Regulatory Governance," in R. Litan, M. Pomerleano and V. Sundararajan (Eds.), *Financial Sector Governance: The Roles of the Public and Private Sectors* (Washington, DC: Brookings Institution Press).

Das, U., M. Quintyn, and K. Chenard (2004), "Does Regulatory Governance Matter for Financial System Stability? An Empirical Analysis," *The Evolving Financial System and Public Policy*, Bank of Canada, Ottawa.

de Haan, J., F. Amtenbrink, and S. Eijffinger (1999), "Accountability of Central Banks: Aspects and Quantification," *Banca Nazionale del Lavoro Quarterly Review* 209: 167–193.

Di Giorgio, G. and C. di Noia (1999), "Should Banking Supervision and Monetary Policy Tasks be Given to Different Agencies?," *International Finance* 3: 361–378.

Eijffinger, S. and P. Geraarts, 2006, "How Transparent are Central Banks?," *European Journal of Political Economy* 22: 1–21.

Fischer, S. (1995), "Central Bank Independence Revisited," *American Economic Review, Papers and Proceedings* 85: 201–206, May.

Freytag, A. and D. Masciandaro (2007), "Financial Supervision Architecture and Central Bank Independence," in D. Masciandaro and M. Quintin (Eds.), *Designing Financial Supervision Institutions: Independence, Accountability and Governance* (Cheltenham, United Kingdom; North Hampton, MA: Edward Elgar).

Frisell L., K. Roszbach, and G. Spagnolo (2004), *Governing the Governors: A Clinical Study of Central Banks*, mimeo.

Goodhart, C. (2002), "The Organization Structure of Banking Supervision," *Economic Notes* 31: 1–32.

Goodhart, C. and D. Schoenmaker (1992), "Institutional Separation between Supervisory and Monetary Agencies," *Giornale degli Economisti e Annali di Economia* 51: 353–439.

  (1995), "Should the Functions of Monetary Policy and Banking Supervision be Separated?," *Oxford Economic Papers* 47: 539–560.

Grilli, V., D. Masciandaro, and G. Tabellini (1991), "Political and Monetary Institutions and Public Financial Policies in the Industrial Countries," *Economic Policy* 13: 341–392.

Hardy, D. (2006), *Regulatory Capture, IMF Working Papers* 34, International Monetary Fund, Washington, DC.

Hayo, B. and C. Hefeker (2001), "Do We Really Need Central Bank Independence? A Critical Re-examination," *WWZ Discussion Papers* 3, University of Basle.

Haubrich, J. G. (1996), "Combining Bank Supervision and Monetary Policy," *Economic Commentary*, Federal Reserve Bank of Cleveland, November.

Hughes, A. and J. Libich (2006), "Central Bank Independence, Accountability and Transparency: Complements or Strategic Substitutes?," *CEPR Discussion Papers* 5470.

Hüpkes, E. H. G., M. Quintyn, and M. Taylor (2005), "The Accountability of Financial Sector Supervisors: Theory and Practice," *European Business Law Review* 16: 1575–1620.

International Monetary Fund and World Bank (2002), "Implementation of the Basel Core Principles for Effective Banking Supervision: Experiences, Influences and Perspectives," *IMF and World Bank Background Papers*, Washington, DC.

Kane, E. (1990), "Principal-Agent Problems in S&L Salvage," *Journal of Finance* 45: 755–764.

Kaufmann, D., A. Kraay, and M. Mastruzzi (2003), *Governance Matters III: Governance Indicators 1996–2002*, World Bank Policy Research Department Working Paper, (Washington, DC: World Bank).

Keefer, P. and D. Stasavage (2001), "Bureaucratic Delegation and Political Institutions: When Are Independent Central Banks Irrelevant?," mimeo.

Kydland, F. E. and E. C. Prescott (1977), "Rules rather than Discretion: The Inconsistency of Optimal Plans," *Journal of Political Economy* 85: 473–492.

La Porta, R., F. Lopez-de-Salinas, A. Shleifer, and R. Vishny (1998), "Law and Finance," *Journal of Political Economy* 106: 1113–1155.

Maciandaro, D. (2006), "E Pluribus Unum? Authorities Design in Financial Supervision: Trends and Determinants," *Open Economies Review* 17: 73–102.

(2007), "Divide et Impera: Financial Supervision Unification and the Central Bank Fragmentation Effect," *European Journal of Political Economy* 23: 285–315.

Masciandaro, D. and M. Quintyn (2008), "Helping Hand or Grabbing Hand? Politicians, Supervision Regime, Financial Structure and Market View," *North American Journal of Economics and Finance* 19: 153–173.

Mihailov, A. and K. Ullricht (2007), "Independence and Accountability of Monetary and Fiscal Policy Committees," mimeo.

Moser, P. (1999), "Checks and Balances, and the Supply of Central Bank Independence," *European Economic Review* 43: 1569–1593.

Oosterloo, S. (2004), "Central Banks and Financial Stability: A Survey," *Journal of Financial Stability* 1: 257–273.

Oosterloo, S. and J. de Haan (2003), *A Survey of Institutional Frameworks for Financial Stability, Occasional Studies*, De Nederlandsche Bank 1 (4).

Peek, J., E. S. Rosengren, and G. M. B. Tootle (1999), "Is Bank Supervision Central to Central Banking?," *Quarterly Journal of Economics* 114: 629–653.

Quintyn, M. (2007a), *Governance of Financial Supervisors and Its Effects—A Stocktaking Exercise*, SUERF Studies 2007/4, Vienna, Austria.

(2007b), *Independent Agencies—More than cheap copies of Independent Central Banks*, paper presented at Conference "Separation of Powers: New Doctrinal Perspectives and Empirical Findings," University of Haifa, Israel, December.

Quintyn, M. and M. W. Taylor (2003), "Regulatory and Supervisory Independence and Financial Stability," *CESifo, Economic Studies* 49: 259–294.

(2007), "Robust Regulators and Their Political Masters," in D. Masciandaro and M. Quintyn (Eds.), *Designing Financial Supervision Institutions: Independence, Accountability and Governance*, (Cheltenham: Edward Elgar).

Quintyn, M., S. Ramirez, and M. W. Taylor (2007), "The Fear of Freedom. Politicians and the Independence and Accountability of Financial Supervisors," in D. Masciandaro and M. Quintyn (Eds.), *Designing Financial Supervision Institutions: Independence, Accountability and Governance* (Cheltenham: Edward Elgar).

Rogoff, K. (1985), "Optimal Degree of Commitment to an Intermediate Monetary Target: Inflation Gains Versus Stabilization Costs," *Quarterly Journal of Economics* 100 (November): 1169–1189.

Shiller, R. J. (1997), "Why do people dislike inflation?" in C. D. Romer and D. H. Romer (Ed.), *Reducing Inflation: Motivation and Strategy* (University of Chicago Press).

Shleifer A. and R. Vishny (1998), *The Grabbing Hand* (Cambridge: Harvard University Press).

Siklos, P. L. (2002), *The Changing Face of Central Banking. Evolutionary Trends since World War II* (Cambridge: Cambridge University Press).

Stiglitz, J. (1998), "Central banking in a democratic society," *De Economist* 146: 199–226.

Stigler, G. (1971), "The Theory of Economic Regulation," *Bell Journal of Economics and Management Science* 6 (2): 114–141.

Tognato, C. (2004), "In the name of money: Central banking as a secular religion," Manuel Ancizar Lecture, Universidad Nacional, Bogotá, October 30.

University of Maryland (2006), *Polity IV* project. Available at
    http://www.cidcm.umd.edu/polity
Westrup, J. (2007), "Independence and Accountability: Why Politics Matter," in D.
    Masciandaro and M. Quintyn (Eds.), *Designing Financial Supervision Institutions:
    Independence, Accountability, and Governance* (Cheltenham, UK: Edward Elgar).
World Bank (2003), *World Development Indicators* (Washington DC: World Bank).

PART III

TRANSPARENCY AND GOVERNANCE IN
CENTRAL BANKING

9

The Economic Impact of Central Bank Transparency: A Survey

Carin van der Cruijsen and Sylvester C.W. Eijffinger

Abstract

Since the move toward more central bank transparency, a lot of research on its desirability from an economic viewpoint has been carried out. We provide an up-to-date overview of this transparency literature. First, we show how the theoretical literature has evolved by looking into branches inspired by Cukierman and Meltzer (1986) and by investigating several, more recent research strands (e.g., coordination and learning). Then, we review the empirical literature that has been growing recently. Last, we discuss whether the empirical research resolves all theoretical question marks, how the findings of the literature match the actual practice of central banks, and where there is scope for more research.

9.1 Introduction

Central banks used to be very secretive, but in the last two decades a lot of central banks have changed their regime into a more transparent one.[1] As central banks became independent, transparency gained importance because it is a necessary prerequisite of accountability, for which the need increased. An additional reason why transparency came into prominence is its likely influence on the formation of expectations. With the

Views expressed are our own and do not necessarily reflect those of the institutions we are affiliated with. We would like to thank De Nederlandsche Bank seminar participants, and Jakob De Haan, Maria Demertzis, Peter van Els, Marco Hoeberichts, Lex Hoogduin, Joris Knoben, Pierre Siklos, Job Swank, two anonymous referees, and participations of the conference "Frontiers in Central Banking" (Central Bank of Hungary, 2007) for helpful comments and suggestions.

[1] Goodfriend (1986) provides a nice summary of, and comments on, the Fed's written defense for secrecy made in 1975 when it was sued to make its policy directive and minutes public immediately after Federal Open Market Committee meetings.

increased importance of financial markets, managing inflation expectations has become key in monetary policymaking. It determines the success
of the transmission of monetary policy. There are several benefits from successfully steering market expectations, like reduced uncertainty, improved
planning of market participants, lower interest rate volatility, and more
effective monetary policy (e.g., Issing 2005). It is, however, not obvious
whether transparency actually improves the steering of market expectations.
Although a lot of research has been conducted in this field, no agreement
has yet been achieved on the desirability of transparency from an economic
viewpoint. These studies vary with respect to the analyzed aspect of transparency and their method of analysis, which makes it difficult to assess an
overall pattern.

Central bank transparency is often defined in the literature as "the
absence of asymmetric information between the central bank and the private sector." According to this narrow definition of transparency, the degree
of transparency automatically increases when the central banks provide
more information. However, in practice, more information does not always
improve the public's understanding. A broader definition of transparency
accounts for this fact and defines transparency as "...the degree of common understanding of monetary policy between the central bank and the
public." (Winkler 2002, 402).

We provide more insight into the transparency literature, refraining
from accountability issues. By doing so, several questions will be answered:
(1) Does the theoretical literature come to a unanimous conclusion with
regard to the desirability of transparency? (2) If not, what causes differences in outcomes? (3) Does the empirical literature provide answers to
some potential theoretical question marks? (4) Is there scope for further
research?

This is not the first overview of the literature on the economic effects of
central bank transparency. Earlier surveys discussed the literature based on
different categorizations of transparency (Geraats 2002; Hahn 2002; Carpenter 2004) or views of transparency (Posen 2003).[2] Since the realization
of these overview papers, however, the literature on central bank transparency has further developed. Moreover, several new theoretical research
strands emerged, such as the work on coordination games, committees,
and the literature on learning. Our survey describes the chronological
development of the theoretical transparency literature to give more insight
into its development. In addition, and only starting to evolve recently, a lot of

---

[2] See Geraats (2006) for an overview of the practice of monetary policy transparency.

empirical research has been performed, and is reviewed as well. To improve the insight into the desirability of more transparency from an economic viewpoint, an up-to-date overview is needed. Note that we focus on the literature that analyzes the effects of longer-lasting transparency changes, and steer clear of works on the effects of day-to-day communication, which is reviewed by Blinder et al. (2008).

Figure 9.1 summarizes the chronological evolution of the theoretical transparency literature.

We start by exploring the theoretical literature based on the seminal work of Cukierman and Meltzer (1986), henceforth CM (1986). Three different branches that are (partly) based on this work are distinguished and discussed in chronological order. They differ in the specific aspect of transparency that is discussed: transparency about preferences, economic transparency, or control-error transparency. Besides the research inspired by CM (1986), we summarize various other strands of the theoretical literature. The research based on reserve targeting models, which dates from the end of the 1980s and the beginning of the 1990s, has become outdated because, nowadays,

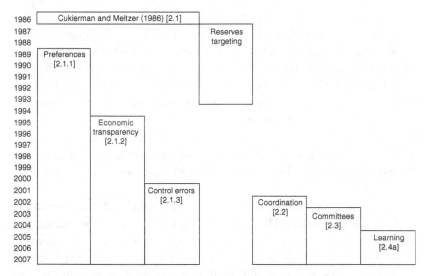

Figure 9.1. Overview of the theoretical transparency literature
Note: This figure summarizes the theoretical transparency literature. We distinguish five different strands: (1) Cukierman and Meltzer (1986), (2) Reserves targeting, (3) Coordination, (4) Committees, and (5) Learning. Strand (1) consists of three separate branches: (a) preferences, (b) economic transparency, and (c) control errors. The numbers in brackets in the figure correspond with the subsections in which these parts of the literature will be discussed. The time line is on the vertical axis.

almost all central banks target interbank or repo-rates instead. Therefore, it is not discussed in detail in this chapter. Recently, several new strands of literature emerged which will be analyzed herein. The analysis of transparency within coordination games is a concept first introduced by Morris and Shin (2002). The idea is that there is public as well as private information about the fundamentals of the economy. Agents want to match these fundamentals, but face a coordination motive as well. Another recently emerged strand of literature analyzes the effect of transparency within monetary policy committees (e.g., Sibert 2003; Maier this volume). The newest strand of research discussed here is the learning literature based on Evans and Honkapohja (2001), which, in contrast to the previous literature on central banking, does not assume rational expectations. After Svensson (2003) pointed out that the effect of transparency on learning was largely neglected, research within this field evolved. This strand of literature assumes that agents engage in learning; for example, about the central bank's policy model. Managing inflation expectations then becomes more important.

The ultimate test for the desirability of transparency from an economic standpoint is empirical research. One requirement for empirical research is to have some measure of transparency at one's disposal. At first, empirical research was hindered by the lack of transparency data. Later on, the construction of several measures of transparency enabled more empirical research. Several researchers have attempted to measure transparency, e.g., Bini-Smaghi and Gros (2001), Siklos (2002), Chortareas et al. (2002a), and Haan et al. (2004). A disadvantage of these measures is that they are time invariant. In contrast, the Eijffinger and Geraats (2006) index contains information about the relative degree of transparency of central banks *and* the timing of transparency events. Dincer and Eichengreen (2007) have used the Eijffinger and Geraats methodology to cover a longer data period (1998–2005 instead of 1998–2002) and included more central banks (100 instead of 9).

This chapter is structured as follows. In Section 9.2 we provide an overview of the theoretical literature. In order of appearance we discuss the findings of: CM (1986) and the research inspired by it (9.2.1), the coordination literature (9.2.2), the committee models (9.2.3), and the learning literature (9.2.4). We conclude on the theoretical literature in Subsection 9.2.5. In Section 9.3, we move to the empirical findings. Anticipation, synchronization, macroeconomic variable effects, and credibility, reputation, and flexibility effects are analyzed in separate subsections (9.3.1 to 9.3.4). A brief cross-country comparison of the results is given in Subsection 9.3.5. Finally, in Section 9.4, we discuss the findings and provide some directions for further research.

9.2 Theoretical Findings

We focus here on the particular aspect(s) of transparency that is (are) changed in a direct manner in the models used and on which more insights into its desirability is provided. We use the classification of Geraats (2002) into five different transparency categories:

1. *Political transparency* includes information provision about the central bank's goals: a formal statement of the target(s), how they are prioritized, and quantified. Institutional arrangements (e.g., central bank independence) lead to higher political transparency because there is less pressure to deviate from these objectives.
2. *Economic transparency* exists when the central bank shares the knowledge about the economy that it uses for monetary policy: the economic data, policy models, and internal forecasts.
3. *Procedural transparency* concerns openness about the procedures used to make monetary policy decisions. It is higher when the central bank is open about its strategy, and when it publishes voting records and minutes.
4. *Policy transparency* is present when the central bank announces and explains its policy decisions immediately and indicates future policy paths.
5. *Operational transparency* considers openness about how well policy actions are implemented. It is higher when the central bank is open about the control errors in realizing its operating instrument or the goal set, and when the central bank discusses the macroeconomic disturbances that influence the transmission process from policy instruments to outcomes.

The relevance of model choice is illustrated by Cukierman (2002), who compares the transmission of monetary policy in three different models: 1) a monetarist Lucas-type expectations augmented Phillips curve, 2) a neo-Keynesian model with backward-looking pricing, and 3) a new Keynesian model with fully forward-looking pricing. In the latter two models, nominal prices are sticky and therefore the nominal interest rate affects the real interest rate. In these three models, monetary policy affects inflation and output levels in different ways. In the first (Lucas-type) model, only unanticipated monetary policy has an effect on output and inflation is directly related to the money supply (quantity theory of money). In the other two models, short-run output is demand determined. Independent of the presence of surprise inflation, interest rate changes can influence output by affecting demand. The effect that the policy choice has on the inflation rate depends on its effect on the size of the output gap. In the backward-looking neo-Keynesian model, current policy can affect the output gap with a one-period lag, and inflation with a 2-year lag. In contrast, in the forward-looking new Keynesian model, current policy can already affect the present values of the output gap and inflation by changing the expectations that currently exist about future variables.

In the next sections we will discuss the various strands of literature in chronological order. A summary of the theoretical literature is provided in Appendix A.

9.2.1 Cukierman and Meltzer (1986)

The theoretical work on the economic effects of central bank transparency started in the 1980s with the work of CM (1986). In this model the central bank determines the extent to which the public observes its targets by setting the quality of inflation control. The higher the latter, the easier it is for economic agents to deduce the central bank's objectives by looking at past inflation. Based on the optimal policy models by Kydland and Prescott (1977), and Barro and Gordon (1983b), CM (1986) conclude that the economic desirability of transparency is ambiguous. To give an idea of how they reach this result, we briefly describe the general structure of their model and discuss the intuition of the results that CM found based on this model.

As is shown by equation (1), period i's realized inflation rate (π_i) is a function of the policymaker's planned inflation rate (π_i^p). Control is imperfect; ψ_i is a stochastic serially uncorrelated normal variate. Its mean is zero and its variance is σ_ψ^2.

$$\pi_i = \pi_i^p + \psi_i \tag{1}$$

Equation (2) is the central bank's multiperiod, state-dependent objective function. The central bank chooses the planned rate of inflation such that this objective function, which depends on both inflation and output, is maximized. Ceteris paribus, lower inflation is preferred. In addition, central banks want to create surprise inflation to stimulate output.[3] In equation (2), β is the central bank's discount factor, E_0 is the expected value operator conditioned on the available information in period 0, including a direct observation of the central bank's period 0 weight (x_0) attached to inflation surprises (e_i) to stimulate output. The policymaker's choice of the planned

---

[3] Variations on this maximization problem are used in other theoretical transparency papers.

inflation rate depends on its weight attached to the benefits of surprise inflation (economic stimulation) and its costs (higher inflation).

$$\max_{\{\pi_i^p, i=0,1,...\}} E_0 \sum_{i=0}^{\infty} \beta^i \left(e_i x_i - \frac{(\pi_i^p)^2}{2} \right) \tag{2}$$

The central bank knows the manner in which the public forms its expectations about inflation, up to a random shock. Therefore the central bank knows the unanticipated rate of inflation (e_i) [as defined in equation (3)] it creates by picking a particular planned inflation rate. $E[\pi_i | I_i]$ is the public's forecast of realized inflation, given the public's information set I_i. This information set includes the realized inflation rate up to and including the previous period.

$$e_i = \pi_i - E[\pi_i | I_i] \tag{3}$$

Equation (4) describes the central bank's shift parameter x_i. It is more likely to be positive than negative and the shift parameter changes in response to unanticipated events. These preferences show some persistence, which is a function of a constant A (which measures the bias toward economic stimulation) and a time-varying component p_i.

$$x_i = A + p_i, \quad A > 0 \tag{4}$$

This time-varying component depends on its past value, with the strength ρ (between 0 and 1), and on a serially uncorrelated normal variate (v) that does not depend on the control error (ψ_i):

$$p_i = \rho p_{i-1} + v_i, 0 < \rho < 1, \quad v \sim N\left(0, \sigma_v^2\right) \tag{5}$$

The public cannot observe the weight attached to surprise inflation (x_i) directly. Control errors can be used to hide shifts in preferences. Based on past observations of inflation, the public then imperfectly infers x_i. For more model details and the derivation of the results, we refer to the CM (1986) paper. For the aim and scope of this review it is sufficient to take a look at the results that they found. The planned inflation rate is described by equation (6).

$$\pi_i^p = \frac{1 - \beta\rho}{1 - \beta\lambda} A + \frac{1 - \beta\rho^2}{1 - \beta\rho\lambda} p_i \tag{6}$$

When equation (6) is put into equation (1) the actual inflation rate turns out to be:

$$\pi_i = \frac{1 - \beta\rho}{1 - \beta\lambda} A + \frac{1 - \beta\rho^2}{1 - \beta\rho\lambda} p_i + \psi_i \tag{7}$$

The actual unconditional mean of the inflation rate is:

$$E(\pi_i) = \frac{1 - \beta\rho}{1 - \beta\lambda}A. \tag{8}$$

When there is some degree of time preference ($\beta < 1$), a higher bias of the central bank toward economic stimulation (A) leads to higher average inflation. When inflation control is less effective (a higher variance of the control errors: σ_ψ^2), the adjustment of expectations is slowed down (the memory of the public of past policies, λ, is higher; i.e., recent developments carry less weight in the formation of current expectations). Because the public is slower in recognizing shifts to a more expansionary policy, the detrimental effects of surprise inflation are delayed and therefore the central bank gains more from current surprise inflation at the cost of future inflation.

The variance of the inflation rate is given by equation (9).

$$V(\pi_i) = \left[\frac{1 - \beta\rho^2}{1 - \beta\rho\lambda}\right]^2 \frac{\sigma_v^2}{1 - \rho^2} + \sigma_\psi^2 \tag{9}$$

From equation (9) it follows that, when there is some degree of time preference, the variance of the inflation rate, $V(\pi_i)$, is higher when inflation rate control is less effective (σ_ψ^2 higher). This impact is both direct (actual inflation rate is more variable for any planned inflation rate) and indirect via λ. Because λ is higher, the public is slower in finding out about shifts in the objectives and, as a result, it is more attractive for the central bank to stimulate the economy more by creating more uncertainty.

A central bank with a relatively high time preference is likely to prefer a higher degree of ambiguity. Given the variance of the inflation rate control error, the lower the discount factor β, the higher $V(\pi_i)$. In this case the costs of future expected inflation are less important in the objective function and, therefore, it is more attractive to stimulate the current economy. This is possible by creating more uncertainty [$V(e)$, which is the variance of the unanticipated inflation rate], partly resulting in higher inflation rate variability.

When the central bank chooses the quality of inflation rate control, the degree of transparency is set. More effective inflation rate control increases transparency and makes it is easier for the public to deduce the central bank's objectives by looking at past inflation. As a result, inflation expectations (which depend both on the policymaker's mean planned inflation and the actual past observations) become more sensitive to past policy outcomes, the public learns faster, credibility is higher, and the inflation bias is reduced.

In addition, however, there is a detrimental effect of more transparency. The policymaker's ability to use surprise inflation to stimulate output is reduced. When this detrimental effect is relatively strong, central banks might prefer ambiguity. It makes it easier to use positive surprise inflation when it is needed the most, and negative surprise inflation in periods in which it is relatively concerned about inflation.

Several branches of literature started by building on the CM model. Based on the particular aspect of transparency that is analyzed in a direct manner, papers are put into three different branches: (1) preference transparency (see "Preferences"), (2) economic transparency (see "Economic Transparency"), and (3) control error transparency (see "Control Errors").

Preferences

Many economists argue in favor of more political transparency because it may improve the reputation and credibility of the central bank (e.g., King 1997; Friedman 2003; Thornton 2003). But transparency about the objective function of the central bank may be difficult to realize, and a role for output in the objective function may confuse the public. It may lead the public to believe that the central bank focuses on counteracting short-run output fluctuations, resulting in higher inflation expectations and higher actual inflation (Mishkin 2004).

Several theoretical papers analyze the desirability of preference transparency. Most of these papers are related to CM (1986). Preference transparency concerns the relative weight attached to the goals in the central bank's objective function (in terms of the CM model, transparency about x_i). In addition, some papers look at transparency about the central bank's targets (in the CM model, e_i or π_i^p, but in an open economy model it could be the target for the exchange rate). Transparency about the weights in the objective function and transparency about the targets are two of the components of political transparency, as defined by Geraats (2002).

Instead of looking at information given by actions of the central bank as CM (1986) do, Stein (1989) analyzes the provision of information using words. He argues that there is a reason why the central bank will not be completely transparent about its target for the exchange rate. The idea in this open-economy model is that, although transparency about objectives potentially leads to a more swift market reaction, the market knows the central bank is tempted to manipulate inflation expectations and would therefore never belief precise announcements by the central bank. In contrast, when given only the opportunity to talk less precisely (e.g., announce a range within which the target lies), the central bank's ability to manipulate expectations has become crude (big lies are needed if it wants to lie) and has the potential to do more harm than good.

Lewis (1991) shows why secrecy of central banks might be desirable from society's point of view, as well. First, secrecy about policy intentions (CM model, v_i is only known by the central bank and therefore p_i and through it x_i) prevents central banks from being secretive in other more costly ways (greater monetary noise, ψ_i). Second, secrecy might be beneficial when the social trade-offs between policy objectives change over time. The central bank is then able to use surprise inflation when society prefers it the most.

Another argument why uncertainty about the preferences of the central bank might be desirable is that it could lead to wage moderation to limit real wage uncertainty as it is unclear in which way the central bank might react to wage claims (Sørensen 1991). More wage discipline lowers inflation and boosts output. In case of an unemployment problem that is large enough and exogenous shocks to unemployment that are not too big, these effects outweigh the resulting higher variability of inflation and unemployment. Using a model very similar to Sørensen's (1991), Grüner (2002) too argues in favor of limited central bank transparency based on lower wages and, as a consequence, average inflation and unemployment. But, in addition, it is shown that even when the only objective is to have low inflation uncertainty, transparency might not be desirable because, under bounded rationality of the public, it may lead to a higher variance of inflation.

Several other papers argue in favor of secrecy, too, because their models show lower resulting inflation rates as well. Cukierman (2002), using a new Keynesian model setting, shows that when the central bank is a flexible inflation targeter, the absence of transparency about the loss function and the weight attached to output gap stabilization is important to maintain credibility. Even when policymakers target the average natural level of employment, flexible inflation targeting in conjunction with asymmetric output gap objectives leads to credibility problems. The higher the flexibility of the central bank in targeting inflation, the higher the inflation bias. Secrecy about preferences can prevent an increase in inflation expectations, which affects current pricing decisions.

According to Sibert (2002), secrecy about the preferences of central bankers leads them to inflate less because they want to signal that they are of a good type (relatively low weight on output) so as to obtain lower inflation expectations.[4] These lower inflation expectations make the trade-off

---

[4] Only for the central banker with the highest weight on output does this mechanism not function. This type will be revealed and, therefore, inflation expectations cannot be improved.

between inflation and output favorable, which makes it possible to respond more strongly to shocks.

In contrast, various other papers point out that preference transparency may, in fact, be beneficial for the level of inflation. In the majority of these papers, however, this benefit comes at the cost of the flexibility to stabilize the economy, which could still make transparency undesirable from an overall welfare perspective.

Transparency could reduce the inflation bias for countries with a bad inflation history or relatively little independence, as argued by Schaling and Nolan (1998). The benefit from greater transparency is higher when the degree of inflation aversion of the central bank is relatively low. In Walsh (1999), inflation targeting lowers the average inflation bias when the announced target is equal to the socially optimal inflation rate (which is a function of the supply shocks that are unknown to the public). The central bank's response to supply shocks would be distorted if there were a noncontingent explicit inflation target that is equal to the expected socially optimal rate. Instead, the central bank could set an inflation target that is based on unverifiable internal forecasts of supply shocks and announce it before the private sector forms its inflation expectations. This announcement reveals private information about supply shocks. The imperfectly credible inflation target that is announced by the central bank could lead to a lower inflation bias without affecting the stabilization policy.

In Eijffinger et al. (2000), transparency lowers inflation as well, because wage setters perceive the central bank as more conservative, and less uncertainty reduces the volatility of inflation.[5] However, it increases the volatility of output in response to supply shocks, which is harmful for society's welfare. When the need for output stabilization policy is large compared to the severity of the time-inconsistency problem, secrecy may be desirable. This trade-off is confirmed by Eijffinger and Hoeberichts (2002), who find improved independence associated with more transparency. However, Beetsma and Jensen (2003) show that the findings of Eijffinger et al. (2000) are not robust to changes in the way in which preference uncertainty is modeled. In addition, they note that one would reach superior outcomes with other arrangements (e.g., an inflation contract or target) or immediately choosing the optimal degree of conservatism. This prevents the need for secrecy to stabilize the inefficiently high output variability associated with a suboptimal degree of conservatism.

---

[5]   The result remains intact when Eijffinger et al. (2000) correct for computational mistakes (Eijffinger et al. 2003), in response to Beetsma and Jensen (2003). Also, see the discussion that follows.

According to Hughes Hallett and Viegi (2003), the central bank wants to limit the amount of transparency about the relative weights in its objective function to benefit from lower inflation (that comes at the cost of fiscal stability). In contrast, the private sector would benefit from this form of transparency because their decisions become better informed. The same holds for transparency about the central bank's output target. Instead, assuming reasonable parameter values, reducing this form of transparency does not deliver any strategic benefits for the central bank, although it might be a substitute for credibility.

Hughes Hallett and Libich (2006) show that goal transparency, which is preferred over goal independence, works as a commitment device. It makes the policymakers more accountable for price stability by threats of punishment, which lowers inflation and improves credibility. Demertzis and Hughes Hallett (2007) demonstrate that political transparency leads to a reduction of the variability of inflation and the output gap, but has no implications for their average levels.

When the public is uncertain about the amount of central bank transparency, a discrepancy between actual and perceived transparency might exist and this will affect the economy (Geraats 2007). Actual transparency makes the noise of communication smaller, which is beneficial. However, perceived transparency is not always beneficial because markets become more sensitive to information. Whereas clarity about the inflation target is desirable, clarity about the output gap target and supply shocks is not.

In summary, the theoretical research on the effects of preference transparency does not give a unanimous answer with regard to its desirability.

Economic Transparency

The feasibility and desirability of economic transparency is heavily debated as well. Regarding its feasibility, some forms of economic transparency may not be so easy to realize in practice. For example, transparency about the economic model used may not be feasible because there is no consensus on the correct model of the economy (Cukierman 2001). Even when some form of economic transparency is assumed to be feasible, it is not clear whether transparency is actually desirable. For example, opponents of economic transparency argue that when forecasts are published, the danger exists that the public attaches too much weight to them (Issing 1999); similarly, when forecasts are provided, too often they could undermine the central bank's credibility as an inflation targeter (Cukierman 2001). Proponents of transparency argue, however, that more economic transparency may improve the markets' understanding of the central bank's actions (e.g., Blinder et al. 2001), and improve the forecasting quality and credibility (e.g. Mishkin 2004).

Several theoretical papers on economic transparency discussed in the following are (partly) inspired by CM (1986). They analyze the desirability of releasing the central bank's information on economic shocks, and the model and outcomes of forecasts. Therefore, all components of economic transparency as defined by Geraats (2002) are covered. Economic information could, for example, make it easier to discover the intentions of the central bank (e.g., m_i^p in terms of the CM model).

Noisy announcements (those that provide a range on its forecast of the money-demand disturbance) may make the trade-off between flexibility (to stabilize output) and credibility (to eliminate the inflation bias) more favorable to the extent that the noisy announcements reveal the monetary authority's private forecast (Garfinkel and Oh 1995). By influencing expectations, the monetary authority can stabilize employment even when there is a monetary rule.

Cukierman (2001) points out that transparency about economic shocks might lead to social inefficiencies. He presents two different models. The first is a model with a simple stochastic Lucas-supply function. Transparency exists when information about supply shocks is provided before inflation expectations are being formed. Then the central bank looses its information advantage and can no longer stabilize these disturbances. The second model presented is neo-Keynesian. In this model, the central bank's instrument is the nominal interest rate that, because of inflation expectations that are already formed, determines the real interest rate. Changes in the real interest rate affect demand then affects inflation with a one-period lag. Transparency is still defined as before, but in this model monetary policy plays a role under transparency. Transparency makes inflation expectations more sensitive to policy actions and, as a result, the central bank needs to change the nominal interest rate more often to achieve the same level of stabilization of output and inflation. Transparency is still disadvantageous if society dislikes variability of the nominal interest rate.

According to Gersbach (2003) transparency about supply shocks that affect unemployment (e.g., through publishing forecasts and forecasting models or through releasing minutes) is detrimental because it eliminates the central bank's possibility to stabilize employment.

Several more-recent papers, however, highlight that economic transparency may be beneficial. In Chortareas et al. (2003), transparency about economic shocks (the part of the demand shock that the central bank forecasts correctly) can lower the sacrifice ratio of disinflation efforts, the reason being that it is easier for the public to find out the central bank's preferences (also see Chortareas and Miller, this volume).

In Hoeberichts, Tesfaselassie, and Eijffinger (2004), when the central bank is transparent about the manner in which it assesses the private sector's inflation and output-gap expectations, the public can forecast the errors that the central bank makes with this assessment. In their model, transparency may improve output stabilization, and increasingly so depending upon how central bank is. However, it makes the stabilization of the inflation rate more difficult because the central bank will use the interest rate to stabilize the effect of the error on the output gap. Nevertheless, overall social welfare is increased.

In Geraats's (2005) model, transparency about the forecasts makes the interest rate a better signaling device of the central bank's preferences. Therefore, inflation expectations will react more to interest rates, which indicates the reputation of the central bank. Central bankers become more interested in building up a reputation, because it is easier to do so when the markets watch the signals more closely. As a result the inflation bias will be lower. When the central bank can choose how much transparency to provide, it is more likely that even when the central bank is weak, concerns about its reputation will make it choose to become transparent. Otherwise the market will punish the central bank with a larger inflation bias. Note that this analysis is desired from forecasts that are based on an explicit interest rate (path) to ensure that transparency creates beneficial incentive effects. In case of unconditional forecasts, the inflation target is directly revealed and the inflation bias is not necessarily reduced because the behavioral incentive (reputation building) is not present.

Gersbach and Hahn (2006) show that transparency about private information about macroeconomic shocks can reduce the margin between the targets announced by the central bank and future inflation. Prerequisite is that this private information is verifiable, otherwise the central bank has an incentive to lie.

Another paper that argues in favor of more transparency is the research by Eijffinger and Tesfaselassie (2007). When combined with political transparency, economic transparency turns out to be desirable. It stabilizes current inflation and output.

Recently some central banks started publishing their interest rate forecasts. Rudebusch and Williams (2008) show that this transparency change might help align financial market expectations and improve macroeconomic outcomes. Prerequisite is that the central bank communicates clearly that interest rate projections are conditional and surrounded by uncertainty. Otherwise the public might interpret the interest rate forecast as an unconditional commitment of the central bank and might put too much weight on it, with all the effects it implies.

Overall, although the results found are mixed, we observe a trend of subsiding disagreement; more recent articles on economic transparency are in favor of it.

Control Errors

Several papers analyze the economic implications of transparency about control errors (in the CM model, ψ_i), and thereby build upon CM (1986). Transparency about control errors in achieving the operating targets is one aspect of operational transparency, as defined by Geraats (2002).[6]

Faust and Svensson (2001), henceforth FS, modified the model of CM (1986) by making the loss-function quadratic in the output gap and distinguishing between imperfect monetary control and operational transparency, which measures the degree to which control errors are made public. Given the level of monetary control, and assuming secrecy about the output targets of the central bank, operational transparency will be beneficial for the central bank's reputation. Inflation expectations of the public will be more strongly linked to realized inflation, which makes deviations from the announced zero inflation path more costly for the central bank. Therefore the central bank is less likely to engage in inflation surprises, resulting in lower variability of both inflation and output. When, instead, it is assumed that there is transparency about the central bank's goals, then its actions do not affect its reputation. Inflation will be higher on average and so will the variability of inflation and employment. However, it is pointed out that, in a more complete model, it could well be that this form of transparency is beneficial, for example, when the public is able to force the central bank to obtain the public's goals.

In contrast to FS (2001), FS (2002) take up the endogenous choice of transparency and monetary control. Most likely there will be commitment about the choice of transparency, whereas there will be discretion about the choice of control. Then the likely outcome is that the degree of control is maximized, whereas the choice of transparency depends on the type of central bank. If the central bank cares enough about the future and has a relatively low inflation bias, then it will commit to minimum transparency. The public can punish this patient central bank relatively heavily by reducing future reputation ex post for inflation surprises. Therefore, lower transparency need not lead ex ante to a similar increase in the inflation bias. In addition, when the central bank targets the natural rate of employment in

---

[6] In addition, operational transparency covers a discussion of how the transmission of monetary policy is influenced by (unanticipated) macroeconomic shocks and consist of an analysis of the central bank's performance.

the absence of shocks, then there is no inflation bias independent of the degree of transparency. In contrast, a central bank is likely to commit to maximum transparency when it has a history of high inflation because the benefits in terms of improved monetary performance are relatively large.

Jensen (2002) shows that, within a forward-looking model, some intermediate degree of transparency may be optimal. Transparency about the control errors makes it easier for the public to deduce the central bank's intentions, which makes inflation expectations, and therefore inflation, more sensitive to policy actions. As a consequence, the central bank is likely to pay more attention to inflation. Although beneficial for a central bank that faces a low degree of credibility, this could be detrimental for a highly credible central bank because it makes stabilizing output more costly in terms of inflation. The optimal degree of transparency is determined by the trade-off between credibility (and the related degree of inflation) and the flexibility to stabilize output. If the central bank instead reveals its preferences for output directly, the full information case, then expectations do not react to central bank's actions, and therefore the central bank would remain flexible to stabilize output.

Sibert (2006a) shows that in the absence of nontransparency (control errors not observed), private information about the preferences (weights in the objective function) leads to lower inflation and the ability to react to shocks is better. When private information about preferences exists, an increase in the degree of transparency has the beneficial effect of lowering equilibrium-planned inflation (both level and variance) without affecting the ability to respond to shocks. When the central bank is transparent, the public can deduce the central bank's actions by looking at realized inflation. Instead, it need not be easier for the public to find out what the central bank's preferences are. Numerical simulations show that complete transparency is always preferred.

To conclude, whether more transparency about control errors is beneficial or not is still open to debate. The earlier papers within this branch of literature find a trade-off between credibility (the level of inflation) and flexibility (the degree of output stabilization), as did CM (1986), whereas according to the most recent paper, this trade-off is nonexistent and transparency is desirable.

9.2.2 Coordination

Through its effect on the formation of inflation expectations, transparency influences economic outcomes. The manner in which agents form expectations is therefore crucial when determining whether transparency is desirable or not. A relatively new strand of literature that analyzes the effects of transparency on the formation of expectations is the work based on coordination games.

Morris and Shin (2002), henceforth MS (2002), analyze the social value of public information based on a model in which agents have public and private information about the underlying fundamentals that they want to match. In addition, they second guess the actions of other agents (coordination motive). The smaller the distance between a player's own action and the actions of other players, the greater is the individual reward. But from an aggregate viewpoint, this coordination does not improve welfare. When public information is the only source of information about the economic fundaments, greater precision in providing this kind of information always leads to higher social welfare because it helps agents align their actions with economic fundamentals. Instead, when some private information is available, and this information is very precise, more public information is likely to lower social welfare. The coordination motive causes agents to put too much weight on the public signal (compared to the private signal) than is justified by the level of its precision. Damage resulting from noise in the public information (worsening the forecast of the economic fundamentals and thereby harming the actions taken by the economic agents) might be magnified as a consequence.

Svensson (2006) shows that for empirically reasonable parameter values, the research performed by MS (2002) actually favors greater transparency. The only circumstance in which the welfare is locally decreasing in case of additional transparency (higher precision of the public signal) is when (1) each agent gives more weight to the beauty contest (coordinating its actions with others) than to bringing its actions in line with economic fundamentals, and (2) the noise in the public signal is at least eight times higher than the noise of the private signal. The latter is not likely because, compared to an individual, central banks devote a considerable amount of resources to collecting and interpreting data. In addition, Svensson uses a global analysis, assuming the public signal is at least as precise as the private signal, to show that no public information at all is never desirable.

Morris et al. (2006) are inclined to agree with Svensson's analysis, but note in response to the global analysis that when the weight to coordination becomes close to one in the utility function, then the precision of public information need not be that low for the absence of public information to be preferred. Morris et al. shift the debate to the empirical question of whether the degree of precision of the public signal is sufficient enough to be in favor of transparency. The authors highlight that, in addition to looking at alternative welfare functions, it is important to analyze the correlations between signals:

> The central bank holds a mirror to the economy for cues for its future actions, but the more effective it has been in manipulating the beliefs of the market, the more the central bank will see merely its own reflection (Morris et al. 2006, 464).

In another paper Morris and Shin (2005) argue that providing too much information to steer market expectations might be harmful. It could lower the informativeness of financial markets and prices and, therefore, worsen public information (which is thus endogenous).

Angeletos and Pavan (2004) assume that there are investment complementarities, which imply that the individual gain from investment is increasing in the total level of investment. When these complementarities are weak, no matter the structure of information, the equilibrium is unique, and more public information (either relative or absolute precision) is desirable because it improves coordination (although it might increase aggregate volatility). What drives this result is the assumption that, in contrast to the assumption in the MS (2002) paper, more effective coordination is socially valuable. Increased precision of private information might reduce welfare by increasing the heterogeneity of expectations, which makes coordination more problematic. When complementarities are strong, two equilibria, one good and the other bad, are possible. Increased transparency facilitates more effective coordination on either one of these equilibria. The only case in which transparency might not be a good idea is when the market is likely to coordinate on the bad equilibrium.

Walsh (2007) agrees that the reduction of price dispersion is desirable from an aggregate point of view. His analysis shows that while increased precision of central banks' forecasts of *cost* disturbances (or lower persistence of these shocks) increases the optimal degree of economic transparency, the optimal level is lower when the central bank is better able to forecast *demand* disturbances (or these disturbances become less persistent).

Several other papers argue in favor of transparency based on coordination games. Pearlman (2005) argues that the central bank should disclose as much economic information about aggregate demand shocks as possible, and without noise, because it leads to higher welfare. The optimal degree of transparency is positive under all circumstances in Cornand and Heinemann (2004). Sometimes, to prevent overreaction to public information, however, it is better to withhold information from some agents.

Demertzis and Hoeberichts (2007) show that, when introducing costs to information precision into the MS (2002) framework and for reasonable parameter values, a trade-off exists between increasing the precision of public information and the accuracy of private information. Increasing the degree of transparency is not necessarily desirable in all circumstances.

Demertzis and Viegi (2008) argue that it can be beneficial for the central bank to provide numerical inflation targets because it can be effective in coordinating expectations of the private sector toward the central bank's goal. Necessary conditions are that the supply shocks that hit the economy are not large and all other public information does not give a clear signal of what inflation is intended to be.

In Lindner (2006) more transparency about the way in which the central bank has assessed the strength of the economy, does not affect public information about the assessment itself but increases the precision of private information. Multiple equilibria are less likely, which makes currency markets more stable.

Overall, we conclude that although, at a first glance, it seems that the work of MS (2002) argues against transparency, it turned out that for reasonable parameter values, their approach actually favors transparency. Indeed, most of the research that has been built upon MS's work is in favor of (at least some degree of) transparency. It is important to note, however, that for the social welfare effect to be positive, it matters *what* the central bank talks about. Although the central bank might wish to coordinate expectations about its monetary policy, it does not want to coordinate expectations about possible problems in the financial system. Cukierman (2008) shows that doing so would increase the chance of a financial crises, which would harm the risk sharing of liquidity shocks and also long-term investments.

9.2.3 Committees

A separate strand of literature models decision making within committees to analyze whether more procedural transparency is desirable. The publication of minutes could be desirable because it leads to accountability, but these minutes should preferably be nonattributed to stimulate open debate (Buiter 1999). On the other hand, the publication of minutes may be harmful, as disagreement within the council would become public, which could harm the central bank's credibility. In addition, it could lead to less exchange of information and viewpoints, informal group meetings, and manipulation of the minutes to make them less informative (Cukierman 2001). The publication of individual votes makes it possible to assess the competence of individual members (Buiter 1999), but may damage the collective responsibility and may come at the cost of clarity, predictability, and coherence of the policy signaled by the committee (Issing 1999). The efficiency and quality of policymaking may decrease when individual members worry about national and personal interests (Issing 1999; Cukierman 2001).

Blinder et al. (2001) argue that the manner of communication depends on the policymakers in place. With one central banker, a clear statement with the reasoning behind the decision is enough. In case of an individualistic committee, everyone votes in his or her own interest, therefore it is difficult to agree on one statement, but detailed minutes should be available as soon as possible. When the committee is collegial, it can more easily combine immediate statements and minutes. It is important that the message brought about should be consistent.

Sibert (2006b) shows that, as the number of committee members increases (something of practical relevance for the ECB), individual's effort decreases. This effect can be prevented by making sure that individual's contributions can be identified and assessed. Prerequisites are a clear objective, publication of voting records, and, at the most, five committee members. It is desirable to have a structure such that committee members do not act as a group member, because too much striving for consensus might lead members to give not enough attention to alternative actions.

The arguments in favor and against procedural transparency have formalized by constructing models of the committee decision-making process. Sibert (2003) models reputation building in monetary policy committees, and shows that it is important to publish the individual votes immediately. It raises the expected social welfare because the incentive of junior policymakers to vote in favor of policy against inflation is increased, as it now helps building up reputation. In addition, she finds that putting more weight to senior policymakers' votes, via increased incentives for the junior policymakers to build up reputation, is beneficial for welfare because they are then more likely to vote against inflation.[7]

Gersbach and Hahn (2004) demonstrate as well that it is desirable to publish voting records. In their model, transparency makes the selection of central bankers with desirable preferences easier, which leads to lower social losses. It should be noted, though, that only central bankers with preferences similar to the public would favor more transparency.

In contrast, when one assumes monetary policy within a monetary union, transparency might not be desirable. It makes it easier for national

---

[7] Under the precondition that the young policymakers sometimes vote for inflation.

governments to appoint central bankers who have preferences that are in line with national interests, but this might not be desirable for the aggregate monetary union social welfare. Gersbach and Hahn (2005) show that voting transparency can lead to more weight on national instead of supranational interests, which could make this kind of transparency undesirable when the central bankers' private benefits are relatively high (such that they care more about reappointments than about beneficial policy outcomes).

In Gersbach and Hahn (2008), procedural transparency makes it easier to reelect central bankers that are highly efficient (good at choosing the right interest rate), such that the competence level of the central bank governing council is increased. But central bankers who are less efficient try to imitate the more efficient ones, because they want to keep their jobs. Their interest rate guess is very likely wrong, and, therefore, it is less probable that the central bank will adopt the right interest rate policy. This detrimental effect of transparency makes procedural transparency undesirable.

In short, the theoretical literature on the procedural transparency does not reach a unanimous conclusion (also see Maier, this volume).

9.2.4 Learning

In the 1970s, the rational expectations hypothesis gained popularity. More recently, however, doubts about the rational expectations hypothesis have emerged because it is hard to believe that every economic agent behaves rationally. In reaction to this criticism, models that include learning agents were constructed. Agents are provided with learning algorithms that they update based on past data (e.g., Evans and Honkapohja 2005). For example, the private sector could be learning about the model used by the central bank uses in conducting monetary policy, whereas both the central bank and the public may have to learn about the way the economy works.

When one incorporates learning in models, managing inflation expectations becomes more important to central bankers (e.g., Orphanides and Williams 2005a). Svensson (2003) put forward the idea that transparency may improve learning by the private sector to form the right expectations about the economy and inflation, and as a result the decisions they make. Up to then, transparency was largely neglected in the learning literature.

Most papers in this strand of literature argue that more transparency is desirable. In Eusepi (2005), transparency about the policy rule can be helpful in reducing uncertainty and in stabilizing the learning process and expectations of the private sector. Without enough transparency, the economy might be destabilized through expectation-driven fluctuations, even when the central bank is not subject to an inflation bias. The effectiveness of monetary policy is lower so that interest rate changes need to occur more often and be larger. The weight that the central bank attaches to output will be higher than optimal (to stabilize the expectations) and the policy rule will prescribe the wrong type of history dependence (how current policy decisions are influenced by past conditions). In addition, it is shown that the publication of forecasts is also desirable. When the central bank and the private sector have different variables in their forecasting models, it enables market participants to learn about the monetary policy strategy.

Orphanides and Williams (2005b) find that when the central bank reveals its inflation target, it becomes easier for the public to learn the rational expectations equilibrium and to converge faster to an equilibrium. During disinflation periods, transparency helps in reducing inflation and unemployment persistence, as demonstrated by Westelius (2005) who combines the Barro and Gordon model with incomplete information and learning.

Some papers, however, show mixed results. Cone (2005) argues that transparency is undesirable if, and only if, the private sector's initial inflation forecast is in a certain interval near the equilibrium. The central bank observes the inflation expectations of the public before setting the inflation rate. Over time the public will learn the rational expectations equilibrium. Instead, when market beliefs differ too much from the rational expectations equilibrium, the central bank may be better off not basing policy on these expectations. In contrast, the central bank should be transparent about the true model and therewith influence the private sector beliefs directly.

In Berardi and Duffi (2007) the desirability of transparency in case of discretion is unclear and depends on the policy rate targets. For example, when a central bank has an output target larger than the natural rate and an inflation target of zero, it could be beneficial for the central bank to be secret and to fool the private sector by saying that it targets the natural rate of output. The resulting restricted perceptions equilibrium ensures that the private sector does not question the model. But, as an opposite example, when the central bank wants to achieve the natural rate of output and it has a target of inflation larger than zero, being transparent works better because it will help coordinate the private sector expectations toward this target, whereas fooling the market is of no use. Under commitment, Berardi and Duffi (2007) find that it is always desirable to be transparent, because the gain from commitment is larger when the public is able to adopt the right forecasting rule.

Overall, a majority of the papers that analyze the effects of transparency when agents learn, find that it can be a helpful tool to improve private sector learning and thereby the decisions that it makes. However some papers show that the finding in favor of transparency is conditional on further assumptions. This strand of research is still in its infancy, so more research in this field is both necessary and to be expected.

9.2.5 Conclusion on Theory

One finding that becomes clear from the survey of the theoretical literature is the fact that the debate on the desirability of central bank transparency continues to be a lively one. Since the theoretical research on the economic effects of central bank transparency began, the literature has evolved considerably. Theoretical papers are not overly concerned with the exact meaning of transparency (e.g., a link to concrete communication is often missing), but focus mainly on the effects of various degrees of transparency. From our review it is clear that increases in transparency have effects on both the sender of the information (the central bank), as well as the receiver of the information (the public).

One of the branches inspired by Cukierman and Meltzer's (1986) work looks into the effects of preference transparency and finds mixed results. While some papers discuss the effect of transparency on inflation, others dispute the effect on the central bank's ability to stabilize the economy. When economic transparency is considered we find that, although earlier papers argue against more transparency, more recent work favors it. A similar trend appears when control error transparency is regarded. Whereas earlier papers within this branch of literature report a trade-off between the central bank's credibility and flexibility to offset shocks, the most recent paper rejects this trade-off and shows that transparency is desirable.

More recently, three completely new strands in the literature have emerged, and research has focused on the way in which individuals take actions.

One strand is based on the work of Morris and Shin (2002). Most of the work building on the idea of coordination games is in favor of more public information. Some papers show, however, that there might be circumstances (e.g., when information provision is costly) or topics (such as financial stability) that make transparency undesirable.

Another strand of research analyzes decision making within committees. The discussion on the desirability of procedural transparency is mostly based on accountability arguments. Theoretical work on the economic implications gives mixed results. The manner in which committee members are modeled is pivotal. Probably a mixture of model assumptions used in the various committee models would be more realistic. For example, committee members might not only have different preferences, but also various qualities and national and supranational interests. However, such a combination would complicate the analysis and therefore make it difficult to come to an overall conclusion on procedural transparency.

The most recent literature deals with learning. Here, a more realistic idea is adopted, namely that the assumption of rational expectations is too strong. Hence, agents need to learn how the economy works. The majority of the work within this strand supports more transparency because it improves learning. One additional benefit of transparency could be that as agents are learning, transparency helps them to learn in the same direction so as to build consensus; for example, a consensus that keeping wages low is desirable. This strand of literature is still in its infancy.

Even small model differences can lead to a diversity of results. For example, in most papers that analyze the effects of political transparency, only unanticipated monetary policy has an effect on output. Additional assumptions dealing with the importance of reputation building, the manner in which wages are set, and the precise definition of transparency, do differ, however, and can account for differences in outcomes. One needs to keep in mind that while one particular mix of transparency might work for one type of central bank, it might not work for another, as Blinder (2007) emphasizes.

As time passes, models become more and more sophisticated. We observe a tendency that more recent work is in favor of transparency although some disagreement still persists about the benefits of procedural and preference transparency. Nevertheless, the ultimate answer to the question as to whether transparency is desirable depends on the findings of the empirical evaluations of transparency.

9.3 Empirical Evaluations of Transparency

The development of explicit indices for central bank transparency has enabled empirical research on theoretical specifications. In the following sections we review the empirical evidence to date. A summary of the empirical literature is provided in Appendix B.

9.3.1 Policy Anticipation

One aspect that the empirical literature has reviewed is the effect of transparency on the ability of economic agents to forecast the central bank's monetary policy decisions. Several researchers have analyzed financial market prices to check the predictability of the central bank's interest rate decisions in relation to its degree of transparency.

An improvement of monetary policy anticipation is found by the majority of papers in this field. This holds both for research about transparency in general (Muller and Zelmer 1999; Siklos 2003; Coppel and Connolly 2003; Swanson 2006; Lange et al. 2003; Drew and Karagedikli 2007), as well as for research that considers the anticipation effects of a change in a particular aspect of transparency. In this respect, all areas of transparency are covered. Evidence for improved predictability has been found as a result of political transparency (Haldane and Read 2000; Clare and Courtenay 2001; Lildholdt and Wetherilt 2004; Biefang-Frisancho Mariscal and Howells 2007), the publication of forecasts (Fujiwara 2005), voting records (Gerlach-Kristen 2004), and higher quality inflation reports (Fracasso et al. 2003). However, the latter could be due to better policymakers that cause both improved predictability and better quality of inflation reports. Results indicate that policy transparency has been beneficial for the predictability of monetary policy as well (Demiralp 2001; Poole et al. 2002; Kohn and Sack 2003; Poole and Rasche 2003; Rafferty and Tomljanovich 2002; Tuysuz 2007). Research in this field focuses mainly on the transparency increase at the U.S. Fed beginning in 1994. Since that time, interest rate decisions take place following a scheduled meeting of the Federal Open Market Committee (FOMC), and are immediately disclosed by a press statement. Ehrmann and Fratzscher (2007) show that the introduction of balance-of-risk assessments by the Fed in 1999 led the private sector to anticipate monetary policy decisions earlier.

Not all papers find improved anticipation effects. Reeves and Sawicki (2007) present evidence that near-term interest rate expectations are significantly affected by minutes and the inflation report. The timeliness with which minutes are published seems to matter. In contrast, it is harder to find significant effects of speeches and testimonies to parliamentary committees; perhaps because these provide information covering a larger array of topics, its effect is more subtle and more difficult to pick up. In addition, testimonies to parliamentary committees are especially backward-looking and do not contain much new information. Another finding of this empirical strand in the transparency literature is that it matters *what* the central bank is actually transparent about. Ehrmann and Fratzscher (2005) show that although transparency about different points of view about the economic outlook can improve anticipations of future monetary policy, this is not the case for transparency about committee members' disagreement about monetary policy.

9.3.2 Synchronization of Forecasts

Transparency has not only affected the quality of forecasts (e.g., Crowe and Meade 2008), but also their degree of synchronization. Biefang-Frisancho Mariscal and Howells (2007) show that transparency has improved consensus among forecasting agents about future monetary policy (measured by looking at the cross-sectional dispersion of agents' anticipation). However, further tests show that this decrease in dispersion is more likely caused by a fall in the dispersion of inflation rate forecasts. Bauer et al. (2006) demonstrate that forecasts of the private sector about economic conditions and policy decisions have become more synchronized (the idiosyncratic errors of macroeconomic variables decreased). However, they could not find evidence that the common forecast error, which drives the overall forecast errors, has become smaller. Finally, several papers find lower interest rate volatility associated with transparency (e.g., Haldane and Read 2000; Coppel and Connolly 2003).

9.3.3 Macroeconomic Variables

Within this subsection we focus on longer-lasting effects of transparency on macroeconomic variables. Several papers look at these longer-lasting effects. The overall measure of transparency constructed by Fry et al. (2000) is related to lower inflation (Cecchetti and Krause 2002). A drawback of this paper is that transparency is measured in 1998, while the data period examined is 1990–1997. Therefore, causality could run the other way. In this respect, the use of detailed, time-series data on transparency has been helpful. Demertzis and Hughes Hallett (2007) look at correlations between the Eijffinger and Geraats index and the levels and variability of inflation and output, and find no significant relation between transparency and average levels of inflation, average levels of output, and the variability of output (at a 95% confidence level). Instead, the total index, and several components of transparency (the economic, alternative economic, and operational index) are significantly correlated with lower inflation variability. Recently, Dincer and Eichengreen (2007) find beneficial effects of transparency on inflation and output volatility, using transparency indices for one hundred countries, which they constructed in the same way as the Eijffinger and Geraats index.

Higher political transparency (about the target) has been beneficial for both the level of inflation (Kuttner and Posen 1999; Fatás et al. 2007) and its persistence (e.g., Kuttner and Posen 1999; Levin et al. 2004). Inflation expectations are relatively better anchored, especially for the longer-term horizons (Levin et al. 2004), inflation expectations are lower, and inflation is easier to predict, which holds for transparency about inflation reports as well (Siklos 2003). Fatás et al. (2007) show that if central banks communicate a quantitative target and successfully hit this target, then the resulting output volatility is less.

Empirical research finds some cost detriment from increasing procedural transparency: the quality of discussion and debate could decrease (Meade and Stasavage, 2004) although it is not clear what effect voicing less dissent with Greenspan's policy proposals has had on the economy. This could have a detrimental effect on policy decisions and, therefore, on the economy.

Chortareas et al. (2002a) find that increased transparency about the forecasts of central banks leads to lower average inflation when the domestic nominal anchor is based on an inflation or money target but not for those countries with an exchange rate target. In addition, there is no evidence that transparency would go hand-in-hand with higher output volatility. Chortareas et al. (2002b) use the same data as Chortareas et al. (2002a) but focus on transparency about policy decisions in addition to transparency about forecasts. Again, they show that higher transparency leads to lower average inflation. Furthermore, their results portray that transparency reduces the sacrifice ratio (the costs of disinflation in terms of lost output and employment). The intuition is that when the public is able to observe the intentions of the central bank more directly through transparency, inflation expectations move fast in reaction to policy changes by the central bank, which reduces the sacrifice ratio. That both forms of transparency are related to lower sacrifice ratios is confirmed by Chortareas et al. (2003), who estimate short-run Phillips curves to get country-specific sacrifice ratios. Publishing detailed forecasts, including a discussion of the forecasts errors and risks, and the minutes and voting records seems to help reducing the sacrifice ratio.

Because a lot of central banks have become more transparent, researchers have started to investigate whether additional transparency would be desirable. van der Cruijsen et al. (2008) argue that there is likely to be an optimal intermediate degree of central bank information. A lot of transparency is likely to be detrimental because it could confuse people and worsen their inflation forecasts. Under these circumstances, price setters will rely more on past inflation (something they are sure about), resulting in higher inflation persistence. Using data on seventy countries, it appears that inflation persistence is indeed minimized at an intermediate degree of central bank transparency. Ehrmann and Fratzscher (2008) also show that central banks would be wise not to strive for full transparency. Limiting transparency in the week before FOMC meetings turns out to be a useful way to prevent market volatility and speculation.

9.3.4 Credibility, Reputation, and Flexibility

Some empirical papers look into the effects of transparency on the central bank's credibility, reputation, and flexibility. Transparency has the potential to improve the degree to which inflation expectations are anchored. This idea is supported by the country-specific and panel data regressions in van der Cruijsen and Demertzis (2007), who make use of detailed time-series and expectations derived from surveys. They show that transparency helps weaken the link between changes in expected inflation and changes in realized inflation, which indicates better anchored inflation expectations. Gürkaynak et al. (2006) find better-anchored inflation expectations accompanied with transparency as well, but they use forward rates on nominal and inflation indexed bonds to determine forward inflation compensation. It turns out that the latter has been sensitive to economic news in the United States (a noninflation targeter) and the United Kingdom before 1997 (implying that inflation expectations were not well anchored). In contrast, this is not the case in the United Kingdom after it became independent and in Sweden (an inflation targeter). Improved anchoring of inflation expectations is an indication of improved credibility. Demiralp (2001) provides some indication of improved credibility as well. Drew and Karagedikli (2007) show that transparency has been beneficial in New Zealand too: market reactions to new data are in line with the inflation target of the Reserve Bank of New Zealand.

Lower interest rates may be interpreted as improved reputation and flexibility of central banks. In case of transparency, the central bank has more flexibility to offset economic shocks because it does not harm its credibility. The private sector knows when the central bank's decisions are intended to offset economic disturbances, therefore long-run inflation expectations, and the long-term nominal interest rates are unaffected by this stabilization policy. In addition, transparency could enhance the reputation of the central bank. It is easier for the private sector to infer the inflation target of the central bank from the policy rate or by looking at inflation outcomes. Assuming that central banks initially have a reputation problem, transparency could lower inflation expectations and through it the long-term nominal interest rates.

Siklos (2004) finds that nominal interest rates are lower for countries with a clear inflation objective. Geraats et al. (2006) use detailed time-series information to analyze the effect of various transparency changes on the levels of interest rates. They find that many transparency increases have had a significant beneficial effect on the level of interest rates (policy, short, and long rates), frequently by over 50 basis points, although not all increases in transparency were desirable, and sometimes there was a trade-off between flexibility (lower short-term and policy rates) and reputation (lower long-term rates).

On the basis of the outcome of a questionnaire, van der Cruijsen and Eijffinger (2007) show that high-transparency perceptions are accompanied by a high degree of trust in the central bank and better aligned inflation expectations. Transparency perceptions are, however, difficult to influence because they do not only depend on a persons degree of transparency knowledge but also on psychological factors.

9.3.5 Cross-Country Comparisons

Although the empirical papers cover many central banks, some receive more attention than others (e.g., the Federal Reserve Bank of the United States). In most cases, it does not matter which central bank is considered, because the majority of articles find beneficial outcomes. Most papers either analyze only one country or a large group of countries in a cross-country analysis, while some perform case studies for a couple of countries. Some of the latter papers find beneficial effects for all countries examined (e.g., Haldane and Read 2000), but not all. Transparency about different points of view about the economy improved anticipations of monetary policy in the United States, but no significant effects could be found for the Bank of England and the European Central Bank (Ehrmann and Fratzscher, 2005). Possible explanations may be due to differences in objectives across these central banks, as well as Romer and Romer's (2000) finding that the Fed has better knowledge and information about the economy than the markets have. van der Cruijsen and Demertzis (2007) also report improved anchoring after several transparency increases in some countries of their sample. In addition, Geraats et al. (2006) report lower interest rates in a many, but not all, cases of increased transparency. One explanation for this finding is that it may matter what type of transparency change is analyzed, as well as the particular central bank in question. The central bank's initial level of transparency and credibility may play an important role. More research is needed to analyze whether this is indeed the case.

9.4 Overall Conclusion

We have shown that the empirical research on the economic effects of more transparency is of a more recent origin than the theoretical work. It begins in 1999 when data about transparency changes became available. Several years later the empirical research received an extra impulse when measures of transparency were constructed. In contrast to the theoretical research, empirical evaluations attach greater weight to the exact meaning of transparency and how it can be measured. The economic effects of transparency are analyzed both by comparing the economic outcomes of central banks with different levels of transparency (in cross-country analyses), as well as by investigating the effects of particular transparency increases (in country-specific analyses). In Table 9.1 we briefly summarized the empirical findings.

While the results of the theoretical transparency literature are quite mixed, although increasingly less contentious over time, the empirical results on almost all aspects of transparency are unanimously in favor of it. Transparency has the potential to improve the anticipations of future monetary policy, which makes monetary policy more efficient. This holds not only for transparency in general, but for all aspects individually as well. In addition, transparency improvements can reduce interest rate volatility, make forecasts more synchronized, and lead to better macroeconomic outcomes and improved credibility.[8] However, central banks would be wise not to strive for full transparency, otherwise agents will not be able to see the forest for the trees anymore.

A large part of the literature focuses on political transparency. From this literature we conclude that, although the theoretical results are mixed, the empirical results are clearly in favor of more political transparency. This is not the case for procedural transparency, which could have some detrimental side effects, such as a lower quality of discussion and debate. All other aspects of transparency empirical analyses show desirable effects, which support the more recent theoretical research.

Despite the recent growth of empirical research, there is still scope for more empirical work. Not all combinations of aspects of transparency in relation to possible economic effects are analyzed as yet. In addition, the evidence on flexibility and reputation do not unanimously point in one direction. Furthermore, several research areas are not yet explored, for example, the way in which the initial level of credibility affects the impact of

---

[8]   Of course there are other possible ways to build up credibility as well, like having a history of low inflation.

Table 9.1. *Overview of empirical findings*

	Political	Economic	Procedural	Policy	Operational	Total
Macroeconomic outcomes	+	+	+	+	+	+
Predictability of future economy				+		
Predictability of inflation	+	+			+	
Level of inflation expectations	+	+			+	
Anchoring of inflation expectations	+					+
Inflation persistence	+					+***
Predictability of monetary policy	+	+	+*	+	+	+
Degree of synchronization of forecasts	+		+	+		
Accurateness of inflation forecasts		+			+	+
Market volatility						+
Flexibility						+**
Credibility				+		+**
Premeetings and quality of monetary policy making			−			
overall	+	+	?	+	+	+

Note: A beneficial effect is defined as a +, a detrimental effect as a − and unclear effects get a ?. More information about how the concepts in the first column have been operationalized is provided in Appendix B.
* Except when transparent about monetary policy disagreement.
** In the majority of cases, but sometimes detrimental effects or a trade-off is found.

transparency increases on economic outcomes. One area closely linked to transparency, but not included in this survey, is communication. With the move toward more transparency, the role of communication in managing inflation expectations has become more important. It is therefore likely that more research will focus on central bank communication.

Furthermore, future empirical literature should look into the robustness of the results. This is especially important because it is difficult to measure transparency, and there are some specific drawbacks in the construction of indices. For example, it is unclear which components should be included and with what weight. Future research could try to find out which aspects matter the most and how they should be weighted accordingly. Papers that abstain from using indices but use a before–after analysis face several downsides as well. It is difficult to refute the idea that other factors might have driven economic changes. Another empirical problem is reverse causality, which refers to the question: Good economic performance or improvements in transparency, which comes first? Additional research into the determinants of transparency would be helpful. Lastly, it would be helpful to know more about the optimal degree of central bank transparency.

What do we see when we contrast the findings of the transparency litera- ture with the actual practice of central banking? The degree of transparency of nine major central banks in 2002 is presented in Figure 9.2 (based on Eijffinger and Geraats 2006).

Although central banks have increased their level of transparency, there is still some room left for further transparency increases. The maximum degree of transparency (15.3 for each of the five aspects) is not yet achieved. In line with the theoretical and empirical findings that support political transparency the most, we observe in practice that it is the aspect of trans- parency on which central banks score the highest (an average score of 2.6),

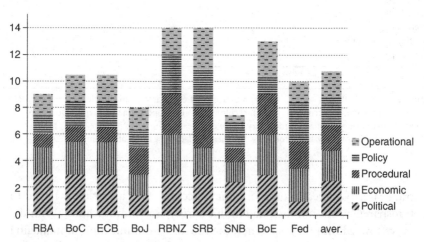

Figure 9.2. Actual degree of transparency (measured in 2002)
Source: Eijffinger and Geraats (2006).
Note: This figure provides an overview of the degree of transparency of the following nine central banks: the Reserve Bank of Australia (RBA), the Bank of Canada (BoC), the European Central Bank (ECB), the Bank of Japan (BoJ), the Reserve Bank of New Zealand (RBNZ), the Swedish Riksbank (SRB), the Swiss National Bank (SNB), the Bank of England (BoE), and the U.S. Federal Reserve (Fed).

but there is still some room for transparency increases for three central banks. Economic transparency ranks second (an average score of 2.3), and policy transparency third (2.2 on average). Although the literature shows that both forms of transparency seem to be desirable, only the Reserve Bank of New Zealand achieves the maximum score on both. Concerning procedural transparency, the literature is not decisive. This might explain why, in practice, the score on procedural transparency is relatively low (the average score is 1.9). But central banks score the lowest on operational transparency (1.8 on average). Only the Swedish Riksbank scores the maximum of 3. This can be explained by the fact that the theoretical literature is not decisively in favor of more operational transparency. In addition, although the empirical literature is in favor of it, relatively little empirical research focuses on this aspect of transparency, and it originates only from 2003 onward.

We can now briefly summarize our findings: (1) The theoretical literature does not come to a unanimous conclusion. Although the more recent theoretical literature argues in favor of more transparency, exceptions are procedural and political transparency. (2) Differences in outcomes occur because of differences in the models used. More recent, microdirected research tends to favor transparency. (3) The empirical literature shows that more transparency is indeed desirable. The only remaining question mark is procedural transparency. (4) There is still scope for some more research on transparency. Now that most central banks have already become more transparent, it is likely that the research will shift more toward the limits to transparency and toward communication, a trend that is already observable.[9] As Winkler (2002) points out, the abolition of asymmetric information is not enough: communication should provide clarity to make sure that the release of information leads to common understanding between the public and the central bank. However, it is not easy to do so, as is illustrated by Kafka (1917): "Prescribing is so easy, understanding people so hard."[10] van der Cruijsen and Eijffinger (2007) show that this applies also to central banking. They find a discrepancy between transparency perceptions and the actual transparency practice of the European Central Bank. This misalignment is the result of psychological biases and lack of knowledge about the actual central bank disclosure practice, which differs for different groups of people (e.g., laymen versus economic experts). Therefore, the best communication strategy is likely to depend on the recipient.

---

[9] For a discussion of the limits to transparency, we refer to Cukierman (2008).
[10] We would like to thank Vitor Gaspar for suggesting to use this quote.

References

Angeletos, G. M. and A. Pavan (2004), "Transparency of Information and Coordination in Economies with Investment Complementarities," *American Economic Review* 94(2): 91–98.

Barro, R. J. and D. B. Gordon (1983a), "A Positive Theory of Monetary Policy in a Natural Rate Model," *Journal of Political Economy* 91(4): 589–610.

(1983b), "Rules, Discretion, and Reputation in a Model of Monetary Policy," *Journal of Monetary Economics* 12(1): 101–21.

Bauer, A., R. Eisenbeis, D. Waggoner, and T. Zha (2006), "Transparency, Expectations, and Forecasts," ECB Working Paper Series No.637.

Beetsma, R. M. and H. Jensen (2003), "Why Money Talks and Wealth Whispers: Monetary Uncertainty and Mystique: Comment," *Journal of Money, Credit, and Banking* 35(1): 129–36.

Berardi, M. and J. Duffy (2007), "The Value of Central Bank Transparency When Agents Are Learning," *European Journal of Political Economy* 23(1): 9–29.

Biefang-Frisancho Mariscal, I. and P. Howells (2007), "Monetary Policy Transparency in the UK: The Impact of Independence and Inflation Targeting," *International Review of Applied Economics* 21(5): 603–18.

Bini-Smaghi, L. and D. Gros (2001), "Is the European Central Bank Sufficiently Accountable and Transparent?," CEPS Working Paper No. 7.

Blinder, A., C. Goodhart, P. Hildebrand, D. Lipton, and C. Wyplosz (2001), *How Do Central Banks Talk? Geneva Reports on the World Economy 3* (London: CEPR).

Blinder, A. S. (2007), "Monetary Policy by Committee: Why and How?," *European Journal of Political Economy* 23(1): 106–23.

Blinder, A. S., M. Ehrmann, M. Fratzscher, J. De Haan, and D. Jansen (2008), "Central Bank Communication and Monetary Policy: A Survey of Theory and Evidence," *Journal of Economic Literature* 46(4): 910–45.

Buiter, W. H. (1999), "Alice in Euroland," *Journal of Common Market Studies* 73(2): 181–209.

Carpenter, S. B. (2004), "Transparency and Monetary Policy: What Does the Academic Literature Tell Policymakers?," Finance and Economics Discussion Series: 2004–35, Board of Governors of the Federal Reserve System (U.S.).

Cecchetti, S. G. and S. Krause (2002), "Central Bank Structure, Policy Efficiency, and Macroeconomic Performance: Exploring Empirical Relationships," *Federal Reserve Bank of St. Louis Review* 84(4): 47–59.

Chadha, J. S. and C. Nolan (2001), "Inflation Targeting, Transparency and Interest Rate Volatility: Ditching "Monetary Mystique" in the UK," *Journal of Macroeconomics* 23(3): 349–66.

Chortareas, G. E., D. Stasavage, and G. Sterne (2002a), "Does It Pay To Be Transparent? International Evidence From Central Bank Forecasts," *Federal Reserve Bank of St. Louis Review* 84(4): 99–117.

(2002b), "Monetary Policy Transparency, Inflation and the Sacrifice Ratio," *International Journal of Finance and Economics* 7(2): 141–55.

(2003), "Does Monetary Policy Transparency Reduce Disinflation Costs?," *The Manchester School* 71(5): 521–40.

Clare, A. and R. Courtenay (2001), "Assessing the Impact of Macroeconomic News Announcements on Securities Prices under Different Monetary Policy Regimes," Bank of England Working Paper Series No. 125.

Cone, T. E. (2005), "Learnability and Transparency with Time Inconsistent Monetary Policy," *Economic Letters* **87**: 187–91.

Coppel, J. and E. Connolly (2003), "What Do Financial Market Data Tell Us About Monetary Policy Transparency," RBA Research Discussion Paper: 2003–05.

Cornand, C. and F. Heinemann (2004), "Optimal Degree of Public Information Dissemination," CESifo Working Paper No. 1353.

Cosimano, T. F. and J. B. Van Huyck (1993), "Central Bank Secrecy, Interest Rates, and Monetary Control," *Economic Inquiry* **31**(3): 370–82.

Crowe, C. and E. E. Meade (2008), "Central Bank Independence and Transparency: Evolution and Effectiveness," IMF Working Paper 08/119.

Cruijsen, C. van der and M. Demertzis (2007), "The Impact of Central Bank Transparency on Inflation Expectations," *European Journal of Political Economy* **23**(1): 51–66.

Cruijsen, C. van der and S. C. W. Eijffinger (2007), "Actual versus Perceived Central Bank Transparency: The Case of the European Central Bank," CEPR Discussion Paper No. 6525.

Cruijsen, C. van der, S. C. W. Eijffinger, and L. H. Hoogduin (2008), "Optimal Central Bank Transparency," CEPR Discussion Paper No. 6889.

Cukierman, A. (2001), "Accountability, Credibility, Transparency and Stabilization Policy in the Eurosystem," in C. Wyplosz (Ed.), *The Impact of EMU on Europe and the Developing Countries* (Oxford University Press), pp. 40–75.

(2002), "Are Contemporary Central Banks Transparent About Economic Models and Objectives and What Difference Does It Make?," *Federal Reserve Bank of St. Louis Review* **84**(4): 15–35.

(2008), "The Limits of Transparency," unpublished.

Cukierman, A. and A. Meltzer (1986), "A Theory of Ambiguity, Credibility and Inflation under Discretion and Asymmetric Information," *Econometrica* **54**: 1099–1128.

Demertzis, M. and M. Hoeberichts (2007), "The Costs of Increasing Transparency," *Open Economies Review* **18**(3): 263–80.

Demertzis, M. and A. Hughes Hallett (2007), "Central Bank Transparency in Theory and Practice," *Journal of Macroeconomics* **29**(4): 760–89.

Demertzis, M. and N. Viegi (2008), "Inflation Targets as Focal Points," *International Journal of Central Banking* **4**(1): 55–87.

Demiralp, S. (2001), "Monetary Policy in a Changing World: Rising Role of Expectations and the Anticipation Effect," Board of Governors of the Federal Reserve System. Finance and Economics Discussion Series: 2001–55.

Dincer, N. and B. Eichengreen (2007), "Central Bank Transparency: Why, Where, and With What Effects?," NBER Working Paper No. 13003.

Drew, A. and Ö. Karagedikli (2007), "Some Benefits of Monetary-Policy Transparency in New Zealand," *Czech Journal of Economics and Finance* **57** (11–12): 521–39.

Dotsey, M. (1987), "Monetary Policy, Secrecy, and Federal Funds Rate Behavior," *Journal of Monetary Economics* **20**(3): 463–474.

Ehrmann, M. and M. Fratzscher (2005), "How Should Central Banks Communicate?," European Central Bank Working Paper No. 557, November.

(2007), "Transparency, Disclosure, and the Federal Reserve," *International Journal of Central Banking* 3(1): 179–225.

(2008), "Purdah. On the Rationale for Central Bank Silence Around Policy Meetings," European Central Bank Working Paper No. 868.

Eijffinger, S. C. W. and M. Hoeberichts (2002), "Central Bank Accountability and Transparency: Theory and Some Evidence. *International Finance* 5(1): 73–96.

Eijffinger, S. C. W. and M. F. Tesfaselassie (2007), "Central Bank Forecasts and Disclosure Policy: Why It Pays to be Optimistic," *European Journal of Political Economy* 23(1): 30–51.

Eijffinger, S. C. W., M. Hoeberichts, and E. Schaling (2000), "Why Money Talks and Wealth Whispers: Monetary Uncertainty and Mystique," *Journal of Money, Credit, and Banking* 32(2): 218–235.

(2003), "Why Money Talks and Wealth Whispers: Monetary Uncertainty and Mystique: Reply," *Journal of Money, Credit, and Banking* 35(1): 137–139.

Eijffinger, S. C. W. and P. M. Geraats (2006), "How Transparent Are Central Banks?," *European Journal of Political Economy* 22(1): 1–21.

Eusepi, S. (2005), "Central Bank Transparency under Model Uncertainty," Federal Reserve Bank of New York Staff Report No. 199.

Evans, G. W. and S. Honkapohja (2001), *Learning and Expectations in Macroeconomics*, (Princeton, NJ: Princeton University Press).

(2005), "An Interview With Thomas J. Sargent," *Macroeconomic Dynamics* 9(4): 561–583.

Fatás, A., I. Mihov, and A. K. Rose (2007), "Quantitative Goals for Monetary Policy," *Journal of Money, Credit, and Banking* 39(5): 1163–1176.

Faust, J. and L. E. O. Svensson (2001), "Transparency and Credibility: Monetary Policy with Unobservable Goals," *International Economic Review* 42: 369–397.

(2002), "The Equilibrium Degree of Transparency and Control in Monetary Policy," *Journal of Money, Credit, and Banking* 34(2): 520–539.

Ferreira de Mendonça, H. and Filho J. S. (2008), "Macroeconomic Effects of Central Bank Transparency: The Case of Brazil," *Cato Journal* 28(1): 117–137.

Fracasso, A., H. Genberg, and C. Wyplosz (2003), "How Do Central Banks Write? An Evaluation of Inflation Targeting Central Banks," Special Report 2 of Geneva Reports on the World Economy, Centre for Economic Policy Research.

Friedman, B. M. (2003), "The Use and Meaning of Words in Central Banking: Inflation Targeting, Credibility and Transparency," in P. Mizen (Ed.), *Central Banking, Monetary Theory and Practice: Essays in Honour of Charles Goodhart, Vol. 1* (Cheltenham: Edward Elgar), pp. 111–24.

Fry, M., D. Julius, L. Mahadeva, S. Roger, and G. Sterne (2000), "Key Issues in the Choice of Monetary Policy Framework," in L. Mahadeva, and G. Sterne (Eds.), *Monetary Policy Frameworks in a Global Context* (London: Routledge), pp. 3–17.

Fujiwara, I. (2005), "Is the Central Bank's Publication of Economic Forecasts Influential?," *Economics Letters* 89: 255–261.

Garfinkel, M. R. and S. Oh (1995), "When and How Much to Talk: Credibility and Flexibility in Monetary Policy with Private Information," *Journal of Monetary Economics* 35: 341–357.

Geraats, P. M. (2002), "Central Bank Transparency," *Economic Journal* 112(483), F532-F565.

(2005), "Transparency and Reputation: The Publication of Central Bank Forecasts," *Topics in Macroeconomics* 5(1): 1–26.

(2006), "Transparency of Monetary Policy: Theory and Practice," *CESifo Economic Studies* 52(1): 111–152.

(2007), "The Mystique of Central Bank Speak," *International Journal of Central Banking* 3(1): 37–80.

Geraats, P. M., S. C. W. Eijffinger, and C. A. B. van der Cruijsen (2006), "Does Central Bank Transparency Reduce Interest Rates?," CEPR Discussion Paper No. 6625, March.

Gerlach-Kristen, P. (2004), "Is the MPC's Voting Record Informative About Future UK Monetary Policy?," *Scandinavian Journal of Economics* 106(2): 299–313.

Gersbach, H. (2003), "On the Negative Social Value of Central Bank's Knowledge Transparency," *Economics of Governance* 4: 91–102.

Gersbach, H. and V. Hahn (2004), "Voting Transparency, Conflicting Interests, and the Appointment of Central Banker," *Economics and Politics* 16(3): 321–345.

(2005), "Voting Transparency in a Monetary Union," CEPR Discussion Paper No. 5155.

(2006), "Signaling and Commitment: Monetary versus Inflation Targeting," *Macroeconomic Dynamics* 10(5): 595–624.

(2008), "Should the Individual Voting Records of Central Bankers be Published?," *Social Choice and Welfare* 30(4): 655–683.

Goodfriend, M (1986), "Monetary Mystique: Secrecy and Central Banking," *Journal of Monetary Economics* 17: 63–92.

Grüner, H. P. (2002), "How Much Should Central Banks Talk? A New Argument," *Economic Letters* 77: 195–198.

Gürkaynak, R. S., A. T. Levin, and E. T. Swanson (2006), "Does Inflation Targeting Anchor Long-Run Inflation Expectations? Evidence from Long-Term Bond Yields in the U.S., U.K., and Sweden," CEPR Discussion Paper No. 5808.

Haan, J. De, F. Amtenbrink, and S. Waller (2004), "The Transparency and Credibility of the European Central Bank," *Journal of Common Market Studies* 42(4): 775–794.

Hahn, V. (2002), "Transparency in Monetary Policy: A Survey," *Ifo Studien Zeitschrift für empirische Wirtschaftsforchung* 48(3): 429–455.

Haldane, A. G. and V. Read (2000), "Monetary Policy Surprises and the Yield Curve," Bank of England Working Paper No. 106.

Hoeberichts, M., M. Tesfaselassie, and S. C. W. Eijffinger (2004), "Central Bank Communication and Output Stabilization," CEPR Discussion paper No. 4408.

Hughes Hallett, A. and J. Libich (2006), "Central Bank Independence, Accountability and Transparency: Complements or Strategic Substitutes?," CEPR Discussion Paper No. 5470.

Hughes Hallett, A. and N. Viegi (2003), "Imperfect Transparency and the Strategic Use of Information: An Ever Present Temptation for Central Bankers?," *The Manchester School* 71(5): 498–520.

Issing, O. (1999), "The Eurosystem: Transparent and Accountable or 'Willem in Euroland'," *Journal of Common Market Studies* 37(3): 503–519.

(2005), "Communication, Transparency, Accountability: Monetary Policy in the Twenty-First Century," *Federal Reserve Bank of St. Louis Review* 87(2): 65–83.

Jensen, H. (2002), "Optimal Degrees of Transparency in Monetary Policymaking," *Scandinavian Journal of Economics* 104(3): 399–422.

Kafka, F. (1917), *A Country Doctor. The Penal Colony, Stories and Short Pieces* (translated by W. & E. Muir, 1961) (New York: Shocker Books), p.140.

King, M. (1997), "Changes in UK Monetary Policy: Rules and Discretion in Practice," *Journal of Monetary Economics* 39: 81–98.

Kohn, D. L. and B. P. Sack (2003), "Central Bank Talk: Does it Matter and Why?," Board of Governors of the Federal Reserve System (U.S.), Finance and Economics Discussion Series: 2003–55.

Kuttner, K. N. and A. S. Posen (1999), "Does Talk Matter After All? Inflation Targeting and Central Bank Behavior," Federal Reserve Bank of New York Staff Report No. 88.

Kydland, F. E. and E. C. Prescott (1977), "Rules Rather than Discretion: The Inconsistency of Optimal Plans," *Journal of Political Economy* 85(3): 473–491.

Lange, J., B. Sack, and W. Whitesell (2003), "Anticipations of Monetary Policy in Financial Markets," *Journal of Money, Credit, and Banking* 35(6): 889–909.

Levin, A. T., F. M. Natalucci, and J. M. Piger (2004), "The Macroeconomic Effects of Inflation Targeting," *Federal Reserve bank of St. Louis Review* 86(4): 51–80.

Lewis, K. K. (1991), "Why Doesn't Society Minimize Central Bank Secrecy?," *Economic Inquiry* Vol. XXIX: 403–415.

Lildholdt, P. and A. V. Wetherilt (2004), "Anticipation of Monetary Policy in UK Financial Markets," Bank of England Working Paper No. 241.

Lindner, A. (2006), "Does Transparency of Central Banks Produce Multiple Equilibria on Currency Markets?," *Scandinavian Journal of Economics* 108(1): 1–14.

Lohmann, S. (1992), "Optimal Commitment in Monetary Policy: Credibility versus Flexibility," *American Economic Review* 82: 273–286.

Lucas, Jr., R. E. (1973), "Some International Evidence on Output-Inflation Tradeoffs," *American Economic Review* 63: 326–334.

Meade, E. E. and D. Stasavage (2004), "Publicity of Debate and the Incentive to Dissent: Evidence from the US Federal Reserve," CEP Discussion Paper, Center for Economic Performance, LSE.

Mishkin, F. S. (2004), "Can Central Bank Transparency Go Too Far?," NBER Working Paper No. 10829.

Morris, S. and H. S. Shin (2002), "Social Value of Public Information," *American Economic Review* 92(5): 1521–1534.

(2005), "Central Bank Transparency and the Signal Value of Prices," *Brookings Papers on Economic Activity* 2005(2): 1–43.

Morris, S., H. S. Shin, and H. Tong (2006), "Social Value of Public Information: Morris and Shin (2002) Is Actually Pro-Transparency, Not Con: Reply," *American Economic Review* 96(1): 453–455.

Muller, P. and M. Zelmer (1999), "Greater Transparency in Monetary Policy: Impact on Financial Markets," Bank of Canada Technical Report 86.

Orphanides, A. and J. C. Williams (2005a), "Inflation Scares and Forecast-Based Monetary Policy," *Review of Economic Dynamics* 8: 498–527.

(2005b), "Imperfect Knowledge, Inflation Expectations, and Monetary Policy," in
B. S. Bernanke, and M. Woodford (Eds.), *The Inflation-Targeting Debate* (Chicago:
University of Chicago), pp. 201–234.

Pearlman, J. G. (2005), "Central Bank Transparency and Private Information in a
Dynamic Macroeconomic Model," ECB Working Paper Series No. 455.

Poole, W. and R. H. Rasche (2003), "The Impact of Changes in FOMC Disclosure
Practices on the Transparency of Monetary Policy: Are Markets and the FOMC
Better "Synched"?," *Federal Reserve Bank of St. Louis Review* **85**(2): 1–9.

Poole, W., R. H. Rasche, and D. L. Thornton (2002), "Market Anticipation of Monetary
Policy Actions," *The Federal Reserve Bank of St. Louis Review* **84**(4): 65–94.

Posen, A. S. (2003), "Six Practical Views of Central Bank Transparency," in P. Mizen
(Ed.), *Central Banking, Monetary Theory and Practice: Essays in Honour of Charles
Goodhart Vol.1* (Cheltenham: Edward Elgar), pp. 153–172.

Rafferty, M. and M. Tomljanovich (2002), "Central Bank Transparency and Market
Efficiency: An Econometric Analysis," *Journal of Economics and Finance* **26**(2):
150–161.

Reeves, R. and M. Sawicki (2007), "Do Financial Markets React to Bank of England
Communication?," *European Journal of Political Economy* **23**(1): 207–227.

Rogoff, K. (1985), "The Optimal Degree of Commitment to a Monetary Target,"
Quarterly Journal of Economics **100**(4): 1169–1190.

Romer, C. and D. Romer (2000), "Federal Reserve Information and the Behavior of
Interest Rates," *American Economic Review* **90**: 429–457.

Rosa, C. (2008), "Talking Less and Moving the Market More: Is this the Recipe for
Monetary Policy Effectiveness? Evidence from the ECB and the Fed," Center for
Economic Performance Discussion Paper No. 855.

Rudebusch, G. D. and J. C. Williams (2008), "Revealing the Secrets of the Temple: The
Value of Publishing Central Bank Interest Rate Projections," in J. Y. Campbell
(Ed.), *Asset Prices and Monetary Policy* (Chicago: University of Chicago Press).

Rudin, J. R. (1988), "Central Bank Secrecy, 'Fed Watching', and the Predictability of
Interest Rates," *Journal of Monetary Economics* **22**(2): 317–334.

Schaling, E. and C. Nolan (1998), "Monetary Policy Uncertainty and Inflation: The
Role of Central Bank Accountability," *De Economist* **146**(4): 585–602.

Sibert, A. (2002), "Monetary Policy with Uncertain Central Bank Preferences,"
European Economic Review **46**: 1093–1109.

(2003), "Monetary Policy Committees: Individual and Collective Reputations,"
Review of Economic Studies **70**: 649–655.

(2006a), "Is Central Bank Transparency Desirable?," CEPR Discussion Paper
No. 5641, April.

(2006b), "Central Banking by Committee," *International Finance* **9**(2): 145–168.

Siklos, P. L. (1999), "Inflation-Target Design: Changing Inflation Performance and
Persistence in Industrial Countries," *Review Federal Reserve Bank of St. Louis*
81(2): 47–58.

Siklos, P. L. (2002), *The changing face of central banking: Evolutionary trends since World
War II.* (New York: Cambridge University Press).

(2003), "Assessing the Impact of Changes in Transparency and Accountability at the
Bank of Canada," *Canadian Public Policy -Analyse de Politiques* **29**(3): 279–299.

(2004), "Central Bank Behavior, the Institutional Framework, and Policy Regimes: Inflation Versus Noninflation Targeting Countries," *Contemporary Economic Policy* 22(3): 331–343.

Sørensen, J. R. (1991), "Political Uncertainty and Macroeconomic Performance," *Economics Letters* 37: 377–381.

Stein, J. C. (1989), "Cheap Talk and the Fed: A Theory of Imprecise Policy Announcements," *American Economic Review* 79(1): 32–42.

Svensson, L. E. O. (2003), "Monetary Policy and Learning," Federal Reserve Bank of Atlanta Economic Review, Third Quarter: 11–16.

(2006), "Social Value of Public Information: Comment: Morris and Shin (2002) is Actually Pro-Transparency, Not Con," *American Economic Review* 96(1): 448–452.

Swank, J., O. H. Swank, and B. Visser (2008), "How Committees of Experts Deal with the Outside World: Some Theory, and EvidenceFrom the FOMC," *Journal of the European Economic Association* 6(2–3): 478–486.

Swanson, E. T. (2006), "Have Increases in Federal Reserve Transparency Improved Private Sector Interest Rate Forecasts?," *Journal of Money, Credit, and Banking* 38(3): 791–819.

Tabellini, G. (1987), "Secrecy of Monetary Policy and the Variability of Interest Rates," *Journal of Money, Credit, and Banking* 19(4): 425–436.

Thornton, D. L. (2003), "Monetary Policy Transparency: Transparent About What?," *The Manchester School* 71(5): 478–497.

Tomljanovich, M. (2007), "Does Central Bank Transparency Impact Financial Markets? A cross-country econometric analysis," *Southern Economic Journal* 73(3): 791–813.

Townsend, R. M. (1983), "Forecasting the Forecasts of Others," *Journal of Political Economy* 91: 546–588.

Tuysuz, S. (2007), "Central Bank Transparency and the U.S. Interest Rate Level and Volatility Response to U.S. News," Munich Personal RePEc Archive Paper No. 5217.

Walsh, C. E. (1999), "Announcements, Inflation Targeting and Central Bank Incentives," *Economica* 66: 255–269.

(2007), "Optimal Economic Transparency," *International Journal of Central Banking* 3(1): 5–36.

Westelius, N. J. (2005), "Discretionary Monetary Policy and Inflation Persistence," *Journal of Monetary Economics* 52(2): 477–496.

Winkler, B. (2002), "Which Kind of Transparency? On the Need for Effective Communication in Monetary Policy-Making," *Ifo Studien* 48(3): 401–427.

A. *Theoretical Summary Table*

Author(s)	Aspect(s)	Used model	Brief description	Outcome
Cukierman and Meltzer (1986)	Operational	ML	Infinite horizon. Based on optimal policy models of KP (1977) and BG (1983b). Multiperiod state dependent objective function (weights shift in unpredictable ways), that is linear in output. Rational expectations. Noisy monetary control: public cannot separate persistent shifts in objectives from transitory control deviations.	Might be undesirable (lower inflation bias, but worse stabilization of shocks)
Dotsey (1987)	Policy	RTM	Equilibrium model of the federal funds rate in case of nonborrowed reserve targeting. Cbt about its monetary targets	Trade-off (lower variance of forecast errors, but higher variability of the federal funds rate)
Tabellini (1987)	Policy	RTM	Based on Dotsey (1987). Lack of information is parameter uncertainty. cb has a constant nonborrowed reserves target. Opacity: the financial market uses the interbank rate to update their prior of the policy target	Desirable (lower variability of interest rates)
Rudin (1988)	Policy	RTM	Based on Dotsey (1987). Only part of the agents engage in Fed watching	Undesirable (worse predictability of the interbank rate)
Stein (1989)	Political	Open economy model, cheap talk game theoretic mechanism.	Two periods. Cb cares about period 1 interest rate (target is zero and known) and the real exchange rate (unknown target, same in both periods, drawn from uniform distribution). Price stickiness. Fed cannot precommit. Time-inconsistent policy then higher utility. Different types of cb-ers with different preferences	Desirable, but statements should be imprecise: providing a range within which the targets lies (more swift market reactions)

(*continued*)

A. (*Continued*)

Author(s)	Aspect(s)	Used model	Brief description	Outcome
Lewis (1991)	Political	ML	Infinite horizon. Based on CM (1986). Cb is transparent about the weights attached to the objectives	Might be desirable (prevents other more costly forms of secrecy, and enables the use of expansionary policy when it is desired the most)
Sørensen (1991)	Political	Two-stage model with a cb and a labor union	Labor union sets the nominal wage rate before the policymaker sets the inflation rate, and cares about the unbiasedness of inflation expectations and risk aversion. Cb knows the actual shock to unemployment and its own weights (on unemployment and inflation stabilization) in the objective function, the union does not	Might be undesirable (lower variance of inflation and unemployment, but higher level of inflation and unemployment)
Cosimano and Van Huyck (1993)	Policy	RTM	Dynamic rational expectations model of the federal funds and deposit market. Secrecy reduces the effect of monetary control policy on interest rates which is valued by the Trading Desk	Undesirable
Garfinkel and Oh (1995)	Economic	ML	Static model. Based on Stein (1989). Cb wants to stabilize both output and inflation, and stimulate output above the natural output. Cb has private forecasts about the money demand disturbance before wages are set. Public cannot distinguish between the forecast and the forecast error	Desirable, but should be noisy by giving a range on the cb's forecast of the money demand disturbance (improved predictability of mp and lower variability of output)
Schaling and Nolan (1998)	Political	ML	Based on CM (1986). Standard mp-game extended with uncertainty about the cb's preferences for inflation stabilization. Wage-setters unilaterally choose the nominal wage every period and the cb controls mp	Might be beneficial (could reduce the inflation bias)

302

Walsh (1999)	Political	ML	Static mp-model based on CM (1986), but simplified (all random elements are serially uncorrelated). Cb has private information about shocks. Relative weight on output target is unknown. Reputational considerations ignored. Focus on information revealed by announcements of a target instead of the past history of actions of the cb. Penalty for deviations from the target. Economic information can be revealed by the announced target. A low target would be desirable for creating surprise inflation but not for evaluation	Might be beneficial (lower inflation bias without distorting stabilization policy)
Cukierman (2001)	Economic	1) ML, and 2) neo-Keynesian	Cbt: info about shocks provided before inflation expectations are formed.	Might be undesirable
Eijffinger et al. (2000, 2003)	Political	ML	Mp-game with uncertainty about the relative weights in the objective function. Nominal wage contracts are signed before shocks to cb preferences realize (only the variance is known by wage setters and taken into account when forming expectations). The productivity shocks occur (also unknown when signing contracts). Cb sets mp, output is determined. Cb loss function is quadratic in output	Trade-off (lower level and volatility of inflation, higher output volatility)
Faust and Svensson (2001)	Operational, political	ML	Infinite-horizon. Based on CM (1986). Standard quadratic cb loss function. Time-varying, serially correlated preferences of cb-ers. Distinction between imperfect monetary control and operational transparency (the extent to which the monetary control errors are disclosed to the ps)	Operational transparency is likely to be desirable (better outcomes through more concern about reputation). Political transparency is not (worse outcomes because actions do not affect its reputation), although it could be in a richer model

(continued)

303

A. *(Continued)*

Author(s)	Aspect(s)	Used model	Brief description	Outcome
Cukierman (2002)	Political	NK	The cb is a flexible inflation targeter and is transparent about its loss function and the weight attached to output gap stabilization	Undesirable (detrimental for credibility)
Eijffinger and Hoeberichts (2002)	Political	ML	Based on Lohmann (1992), Schaling and Nolan (1998), Eijffinger et al. (2000). Conservative cb-er. Weight on output stabilization unknown to government and society. After the cb proposes its preferred rate of inflation, the government is able to override the cb at a fixed cost	Trade-off (improved credibility, but worse flexibility)
Faust and Svensson (2002)	Operational	ML	Infinite-horizon model. Based on CM(1986). Cbt: the degree to which cb preferences (serially correlated) can be inferred by the public. Control: extent to which outcomes match intentions. Standard cb loss function. More cbt then inflation expectations are more sensitive to policy actions. Current policy decisions influence future inflation expectations. No implication for current aggregates (not forward looking). Cbt introduces a constant marginal cost of loose m, but the marginal costs of current inflation are the same. Given that the cb is aiming at an output level above the natural level, resulting in a BG (1983b) inflation bias, cbt is beneficial. It implies that no costs are incurred in terms of stabilization policy	Might be desirable (for cb's with a bad inflation record)

Grüner (2002)	Political	Two-stage model with a cb and a labor union	Union sets nominal wage before cb sets inflation. Crucial distinction between uncertainty about the objectives (influenced by disclosure of information) and uncertainty about inflation (affected by cb's objectives, and actions of all players)	Might be undesirable (higher wages, average inflation and unemployment, possibly higher variance of inflation)
Jensen (2002)	Operational	NK	Infinite-horizon model. Shocks to the preferred value of the output gap (time-varying, serially correlated) of cb-ers are unknown. Cb has imperfect control about its policy outcomes. Cbt: error is made known. Full information: price setters get direct information about the preferences	Trade-off (improved credibility, but worse flexibility)
Morris and Shin (2002)	Economic	Coordination	Agents face a coordination motive (coordination does not improve social welfare) as well as a wish to match the fundamentals, about which there is public and private information	Might be undesirable
Sibert (2002)	Political	Expectations augmented Phillips curve	Basic model: two-periods. Either nominal wage contracting and rational expectations as in BG (1983a) or Lucas (1973) expectations view of aggregate supply. Continuum of policymaker types (weights in objective function differs) which is unknown. Public forms expectations. Then stochastic shocks occur. Then mp is made.	Undesirable (higher inflation and worse stabilization)
Beetsma and Jensen (2003)	Political	ML	Based on Eijffinger et al. (2000). Model preference uncertainty somewhat different (isolating the effects of preference uncertainty on policy uncertainty)	Might be beneficial (even when the flexibility problem is relatively large)

(continued)

A. (Continued)

Author(s)	Aspect(s)	Used model	Brief description	Outcome
Chortareas et al. (2003)	Economic	ML	Based on BG. Simple model of disinflation costs under incomplete information. Cb has private info about the control error (demand shock), which it partly forecasts	Desirable (lower sacrifice ratio)
Gersbach (2003)	Economic	ML	One-period model. Based on BG (1983a). Two agents: cb and ps. Cb's objectives are known to the ps (and the same as theirs). Supply shocks should be stabilized around a set goal. Cbt: the ps receives the economic information (economic judgment, forecasts, models) before forming expectations.	Undesirable (eliminates the possibility to stabilize employment)
Hughes Hallett and Viegi (2003)	Political	ML	Two-period. Based on BG (1983a) Microfoundations of monopolistic competition, sticky prices (Calvo contracts), quadratic adjustment costs. The government and the cb (independent) simultaneously decide about inflation and net tax revenues (which is assumed to have a positive effect on output). The government and the ps both have asymmetric information about the relative weights in the cb's objective function or the output target	Cbt about the relative weight put on output is desirable for the ps (better informed decisions), but undesirable for the cb (cannot manipulate expectations). Cbt about the output target is desirable for the ps. For the cb it does not affect its ability to manipulate expectations, but secrecy could still be desirable as it works as a substitute for credibility

306

Sibert (2003)	Procedural	Committee	Based on a standard time-inconsistency framework. Two cb-ers: one in his first term and one in its second, last, term. Voting signals whether they are opportunistic or not. Because there is some utility attached to keeping the job, an opportunistic junior member will want to pretend that he is not	Might be desirable to publish individuals' votes immediately (lower incentive to inflate raises the expected social welfare)
Angeletos and Pavan (2004)	Total	Coordination	Investment complementarities: the individual gain from investment increases in the aggregate level. More effective coordination is socially valuable	Depends on circumstances
Cornand and Heinemann (2004)	Total	Coordination	MS(2002) with the possibility of intermediate degrees of cbt	Desirable (but sometimes only to part of the ps)
Gersbach and Hahn (2004)	Procedural	Committee	Cb-ers: different preferences. Incentive to misrepresent them (when different from the public) to be reelected in period 2. But utility loss of strategically voting in period 1 is larger. Adjustment to this model: national governments appoint the national cb-ers that decide on mp within a monetary union	Desirable (but it might not be in case of a monetary union)
Hoeberichts et al. (2004)	Economic	NK	Cb is sufficiently conservative. Cbt: about cb's assessment of the expectations of the ps	Desirable (the increase in output stabilization > the decrease in inflation stabilization)
Cone (2005)	Economic	Learning	Canonical time-inconsistency mp-model	Depends on circumstances

(continued)

307

A. *(Continued)*

Author(s)	Aspect(s)	Used model	Brief description	Outcome
Eusepi (2005)	Political	Learning. Microfunded general equilibrium model with nominal rigidities	The cb and ps have to learn the correct model of the economy. Cbt: then no uncertainty about the policy strategy	Desirable (reduces uncertainty, stabilizes inflation expectations)
Geraats (2005)	Economic	Real interest rate transmission mechanism with backward-looking pricing	Two-periods. Based on BG (1983a). The ps tries to infer the intentions of the cb by looking at the long-term nominal interest rate (=policy instrument). Cbt: the publication of (truthful) cb forecasts, which contain information about demand and supply shocks that influence their mp decisions	Desirable (lower inflation bias)
Gersbach and Hahn (2005)	Procedural	Committee	Two-periods. Monetary union with members appointed by national governments	May be undesirable
Morris and Shin (2005)	Economic	Coordination	Based on MS(2002). Dynamic. The quality of public information is endogenous	Unclear (trade-off: improved steering of expectations but worse signal value of prices)
Orphanides and Williams (2005b)	Political	Learning	Ps has the correct reduced form model but uses a truncated sample of the data	Desirable

308

Pearlman (2005)	Economic	Coordination Townsend's (1983) model of an industry	Heterogeneous agents with different levels of information. They know the prices of other firms, but not their current output. Idiosyncratic demand shocks and aggregate demand (money supply) shocks. A noisy public information signal is given about the money supply. Firms need to find out their own information by guessing the information of other firms	Desirable
Westelius (2005)	Operational	Neoclassical expectations augmented Phillips curve Learning	Combining BG (1983a) with incomplete information and learning	Desirable (lower inflation and unemployment persistence during periods of disinflation)
Gersbach and Hahn (2006)	Economic	ML	One-period model. Based on BG (1983a) and KP (1977). CB's objectives are representative for the public. Cbt: publication of private information about macroeconomic shocks	Desirable (lower difference between targeted and realized inflation)
Hughes Hallett and Libich (2006)	Political	ML	Based on BG (1983b) and KP (1977). Cb, ps and the government (strong or weak) are rational and have common knowledge of rationality. Extensions: monitoring costs, authorities dislike accountability punishments, control over mp depends on degree of goal independence enjoyed by the cb. Focus on goal cbt: how explicit goals are stated in legislation or statutes	Desirable (lower inflation)

(*continued*)

A. (Continued)

Author(s)	Aspect(s)	Used model	Brief description	Outcome
Lindner (2006)	Economic	Coordination	Two-period model of currency attack based on global games. Period 0: cb provides its assessment of the current economic strength. Period 1: traders decide whether to attack the currency. Success depends on economic strength in period 1 assessed by cb. This is unobservable but estimated based on cb's assessment of period 0, and private information	Desirable (currency markets more stable)
Morris et al. (2006)	Economic	Coordination	MS (2002)	Desirable (for reasonable parameter values)
Sibert (2006a)	Operational	Expectations augmented Phillips curve	Two-periods. Either nominal wage contracting and rational expectations as in BG (1983a), or Lucas expectations view of aggregate supply. Building on CM (1986). For a simple stochastic structure it is possible to solve the model analytically, for a different stochastic structure this is done numerically. Cbt: control errors observed. Private information: about the weights in the objective function	Desirable (lower inflation, same ability to stabilize shocks)
Svensson (2006)	Economic	Coordination	MS (2002)	Desirable (for reasonable parameter values)
Berardi and Duffi (2007)	Political	Learning NK	The ps uses a misspecified reduced form forecast model when cb's policy is not transparent, but is not aware of this misspecification. Distinction between a discretionary and a commitment regime (possible to disentangle transparency from the time-inconsistency problem)	Might be desirable under discretion (depends on targets), desirable under commitment

Demertzis and Hoeberichts (2007)	Economic	ML Coordination	Mp-game based on Demertzis and Viegi (2008) and MS(2002). Costs introduced	Might be desirable (depends on circumstances, trade-off between public and private information)
Demertzis and Hughes Hallett (2007)	Political	ML	Mp-model based on Rogoff (1985). Look at two forms of cbt: 1) about the relative weight in the cb's objective function, and 2) about the output target of the cb	Desirable (lower variability of inflation and the output gap, averages unaffected)
Eijffinger and Tesfaselassie (2007)	Economic	NK	Cb has private information on the state of the economy, which under a transparent regime is disclosed. Cbt: cb discloses forecasts of future shocks	Desirable (stabilization of current inflation and output, prerequisite: no credibility problem and/or preferences of the cb known)
Geraats (2007)	Political/ economic	Keynesian (robust to the use of ML or NK)	Imperfect common knowledge about the degree of cbt. Both actual and perceived transparency affect economic outcomes	Actual transparency is desirable, perceived transparency only about the inflation target not about the output target and supply shocks
Walsh (2007)	Economic	NK and coordination	Focus on cb's that have a good inflation reputation. Economic information that individual firms receive is diverse	Optimal degree is increasing when cost shocks are less persistent or better forecastable and decreasing when demand shocks are less persistent or better forecastable
Demertzis and Viegi (2008)	Political	Coordination	MS (2002) with Bacharach's variable universe games approach. The latter provides a description of how players evaluate the alternatives they can choose from by taking into account what all other players might believe about them	Desirable

(continued)

A. (*Continued*)

Author(s)	Aspect(s)	Used model	Brief description	Outcome
Gersbach and Hahn (2008)	Procedural	Committee	Cb-ers have different degrees of economic knowledge (ps is unaware of this). Cb-ers can participate actively in the discussion and decision making or wait and listen to the information and views provided by other cb-ers before voting. Cbt: various interest rate proposals and the individual voting records are made public	Undesirable
Rudebusch and Williams (2008)	Economic	NK	ps and cb know the structure and parameters of the equations describing output, inflation and the inflation target, and the functional form of the equation describing mp. Publication of interest rate forecasts might help reducing either policy rule uncertainty or inflation target uncertainty	Desirable (prerequisite: emphasize conditionality and uncertainty)

Note: Column 2: aspects of transparency based on Geraats (2002). Political transparency = information about the cb's goals, how they are prioritized, and quantified, and explicit institutional arrangements or a contract with the government. Economic transparency = information about the economy for example by providing economic data, the models used, and the economic forecast made. Procedural transparency = openness about the procedures used within the central bank to make a monetary policy decision (strategy, voting record, minutes). Policy transparency = the absence of asymmetric information regarding the policy of the central bank (policy decisions are clearly explained, changes are immediately announced, and future policy paths are indicated). Operational transparency = when there is a regular assessment of how well the central bank performed by looking at the achievement of operating targets, policy outcomes, and when the central bank is open about the macroeconomic disturbances that influence the policy transmission process. Column 3: ML = A model in which output is increasing in unexpected inflation (Monetarist Lucas-type transmission mechanism), NK = New Keynesian model, RTM = reserve targeting model. Columns 4 and 5: cbt = central bank transparency, cb = central bank, ps = private sector, mp = monetary policy, BG = Barro and Gordon, KP = Kydland and Prescott, MS = Morris and Shin.

B. *Empirical Summary Table*

Author(s)	Aspect(s)	Country(ies)	Period(s)	Index	Conclusion(s)
Kuttner and Posen (1999)	Political	UK, CA, NZ	1984–99, 1984–98, 1982–98	–	Desirable (decreased level and persistence of inflation)
Muller and Zelmer (1999)	Total	CA	1994–99	–	Desirable (improved anticipation of mp = future mp is better incorporated by financial asset prices)
Siklos (1999)	Political	7 IT: AU, CA, FI, NZ, ES, SE, UK and 3 non-IT: US, DE, CH	1958–97	–	Desirable (inflation persistence an lt interest rates sign. lower after the adoption of inflation targets for a majority of IT countries, no evidence for effect on inflation performance/inflation expectations)
Haldane and Read (2000)	Political, policy	UK, US	1984–97, 1990–97	–	Desirable (less yield curve surprises at the short end for the UK after 1992 and US after 1994)
Chadha and Nolan (2001)	Total	UK	1987–99	–	No effect (increased financial market volatility cannot be attributed to more cbt since May 1997)
Clare and Courtenay (2001)	Political	UK	1994–99	–	Desirable (increased speed of reaction of financial prices to interest rate announcements, but the size of the reaction remained the same or decreased, indicating that the news content of macroeconomic announcements may have fallen)
Demiralp (2001)	Policy	US	1994	–	Desirable (improved market anticipation (adjustment of market rates to future mp actions before policy announcement) and credibility (immediate reaction to surprise mp announcement without waiting for the actual mp move)

(continued)

313

B. *Continued*

Author(s)	Aspect(s)	Country(ies)	Period(s)	Index	Conclusion(s)
Cechetti and Krause (2002)	Total	22	1995–99, 1990–97, 1990–97	F	Desirable (lower average inflation (sign.); better macroeconomic performance and less policy inefficiency (not. sign.); measured using the inflation-output variability trade-off)
Chortareas et al. (2002a)	Economic	87	1995–99	Own based on F	Desirable (lower average inflation (for countries with a domestic nominal anchor based on an inflation or a money target, not for those with an exchange rate target) and unchanged output volatility)
Chortareas et al. (2002b)	Economic, procedural, policy	87	1995–99	Own based on F	Desirable (lower average inflation, lower sacrifice ratio (= unemployment costs of disinflation)
Poole et al. (2002)	Policy	US	1987–2001	–	Desirable (improved anticipation after 1994, response of lt treasury rates to unexpected funds rate target changes has become lower)
Rafferty and Tomljanovich (2002)	Policy	US	1983–98	–	Desirable (improved predictability (lower forecasting error interest rates on US bonds), lower interest rate volatility)
Chortareas et al. (2003)	Economic, procedural, policy	21 OECD	1990–2000	Own based on F	Desirable (lower sacrifice ratio)
Coppel and Connolly (2003)	Total	AU	1986–2002	–	Desirable (improved anticipation of mp: less interest rate volatility at the short end and quicker reactions to mp decisions)
Fracasso et al. (2003)	Economic/operational	20	2000–02	Own measure	Desirable (using short-term interest rates to show improved predictability of mp through higher quality inflation reports)

Study	Type	Country	Period		Assessment
Lange et al. (2003)	Political, policy	US	1983–2000	—	Desirable (improved predictability of monetary policy/lt and futures rate now incorporate changes in the federal funds rate a couple of months in advance)
Kohn and Sack (2003)	Policy	US	1989–93	—	Desirable (use various financial variables to show improved anticipation of future policy and economy, which improves policy effectiveness)
Poole and Rasche (2003)	Policy	US	1988–2002	—	Desirable (show lower market surprises using the federal funds futures rate)
Siklos (2003)	Political, economic/ operational	5 non-IT (US, DE, CH, NL, AT) and 6 IT (AU, CA, SE, NZ, ES, UK)	1988–99	—	Desirable (lower inflation expectations (survey data), improved predictability of inflation)
Gerlach-Kristen (2004)	procedural	UK	1997–2003	—	Desirable (improved predictability of mp (= repo rate changes))
Levin et al. (2004)	Political	5 IT (AU, CA, NZ, SE, UK) and 7 non-IT (US, JP, DK, FR, DE, IT, NL)	1994–2003	—	Desirable (lower inflation persistence, better anchored inflation expectations (weaker link between changes in survey inflation expectations to changes in realized inflation), especially for the lt horizons)
Lildholdt and Wetherilt (2004)	All	UK	1975–2003	—	Desirable (use a simple term structure model to show improved predictability of monetary policy, especially after the introduction of IT)
	Total	CA, UK	1994–2001, 1997–2001	—	Desirable (decreased market volatility and uncertainty using daily financial asset prices and interest rate spreads)
Meade and Stasavage (2004)	Procedural	US	1989–97	—	Undesirable (decreased quality of the FOMC's discussion and debate)

(continued)

B. *Continued*

Author(s)	Aspect(s)	Country(ies)	Period(s)	Index	Conclusion(s)
Siklos (2004)	Political	20 OECD countries	1967–99	–	Desirable (sign. lower nominal interest rates)
Ehrmann and Fratzscher (2005)	Procedural	UK, US, EU	1999–2004	–	Desirable (cbt about different points of views about the economic outlook improves anticipation of monetary policy, only for the US) and undesirable (cbt about disagreement about monetary policy could worsen it). Two methods used to measure surprise: (1) absolute value of difference between the actual mp decision and the mean of Reuters survey expectations and (2) absolute change of the 1-month interest rate on the day of the mp meeting.
Fujiwara (2005)	Economic	JP (41 forecasting institutions)	1998–2003	–	Desirable less uncertainty, improved understanding of future monetary policy (using forecasts obtained from newspapers and the internet)
Bauer et al. (2006)	Policy	US	1986–2004	–	Desirable; more synchronized private sector forecasts about the economy and policy decisions (survey data), but common forecast error unchanged
Geraats et al. (2006)	All	AU, EU, JP, NZ, SE, CH, UK, US	1993–2002	EG	Most of the times desirable (lower policy, short and long interest rates indicating increasing flexibility and reputation), although several times no effect, detrimental, or a trade-off
Gürkaynak et al. (2006)	Political	US, UK, SE	1994–2005, 1993–2005, 1996–2005	–	Desirable (better anchored inflation expectations = forward inflation compensation insensitive to economic news)

Study	Aspect	Sample	Period	Code	Result
Swanson (2006)	Total	US	1985–2003	–	Desirable (improved predictability of monetary policy using financial market data and private sector forecasts)
Biefang-Frisancho Mariscal and Howells (2007)	Political, procedural	UK	1984–2003	–	Desirable (improved policy anticipation after 1992 (inflation targeting), and more interest rate consensus among forecasters after 1997 (independence + procedural transparency), although this is more likely caused by a fall in the dispersion of inflation rate forecasts. Money market data is used.
van der Cruijsen and Demertzis (2007)	All	AU, CA, EU, JP, NZ, SE, CH, UK, US	1989–2004	EG, BSG, S, and D	Desirable; better anchored inflation expectations (= weaker relationship between changes in inflation expectations and changes in realized inflation) and less inflation persistence)
van der Cruijsen and Eijffinger (2007)	All aspects	EU (1800 respondents)	June 2007	EG	Desirable (higher transparency perceptions result in more trust, better aligned inflation perceptions and expectations)
Demertzis and Hughes Hallett (2007)	All aspects	AU, CA, EU, JP, NZ, SE, CH, UK, US	Early 90s–end 2001	EG	Desirable (not sign, correlated with average levels of inflation and output, and variability of output, but total, economic, and operational transparency are sign, correlated with lower inflation variability, 95% confidence level)
Dincer and Eichengreen (2007)	Total	100	1998–2005	DE	Desirable (better macroeconomic outcomes, e.g., lower inflation and output volatility)
Drew and Karagedikli (2007)	Total	NZ	2000–2007	–	Desirable (market reactions to new data are in line with the central bank's policy and inflation target)

(continued)

B. *Continued*

Author(s)	Aspect(s)	Country(ies)	Period(s)	Index	Conclusion(s)
Ehrmann and Fratzscher (2007)	Policy	US	1994–2004	–	Desirable (ps anticipates monetary policy decisions earlier). Daily treasury rates are used
Fatás et al. (2007)	Political	42	1960–2000	–	Desirable (lower inflation rates and output volatility)
Reeves and Sawicki (2007)	Procedural, economic/ operational, policy	UK	1997–2004	–	Desirable (Minutes and the inflation report have a significant effect on near term interest rate expectations. The timeliness with which the minutes get published seems to matter. It is harder to find significant effects of speeches and testimony to parliamentary committees, perhaps because these provide information covering a larger array of topics, its effect is more subtle and more difficult to pick up.)
Tomljanovich (2007)	Total	AU, CA, DE, JP, NZ, UK, US	1990–2003	–	Desirable (using interest rates on government bonds with various maturities shows slightly larger reductions in volatility and increased efficiency of financial markets)
Tuysuz (2007)	Policy	US	1990–2004	–	Desirable (improved market understanding)
Crowe and Meade (2008)	All	28	1998 and 2006	Own	Desirable (more accurate private sector inflation forecasts)

Study	Aspect		Period		Finding
van der Cruijsen et al. (2008)	Total	70	1998–2005	DE	Desirable (inflation persistence is minimized at an intermediate degree of transparency)
Ehrmann and Fratzscher (2008)	Policy	US	1994–2007	–	Undesirable (higher market volatility)
Ferreira de Mendonça and Filho (2008)	Economic, procedural	BR	2002–2006	–	Desirable
Rosa (2008)	Policy	US, EU	1999–2006	–	Desirable (easier to affect interest rates)
Swank et al. (2008)	Procedural	US	1989–1997	–	Undesirable (move of some deliberations to premeetings)

Note: Column 2: aspects of transparency based on Geraats (2002). Political transparency = information about the cb's goals, how they are prioritized, and quantified, and explicit institutional arrangements or a contract with the government. Economic transparency = information about the economy for example by providing economic data, the models used, and the economic forecast made. Procedural transparency = openness about the procedures used within the central bank to make a monetary policy decision (strategy, voting record, minutes). Policy transparency = the absence of asymmetric information regarding the policy of the central bank (policy decisions are clearly explained, changes are immediately announced, and future policy paths are indicated). Operational transparency = when there is a regular assessment of how well the central bank performed by looking at the achievement of operating targets, policy outcomes, and when the central bank is open about the macroeconomic disturbances that influence the policy transmission process.

BSG = Bini-Smaghi and Gros (2001), D = De Haan et al. (2004), DE = Dincer and Eichengreen (2007), EG = Eijffinger and Geraats (2006), F = Fry et al. (2000) and S = Siklos (2002). IT = inflation targeting, cbt = central bank transparency, lt = long term. Country codes: AT (Austria), AU (Australia), BR (Brazil), CA (Canada), CH (Switzerland), DE (Germany), DK (Denmark), ES (Spain), FI (Finland), FR (France), IT (Italy), JP (Japan), NL (Netherlands), NZ (New Zealand), SE (Sweden), UK (United Kingdom), US (United States).

10

How Central Banks Take Decisions:
An Analysis of Monetary Policy Meetings

Philipp Maier

Abstract

More than eighty central banks use a committee to take monetary policy decisions. The composition of the committee and the structure of the meeting can affect the quality of the decision making. In this chapter we review economical, experimental, sociological, and psychological studies to identify criteria for the optimal institutional setting of a monetary committee. These include the optimal size of the committee, measures to encourage independent thinking, a relatively informal structure of the meeting, and abilities to identify and evaluate individual members' performances. Using these criteria, we evaluate the composition and operation of monetary policy committees in more than forty central banks worldwide. Our findings indicate that, for example, the monetary policy committee of the Bank of England follows committee best practice, while the committee structure of other major central banks could be improved.

10.1 Introduction

In recent decades, central banks have undergone substantial transformations. One of the elements of the "quiet revolution" (Blinder 2004) in central banking has been a change in the way monetary policy decisions are taken: the "dictatorial central bank governor" of the past increasingly has been replaced by committees taking monetary policy decisions. Today, more than eighty central banks take monetary policy decisions in a committee. No country has ever replaced a monetary committee by a single decision maker (Mahadeva and Sterne 2000). In addition, central banks have become much more transparent (see van der Cruijsen and Eijffinger, this volume).

We view the structure of the monetary policy committee as an important part of the overall institutional framework of the central bank. The structure and composition of a committee can affect the outcome of the meeting and, possibly, the quality of decisions (Blinder 1998). Improvements to the decision-making process can have effects similar to making a central bank more transparent, as both can make monetary policy more predictable. Consequently, following best practices in setting a framework for monetary policy decisions can result in an environment where inflation expectations are better anchored or anchored at lower levels.[1]

When designing a monetary policy committee, decisions need to be taken on aspects such as its size, or whether voting records should be disclosed. To guide these decisions, theoretical models, as well as findings from the social, psychological, and experimental literature on committee decision making can provide important insights. The insights from theoretical models are summarized in studies by Fujiki (2005) and Gerling et al. (2005), who focus on game-theoretic insights for the design of committees. There is, however, an important limitation: While theoretical studies can yield recommended mechanism to, say, limit strategic voting in committees, they have to rely on assumptions concerning human behavior (i.e., the degree to which committee members are inclined to pursue private interests). How members of a committee behave "in real life" is examined not in theoretical models, but in the social, psychological, and experimental literature. In addition, this strand of the literature has uncovered that when groups take decisions, group processes such as group think might interfere in the decision making. These are not easily captured in theoretical models. Consequently, regarding, for example, the optimal size of the committee, Fujiki (2005) cannot give a definitive answer.

Against this backdrop, we review empirical and experimental studies in the fields of economics, psychology, and sociology to identify recommendations for setting up a committee "optimally." As of yet, there is no overarching theory or consensus about what constitutes an optimal structure of the decision-making committee of a central bank. However, to guide these decisions, these studies can provide important insights. Our focus lies on issues relevant for monetary policymaking in central banks, but clearly this discussion applies for other types of committees as well. Our study follows Sibert (2006) and Vandenbussche (2006), but in addition, we also provide new data on the setup of monetary committees in many central banks.[2] On the basis of the review of empirical and experimental studies, we derive a number of criteria about how monetary policy committees should

---

[1]   Chortareas et al. (2001) find that higher transparency is correlated with lower inflation.
[2]   This extends the empirical work of Mahadeva and Sterne (2000) and Wyplosz et al. (2003).

be set up, and how meetings should be structured, and, using these criteria, we then analyze the institutional setup of monetary policy committees in various central banks in the world.

To preview the conclusions, we find that some central banks have taken measures that are likely to increase the effectiveness of their monetary committees. A vast majority of central banks, however, could probably improve their committee framework by making it possible, for example, to identify and evaluate individual contributions to counter free-riding on information provided by others.

We proceed as follows. In the next section we outline the main benefits and costs of taking monetary decisions by committee. We identify a number of criteria for "good" committees, and use them to evaluate real-life monetary committees in Section 3. The final section summarizes our main conclusions.

10.2 The Impact of Committees on Decision Making

Consider a central bank with a clear target and instruments suitable to achieve the target. Also, the central bank is independent in its use of instruments, that is, it is effectively shielded from outside pressure.[3] As it is impossible to foresee all contingencies, the central bank retains a degree of discretion (otherwise monetary policy could be set by a computer). The central bank's success will depend on the quality of its decisions. And if these decisions are taken by a committee, the structure of the committee will matter.

My experience as a member of the FOMC [Federal Open Market Committee] left me with a strong feeling that the theoretical fiction that monetary policy is made by a single individual . . . misses something important. In my view, monetary theorists should start paying attention to the nature of decision making by committee. . . (Blinder 1998, 22).

We define the monetary policy committee as the body taking monetary decisions.[4] Ideally, we can think of the monetary policy committee as a

---

[3] In the words of Goodfriend (2005), assume that an "overarching guidance" exists that supplements formal central bank independence and that enables the central bank to use its monetary policy power efficiently to stabilize the economy.

[4] When referring to the body taking monetary policy decisions, we use the terms "monetary (policy) committee," "committee" or "group" interchangeably. The head of the committee will be called "chairman." The discussion will primarily focus on the monetary policy aspect, as this is the most visible aspect of central banking.

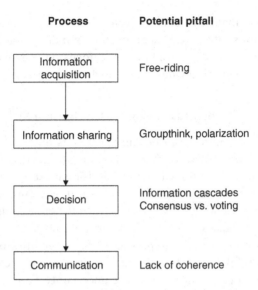

Figure 10.1. Decision making and potential pitfalls

group of people sharing information and taking a decision together, on the basis of the information reviewed (and revealed).

Assume that all committee members genuinely want the committee to take good decisions, which we define here as the optimal monetary policy in the face of an uncertain economic environment.[5] However, the committee operates in a uncertain environment, as the state of nature or the state of the economy is not readily observable. Hence, committee members need to gather, share, and discuss information, on which the group decision will be based. Figure 10.1 shows how a group decision is taken. On the right of the figure, we show how, at each of these stages, group processes might interfere in the decision-making process. Examples of such processes include adoption of extreme preferences (polarization), the need to achieve consensus, or free-riding on information provided by others (Kerr et al. 1996). The structure of the committee can either facilitate taking good decisions, for example, by providing incentives to be well prepared – or induce frictions, because, for example, the committee is too large to allow for a genuine exchange of views.

[5] As we focus on the decision making in committees, we abstract from the possibility that committee members pursue private interests or have strong political preferences. In practice, however, such considerations may matter (Siklos 2002).

To expose the main elements of group decision making more clearly, we abstract from strategic considerations or from analyzing the merits of different decision rules.[6] This allows us to focus on our main objective, namely examining how individuals behave when taking a decision together.

10.2.1 The Benefits of Committee Decision Making

The virtues of committees can be summarized as follows. First, if every member of a committee exerts effort to become informed, committees can gather more information than individual decision makers. Better information can lead to better decisions. Second, even if all committee members have identical information, they need not reach the same (individual) conclusion. This is because committee members typically have different skills, different backgrounds and preferences, and different abilities to process data and to extract useful information. Third, if information may contain errors, a committee can pool signals and reduce uncertainty. Fourth, committees provide an "insurance" against extreme preferences.

Information gathering

Committee members can possess different information sets. Central bankers might, for example, have links to key sectors in the business community (Goodfriend 2005) or to international fora, from which they gain private information. This holds, in particular, if central banks have regional branches. Also, within a central bank, committee members might have different functions, for example, one being in charge of (domestic) research, one in charge of financial supervision, and so on. Group discussion enables participants to share information, such that the committee as a whole can access a larger pool of information than any one person acting alone (Shaw 1981).

Information processing

Individuals differ in terms of their ability to process information. *Homo economicus* is an efficient calculating machine; *homo sapien* is not (Blinder 2007a). Diverse groups can outperform individuals or homogeneous groups in solving problems (Hong and Page 2004).[7] Blinder and Morgan (2005, 2007) and Lombardelli et al. (2002) show that groups outperform

---

[6] An extensive overview is given in Mueller (2003).
[7] Odean (1998) cautions on the value of "expert knowledge" when experts are individuals. He reports that physicians, nurses, lawyers, engineers, entrepreneurs, and investment bankers typically overestimate their own knowledge. However, the *average* prediction of experts –

individuals in an experiment designed to mimic monetary policy when the state of the economy is uncertain.

Applied to monetary committees, variations in information-processing skills can result, for example, from employing different economic models to evaluate the state of the economy, or from different methods for making forecasts (Gerlach-Kristen 2006). Pooling knowledge leads to better forecasts and potentially better decisions.

Removing noise from signals

Consider the following stylized setting (Sibert 2006): A committee of n members has to take a binary decision. Prior to the meeting, every committee member receives a private signal about which alternative is best. Suppose that, by assumption, the private signals are uncorrelated, informative, but "noisy" – that is although the signals are on average more likely to be correct than incorrect, there is a certain probability that the signal is wrong. Assuming that all members vote according to the signal they receive, and that decisions are taken by simple majority, the probability that the correct alternative is chosen goes to one as the committee size increases. This result is the famous Condorcet jury theorem (Condorcet 1785): If decisions are taken by majority, the committee is more likely to pick the best option than any of its members (i.e., a committee is more than just the sum of its parts). Lastly, in an experimental study, Kocher and Sutter (2005) show that groups are not smarter decision makers per se, but that they learn faster than individuals.

Insurance

Much as a careful investor would not put all his eggs in one basket, having policy set by a group rather than by a single central banker keeps policy from going to extremes (Waller 2000). Hence, committees can provide an "insurance" against strong individual preferences. Also, letting a committee decide – as opposed to having a single monetary decision maker – provides a certain "protection" for the Governor (and all other committee members), who otherwise might be subject to substantial personal pressure (Goodhart 2000). This "protection" helps to promote independence and facilitates the frank discussion of opinions.

that is, if their knowledge is pooled together – is likely to be correct. Surowiecki (2004) provides an example of a weight-judging competition, where members of a crowd placed wagers on the weight of an ox. The average guess of 787 contestants was 1,197 pounds. The crowd missed the actual weight by only one (!) pound.

Implications

An important implication of the first two elements is that to reap the full benefits of committee decision making, its members should be heterogeneous. An optimal committee consists of people that share information to jointly maximize the information available to the group.

Some qualifications apply. First, information gathering and information processing is assumed to be costless (and effortless). Hence, the optimal committee would be infinitively large. As we show in the following, once we allow for costs associated with information gathering, there is likely to be an "upper limit" for the optimal committee size.

Second, the insurance argument assumes that individual preferences are stable, and that group membership does not introduce biases in judgment. This, however, is not necessarily true. The next section shows that there are powerful reasons to believe that committee membership may affect individual preferences or judgment.

10.2.2 The Costs of Committee Decision Making

Large committees do not work

Output of real-world committees is not always as good as one might expect, given the capabilities of the individuals who comprise them. This holds particularly for large committees. The key difference between individual and group decision making is the exchange of information. However, information exchange in group decision making is often done poorly (Stasser 1992). For instance, when information acquisition is costly, group members have incentives to free ride. An appropriate committee structure, however, may alleviate these issues.

Free-riding

Free-riding or shirking refers to behavior where individuals do not exert their full effort in contributing to the group's performance. Shirking can easily be measured in additive tasks, such as pulling a rope.[8] Assuming that there are no coordination problems and that individuals' efforts do not depend on the size of the group, group output should rise linearly as additional group members are added. However, if individuals tend to shirk when they are part of a group (and more so the larger the group), then

---

[8] An additive task is one wherein the group's performance is the sum of individual performances. A disjunctive task is one wherein the committee's performance depends on its most competent member (e.g., problem solving).

group performance will be a concave function of the number of members. As Sibert (2006) reports, a vast number of studies have found evidence for shirking across a range of additive tasks such as clapping and shouting.

In a committee context, shirking exists because revealed information becomes a public good. Suppose the correct decision depends on the (unobservable) state of the economy. A member observes a signal if he or she expends effort (the signal is a random draw from a normal distribution with known variance). There is no conflict over objectives, but information is a public good, which is costly to obtain (such "costs" can include reading briefing material distributed prior to the meeting). Hence, each member would prefer to become informed rather than have the committee be completely uninformed; however, each member's most preferred option is for the *other* members to expend effort becoming informed, while he or she free rides (Sibert 2005).

It is not fully understood what determines optimal committee size, but studies by Berger et al. (2007) and Erhart et al. (2007) suggest that country-specific characteristics are important. For instance, more complex economies – that is, larger economies or those with more diverse economic structure – might require a larger committee to gather and process information. Also, the exact nature of the central bank's tasks (for instance, whether the central bank is also supervising the financial sector) can affect optimal committee size. Lastly, political institutions may matter, as larger committee may insulate the central bank better from political pressures. This builds on Lybek and Morris's (2004) idea that the size of a central bank's board is a balance between the central bank's function, simplicity, and country-specific factors, including appointment procedures or terms of the committee members.

Shirking becomes more important as committee size increases: the larger the group, the less noticeable it is if one member does not sufficiently participate in the decision making or if he or she is poorly informed. Hence, if the size of the committee increases, the (marginal) costs arising from shirking increase. At the same time, the additional benefits from more people being able to process information get smaller the larger the committee.

Taken together, when information acquisition is costly, and committee members have incentives to shirk, the optimal size of the committee is finite (Gerling et al. 2005). This means that some of the benefits of (larger) committees in terms of better information processing cannot be reaped. This is visualized in Figure 10.2. The solid line shows the benefits of the committee, or more specifically, the marginal gain in terms of information gathering or processing from adding an additional individual to the committee. The steeper dotted line shows the marginal costs that arise when the committee

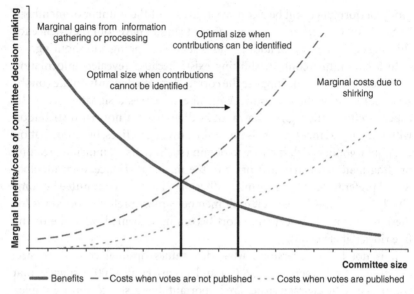

Figure 10.2. Optimal committee size

expands, because additional members increase opportunities and incentives to shirk. Measures to limit shirking are therefore important. There are two ways of dealing with shirking.

- Limiting the size of the committee
- Creating incentives to discourage shirking

Shirking is reduced when individual contributions can be identified and evaluated. For instance, relay team swimmers swim laps faster when individual times were made public, but slower when they were not (Williams et al. 1989). Similar results are found for brainstorming tasks (Harkins and Jackson 1985). Croson and Marks (1998) experimentally examine how information affects behavior. All group members can contribute toward a public good, but participants receive varying amounts of information about contributions made by others (the public good can be compared to information in a committee context). Revealing anonymous information about other contributions leads to a significant decrease in contributions. When individual contributions are clearly identifiable, average contributions increase.[9]

---

[9] A study that comes relatively close to monetary policy analysis is Henningsen et al. (2000): 189 persons worked either alone or in four-person or eight-person groups. Each participant

Applied to the central banking context, an institutional device to discourage free-riding is the publication of the discussion in the form of minutes. An alternative possibility could be that, prior to the meeting, each committee member privately notes his or her preferences and the main arguments for the upcoming decision. This forces individuals to become informed. Again this information could be published in the minutes. Both measures imply a reduction in shirking. This means that the line showing the marginal costs of adding more committee members is now flatter (the flatter dotted line in Figure 10.2). The optimal committee size increases, and more gains from information gathering and processing arise.

Inertia

A common criticism of committee decision making focuses on the difficulties to reach a decision:

Had Newton served on more faculty committees at Cambridge, his first law of motion might have read: A decision-making body at rest or in motion tends to stay at rest or in motion in the same direction unless acted upon by an outside force (Blinder 1998).

Riboni and Ruge-Murcia (2006) formalize this notion. They show that if the status quo is the "default option" in situations where the committee cannot agree, monetary policy tends to be too inert. However, these authors require a number of strong assumptions to generate inertia, such as the committee is not able to take a majority decision. In practice, many central banks [such as the European Central Bank (ECB)] have provisions that, in the event of a tie, the chairman's vote counts double. Also, experimental evidence indicates that groups are not more inert than individuals (Blinder and Morgan 2005, 2007).

An important factor contributing to inertia is whether committees are not "internally transparent." By this we mean that not every committee member is forced to reveal his or her position (i.e., whether he or she votes A or B). Such ambiguities can result in consensus-oriented committees. Also, voting committees need only to convince fewer members to change policy (at the margin, "50 + ϵ" percent is sufficient), whereas consensus-oriented committees need to convince more than 50% of the group members. Simulations show that building consensus can delay the

was asked to read information for the purpose of making a future individual or group decision. Individuals who anticipated working alone recalled more of what they had read.

decision making (Gerlach-Kristen 2005). We return to this issue when we discuss consensus versus voting in committees.

Optimal committee size

As the optimal committee size depends on behavioral considerations, purely theoretical studies (e.g., Fujiki 2005) cannot provide a definite answer. The experimental literature does give some guidance: Slater (1958) had 24 groups of two to seven male undergraduates who were given analytical problems to discuss. He asked the group members whether their group was too large or too small. Groups of five did best.

Oakley et al. (2004) found that with only two people on a team, there may not be a sufficient variety of ideas, skills, and approaches to problem solving for the full benefits of group work to be realized. Also, conflict resolution can be problematic in a pair: whether right or wrong, the dominant partner will win most arguments. On the other hand, if a team has more than five members, at least one is likely to be relatively passive. As monetary policy is a relatively complex task, the benefits from having a large committee might be very important. Hence, the optimal committee size might be moderately larger than these studies suggest. Sibert (2006) concludes that monetary policy committees should probably have at least five members, but they should not be much larger. Beyond seven to nine members, the participation of members decreases and members become less satisfied, and groups of over twelve people find mutual interaction difficult.[10] In view of these considerations, it is encouraging that Erhart et al. (2007) found that, in their sample of 85 central banks, the average MPC consisted of seven members.

"Hub-and-spoke" committees and rotation

The monetary policymaking bodies of the central banks representing the two largest currency areas in the world – the U.S. Federal Reserve and the ECB – have clearly more than 10 members.[11] They are also set up in "hubs" (i.e., the Fed Board in Washington and the ECB in Frankfurt) and "spokes"

---

[10] As an aside, the literature on microbanking also suggests that small group sizes (3–10 people) work best, for example, because small groups can monitor each other's effort better (Morduch 1999).

[11] In their defense, it has been noted that for a large currency area, the committee might benefit from regional representation: "If an economy is complex. . . then it might be useful to have the views of the key sectors represented on the policy committee" (Goodfriend 2005). From a practical perspective, improvements in data collection and better economic statistics may reduce the need for regional or sectoral representation. For the euro area,

(the regional Feds or the national central banks of the euro-area member countries).

- The Federal Open Market Committee (FOMC) comprises the seven Board members and the President of the Federal Reserve Bank of New York. Of the other eleven regional Fed Presidents, only four have the right to vote.[12]
- The ECB Governing Council consists of five ECB Board members, plus all euro-area National Central Bank (NCB) Governors (currently 13).

Both central banks have adopted a rotation system to limit the number of voting members – that is, the right to vote rotates following a predetermined sequence.[13] If rotation is used as a device to shorten the time needed for discussion, then this goal can only be achieved if nonvoting members hardly ever participate in the discussion.

In principle, rotation is a useful device to increase the amount of information without compromising the group size. Note, however, a potential danger of such a system is that, if committee members interests' are not fully aligned, voting members might exploit the nonvoting members. Bosman et al. (2004) show that committee members might be trapped in a "prisoner's dilemma," that is, everyone votes for options that maximize his or her own advantage. Such individualistic voting behavior can result in the committee taking worse decisions than if every member had just voted for the option that maximizes the group's benefit. And lastly, a risk is that rotation can cause spurious changes in policy, simply from rotation of committee members.

Instability of preferences and groupthink
An important assumption underlying committee benefits is that membership in a group does not change members' prior beliefs or preferences. Economists typically downplay the influence of others on people's preferences, and emphasize people's autonomy. In contrast, sociologists and social-network theorists describe people as embedded in particular social

national representation might also be an important issue, for example, because it may facilitate communication (Wellink et al. 2002).
[12] More specifically, the Presidents of the Cleveland and Chicago Banks vote in alternating years. The remaining three FOMC votes rotate annually among the Presidents of the other nine Reserve Banks (see Meade and Sheets, 2005, for details).
[13] The ECB rotation scheme will become effective once the number of NCB Governors rises above 15 (European Central Bank 2003).

contexts. Influence from others is inescapable. The more influence members of a group exert on each other, the more likely it is that group members' preferences align (Surowiecki 2004). Research in social and cognitive psychology has devoted considerable effort to showing that human judgment is imperfect (Kerr et al. 1996).

Are committees any less – or more – subject to judgmental biases than individual decision makers? Several hundred studies demonstrate that belonging to a committee polarizes its members. For example, groups are more likely to support failing projects (Whyte 1993). This could imply that monetary policy set by a committee is overly biased against inflationary pressures, or less likely to correct past mistakes (note that in this case, the failure to correct past mistakes is not due to inertia, but to biased, polarized views).

A particularly harmful form of group polarization occurs when committee members stop paying sufficient attention to alternatives, because they are striving for consensus. This is also called groupthink (Janis 1973). The following factors have been identified as leading to groupthink (Sibert 2006):

- insulation from outsiders;
- lack of diversity in viewpoints; and
- leaders actively advocating solutions.

Key to avoiding groupthink is independence, that is, to encourage committee members to think for themselves. Encouraging independence has two positive effects (Surowiecki 2004): first, it avoids errors in judgment becoming correlated.[14] Second, independent committee members are more likely to gather new, additional information or interpret existing information differently. This might lead them to question the group consensus and thus, ultimately, limit groupthink (Morck 2004). In line with these considerations, the experimental study by Blinder and Morgan (2007) finds that committees do *not* perform better when they have a designated chairman.

An institutional arrangement to avoid groupthink is to appoint committee members with different personal backgrounds. Clearly, members of a monetary committee should have some knowledge about what monetary

---

[14] Errors in individual judgment do not wreck the collective judgment, as long as these errors are not systematically correlated (i.e., all pointing in the same direction). Note, however, that the collective decision might be biased if the signals are correlated, for example, because all committee members base their judgment on the same forecast. This underlines the importance of independent information gathering.

policy can achieve. However, a committee consisting of only economists (possibly with Ph.D.s from a small handful of universities, which aligns their ways of thinking even more), or only "career" central bankers, is more likely to exhibit groupthink than a more diverse group. Similarly, having external members on the committee – that is, members not working at the central bank, like academics or business representatives – might help. This is not to say that the monetary policy committee should *only* be staffed by members without a background in economics. In fact, as Göhlmann and Vaubel (2005) have shown, former trade unionists and politicians seem to have higher inflation preference than former bankers, former members of central bank staff, or businessmen (note that their results regarding education are less clear). However, having some "noneconomists" on the committee can play an important role in avoiding groupthink. Consistent with this view is that an analysis of voting records of the Bank of England's MPC has found that noncentral bankers dissent more often than central bankers. The value of their dissenting views can be inferred from the observation that their dissents seem to perform well in forecasting future interest rate changes (Gerlach-Kristen 2003).

Note, however, two caveats: First, if group members are "too independent," the monetary committee may run the danger of speaking with too many voices when communicating externally (Blinder 2007b). The monetary committee should be individualistic enough to benefit from diversity, yet collegial and disciplined enough to project a clear and transparent message. Second, while diversity is likely to have a positive impact on group processes, it may be detrimental for the conduct of monetary policy, if the composition of the group impedes the central bank's independence. Such a situation can occur when a monetary committee is dominated by government officials, who may care about their reelection (Tuladhar 2005). This bears the risk that despite the central bank being formally independent, its policy nevertheless reflects electoral constraints.

Structuring the meeting
Avoiding information cascades

A different institutional device to counter groupthink is related to how meetings are structured. Assume a committee taking a binary decision (Bikhchandani et al. 1992). Prior to the meeting, each member receives an independent signal. The chairman makes the first proposal. If the first person after the chairman has received a similar signal, that person will support the chairman. If not, that person might flip a coin. The important issue is that if the second person chooses to support the proposal, the third person has strong incentives to agree to the proposal, too: even if the third person received a different signal prior to the meeting, having observed (on the basis of their voting behavior) that the first two persons have both received the other signal, it is safer to assume that his or her own signal is wrong. Similar considerations hold, of course, for all other committee members.

In other words: the "hurdles" to expressing a contrary view increase as more members have previously voiced identical opinions. Such a group process is called an "information cascade." In an experimental setup, Anderson and Holt (1997) show that wrong initial signals can start a chain of incorrect decisions that is not broken easily by correct signals received later. Repeated information cascades can lead to groupthink. Experiments by Milgram (1974) show that individuals may have a psychological predisposition to obey authority. Applied to monetary policy decision making, this means that if the chairman (or the person to speak first) is a very powerful or "authoritarian" person, the tendency for conformity may be high.

The fundamental problem with information cascades is that choices are made sequentially, instead of all at once. There are two ways to avoid information cascades: first, by promoting independent thinking among committee members. Independence can be promoted by not making the meeting structure too formal. For instance, it is preferable that the same person does not always open the discussion, or that the same person does not always make the interest rate proposal. A device to implement this is not to have a fixed order for speakers. Alternatively, one might consider removing the sequential element of the decision making by letting all people decide simultaneously. One way of doing this is to vote.

Consensus or voting?

A long-standing debate among central bankers is whether a committee should use voting or operate consensus based. *A priori*, there is no reason to believe that either of the two options always delivers better results. Voting has the advantage that every group member has to reveal his or her preference. Also voting can act as a device to reduce free-riding, especially if individual voting patterns are published. A similar arrangement can, however, be implemented in a consensus-oriented approach, when the contribution of individual committee members is identifiable.

Several disadvantages of voting have been mentioned. First, members on the losing side can become dissatisfied (particularly if they are regularly losing), or "winning" members can become concerned with maintaining group harmony (Janis 1973). This could lead them not to vote sincerely. Second, if individual voting patterns are published, external pressure on committee members might increase.[15] Lastly, group members might be concerned about appearing "competent." This might discourage asking questions challenging the conventional wisdom. This needs to be taken seriously, as in, for example, the study of Schweiger et al. (1986), which shows that "dialectical inquiry" and playing the "devil's advocate" can greatly improve the decision.[16] Hence, it is important that the discussion is frank and open. This concern could be dealt with by publishing a detailed transcript of the discussion, but not mentioning names.

How well consensus-oriented committees perform depends on whether the committee is evidence-based or verdict-based (Surowiecki 2004): Evidence-based juries spend time to sift through the evidence and explicitly contemplate alternative explanations before they take a vote. Verdict-based juries see their mission as reaching a decision as quickly as possible by taking a vote before any discussion (and the debate concentrates on getting those who do not agree to agree). If evidence-based, the consensus-oriented approach may encourage members more to engage in a discussion than voting. Pressure to reach a consensus quickly, as in verdict-based juries, often leads to poor choices (Priem et al. 1995).

While we focus primarily on interaction *within* the committee throughout this study, the discussion on consensus versus voting is also affected by the way the committee interacts with the outside world. Communication with financial markets has become an important issue during the past 15 years (Woodford 2005).[17] Greater transparency and clarity are thought to limit surprises for financial markets, thereby reducing uncertainty and generating less volatility (Kohn and Sack 2003; van der Cruijsen and Eijffinger, this volume). Central banks can provide information on the decision itself,

---

[15] This concern has been particularly emphasized in the European context, where NCB Governors might be subject to political pressure in their home country (Issing 1999). Another concern about publication of votes is that market participants might use them to predict individual members' voting patterns.

[16] In its purest form, dialectical inquiry uses debates between diametrically opposed sets of recommendations and assumptions, whereas devil's advocacy relies on critiques of single sets of recommendations and assumptions (Schweiger et al. 1986).

[17] Good communication is important for central banks not only for reasons of democratic legitimacy, but also in the interest of the central bank itself: central banks can only influence short-term interest rates, whereas the effectiveness of monetary policy depends on the degree to which economic variables, such as long-term interest rates, exchange rates, equity price, and so on respond to central bank's actions. Better communication with the public, in particular clarity about the expected future path of short-term rates over coming months, strengthens the relationship between these variables and central bank's policy steps. Therefore, good communication improves the effectiveness of monetary policy (see Blinder et al. 2008).

on inputs for the decision, on how the decision was reached, or even disclose transcripts of the meeting or plans for future policy. The ways central banks organize their communication with financial markets is arguably not independent of their decision making: If decisions are taken by committee, the question arises whether committee members should communicate in a collegial manner – that is, by conveying the consensus or majority view of the committee – or in an individualistic way, by stressing and conveying the diversity of views among the committee members (Blinder 2007b).

Consensus-oriented: When monetary committees operate consensus-based, it is not evident why they should discuss "conflicts" in public. After all, a collegial committee wants to project an "aura of agreement" (Blinder and Wyplosz 2004) in its disclosures. Therefore, under this model, central banks are likely to emphasize unanimous agreement. In principle, they could still decide to discuss different policy options in public, or to disclose whey they preferred, say, option A over option B. In practice, though, not all consensus-based committees provide detailed information on options they dismissed (the ECB is an obvious example here). To some extent, this might be regarded as lacking transparency if it masks disagreements within the committee.

Voting: When monetary committees vote, central banks can choose to disclose the results of the votes (possibly also disclosing who cast dissenting votes); and in many cases, dissenting members of the committee also talk in public – or even in parliament – about their reasons for dissenting. For example, the U.S. Federal Reserve is relatively individualistic in its communication, as FOMC members regularly express personal views. Similarly, members of the Bank of England's MPC have discussed their reasons for dissenting in public (e.g., Nickell 2000).

Which of the two is preferable is not clear. Blinder (2007a) highlights the danger that voting may pose difficulties for communication. Voting highlights differences in opinion, even if in practice the differences are relatively small. A consensus-oriented approach may make it easier when addressing the public: "If the result is a cacophony rather than clarity, that may confuse rather than enlighten the markets and the public" (Blinder 2007a). Empirically, however, the results are more mixed: for instance, Siklos (2003) finds that for the United Kingdom, volatility in key interest rates is actually *lower* when minutes reveal disagreement in the committee than when decisions are taken unanimously. This could indicate that bonds markets could actually benefit from the additional information revealed, if disagreement among committee members is made explicit by disclosing voting patterns. Ehrmann and Fratzscher (2005) find that the ECB and the Federal Reserve, despite the differences in their decision-making and communication strategies, are equally predictable in terms of their policy decisions. Also, the responsiveness of financial markets to communication from these central banks is equally good. This suggests that in practice, both decision-making and communication strategies can be equally effective.

10.2.3 Implications for Committee Design

Committees can offer the classic benefit of diversification: a higher mean with a lower variance. To function properly, the committee should have an overarching framework, that is, a clearly defined target and freedom to adjust its instruments in order to achieve that goal. But additional arrangements may be required to facilitate information sharing and aggregation, and avoid polarization of group members.

As mentioned before, there is no overarching theory on decision making, and recommendations regarding the structure of a "good" committee are not based on first principles. However, the studies reviewed suggest a number of criteria, which can be thought of as "best practice." Table 10.1 summaries the main design implications of the preceding discussion. First, the body taking monetary decisions should be small enough to allow for an exchange of views. Second, encouraging group members to act and think independently is crucial to avoid polarization and groupthink. Having

Table 10.1. *Criteria for "good" committees*

Clear objectives and independence
* Clearly defined goal and efficient instruments
* High score of central bank independence

Size of the monetary policy committee
* Not much larger than five members
* Rotation can lead to better information and limit the group size

Measures to avoid free-riding
* Possibility to identify and evaluate individual contributions

Polarization and groupthink
* Encouraging group members to think for themselves
* Different personal backgrounds
* Having a mix of internal and external members
* No fixed speaking order to avoid information cascades

---

group members with different personal backgrounds – that is, different nationalities or different professions – might help. Lastly, the literature offers no clear preference for voting or consensus – both can work well, provided that arrangements exist to identify and evaluate individual contributions to avoid shirking.

10.3 Monetary Policy Committees in Practice

Before we review how real-life monetary committees operate, we should stress that committees organized very differently can nevertheless take good decisions. Each central bank operates differently, and different traditions may justify different setups. However, on the basis of the studies reviewed we would argue that the likelihood for committees to consistently take good decisions is higher if the setup of the committee follows the lines we outline in the following.

10.3.1 Clear Objectives and Independence

Few studies provide detailed information about the structure of monetary policy committee meetings, but various studies have compiled evidence about central banks' objectives and their degree of independence. Among the most comprehensive is the survey by Mahadeva and Sterne (2000). Other studies have covered either a more limited set of countries (Siklos 2002, provides information on the governance of 20 OECD central banks; Tuladhar 2005, focuses on inflation targeting countries) or have a slightly different focus (e.g., Wyplosz et al. 2003, focus on central bank communication, but they also provide information on decision making for 19 central banks in their study; Berger et al. 2007, and Erhart and Vasquez-Pas 2007, provide evidence on the size of monetary policy committees in 85 central banks). We, therefore, take Mahadeva and Sterne (2000) as our starting point.

Consider central banks' institutional structure first. Regarding the clarity of objectives, Mahadeva and Sterne (2000) report that of the 94 central banks in their sample, 90 had monetary stability as a legal objective. Approximately 95% have operationalized this by translating it into a definition of price stability, an inflation target or a monitoring range – which is an improvement over 1990, when only 57% had an explicit nominal target or monitoring range.[18] Seventy-seven central banks can be classified as having

---

[18] Note that in the 1990s, many central banks had exchange rate targets or target ranges.

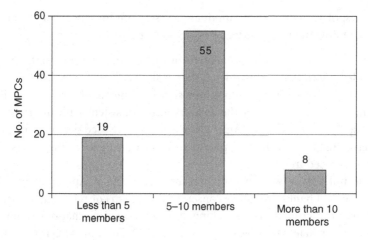

Source: Mahadeva and Sterne (2000)

Figure 10.3. Size of the monetary policy board

instrument independence.[19] Seventy-nine central banks take decisions in a committee. The most common committee size is between five and ten members (see Figure 10.3).

10.3.2 The Structure of the Monetary Policy Meeting

Mahadeva and Sterne (2000) provide information on central bank governance, but their study does not give a comprehensive picture of how decision making in central banks actually takes place. Also, as mentioned above, other studies either focus on other issues, or have a more restrictive coverage. We seek to make our sample as broad as possible, covering all central banks on the BIS web site (currently 149). To be able to evaluate central banks against the criteria we set out in Table 10.1, we gather our own data. We rely on three sources:

- speeches from senior bank officials, in which they discuss the process of monetary policy decision making;
- information on monetary policy committees on central banks' web sites; and

---

[19] Their score ranges from 0 (no instrument independence) to 1 (full independence). Seventy seven have a score of 0.66 or more, indicating that the central bank is the "leading body" to set monetary policy. Note that the number of observations differs between Figure 10.3 and Figure 10.4, as not all central banks have committees or disclose their size.

- responses to a brief questionnaire we sent out to central banks to find out how their committee meetings are structured.

All three sources have been used, but given that central banks differ considerably in terms of the detail they make available in English through web sites and speeches, we took our survey results as the starting point. Then, we checked whether the answers were consistent with information from speeches or web sites. Also, where available, we used personal contacts to verify that the information provided an accurate picture of the decision-making procedure.[20]

The full survey we sent out by e-mail is given in Appendix A.[21] As many central banks are rather conservative in terms of releasing information about internal decision making, it is not surprising that our response rate is lower than Mahadeva and Sterne (2000). In total, 44 central banks responded, and we list key elements of their responses in Table 10.3. We report the following.

- The size of the monetary policy committee (column 2). This allows checking whether the committee is too big. Where available, column 2 also reports the number of external and internal members in brackets (external members are not working for central banks, internal members are central bankers). Together with the information about personal backgrounds of committee members given in column 3, this serves as an indication of the diversity of the committee.

- Column 4 reports whether decisions are taken by consensus (C) or voting (V); column 5 shows whether (individual) votes are published. This information is a proxy for the degree to which individual contributions can be identified and evaluated – that is, for the degree to which the committee setup discourages shirking.

- The remaining columns summarize information on measures to counter information cascades and groupthink. Column 6 provides

---

[20] Clearly, all of these sources have limitations. Given most central banks' secrecy when it comes to the details of monetary policy decision making, we have few possibilities to verify whether the information gathered from the sources conveys the full picture. To limit errors, we only included central banks for which we could verify the information provided in the survey. This also means that central banks that did not respond to the survey are not included in our study. Lastly, where answers were ambiguous, we clarified by asking more precise questions (e-mails are available upon request).

[21] A first e-mail was sent out to all 149 central banks on the BIS web site on June 20, 2006; all central banks that did not respond to the initial e-mail were contacted again on February 12, 2007. In addition, where available, we pursued personal contacts to gather information or to verify answers we received to the questionnaire.

information about the organization of the meeting, column 7 reports who makes the interest rate proposal, and column 8 reports if the Governor has been on the losing side of a vote (the idea here is that an authoritarian Governor is never on the losing side of a vote). Lastly, column 9 provides how committee members are encouraged to act and think independently.

It is apparent that many central banks have diverse monetary committees, some of which are staffed with central bankers, academics, and/or representatives of the business community or ministries (see Figure 10.4).[22] Figure 10.5 shows a relatively even distribution of voting versus consensus, but note that some central banks have tried to augment consensus decision making by making the Governor solely responsible for the decision. This provides strong incentives for the Governor to ensure that all committee members have an open and frank discussion to reap the benefits of information sharing and evaluation. And our results suggest that while many central banks publish votes, few publish individual votes (Figure 10.6).

Another apparent feature is that few central banks have fixed speaking orders, but at the same time, few central banks have institutional mechanisms to effectively encourage independent thinking. Moreover, most central banks have fairly strict rules on who makes the interest rate proposal

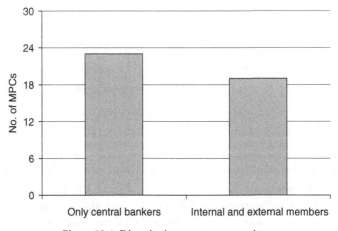

Figure 10.4. Diversity in monetary committees

---

[22] The Figures 10.6–10.8 are based on information contained in Table 10.3.

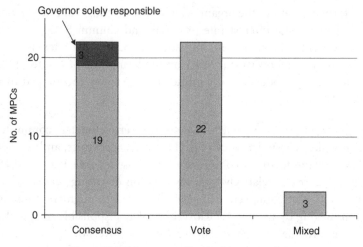

Figure 10.5. Monetary policy decision procedures

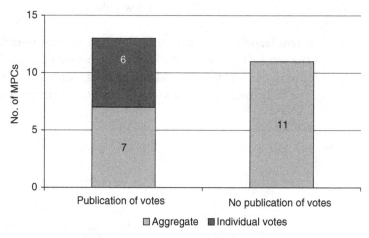

Figure 10.6. Are votes published?

(see Figure 10.7) – which, as indicated above, bears a severe risk of information cascades. And lastly, many central banks are reluctant to disclose whether the Governor has a lost a vote during the last 5 years (see Figure 10.8). However, some central banks provide that information, and it seems that among these, the Governor being on the losing side of a vote is the exception.

Next, we convert some of the qualitative indicators we collected into quantitative measures in the following way: the variable "Diversity" is zero

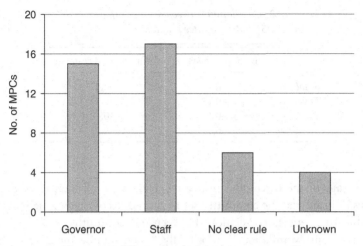

Figure 10.7. Who makes the interest rate proposal?

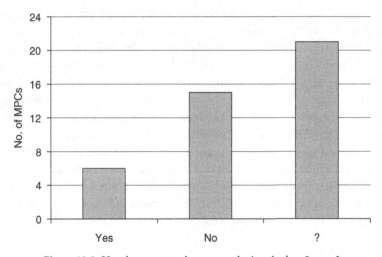

Figure 10.8. Has the governor lost a vote during the last 5 years?

for committees that are staffed only with central bankers; more diverse committees are assigned 1. "Proposal" indicates who makes the first interest rate proposal. Higher values indicate less likelihood of information cascades: the variable takes values of 1 if Staff makes the first proposal, 2 if there is no clear rule, and 0 if the Governor always makes the first proposal. "Governor" measures whether the Governor has lost a vote during the last 5 years, taking the value 0 if he has not (and 1 otherwise). Lastly, "Total score" simply takes

Table 10.2. *Correlation between average inflation*
(2000–2006) and committee properties

	Emerging markets	Industrialized countries
Total score	−0.11	−0.47
Diversity	−0.17	−0.33
Proposal	−0.13	−0.48
Governor	0.11	0.34

the average of the three other measures. Hence, for all indicators, higher values indicate that the committee setup is closer to our recommendations.

Table 10.2 reports correlations between our committee indicators and average monthly inflation – admittedly a very simple measure of how well a central bank conducts monetary policy – during the period 2000–2006. Given the difference in economic structure, we report correlations for emerging markets and industrialized countries separately.[23] We see that higher scores on the measures for "Diversity" and "Proposal" are correlated with lower average inflation rates, whereas the correlation between average inflation and whether the Governor has lost a vote has the wrong sign. In addition, we also checked for correlations between average inflation and committee size. As reported, the optimal committee size is likely to be five or slightly higher. Correlation between average inflation and committee of four to six members is −0.20; correlation between average inflation and committees of six to eight members is 0.16.[24] These findings are in line with our recommendations. Note, however, that these simple correlations are not statistically significant, and correlation is not causation. Many other factors (such as the central bank's institutional arrangements, or the frequency and types of shocks hitting the economy) are also likely to affect inflation

---

[23] The industrialized countries group comprises Australia, Canada, the euro area, Japan, New Zealand, Norway, Sweden, Switzerland, the United Kingdom, and the United States; the emerging markets group comprises all other countries (with the exception of Belarus, Bosnia, and Herzegovina, the Eastern Caribbean Central Bank (ECCB) countries, Namibia, South Korea, and United Arab Emirates, for which we did not find inflation data). Quarterly inflation data for Australia and New Zealand were converted to monthly data using a linear adjustment.

[24] Splitting correlations between committee size and average inflation into groups for emerging markets and industrialized countries is not very useful, as the number of observations for industrialized countries for these committee sizes is very low. For emerging markets we find very similar results, as correlations between committees of sizes four to six and seven to nine are −0.23 and 0.14, respectively.

performance. Future work will look more closely at the exact nature of the relationship between central bank performance and committee structure. Let us look more closely at some prominent central banks or at central banks with interesting institutional arrangements.

- In many ways the Bank of England's committee structure follows best practice: it has a clear goal, it is made up of diverse members (academics, business representatives, and central bankers), and it is not too big. Also, individual contributions can be identified and evaluated, and its members are encouraged to think for themselves. Lastly, the Governor has lost votes in 2005 and 2007, which indicates that the Governor is not dominating the committee.

- The Bank of Japan is the only one to explicitly change the speaking order for every meeting. We view this as an effective measure for members to get informed and to limit information cascades. Also, every board member can make an interest rate proposal. However, the committee is exclusively staffed by central bankers (although some have working experience as government officials or in the business community).

- The structure of the FOMC and the Governing Council of the ECB could be improved: Individual contributions cannot be clearly identified and both committees are probably too large. The FOMC also lacks an explicit inflation target, and internal and external transparency of the ECB is low (consensus decision making and no publication of minutes or voting records). Moreover, it is likely that both committees were firmly led by its chairman (FOMC)[25] or its Chief Economist (ECB),[26] although that might change with recent personnel changes.

  On the positive side: the fact that each of the national ECB briefs its own Governor individually, and that each of them uses a different economic model, maximizes the benefits from information gathering and processing. Similarly, the Fed benefits from a "hub-and-spoke" structure, which facilitates gathering and processing regional

---

[25] Alan Greenspan has chaired the FOMC for about 18 years and has never been on the losing side of a vote. The transcript of the February 1994 FOMC meeting shows that a clear majority of the committee favored raising the funds rate by 50 basis points. Greenspan, however, insisted not just on 25 basis points, but on a unanimous vote for that decision. He got both (Blinder 2007a).

[26] The ECB's Chief Economist traditionally starts the debate by giving an overview of recent economic developments. He is also the first to make an interest rate proposal (at the end of his exposition).

Table 10.3. *Monetary policy committees in practice*

Country	Size[a]	Background[b]	C/V[c]	Votes[d]	Organization of meeting	IR proposal[e]	Vote lost[f]	Independence
Armenia	7 (0/7)	CB	V	Yes/No	No fixed order	Monetary policy department	No	No
Aruba[g]	7 (0/7)	CB	C	–	No fixed order, informal meeting	–	–	Unknown
Australia	9 (7/2)	CB, ACA, BC	C (V)	No	No fixed order	Governor	No	Free discussion encouraged
Bahamas	8 (0/8)	CB	C	No	No fixed order	Research department	?	Unknown
Brazil	9 (0/9)	CB	V	Yes/No	First round of discussion has a fixed order	Deputy-Gov's Mon. and Econ. Policy	?	Members are allowed to make own evaluation of scenarios and risks
Canada	6 (0/6)	CB	C[h]	No/No	No fixed order	Staff	–	Board member receive advice from independent advisors
Chile	5 (0/5)	CB	V	Yes/No	Voting: oldest to newest member, then Vice-Governor, Governor	Chief of Research	No	Members present own analysis
Croatia	14 (8/6)	CB, ACA, BC	V	No/No	No fixed order	Governor	No	No special strategies (but only experts are appointed)
Cyprus	7 (3/4)	CB, ACA, BC	V	No	No fixed order	Governor	?	Each member explicitly states his views regarding interest rates

346

Country								
Czech Republic	7 (0/7)	CB	V	Yes/No[i]	Rules exist, but room to raise other issues	Staff	?	Members need no encouragement to think individually
Dominican Republic	9 (6/3)	CB, ACA, BC, GOV	V	No/No	Relatively fixed[j]	Economic department	Yes	Free speech, limited formalities, knowledge that discussions are internal
Euro area (ECB)	18 (0/18)	CB (different nationalities)	C (V)	No	Chief Economist starts the discussion	Chief Economist	–	Governors briefed by own staff (who use different models etc.)
Guatemala	8 (7/1)	GOV, ACA, BC	C (V)	Yes/No	No fixed order; any person can raise any issue	Staff	?	Unknown
Haiti	14 (0/14)	CB	C/V	No	Fixed order for presentations, later anyone can raise any issue at any time	No formal rule	Yes	Everyone is free to raise questions regarding monetary policy
Hungary	9–11 (7–9/2)	CB, ACA, BC	V	Yes/Yes	No fixed order	Any member	Yes	Members express own views without restrictions (also publicly)
Iceland	3 (0/3)	CB	C	No	Unknown	Governor	?	Unknown
India	6 (4/2)[k]	CB, ACA, BC	V	No	Fixed order, starting with Staff presentation	Any board member	No	Individuals can give their own opinion
Iran	13 (10/3)	CB, GOV	C (V)	No	No fixed order	Unclear	Yes	Member can voice personal ideas
Israel	4 (0/4)	CB	C[h]	No/No		Governor	–	Four departments prepare recommendations before the meeting

(continued)

Table 10.3. *Continued*

Country	Size[a]	Background[b]	C/V[c]	Votes[d]	Organization of meeting	IR proposal[e]	Vote lost[f]	Independence
Japan	9 (0/9)	CB, ACA, BC, GOV	V	Yes/Yes	order changes every meeting	All board members	No	Voting induces members to think individually
Jamaica	18 (0/18)[l]	CB	C[h]	No	Agenda, but additional issues can be raised	Staff	No	Members are encouraged to participate in discussions
Kazakhstan	9 (3/6)	CB, GOV	V	No	Unknown	Unknown	?	Unknown
Latvia	8 (0/8)	CB	V	No	No fixed order	Unclear	No	Members are urged to express their individual opinions before voting
Madagascar	7 (0/7)	CB	C	No	No fixed order	Staff	No	Each department makes his own report
Namibia	5 (0/5)	CB	C	No	No fixed order	Governor	–	Individual discussions
New Zealand[m]	9 (2/7)	CB, BC	C[h]	No/No	No fixed order	Governor	No	No applicable
Norway	7 (5/2)	CB, ACA, BC	C	–	Governor starts the discussion, anyone can raise any issue	Governor	–	Committee members are expected to make own contributions
Philippines	7 (1/6)	CB, GOV	V	No	No fixed order	Staff	?	No restrictions on views, issues discussed; interest rate proposal circulated in advance
Poland	10 (9/1)	CB, ACA,	V	Yes/No	No fixed order	Each member can make proposal	Yes	Each member can share his judgement; no restrictions on views
Slovakia	up to 11 (max 3/max 8)	CB, BC	V	Yes/No	No fixed order	Board member for monetary policy	?	Members are individuals and think that way

S. Korea	7 (4/3)	CB, ACA, BC, GOV	V	Yes/No[n]	No fixed order	No formal rule	No	Members are strongly independent, express their opinions actively and explicitly
Sweden	6 (0/6)	CB	V	Yes/Yes	No fixed order	Governor	No	Members "say what they think"
Switzerland	3 (0/3)	CB	C (V)	No	Relatively fixed order	Monetary department	No	Committee members briefed by different departments
Turkey	7 (1/6)	CB[o]	V	No/No	No fixed order[p]	Unknown	?	Free discussions
UAE	7 (0/7)	CB	C	No	No fixed order	Governor	–	Members are free to give opinions
UK	9 (4/5)	CB, ACA	V	Yes/Yes	No fixed order, any person can raise any issue	Governor	Yes	Members make personal speeches and appear in Parliament
Uruguay	6 (0/6)	CB	C (V)	No	No fixed order	Staff	?	?
US	12 (0/12)	CB	V	Yes/Yes	No fixed order Chairman probably dominates	Chairman	No	FED Presidents briefed by their own staff; limited scope for dissent
Countries with fixed exchange rate arrangements or currency boards								
Belarus	10 (0/10)	CB	V	No/No	Order fixed in the agenda	Staff	?	?
Bosnia and Herzegovina	5 (0/5)	CB	C	No	Unanimous decisions	Governor	No	Unknown
ECCB[q]	9/16[r]	CB, BC, GOV	V/C[s]	No/No	No fixed order	Governor	–	All members are equal in their standing

(*continued*)

Table 10.3. *Continued*

Country	Size[a]	Background[b]	C/V[c]	Votes[d]	Organization of meeting	IR proposal[e]	Vote lost[f]	Independence
Estonia	9 (0/9)	CB	C	No	No fixed order	–	No	Every member can express his opinion
Singapore	12 (7/5)	CB, BC, GOV	C	No	No fixed order	Economic policy dep.	–	Not applicable

[a] Total number of MPC members, number of external/internal members in brackets.
[b] Background of committee members (CB = central banker, ACA = academics, BC = business community, GOV = government).
[c] Consensus (C) or voting (V).
[d] Publication of the decision/individual votes.
[e] Who makes the interest rate proposal?
[f] Has the Governor lost a vote during the last 5 years?
[g] No formal monetary policy committee, we provide information on the informal committee discussing monetary issues.
[h] Governor solely responsible.
[i] Individual contributions can be identified with a 6-year delay.
[j] Vice-Governor opens and closes sessions; Finance Department is responsible for presenting open market operations proposals.
[k] Information applies to the Technical Advisory Committee. Note that its proceedings are to be ratified by the Central Board, of which the Governor is the executive member.
[l] Decision can be taken by Operating Targets Committee, comprising 18 members, or the Economic Policy Committee, which consist of 30 persons.
[m] Information applies to the informal advisory body.
[n] In general votes are not published. However, individual members may request their votes be recorded in the minutes. Individual contributions can be identified on minutes.
[o] One additional member with background in economics.
[p] Monetary policy decisions are taken in a three-stage voting process: first vote is whether term interest rates should be changed at all; the second and third stage decides upon the direction and the size of the change.
[q] The ECCB is the multinational central bank for Anguilla; Antigua and Barbuda; Dominica; Grenada; Montserrat; St. Kitts and Nevis; Saint Lucia and St Vincent and the Grenadines.
[r] Monetary decisions are taken by the Monetary Council (MC), comprising eight members. Decisions regarding the fixed exchange rate regime are taken by the Board of Directors (eight voting members), who must unanimously agree to recommend the proposed changes to the MC, and the MC must unanimously agree to the proposed change.
[s] Voting on exchange rate issues, consensus on monetary decisions.

information. Also the ECB has a clear goal,[27] and both ECB Governing Council and FOMC comprise members with diverse backgrounds (all central bankers, but with different nationalities or with diverse past experience).

- The Bank of Canada has a clear objective, and the size of its MPC is probably optimal. However, individual contributions are not identified, and there are no outside members. On the positive side: although all get the same briefing material, board members also receive policy advice from a group of senior advisors, who are encouraged to think independently.
- The Central Bank of the Czech Republic makes it possible to identify individual contributions with a 6-year delay. This provides a compromise between allowing for the evaluation of individual performance and shield against external pressure.
- At the Bank of Chile, the monetary committee votes in a specific order, starting with the oldest, and ending with the newest members. In light of the discussion about groupthink, the voting process could probably be improved. On the positive side: the Governor is the last member to cast its vote.
- At the Bank of Israel, four departments *independently* have to prepare recommendations before the meeting. This forces each department to conduct its own analysis, which counters shirking and groupthink.
- An interesting feature of the Swiss monetary committee is that different group members are briefed by different departments. To some extent this could be viewed as a device to encourage independence. However, their speaking order is relatively fixed,[28] the committee has no outside members, and there is no way to (externally) identify and evaluate individual input for the discussion.
- The National Bank of Poland addresses information cascades by allowing each member to make the first interest rate proposal. Also, the Chairman has been on the losing side of a vote on several occasions. Regarding accountability, neither individual votes nor minutes are published. However, plans exist to modify the inflation report to make

---

[27] The ECB is not an inflation targeter, but it has a relatively clear definition of price stability (inflation "below, but close to two percent"). This is the ECB's overriding objective.

[28] After an informal debate among the members of the Board, their Deputies and economists who prepared the documents, the Chairman of the Governing Board gives the floor to the heads of two other departments. Then the Governor speaks again, although any member can intervene again after one of his or her colleagues has spoken. The Chairman of the Governing Board summarizes the arguments, repeats the decision, and closes the debate.

it "minutes-like" (i.e., to provide a broad picture of the discussions and enabling outsiders to identify views of individual members).

10.4 Conclusions

Typically, reports released to the public to explain monetary policy decisions feature detailed discussions about the state of the economy. While such information is important for financial markets, our discussion suggests that availability of economic information alone is not sufficient to guarantee optimal decision making. Well-structured institutional arrangements can ensure that committee members get informed and adequately process economic information before taking a decision. Do real-life monetary committees feature such arrangements?

Our survey of the literature suggests that encouraging independent thinking and having members with different personal backgrounds may be useful provisions to avoid groupthink. The structure of the meeting should not be too formal (e.g., no fixed speaking order) in order to reduce information cascades. And if individual contributions can be identified and evaluated, free-riding can be eliminated.

We would like to stress that there is no ultimate model, and it is unlikely that one structure dominates all others on all aspects. Each solution also reflects local circumstances and traditions. However, our guidelines for the way monetary policy committees should be set up show that some central banks could probably improve their committee framework. By changing the way the monetary committee works, incentives are created for group members to actively participate in the discussion, to become informed, and to reveal their information. As this is the basis for the gains that decision making by committee can offer, having such institutional arrangements can contribute to the overall quality of the decisions. As this overview has shown, some central banks could reap more of the committee benefits if they had provisions to avoid free-riding or encourage "thinking outside the box."

Appendix A

We contacted all 149 central banks listed on the BIS web site to inquire about their committee structure (if a central bank is not listed in the tables in the main text, it did not respond to our inquiry). Following is a copy of the survey we sent out by e-mail.

I am currently investigating how central banks make monetary policy decisions. In many central banks, monetary policy decisions are not taken by a single decision maker, but by a committee. I am interested in how exactly the committee reaches a decision – that is, how the committee functions. I would also like to clarify that I am only interested in monetary policy decisions, not other central banking matters (e.g., payment systems). I would kindly like to ask you the following questions:

1. How many people are directly involved in making the monetary policy decision in your central bank? That is, if the decision is taken in a committee, how many members does the committee comprise?
2. Does the committee vote, or is the decision taken by consensus?
3. If the committee votes: Are votes published? Are individual votes published?
4. Are there ways to identify individual contributions to the discussion?
5. Do all committee members share similar background (i.e., are all central bankers), or are some of the members from the academic world or the business community?
6. Is there a fixed speaking order in the committee (e.g., alphabetical or by rank), or can any person raise any issue at any time?
7. Who makes the proposal how interest rates should be set?
8. Does the committee release minutes?
9. Provided that the Governor is a member of the committee: Has he ever been on the losing side of a vote during the past 5 years?
10. Is individual thinking encouraged among committee members? How?

Please feel free to bring any other matters of relevance about the functioning of the monetary committee to my attention.

References

Anderson, L. and C. Holt (1997), "Information cascades in the laboratory," *The American Economic Review* 87(5):847–862.
Berger, H., V. Nitsch, and T. Lybek (2007), "Central bank boards around the world: Why does membership size differ?" *IMF Working Paper* 06/281.
Bikhchandani, S., D. Hirshleifer, and I.Welch (1992), "A theory of fads, fashion, custom, and cultural change as informational cascades," *Journal of Political Economy* 100(5):992.
Blinder, A. S. (1998), *Central Banking in Theory and Practice* (Cambridge: MIT Press).
(2004), *The Quiet Revolution: Central Banking Goes Modern* (Yale University Press).
(2007a), "Monetary policy by committee: Why and how?" *European Journal of Political Economy* 23(1):106–123.
(2007b), "On the design of monetary policy committees," CEPS Working Paper 153.

Blinder, A. S., M. Ehrmann, M. Fratzscher, J. De Haan, and D.-J. Jansen (2008), "Central bank communication and monetary policy: A survey of theory and evidence," NBER Working Paper 13932.

Blinder, A. S. and J. Morgan (2005), "Are two heads better than one? An experimental analysis of group vs. individual decisionmaking," *Journal of Money, Credit and Banking* 37(5):789–812.

(2007), "Leadership in groups: A monetary policy experiment," CEPS Working Paper 151.

Blinder, A. S. and C. Wyplosz (2004), "Central bank talk: committee structure and communication policy," Paper presented at the 2005 meetings of the American Economic Association.

Bosman, R., P. Maier, V. Sadiraj, and F. van Winden (2004), "Let Me Vote! An experimental study of the effects of vote rotation in committees," De Nederlandsche Bank Working Paper Series 23.

Chortareas, G., D. Stasavage, and G. Sterne (2001), "Does it pay to be transparent? International evidence from central bank forecasts," Bank of England Working Paper 143.

Condorcet, M. (1785), *Essai sur l'application de l'analyse 'a la probabilité des decisions rendues à la pluralité des voix* (Paris: L'imprimerie royale).

Croson, R. and M. Marks (1998), "Identifiability of individual contributions in a threshold public goods experiment," *Journal of Mathematical Psychology* 42(2):167–190.

Ehrmann, M. and M. Fratzscher (2005), "How should central banks communicate?" European Central Bank Working Paper 557.

Erhart, S. and J. L. Vasquez-Pas (2007), "Optimal monetary policy committee size: Theory and cross-country evidence," Kiel Advanced Studies Working Paper 439.

European Central Bank (2003), "The adjustment of voting modalities in the Governing Council", *Monthly Bulletin* 3:73–74.

Fujiki, H. (2005), "The monetary policy committee and the incentive problem: A selective survey," *Monetary and Economic Studies October* (Special edition): 37–82.

Gerlach-Kristen, P. (2003), "Insiders and outsiders at the Bank of England," *Central Banking* XIV (1):96–102.

(2005), "Too little, too late: Interest rate setting and the cost of consensus," *Economics letters* 88(3):376–381.

(2006), "Monetary policy committees and interest rate setting," *European Economic Review* 50:487–507.

Gerling, K., H.P. Grüner, A. Kiel, and E. Schulte (2005), "Information acquisition and decision making in committees: A survey," *European Journal of Political Economy* 21:563–597.

Göhlmann, S. and R. Vaubel (2005), "The educational and professional background of central bankers and its effect on inflation—an empirical analysis," RWI Discussion Paper 25.

Goodfriend, M. (2005), "Comment," *Monetary and Economic Studies* October (Special edition):83–86.

Goodhart, C. A. (2000), "The role of the monetary policy committee: Strategic considerations and operational independence," in L. Mahadeva and G. Sterne

(Eds.), *Monetary Frameworks in a Global Context* (London: Routledge), pp. 226–242.

Harkins, S. and J. Jackson (1985), "The role of evaluation in eliminating social loafing," *Personality and Social Psychology Bulletin* 11(4):457–465.

Henningsen, D., M. Cruz, and M. Miller (2000), "Role of social loafing in predeliberation decision making," *Group Dynamics: Theory, Research, and Practice* 4(2):168–275.

Hong, L. and S. Page (2004), "Groups of diverse problem solvers can outperform groups of high-ability problem solvers," *Proceedings of the National Academy of Sciences* 101(46):16385–16389.

Issing, O. (1999), "The eurosystem: Transparent and accountable or 'willem in euroland,'" *Journal of Common Market Studies* 37(3):503–519.

Janis, I. (1973), "Victims of Groupthink: A Psychological Study of Foreign-Policy Decisions and Fiascoes," *Annals of the American Academy of Political and Social Science* 407:179–180.

Kerr, N. L., R.J. MacCoun, and G. P. Kramer (1996), "Bias in judgment: Comparing individuals and groups," *Psychological Review* 103(4):687–719.

Kocher, M. and M. Sutter (2005), "The decision maker matters: Individual versus group behaviour in experimental beauty-contest games," *The Economic Journal* 115(500):200–223.

Kohn, D. L. and B. Sack (2003), "Central bank talk: does it matter and why?" Finance and Economics Discussion Series 2003–55.

Lombardelli, C., J. Proudman, and J. Talbot (2002), "Committees versus individuals: An experimental analysis of monetary policy decision-making," Bank of England Working Paper 165.

Lybek, T. and J. Morris (2004), "Central bank governance: A survey of boards and management," IMF Working Paper 04/226.

Mahadeva, L. and G. Sterne (2000), *Monetary Policy Frameworks in a Global Context* (London: Routledge).

Meade, E. E. and D. N. Sheets (2005), "Regional influences on U.S. monetary policy," *Journal of Money, Credit, and Banking* 37(4):661–677.

Milgram, S. (1974), *Obedience to authority* (New York: Harper & Row).

Morck, R. (2004), "Behavioral finance in corporate governance-independent directors and non-executive chairs," *NBER Working Paper* 10644.

Morduch, J. (1999), The Microfinance Promise, *Journal of Economic Literature* 37(4):1569–1614.

Mueller, D. C. (2003), *Public Choice III* (Cambridge: Cambridge University Press).

Nickell, S. (2000), "Some problems facing the MPC," Speech to the Wessex Institute of Directors October 10.

Oakley, B., R. Felder, R. Brent, and I. Elhajj (2004), "Turning student groups into effective teams," *Journal of Student Centered Learning* 2(1):8–33.

Odean, T. (1998), "Volume, volatility, price, and profit when all traders are above average," *The Journal of Finance* 53(6):1887–1934.

Priem, R., D. Harrison, and N. Muir (1995), "Structured Conflict and Consensus Outcomes in Group Decision Making," *Journal of Management* 21(4):691–710.

Riboni, A. and F. Ruge-Murcia (2006), "The dynamic (in) efficiency of monetary policy by committee," mimeo (University of Montreal).

Schweiger, D., W. Sandberg, and J. Ragan (1986), "Group approaches for improving strategic decision making: A comparative analysis of dialectical inquiry, devil's advocacy, and consensus," *The Academy of Management Journal* 29(1):51–71.

Shaw, M. (1981), *Group dynamics:The psychology of small group behavior (3rd ed.)*, (New York: McGraw-Hill).

Sibert, A. (2005), "Is the structure of the ECB adequate for the new challenge?" in F. Breuss and E. Hochreiter (Eds.), *Challenges for Central Banks in an Enlarged EMU* (Wien: Springer), pp. 95–118.

——— (2006), "Central banking by committee," De Nederlandsche Bank Working Paper 91.

Siklos, P. L. (2002), *The Changing Face of Central Banking: Evolutionary Trends Since World War II* (Cambridge: Cambridge University Press).

——— (2003), "Assessing the impact of changes in transparency and accountability at the Bank of Canada," *Canadian Public Policy* 29(3):279–299.

Slater, P. (1958), "Contrasting correlates of group size," *Sociometry* 21(2):129–139.

Stasser, G. (1992), "Information salience and the discovery of hidden profiles by decision-making groups: A 'thought experiment,'" *Organizational behavior and human decision processes* 52(1):156–181.

Surowiecki, J. (2004), *The wisdom of crowds: why the many are smarter than the few and how collective wisdom shapes business, economies, societies, and nations* (New York: Doubleday).

Tuladhar, A. (2005), "Governance structures and decision-making roles in inflation targeting central banks," IMF Working Paper WP/05/183.

Vandenbussche, J. (2006), "Elements of optimal monetary policy committee design," IMF Working Paper WP/06/277.

Waller, C. J. (2000), "Policy boards and policy smoothing," *Quarterly Journal of Economics* 115(1):305–339.

Wellink, A., B. Chapple, and P. Maier (2002), "The role of national central banks within the European System of Central Banks: The example of De Nederlandsche Bank", *Bank of Austria, 30th Economics Conference, Conference Volume:*169–189.

Whyte, G. (1993), "Escalating commitment in individual and group decision making: A prospect theory approach," *Organizational behavior and human decision processes* 54:430–455.

Williams, K., s. Nida, L. Baca, and B. Latané (1989), "Social loafing and swimming: Effects of identifiability on individual and relay performance of intercollegiate swimmers," *Basic and Applied Social Psychology* 10:73–81.

Woodford, M. (2005), "Central-bank communication and policy effectiveness," NBER Working Paper 11898.

Wyplosz, C., H. Genberg, and A. Fracasso (2003), "How do central banks write?" *Geneva Reports on the World Economy Special Report 2*.

11

Institutional Rules and the Conduct of Monetary Policy
Does a Central Bank Need Governing Principles?

Pierre L. Siklos

Abstract

This chapter suggests that good governance should enhance the trustworthiness of a central bank. Trust is determined by the performance of a central bank over time and is estimated by the absolute value of accumulated inflation surprises. The latter is estimated for a cross-section of over 100 countries. The empirical evidence reveals that all principles of good governance matter, and that no single indicator of central bank behavior, such as its autonomy, suffices to explain inflation performance. Moreover, there is no unique combination of good governance principles that works for every single country. Institutional and socioeconomic differences across countries mean that one size does not fit all.

11.1 Introduction

As the 1990s began, the movement to grant either de facto or de jure central bank autonomy gathered speed, prompted in part by the view that there was a correlation but not, as it turns out, causation between inflation and central bank independence. There was an even weaker relationship between real economic growth and central bank independence (Alesina and Summer 1993; Forder 2005). Figure 11.1 plots the relationship between average inflation for the years 1990–2004 in over 100 countries against an index of central bank autonomy that is comparable, though not identical, to the

A previous version of this chapter was presented at the first FINLAWMETRICS Conference, Bocconi University, May 2006, and the Conference "Does Central Bank Independence Still Matter?, Bocconi University, September 2007. Comments by Carsten Hefeker and three anonymous referees are gratefully acknowledged. Some of the research for this chapter was conducted while I was Bundesbank Professor at the Freie Universität, Berlin.

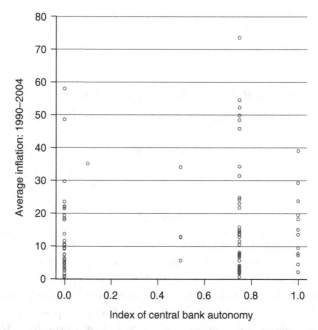

Figure 11.1. Central bank autonomy and average inflation, 1990–2004
Note: Average inflation in the CPI is evaluated on an annual basis for the countries listed in the Appendix. Data are from the International Monetary Fund's *International Financial Statistics* CD-ROM (March 2006 edition). The index of central bank autonomy is from Cukierman (1992), and Siklos (2002).

many indicators that have been published over the past several years (e.g., see Cukierman 1992; Siklos 2002, Chapter 6 and references therein).[1] No clearly identifiable negative relationship between these two variables is apparent.

The mantra of central bank independence has spread worldwide (e.g., Cukierman 1992; Mahadeva and Sterne 2000; Siklos 2002), but it is also becoming evident that central bank independence alone does not suffice to deliver good monetary policy (also see Hayo and Hefeker, Chapter 7, this volume). Even an independent central bank has to follow a particular monetary policy strategy. For example, inflation targeting has now emerged as a favorite strategy because it is a coherent policy, especially when paired with a floating exchange rate.[2]

---

[1] The index is constructed on the basis of information collected between 2004 and 2006. An appendix available for downloading, contains the details. Go to www.wlu.ca/sbe/psiklos/

[2] Not surprisingly, an earlier literature that sought to distinguish between de facto and de jure central bank independence would be followed by a parallel literature that attempts

Choosing a monetary policy strategy, and giving the central bank auton-omy over day-to-day policy decisions, also led policymakers to realize that measures to assign responsibility for monetary policy outcomes provide a quantifiable assessment about whether a chosen monetary policy strat-egy was being carried out satisfactorily, and whether the development of policies to publicly explain central bank actions, since known as the twin requirements of transparency and accountability, are also essential ingre-dients in the mix that constitute the core principles of good monetary policy. While the preference for granting central bank autonomy is widely accepted and comparatively easy to define, at least in broad terms,[3] there appears to be less of a consensus about how to define accountability and how best to ensure it. Similarly, differing degrees of transparency have emerged, tied to the type of monetary regime in place or possibly to other factors, such as views about how much guidance to offer to financial markets and the public more generally, either via the provision of forecasts or other forms of communication (van der Cruijsen and Eijffinger, Chapter 9, this volume).

Perhaps inspired by scandals in the corporate sector and the swift – and some would say heavy-handed – reaction of policymakers to public outrage over transgressions of the public's trust, especially in the United States,[4] attention has shifted to the governance of central banks. What is effectively being debated is whether it is possible to specify a common set of institutional rules that would constitute a code of good conduct permitting the central bank to deliver its monetary policy responsibilities in as effective a manner as possible. Some would no doubt consider this yet another manifestation of the globalization phenomenon.

Adapting the World Bank's definition[5] as a guide, governance refers to the set of rules that stimulate the building up of trust in the central bank. What remains unclear are the ingredients, or combination of ingredients, that guarantee that the process by which central banks make decisions,

to classify de facto versus de jure exchange rate regimes along a continuum from fixed to freely floating (e.g., Reinhart and Rogoff 2004; Levy-Yeyati and Sturzenegger 2005).

[3] While some countries over the past decade or so opted for the de facto form of central bank autonomy, a larger numbers of countries chose the de jure approach. As we shall see, one proximate reason may be the legal origins of the country in question.

[4] As in the much discussed and maligned Sarbanes–Oxley legislation in the United States passed to remedy real and perceived deficiencies in corporate governance standards. More recently, of course, it is the failure of banking supervisors to monitor or regulate the exotic financial instruments that are at the centre of the financial crisis of 2007–2008, which are prompting demands for reforms of the global financial architecture.

[5] See http://info.worldbank.org/etools/docs/library/18388/quinghua_presentation.pdf

and publicly announce them, contribute to the maintenance of trust in the institution itself, perhaps the ultimate indication that good governance principles are in place. Trust contains both a "stock" and a "flow" element. The stock is the trustworthiness of the central banking institution perceived by the government and the public, while the flow component represents the credibility of policy decisions taken over time. How trust translates into measurable economic variables is not obvious. Nevertheless, experience suggests that monetary policy failures show up as poor inflation performance and, perhaps more importantly, in an inability to anchor inflationary expectations. In addition, choosing a monetary policy strategy, and how accountable and transparent a central bank is, must surely also be front and center in explaining the trustworthiness of the monetary policy authority.

This chapter is concerned with the role of governance principles as a determinant of central bank performance. Central bank performance, in turn, is thought to be a function of the trust the public has in the institution responsible for monetary policy. Trust is proxied as the accumulated absolute value of inflation surprises over some interval of time. Next, we also ask whether our measure of trust can be explained by a set of key institutional characteristics thought to represent the essence of core governance principles in central banking. The basic hypothesis of this chapter is a straightforward one, namely, that good governance principles translate into building up trust in the institution. While the establishment of good governance principles at the outset can accelerate the development of trust in the central bank, it can never substitute for it.

Generally, the literature on institution building, as well as research dealing with some of the qualitative aspects of central banking, has focused on the experiences of industrial countries. This chapter considers a much wider set of countries, updating and extending the data set introduced in Siklos (2005). It is argued that such an approach is essential to demonstrate empirically that good governance principles matter on a global scale.

The chapter is organized as follows. The following section examines the rules versus discretion debate in an institutional setting, and considers the implications for our understanding of the principles of good central bank governance. The next section defines the empirical proxy for trust in the central bank, and briefly describes the various quantitative and qualitative determinants of trust in the central bank. Following a description of the empirical results, the chapter concludes with a summary and draws some policy implications.

11.2 The "Wisdom of Men" Versus Rules

11.2.1 Trustworthiness in the Central Bank and Its Determinants

With inflation seemingly firmly under control in many parts of the world and, at least until 2008, the overall economic environment generally benign, it is hardly surprising that, in matters relevant to central banking, attention turned to central bank governance. King (2004), looking back on his experience as a central banker, opined that good central bank performance relies crucially on the "wisdom of men," not on rules or legislation. Several decades earlier, Milton Friedman (1962) argued that central banks are hostage to the individuals who head these institutions. Central bankers, he argued, generally take credit for economic performance when times are good. When times are bad the head of the central bank deflects or explains away criticisms as being due to circumstances beyond his or her control.[6] None of the foregoing views explicitly evinces a concern for the extent to which personalities at the helm of a central bank, or their policies, are in any way swayed by the institutional environment that defines their responsibilities.

Unlike most shareholder-owned private firms, the government is typically the central bank's only shareholder.[7] Central bank decisions, of course, impact the general public regularly and directly. Hence, in a real sense, the central bank has a dual responsibility, namely, accountability to the government, as well as responsibility to explain its actions and views to the public at large. Satisfactorily meeting these dual responsibilities requires a multifaceted set of principles.

Ultimately, however, the effectiveness of these principles should translate into *trust* in the central banking institution. I argue that good governance translates into greater confidence or trust in the institution. This need not, however, guarantee or imply that policy mistakes will not happen. At the very least, what is essential is clarity in the division of relative responsibilities between the central bank and the government once a monetary

---

[6] One reason this view is flawed is that it makes no allowance for the possibility that the institution can also "form" or discipline the individual. In other words if, ex ante, a newly appointed Governor is seen as a "dove" based on past performance the history and performance of the central bank could conceivably turn the Governor into a "hawk," either to defend the institution's autonomy or to ensure that a particular monetary policy strategy is carried out.

[7] The relationship between the "principal" and "agent" in the case of the European Central Bank is somewhat more complex. For our purposes, however, it makes no difference whether one, or several, governments are the stakeholders.

policy strategy has been adopted, and that its anticipated outcomes are clearly defined. This implies that it is necessary to have more than just rules to ensure the autonomy of the central bank. For example, the division of responsibilities between the central bank and the government must be clear. This can be accomplished by an explicit stipulation that the locus of *ultimate* responsibility for monetary policy must rest with government, while *day-to-day* or short-run accountability for monetary policy must rest squarely with the central bank. Indeed, clarity of the "mission statement" of the central bank can serve as the device that avoids the situation of having to appoint a central banker who is more conservative than the public, as in Rogoff's (1985) model. In addition, the decision to pursue a particular monetary policy strategy ought to be made by the government, in consultation with the central bank, and must be publicly acknowledged by the central bank's executive.[8] There must also be procedures in place to deal with central bank – government conflict. While the foregoing conditions may seem reasonable, if not obvious, relatively few central banks operate under legislation or practice that meet such minimal and, in my opinion, essential requirements (Siklos 2002, 2005, 2006, and see below). Conflict is inherent in all forms of institutional structure. The essential difference between countries is how these are settled when such procedures are absent from legislation. This is usually done via conflict, with negative consequences the trust the public has in the institution. Alternatively, procedures that deal with cases of serious disagreements between the government and the central bank can make a crucial difference, such as when the government has the option to direct the central bank to take a certain action and to shoulder the responsibility for such a decision.

There are potentially other ingredients essential to good governance, namely whether monetary policy decisions are entirely the responsibility of a single individual or delegated to a committee. In the latter case, the number of individuals responsible for such decisions and how these are publicly communicated, the appointment procedure of senior central bankers, and the scope of the responsibilities of the central bank are also critical ingredients to ensuring good governance. Some of these have been emphasized by others, but appointment procedures and the size and make up of monetary

---

8   In an effort to ensure the autonomy of the European Central Bank, the choice of monetary policy strategy has been delegated to the central bank. However, there is indirect pressure and, as a result, less accountability in such an institutional setup. Indeed, this has led to persistent attacks on the European Central Bank. While the level of conflict has been moderate so far the existing institutional setup cannot entirely prevent a serious conflict with possibly disastrous consequences for the euro area.

policy committees are aspects that have either been ignored altogether or underemphasized, at least until very recently (see, however, Siklos 2002; Lybek and Morris 2004; Berger and Nitsch 2008), because of the belief that central bank autonomy, and clear monetary policy objectives, are the only characteristics that are necessary. While setting out in formal terms the requirements that facilitate good governance is useful, this cannot succeed unless markets, and the public more generally, trust or believe that the institution will deliver on these principles. Trust is built on a proven record of performance. This requires that the data necessary for such an evaluation be available in a timely manner, and that the data meet some standard of quality. Trust can then be ensured by consistently delivering favorable policy outcomes. We define these outcomes in terms of inflationary surprises. Paraphrasing Lord Hewart,[9] good monetary policy must not only be done but must be seen to be done, and this can only occur if the central bank consistently delivers inflation performance that the public has come to expect.

This chapter proposes indicators of central bank governance based on an expanded data set, covering over 100 countries, compiled by Siklos (2005). Relying on a wide variety of quantitative and qualitative variables, the determinants of trust in central banks, as defined previously, are empirically assessed. Next, the question whether, and in what sense, good governance principles matter is investigated. Rules governing central banks cannot operate in a vacuum. First and foremost, no matter how well they are designed, good governance principles cannot be meaningfully applied if the overall institutional and economic and political environment will not support it. Consequently, poorly established democratic institutions, political instability, endemic amounts of corruption, legal origins, among other factors, may individually, or in some combination, overturn any desiderata of rules. The choice of exchange rate regime and the existing monetary policy strategy are also proximate determinants that create conditions for good governance. As a result, central bank autonomy is not sufficient to explain a significant portion of monetary policy outcomes. Indeed, greater central bank independence across the world has not translated into fewer episodes of financial or economic crises (also see Čihák 2006). Instead, more such crises have emerged in recent decades (e.g., International Monetary Fund 1998; World Bank 2007). Hence, while there is a superficial resemblance

---

[9] "Justice should not only be done, but should manifestly and undoubtedly be seen to be done" Gordon, 1st Baron of Bury Hewart (1870–1943), British judge. Remark, Nov. 9, 1923. "Rex v. Surrey Justices," vol. 1, King's Bench Reports from 1924.

between central bank objectives and autonomy around the world, there is considerably more diversity between central banks along the dimension of governance.

The foregoing discussion leads, therefore, to a testable proposition, namely, that the effectiveness of adopted governance principles must also be partially determined by the particular economic, institutional, and political climate. These are defined by the following characteristics: the existence of democratic institutions, the degree of corruption, and the level of political and economic stability. We show that a linear combination of these factors can also act as an indicator of central bank governance. Because questions have been raised about the reliability and usefulness of the largely qualitative data that serve as determinants of central bank governance, we also propose that the cross-section of governance structures is related to economic distance, measured in terms of aggregate output performance. Hochreiter and Siklos (2002) discuss how economic distance is measured. The measure they use is adapted from Alesina and Grilli (1992) who focus on the role of inflation and output volatility as a means of assessing the costs of a monetary union. In this chapter, a version of this indicator is defined to proxy the potential for a loss of credibility in the conduct of monetary policy. The presumption implicit in the proposed measure is that more volatile economic outcomes are likely to be damaging to a central bank's reputation.

11.2.2 Central Bank Signaling Costs and Trust

It may help fix ideas about the theoretical connection between governance and trust in central banking to rely on the signaling framework. A successful central bank is assumed to be one that enjoys a high level of trust among the public, as previously defined.[10] Trust is costly to deliver, and is assumed to be chiefly signaled through a set of governance principles.[11] The problem for financial markets, and the public more generally, is to determine the level of trust they ought to invest in the central bank based on a mix of institutional and economic characteristics that comprise the largely institutional signals

---

[10] The precise form in which objectives are stated is, of course, important but this is a consideration that is ignored here.

[11] The intellectual debt to Spence's original signaling model (1973) will be obvious. While it is quite likely that signaling costs might be a function of the type of signal, the resulting complication is ignored in what follows. A different version of the arguments used here was also used in Siklos (2002, Chapter 6). Hence, the description that follows will be relatively brief.

and, therefore, constraints on the actions of the central bank. The problem is that institutional characteristics alone need not necessarily deliver good monetary policy. The same problem holds for noninstitutional aspects of central bank behavior (i.e., the choice of exchange rate regimes or the monetary policy strategy of the central bank, the general political and legal environment the central bank operates in). Good governance rules hasten the building of a reputation, and thereby reduce the costs of determining whether to trust the central bank. The relevant principles consist of some aggregation of four characteristics. They are, not in any order of importance: autonomy, disclosure, accountability, and past policy successes. Ultimately, however, the central bank must deliver in a concrete way through monetary policy outcomes. The public assumes that the signaling costs necessary to convince the public to display a particular level of trust in the central bank are also negatively correlated with the overall political and economic environment in which the central bank operates. Hence, for example, in less democratic or free societies, the costs of generating a level of trust in the central bank will be relatively higher than in a freer and more democratic society. Assume that there exist two types of central banks: in one case, the public has a low level of trust (type I), while another exhibits a relatively high level of trust (type II). For a central bank that enjoys a relatively higher level of trust, the costs of signaling to reach a higher level of trust are lower than for a central bank that enjoys a lower level of trust.[12] If signaling costs for a type I central bank are C_I then the optimal solution for central bank type I is not to adopt good governance principles, as defined here, or a subset that is insufficient to permit the public to exhibit a high level of trust in the central bank (i.e., $s = 0$). In contrast, if signaling costs for a type II central bank are C_{II} then it is optimal to signal $s^* > 0$. Clearly, there are an infinite number of signaling equilibria, that is, an infinite number of s^*. This means that no single element of the vector of characteristics that constitute good governance alone needs explain the high level of trust in a central bank. If signaling costs are exclusively related to statutory factors of the kind that the relevant literature has emphasized in recent years, this may partly explain why it is so difficult to extract meaningful information about central bank behavior

---

[12] The resulting "return" to signaling would then also be relatively lower for a central bank that already enjoys in the present setup. Put differently, the setup here provides an incentive for the central bank with a low level of trust to build it up. However, the costs of doing so are relatively higher. The assumption of linearity in the costs of generating more trust is also relevant.

based upon variables such as whether the central bank is autonomous.[13] The reason is that it is costly to determine the type of central bank based on such an arguably narrow dimension (i.e., this signal is not sufficiently informative). An implication of this result then is that some central banks may incur higher signaling costs. For example, in order to be recognized as a trustworthy central bank, the monetary authority could deliver consistently good monetary policy in the form of fewer inflation surprises.[14] This outcome can be facilitated through policies, statutory or otherwise, that support such outcomes via good governance principles. Clearly, the relationship between good governance and good monetary policy can be an endogenous one.

It may be that a higher *s* is also required because of existing deficiencies in the statutory relationship between the central bank and the government requiring more signaling. This is especially true if principles granting more autonomy, disclosure, or accountability practices are not in place, or if the necessary stamp of approval requires outside bodies (e.g., government or some commission recommending reform). Alternatively, the central bank may be hampered by too few policy successes. An obvious option is to search for other techniques that have the effect of reducing the effective signaling costs. How could this be accomplished? For example, the more specific or clear the inflation target, the greater the incentive for the monetary authority to signal its type. Other devices might include the publication of an inflation report, clarity in the procedures that would follow in case of a conflict with the government, and a committee type decision-making structure that sets the course of monetary policy.

11.3 Data and Econometric Specification

We use annual data since 1990 from a variety of sources. An appendix (available separately) provides sources of data and more detailed definitions. Macroeconomic time series data, such as inflation and real GDP series, are from the March 2006 edition of the International Monetary Fund's (IMF) *International Financial Statistics* CD-ROM. Institutional and qualitative data come from a variety of sources including Siklos (2005), Glaeser et al. (2004), Transparency International (http://www.transparency.org/),

---

[13] Hayo and Hefeker (Chapter 7, this volume) reach a similar conclusions but for different reasons.

[14] Eijffinger et al. (2000) reach the same conclusion but predict that openness will be associated with reduced flexibility. In the above setup this need not be the case because, with greater credibility and an enhanced reputation, the central bank also acquires some flexibility in implementing policies.

the Heritage Foundation (http://www.heritage.org/), the Polity IV data base (http://www.cidcm.umd.edu/polity/), and Lybek and Morris (2004). Data that capture governance principles consist of the following characteristics: the policy objective of the central bank, its autonomy from government, whether decision making about the current stance of monetary policy is the responsibility of an individual or a committee, and the size of that committee, whether the central bank has an explicit numerical target of some kind (i.e., a monetary, inflation, or exchange rate target), whether the central bank is also responsible for financial sector supervision, and whether the country meets the IMF's Special Data Dissemination Standards program introduced in the second half of the 1990s. Siklos (2005) also compiles some of the relevant data from information made available on individual country's central banks web sites. These can be accessed through the web site portal maintained by the Bank for International Settlements (BIS) (www.bis.org). The relevant information was compiled at irregular intervals beginning in 2004 through 2006 and, to the best of my knowledge, reflects the conditions at these central banks as of 2004. Almost all the central banks considered posted information on their web sites in English. However, information, where relevant, posted in French and Spanish was also consulted for completeness. When the information about a particular variable was not posted, it was assumed that the characteristic is not present in that central bank.

It needs to be underscored even though it is well-known (e.g., see Siklos 2002), that many institutional characteristics of central banks and, indeed, of economies more generally, change slowly. There is the added difficulty that not all changes occur at the same time in every central bank surveyed. Nevertheless, the bulk of reforms making central banks more accountable and transparent took place during the period considered in this study, that is, during the 1990s and early 2000s. To be sure, there is something lost due to the averaging of data over several years. Data limitations obviously present some challenges when over a 100 countries are sampled. Moreover, there may well be some useful information contained in annual time series that is ignored in averaging data over time. Nevertheless, there is also something to be gained from the procedure. First, one is able to more clearly exploit the cross-sectional variation of the data which is, after all, a prime motivation of the present empirical exercise.[15] Second, because the results examine

---

[15] Annual data on characteristics that define central bank transparency since 1998, from Dincer and Eichengreen (2007), suggest that there is possibly more useful information in the cross-section of countries sampled than in the time series variation in the variables collected by the authors. I am grateful to Nergiz Dincer for making available their data set.

the determinants of trust over an extended period of time, there is less of a concern that the hypothesized determinants will be endogenous. Third, one can argue that trust takes a long time to build.[16] Hence, averaging of data over several years is the appropriate way to proceed.

Inflation surprises are evaluated as the difference between actual and expected inflation, again using annual data for all countries, where the latter is proxied using data obtained from the IMF's *World Economic Outlook* data base up to the September 2005 edition (http://www.imf.org/external/pubs/ft/weo/2005/02/data/index.htm). Ideally, we should employ forecasts generated by the central bank. Such data are, of course, unavailable for most countries. Nevertheless, the IMF's World Economic Outlook (WEO) forecasts are based on techniques that central banks are likely to use and the staff at the IMF does consult with each central bank in preparing the forecasts.[17] Next, we evaluate the absolute value of accumulated inflation surprises, based on CPI inflation, as

$$|cumsurp_i| = \sum_{t=1991}^{2004} |\pi_t - \pi_{t|t-1}^{WEO}| \tag{1}$$

where π_t is annual inflation, and $\pi_{t|t-1}^{WEO}$ is the WEO's inflation forecast for the same year based on past information.[18] Figure 11.2 plots the relationship between average inflation and accumulated inflation surprises, and reveals

---

[16] In other words, a cross-section time series model may well require more structure than the specifications considered below. Of course, even if a structural model is, in any event, deemed to be more desirable, estimation would be hampered, for example, by the paucity of valid instruments. Some of the estimates below do, however, implement an instrumental variables approach with little impact on the conclusions, an additional issue is that both trust, as well as some of its determinants, are observable but require proxy measures in a statistical investigation. It is true that there is an unobservable element to some of the key variables in the estimated model. In addition, they are likely to be measured with error. Again, resort to averaging helps but does not overcome all of the econometric problems. For more on the relevant issues, see Wansbeek and Meijer (2000).

[17] Timmermann (2006) assesses the quality of WEO forecasts and finds them to be on a par with those published by Consensus Economics. Nevertheless, one cannot entirely overlook the possibility that a political element exists in some of the published forecasts. Unfortunately, for such a large sample of countries, WEO forecasts are the only ones that can be reliably used for the purposes of this study.

[18] Equation (1) is clearly not the only possible definition of "trust," as understood in this paper. For example, one might wish to square the errors to penalize relatively large errors. Alternatively, one might want to scale the measure given in equation (1) by the variance of inflation or some other scaling measures. Lastly, one might even wish to account for any asymmetries in the inflation forecasting performance over time. These alternatives are presently being considered as extensions for future research.

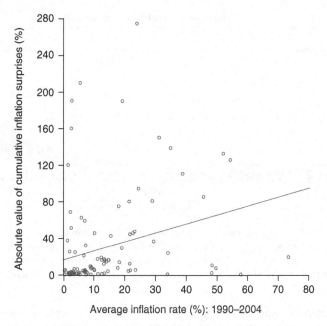

Figure 11.2. Average inflation rates and inflation surprises, 1990–2004
Note: The data measured along the vertical axis are defined by equation (1).

a fairly clear positive correlation between these two variables. Nevertheless, a substantial portion of the countries in our sample are concentrated at the low end of the average inflation scale, and there is considerable dispersion around the fitted regression line. An alternative might be to fit a nonlinear relationship between these two series but this extension is not considered here.

Figure 11.3 plots the measure defined in equation (1) for the countries in our sample. Perhaps unsurprisingly, industrial countries tend to have relatively more trustworthy central banks. Nevertheless, there are many emerging market economies whose cumulative inflation surprises display few differences with their counterparts in the industrial world. Although we began with a total of 115 countries, statistical results presented below are for anywhere from 99 to 111 countries, as we were unable to obtain a complete dataset for every country in the sample. The basic estimated model then is written as follows:

$$|cumsurp_i| = \alpha + \beta\,GOV_i + \gamma Z_t + \varepsilon_t \tag{2}$$

Pierre L. Siklos

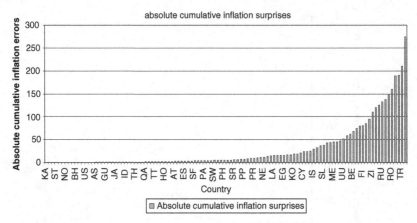

Figure 11.3. Average inflation and absolute cumulative inflation surprises, 1990–2004
Note: See the Appendix for data sources. Absolute cumulative inflation surprises are
defined in equation (1). Not that outlier values for a few countries for inflation surprises
were omitted. Again, see the Appendix for more information and the country code
definitions.

where *cumsurp* was defined previously, and *GOV* is a vector of governance
indicators [OBJ, AUT, DM, AP, NUMT, SANDS, SDDS] where OBJ is an
indicator of the objectives of the central bank, AUT is an index of central
bank autonomy, DM is an indicator of the individual or collective responsibility of the central bank, AP is an indicator of how senior central bank
officials are appointed, NUMT is an indicator of whether and what type of
explicit numerical target the central bank is responsible to meet, SANDS is
an index that indicates whether the central bank is responsible for financial
supervision, and SDDS indicates whether the country has met the IMF's
data dissemination standards. The vector *Z* consists of control variables
that reflect the general political and economic environment in which the
central bank operates. We include regional dummies (e.g., Europe vs. Asia,
Africa, etc.), a measure of how free the society is, the level of corruption
perceived in each country, and either average inflation over the 1990–2004
period or a measure of economic distance originally put forward by Alesina
and Grilli (1992). Because the regressions that include average inflation
produced extremely small coefficients (e.g., of the order of .0000003), only
results that include the measure of economic distance in the various estimated regressions are presented. Economic distance refers to an indicator
of divergence in output performance defined as the ratio of standard deviations adjusted for the correlation in output growth between two countries.
Since Alesina and Grilli (1992) introduce this measure as a short-hand way
of evaluating the likely costs of monetary union, this is a natural variable

to use in the present context to represent some of the economic forces contributing to convergence in the performance of central banks. Presumably, the smaller the differences in output performance between pairs of countries, the smaller are the costs of inflation convergence. More precisely, economic distance is evaluated as

$$((\sigma_i/\sigma_j)^2 + (1 + \rho_{ij}))1/2 \tag{3}$$

where, σ is the standard deviation of output growth in countries i and j, and ρ_{ij} is the simple correlation in output growth between countries i and j. Distance is measured relative to the United States.

Finally, it is possible that the state of governance is not entirely exogenous from our inflation surprise measure. Consequently, we also ran some auxiliary regressions to explain the effect of longer-run institutional factors on each one of the components of the vector *GOV*. Each of these regressions has the form

$$GOV_i = \phi_0 + \phi_1 INST\_SOCIAL_i + \xi_i \tag{4}$$

where *GOV* has previously been defined, and *INST_SOCIAL* represents a vector of institutional and social characteristics that may, albeit perhaps indirectly, influence each one of the central bank governance characteristics we are trying to measure. While it is quite possible that some of the characteristics are relatively more important in some countries than in others, no attempt at weighting was carried out for some countries than for others. The vector consists of the following variables: the fraction of the population that is Catholic, the fraction of the population that is Muslim, both of which are only available for 1980, legal origins which are either French, British, German, or Scandinavian, and an index of political stability. ξ_i is then assumed to be the value of *GOV* net of the impact of these longer-run factors and is then considered as an exogenous proxy for the *GOV* vector in equation (2). Essentially, this procedure amounts to an alternative way of estimating equation (2) where *INST_SOCIAL* and a constant are effectively instruments. Because the results shown below, using the conventional instrumental variables technique, are essentially the same, we only discuss these. However, estimates of equation (4) are of separate interest because there may be common elements that dictate the particular way *GOV* is legislated across countries. Indeed, this turns out to be largely the case, as we shall see.

Finally, to the extent that the separate elements that make up *GOV* have a common set of elements, then the constituents of this variable may not be effectively independent of each other. Quite often central bank reform consists of a simultaneous change in possibly several of the governance characteristics considered in this chapter. Hence, a central bank that becomes more autonomous may also, whether it is mandated to do so or not, undertake steps to become more transparent. Moreover, central bank independence and accountability can often go hand in hand. Occasionally, central bank reforms result in the creation of a new decision-making body, as when the reforms that brought about independence for the Bank of England led to the formation of a monetary policy committee. Therefore, instead of including the components of GOV separately, we can rely on linear combinations of this variable as a proxy determinant of trust in the central bank. In yet another variant of equation (2), then, I also replace the separate elements of *GOV* with its principal components estimated across the entire cross-section of countries in question. Principal component analysis is frequently used to reduce the dimensionality of a regression specification when several variables are believed to contain some common features.

11.4 Empirical Evidence

Table 11.1 provides cross-section estimates for equation (2). The first column of estimates reveals that all governance indicators, save the index that measures whether the central bank is responsible for financial supervision (SANDS), are statistically significant at least at the 5% level of significance. With one exception, all variables also have the expected signs. Thus, central banks with a single objective generate greater cumulative inflation forecast errors. Note, however, that this variable as constructed makes no distinction between an inflation target and a numerical money growth or exchange rate target. All three monetary policy strategies stand on an equal footing in the estimated specification. Yet, it is likely that the form of the objective also matters. Indeed, central banks with a numerical inflation objective (NUMT) deliver fewer inflation surprises over time and generate, therefore, greater trust than central banks with either a money growth or an exchange rate objective, other things being equal.

Central bank autonomy (AUT) also reduces the absolute value of cumulative inflation surprises. Turning to the other governance indicators, it is also found that monetary policy by committee, as well as relatively larger committees, combine to produce smaller cumulative inflation shocks, at least over the sample considered. Interestingly, central bankers appointed by the head of government do more poorly in terms of generating more trust in the central banking institution than when the governor is appointed either by

Table 11.1. *Estimates of equation (2)*

Variable	(1)	(2)	(3)	(4)
	Dependent variable: absolute value of cumulative inflation surprises			
Constant	78.69 (13.52) [.00]		47.60 (5.06) [.00]	35.39 (4.61) [.00]
	Governance indicators			
OBJ	5.32 (2.18) [.03]		0.66 (0.33) [.75]	
AUT	−13.31 (−3.27) [.00]		−4.76 (−1.05) [.30]	
DM	−17.01 (2.22) [.00]		−7.86 (−3.09) [.00]	
AP	22.99 (2.22) [.00]		11.02 (3.35) [.00]	
COMSIZE	−1.05 (−2.10) [.04]		0.04 (0.09) [.93]	
NUMT	−14.83 (−4.16) [.00]		−7.87 (−3.09) [.01]	
SANDS	6.95 (1.52) [.13]		3.03 (0.58) [.57]	
SDDS	19.89 (6.00) [.00]		994 (2.98) [.00]	
1st Princ. Comp.		−1.30 (−2.11) [.04]		−1.54 (−2.81) [.01]
2nd Princ. Comp.		(3.47) [.00]		1.39 (1.85) [.07]
3rd Princ. Comp.		2.20 (3.53) [.00]		0.73 (0.67) [.28]
	Other socioeconomic factors			
Free	−0.47 (−0.16) [.88]	0.79 (0.21) [.83]	0.29 (0.10) [.92]	1.44 (0.46) [.65]
Corruption	−8.39 (−12.80) [.00]	−6.36 (−7.85) [.00]	−5.79 (−7.46) [.00]	−4.95 (−7.45) [.00]
Econ Distance	0.69 (1.85) [.07]	1.11 (2.49) [.01]	1.08 (3.15) [.00]	1.34 (3.04) [.00]
Exchange Rate Reg.	−2.58 (−2.75) [.01]	−3.23 (−4.39) [.00]	−1.18 (−1.27) [.21]	−1.16 (−1.68) [.10]
	Regional dummies			
Accession and new Europe	8.61 (0.53) [.60]	30.98 (2.76) [.01]	23.38 (1.56) [.12]	32.61 (2.71) [.01]
Africa	6.34 (1.31) [.19]	11.89 (2.90) [.00]	7.56 (1.73) [.09]	17.85 (4.17) [.00]
Central and South America	−14.34 (−3.26) [.00]	−6.56 (−1.85) [.07]	−8.23 (−2.05) [.04]	−3.16 (−1.38) [.17]
Middle East	−2.11 (−0.32) [.75]	0.13 (0.02) [.99]	−5.79 (−0.78) [.44]	3.50 (0.48) [.63]

(*continued*)

Table 11.1. *Continued*

Variable	(1)	(2)	(3)	(4)
Orient	−24.80 (9.32)	−11.21 (−3.29)	−17.68 (−7.29)	−4.67 (−1.46)
	[.00]	[.00]	[.00]	[.15]
Pacific	−4.72 (−0.46)	−0.19 (0.02)	0.71 (0.11)	4.15 (0.55)
	[.65]	[.98]	[.91]	[.59]
Rest of Europe	15.21 (5.42)	11.65 (7.31)	11.72 (4.87)	6.75 (4.58)
	[.00]	[.00]	[.00]	[.00]
$\bar{R}^2$	.96	.80	.99	.71
Observations	102	102	99	99

Note: Columns (1) and (2) are estimated via (weighted) OLS; columns (3) and (4) via pooled IVE. See text and Appendix for some variable definitions. *t*-statistics are in parentheses, *p*-values in brackets. Observations represent the number of countries included in each regression. Instruments used include the regressors discussed in the main body of the chapter, as well as a constant.

the head of state or a separate committee. Lastly, adherence to the IMF's data dissemination standards also results in poorer accumulated forecast performance and, therefore, less trust in the central bank. This result could be the short-term response to greater transparency and, possibly, more scrutiny that greater public provision of data provides. Alternatively, the sign on the SDDS variable might reflect the fact that central banks with strong or weak accountability vis-á-vis governments and the public met the data dissemination standards. In other words, the SDDS variable suggests no obvious ranking of inflation performance in a cross-country setting.

Regional differences were also found. For example, on average, cumulative inflation surprises were lower in Central and South America and the Orient, and significantly higher in the rest of Europe, that is, among the European countries that either did not join the Euopean Union or are not, as of 2004, among the EU accession countries. In other words, the decade of the 1990s has seen trust in central banks rise, broadly speaking, in diverse parts of the world. However, as noted earlier, these findings may intermingle regional and period-specific effects since, from the 1990s on, inflation globally was on a downward path. How free a society is does not appear to contribute to cumulative inflation surprise performance, although more corrupt societies display significantly worse cumulative inflation surprise performance.[19] Greater economic distance generates slightly higher cumulative inflation surprises and, consequently, less trust in the central banking

---

[19] The corruption index is constructed in such a way that a higher index implies a less corrupt society.

institution. Because greater economic distance is a proxy for less economic integration vis-á-vis the United States, this result is suggestive of a small, but statistically significant, impact from the global reduction in inflation throughout the 1990s.

Lastly, the exchange rate regime indicator of Levy-Yeyati and Sturzenegger (2005) reveals that countries with pegged exchange rates experience the smallest absolute value of cumulative inflation surprises.[20] In other words, pegging one's exchange rate raises the confidence one has in the central bank's performance. Presumably, this result captures the benefits of tying one's hands to a lower inflation economy. However, the exchange rate regime indicator is uninformative about the credibility of regimes with the least flexible exchange rates. It should be emphasized, then, that such variables can only provide a partial picture of how the choice of exchange rate regimes translates into trust in the central banking institution.

We now turn to the evidence where the elements of *GOV* are replaced with their principal components. The results are shown in column (2) of Table 11.1. Roughly 60% of the variation in the institutional variables considered can be explained by the first three principal components. These consist primarily of OBJ, AUT, and DM. The remaining variables, namely AP, COMSIZE, NUMT, SANDS, and SDDS, each contribute between 4% and 11% of the total variation in these characteristics (results not shown). Retaining the first three principal components, these are then used as a substitute for the *GOV* vector in equation (2). Estimates shown in column (2) of Table 11.1 reveal that all three principal components are statistically significant. The results, therefore, suggest that an aggregation of variables that describe central bank objectives, its autonomy, and its decision-making process, each contribute to explaining the absolute value of cumulative inflation surprises. Because the first principal component is associated with OBJ, we now find that central banks with a single objective do, in fact, deliver fewer inflation surprises and, consequently, more trust in the institution. This contradicts the results reported in column (1) of Table 11.1. The earlier results are also overturned based on the second and third principal components because more autonomous central banks no longer prove relatively more trustworthy; likewise it is not the case that single, decision-maker institutions generate more confidence in the central banking institution.

Which of the two sets of results are we to believe? To partly address this issue I now turn to estimates that recognize the endogenous nature

---

[20] The exchange rate regime indicator ranges from one to five, with five indicating a fixed exchange rate regime and one a floating regime.

of several of the variables in equation (2). Estimates of equation (2) that rely on an instrumental variables approach are shown in columns (3) and (4) of Table 11.1. If one compares columns (1) and (3), the most notable differences are the insignificance of the OBJ, AUT, and COMSIZE variables. Hence, the multiplicity of central bank objectives, central bank autonomy, or the size of the policy-making committee is unable to explain how much trust the public has in the central banking institution. Treating the GOV variable as being endogenous has essentially no impact on the sign or statistical significance of the remaining socioeconomic or geographical variables. The statistical significance of DM, AP, NUMT, and SDDS is robust to the change in estimation procedures. Hence, the decision-making process, appointments procedures, the clarity and precision of the monetary policy strategy, and meeting certain standards in the dissemination of data, remain statistically significant ingredients of *GOV*. It is certainly conceivable that these characteristics that describe how central banks carry out their duties, supplant, or complement, central bank autonomy as it is commonly understood. Consequently, central bank independence is not enough, unless other elements of central bank governance are also put in place.

Turning to estimates that rely on principal components analysis, the only difference relative to the earlier results is that the third principal component now becomes statistically significant. This raises some doubts about the importance of the distinction between central banks where there is a single decision maker versus those where a committee structure is in place.[21]

Clearly, the ability to properly control for endogeneity is dictated by the quality of the chosen instruments. As is well-known, finding relevant instruments is difficult at the best of times, and the choice is likely to be especially hazardous in cross-country studies of this kind. Nevertheless, Table 11.2 shows regression estimates of the seven governance indicators on four sets of instruments that have been used in several such cross-country studies. They are religion, the protection of property rights, legal origins, and the degree of political stability. Although several of the variables are significant, it is the legal origins variables that consistently prove to be statistically and economically significant, followed by the protection of property rights. More generally, these types of characteristics are also highly correlated with all of the various governance indicators. While it is important not to draw excessively strong conclusions from these results, it is interesting to note,

---

[21] Indeed, a complication in interpreting this variable is that several countries (e.g., New Zealand, Canada) do not have committee structures defined in statutes, even though ad-hoc committees ostensibly make monetary policy decisions.

Table 11.2. *Auxiliary equations: socioeconomic determinants of governance principles*

Independent variables	Dependent variables						
	OBJ	AUT	DM	AP	NUMT	SANDS	SDDS
Constant	1.01	0.47	0.78	0.81	0.46	0.49	0.54
	(10.57)	(7.05)	(27.21)	(17.23)	(3.94)	(33.27)	(6.93)
Catholics	−0.002	0.0001	−0.001	−0.001	−0.001	−0.00004	−0.00004
	(−1.15)	(2.43)	(−2.04)	(−2.06)	(−0.60)	(−0.51)	(−0.08)
Muslim	0.005	0.0003	0.001	−0.00003	−0.002	−0.001	−0.002
	(5.16)	(0.52)	(1.81)	(−0.13)	(−2.02)	(−2.98)	(−3.24)
Property rights	0.16	0.03	0.001	0.01	0.04	0.002	0.069
	(12.41)	(4.36)	(0.14)	(2.09)	(2.01)	(0.68)	(5.50)
Legal origin: France	−0.55	0.01	−0.06	−0.33	−0.20	−0.004	−0.23
	(−6.46)	(0.52)	(−1.89)	(−8.20)	(−2.52)	(−0.40)	(−4.13)
Legal origin: UK	−0.71	−0.49	−0.12	−0.37	−0.17	−0.01	−0.48
	(−10.52)	(−12.19)	(−2.88)	(−10.18)	(−3.13)	(−0.92)	(−8.15)
Legal origin: Germany	−0.08	−0.004	0.04	−0.39	0.21	0.02	0.01
	(−0.39)	(−0.05)	(0.72)	(−10.45)	(1.60)	(0.31)	(0.21)
Legal origin: Scandinavia	−0.12	−0.05	0.37	−0.43	0.17	−0.004	0.03
	(−1.29)	(2.68)	(2.28)	(−6.08)	(2.68)	(−0.90)	(0.68)
Political stability	−0.003	−0.01	−0.03	0.002	0.12	−0.002	−0.06
	(−0.22)	(−1.75)	(−2.10)	(0.90)	(4.72)	(−1.06)	(−3.86)
$\bar{R}^2$	.99	.99	.07	.48	.84	.04	.95
Observations	111	111	111	111	111	111	111

Note: All estimates are (weighted) OLS with *t*-statistics in parentheses.

for example, that countries with legal origins inherited from Germany and Scandinavia are more likely to have a numerical inflation target than countries with either French or U.K. legal origins. Also notable is that countries with both U.K. and French legal origins are less likely to have independent central banks, at least based on the Cukierman style of index. This appears to contradict the Anglo-Saxon divide that is sometimes thought to characterize central bank types. Finally, it is interesting to point out that single decision-maker central banks are more common in less politically stable countries.

11.5 Conclusions

This chapter asks whether certain characteristics of central bank governance structures can explain trust in the monetary authority, proxying the absolute value of annual accumulated inflationary surprises over the period 1990–2004. Seven characteristics are thought to contribute to good central bank governance. Over and above the "traditional" indicators of central bank independence, we also add indicators that measure the type of decision-making structure, the scope of central bank responsibilities, an indicator of data availability and quality, as well as indicators of how clear and quantifiable are the objectives of the central bank. All of the reported regressions find that governance principles matter, even after controlling for the variables that measure the overall economic environment and political and social factors, including legal origins.

Much work, however, remains. We did not consider the variability of inflation surprises as an alternative independent determinant of our proxy for trust in the central bank. We did construct, but did not use, a measure of surprises in output performance that may also have played a role in inflation forecast performance. Interactions between governance principles and regional or other effects were also omitted, as are potential asymmetries across regions. These extensions were avoided to prevent the estimation of overparameterized regressions. A role for the frequency and, possibly, the magnitude of financial crises was mentioned but not incorporated into the specification, nor have we considered empirically the pressure that fiscal policy might have on monetary policy performance.

Our principal components analysis is conducted on the entire data set and not on a regional scale. It is quite likely that some of the linear combination of the characteristics considered matter more in some regions (e.g., industrialized vs. emerging markets) than in other parts of the world. Finally, one might imagine that the state of the central banking institution in 2004 reflects a form of imitation, especially of the legal position of central banks in industrial countries where reforms were undertaken much earlier. Indeed, it may be the case that small countries have simply adopted the institutional characteristics of larger and richer countries. In other words, more sensitivity analyses would help.

In spite of the additional work that remains to be done, it is clear that one size does not fit all. While a set of good governance principles can be defined, the particular combination of such principles that best suits a particular country can vary considerably. Those who advocate central bank reform should keep this in mind.

References

Alesina, A. and V. Grilli (1992), "The European Central Bank: Reshaping Monetary Politics in Europe," in M. Canzoneri, V. Grilli, and P. Masson (Eds.), *Establishing a Central Bank: Issues in Europe and Lessons from the US* (Cambridge: Cambridge University Press), pp. 49–77.

Alesina, A. and L. Summer (1993), "Central Bank Independence and Macroeconomic Performance: Some Comparative Evidence," *Journal of Money, Credit, and Banking* 25 (May): 151–62.

Berger, H. and V. Nitsch (2008), "Too Many Cooks? Committees in Monetary Policy", CESIfo working paper 2774, March.

Čihák, M. (2006), "How Do Central banks Write on Financial Stability?," IMF working paper 06/163, May.

Cukierman, A. (1992), *Central Bank Strategy, Credibility, and Independence: Theory and Evidence* (Cambridge, MA: MIT Press).

Dincer, N. and B. Eichengreen (2007), "Central Bank Transparency: Where, Why, and What Effects?," NBER working paper 13003, March.

Eijffinger, S., M. Hoebrichts, and E. Schaling (2000), "Why Money Talks and Wealth Whispers: Monetary Uncertainty and Mystique," *Journal of Money, Credit and Banking*, 32 (May): 218–235.

Forder, J. (2005), "Why Is Central Bank Independence So Widely Approved?," *Journal of Economic Issues*, 39 (December): 843–865.

Friedman, M. (1962), "Should There Be an Independent Monetary Authority?" in L. B. Yeager (Ed.), *In Search of a Monetary Constitution* (Cambridge, MA: Harvard University Press).

Glaeser, E., F. LaPorta, F. López-de-Silanes, and A. Schleifer (2004), "Do Institutions Cause Growth?," *Journal of Economic Growth* 9 (September): 271–303

Hochreiter, E., and P. L. Siklos (2002), "Alternative Exchange Rate regimes: The Options for Latin America," *North American Journal of Economics and Finance* 13 (December): 195–211.

International Monetary Fund (1998), *World Economic Outlook, Financial Crises: Causes and Indicators*. Available from http://www.imf.org/external/pubs/ft/weo/weo0598/index.htm

380   *Pierre L. Siklos*

King, M. (2004), "The Institutions of Monetary Policy," NBER working paper 10400, April.

Levy-Yeyati, E. and F. Sturzenegger (2005), "Classifying Exchange Rate Regimes: Deeds Versus Words," *European Economic Review* 49 (August): 1603–1635.

Lybek, T. and J. Morris (2004), "Central Bank Governance: A Survey of Boards and Management," IMF working paper 04/226.

Mahadeva, L. and G. Sterne (2000), *Monetary Policy Frameworks in a Global Context* (London: Routledge).

Reinhart, C. and K. Rogoff (2004), "The Modern History of Exchange Rate Arrangements: A Reinterpretation," *Quarterly Journal of Economics* 119 (February): 1–48.

Rogoff, K. (1985), "The Optimal Degree of Commitment to an Intermediate Monetary Target," *Quarterly Journal of Economics* 100 (November): 1169–1189.

Siklos, P. L. (2002), *The Changing Face of Central Banking* (Cambridge: Cambridge University Press).

(2005), "Varieties of Central Bank—Executive Relationships," *Current Developments in Monetary and Financial Law* (Washington: International Monetary Fund).

(2006), "Varieties of Central Bank—Executive Relationships: International Evidence," in *Current Developments in Monetary and Financial Law* (Washington, DC: International Monetary Fund).

Spence, M. (1973), "Job Market Signaling," *Quarterly Journal of Economics* 87 (August): 355–374.

Timmermann, A. (2006), "An Evaluation of the World Economic Outlook Forecasts," IMF working paper 06/59.

World Bank (2007), *Financial Crises and Contagion.* Available at http://www.worldbank.org/research/projects/fincrises.htm

Wansbeek, T. J. and E. Meijer (2000), *Measurement Error and Latent Variables in Econometrics* (New York: Elsevier).

Appendix A. Data Availability and Sample: Core Macro Data

Country name	Country code	CPI	POP	Real GDP	Nominal GDP	Nom ER	Int. rate Lend	Int. rate MM	Inflation	WEO forecasts Current account %GDP	Real and nominal p.c. GDP	GDP growth
Albania	AL	91–		–01	–03	92–	92, [97–98]	NA				
Argentina	AR						95–	91–				
Armenia	AM	93–	[91–92]	94–99	94–	93–	95–	96–				
Aruba	AU			95–02	95–02		[98]					
Australia	AS											
Austria	AT					–98		–98				
Azerbaijan	AZ*, +	92–	[91]	95–	95–	92–	99–					
Bahamas	BA			90–95	–95							
Bahrain	BH	–03						[97]				
Bangladesh	BN			–03	–03							
Barbados	BB			–03	–02							
Belarus	BE	93–				95–	93–					
Belgium	BL					–98		–98				
Bolivia	BO							95–				
Botswana	BT											
Brazil	BR						97–					
Bulgaria	BU			–97				91–				
Canada	CA											
Chile	CH							00–				
China P.R.	CI*											
Colombia	CO							95–				

(continued)

381

Appendix A. *Continued*

Country name	Country code	CPI	POP	Real GDP	Nominal GDP	Nom ER	Int. rate		WEO forecasts			
							Lend	MM	Inflation	Current account %GDP	Real and nominal p.c. GDP	GDP growth
Costa Rica	CR							92–				
Croatia	CT					93–	92–	96–				
Cyprus	CY		[91–92]				93–	93–				
Czech R.	CZ	93–		93–	93–	93–						
Denmark	DE							[01]				
Dominican R.	DO				NA		[91]	96–				
Ecuador	EU						–00					
Egypt	EG						92–					
El Salvador	ES			93–		93–	96–02	97–				
Estonia	ET	92–		98–	91–	99–		94–				
Ecb	EC	98–						94–				
Fiji	FI			–02	–01		[03]					
Finland	FN					–98						
France	FR					–98		–98				
Georgia	GE +	94–	95–02		95–02	96–						
Germany	GR	91–					–02	96–				
Ghana	GH			–97		–98	–03	03–				
Greece	GC				–97	–98						
Guatemala	GU											
Honduras	HO											
Hong Kong	HK							97–				
Hungary	HU											

Country	Code							
Iceland	IC							
India	IN							
Indonesia	ID							
Iran	IR			-03				
Ireland	IE					-98	NA	-97
Israel	IS							
Italy	IT			-03		-98	-03	
Jamaica	JA			-03				
Japan	JP							
Jordan	JO			-03				99-
Kazakhstan	KA	93-		94-03				
Kenya	KE				-03			
Korea	KO				93-			
Kuwait	KU			92-03		94-	92-	
Kyrgystan	KY	95-		92-	91-	92-	93-	93-
Latvia	LA	91-			-03			98-01
Lesotho	LS	[97-8,04]		-02				94-
Lithuania	LI	92-				92-	93-	94-
Luxembourg	LU					-98	-98	
Macedonia	MA+	93-		93-03		94-	94-	
Malawi	MW							
Malaysia	ML	93-	[91-92]					
Malta	MT							
Mauritius	MU							
Mexico	ME							
Moldova	MO+	92-		91-	93-	95-	96-	97-
Mongolia	MN			-03	03-		93-	93-
Mozambique	MZ			-03	03-	98-	98-	99-
Namibia	NM	-02		-00		91-	91-	92-

(continued)

Appendix A. *Continued*

Country name	Country code	CPI	POP	Real GDP	Nominal GDP	Nom ER	Int. rate Lend	MM	Inflation	WEO forecasts Current account %GDP	Real and nominal p.c. GDP	GDP growth
Nepal	NE				–01		[91–95]					
Netherlands	NT					–98		–98				
Netherlands Antilles	NA				NA		[91–92]					
New Zealand	NZ											
Nicaragua	NI				91–							
Nigeria	NG											
Norway	NO											
Oman	OM											
Pakistan	PA											
Papua New Guinea	PP											
Paraguay	PR			–03				91–				
Peru	PE											
Philippines	PH											
Poland	PO							91–				
Portugal	PT					–98	–99	–98				
Qatar	QA+						–94	95–				
Romania	RO						96–02					
Russia	RU	91–		92–	92–	93–						
Saudi Arabia	SA	92–										
Senegal	SE						90–92					
Sierra Leone	SL			–03								

384

	Variable Code	cpi	pop	rgdp	ngdp	ner	lr	MMR	pi	ca	rgdppc/gdppc	gdpg
Singapore	SI											
Slovak R.	SO	93–			[91], 93–		93–	00–				
Slovenia	SV	92–					91–	92–				
South Africa	SF											
Spain	SP					–98						
Sri Lanka	SR											
Suriname	SU	–03		–94		94–	91–					
Sweden	SW							–03				
Switzerland	ST											
Tanzania	TA											
Thailand	TH											
Tonga	TO +											
Trinidad and Tobago	TT											
Tunisia	TU											
Turkey	TR											
Uganda	UG			–03			[92–94]					
Ukraine	UR*, +	93–		92–	92–	93–	93–	97–				
United Kingdom	UK											
United States	US											
Uruguay	UU											
Venezuela	VE											
Yemen	YE	–03		–03	03–		96–	94–				
Zambia	ZA	–97		–97	–97			96–				
Zimbabwe	ZI	–02		–00	–01							

Note: Data collected from March 2006 IFS CD-ROM.

*Means raw data in % change format. Filled cells indicate data limitations (year starting –, or – year ending). Otherwise, data are annual for the period 1990–2004, inclusive. + means that the real GDP data are production based, or indexed to 100 in a different year.

Appendix B. *Data Availability and Samples: Institutional and Qualitative Variables*

Country name	Country code	(1) Objective	(2) Autonomy	(3) Decision making	(4) Appointment procedure	(5) Committee size	(6) Num. target	(7) Stability & supervision	(8) Sdds standard	(9) Index of economic freedom	(10) Corruption perception index	(11) Er regime
Albania	AL	■	■	■	■	■						
Argentina	AR	■	■	■	■	■	■	■	■			
Armenia	AM	■		■	■	■	■	■	■			
Aruba	AU	■	■	■	■			■				
Australia	AS	■	■	■	■	■	■	■	■			
Austria	AT	■	■	■	■	■	■	■	■			
Azerbaijan	AZ	■	■	■	■		■					
Bahamas	BA	■		■	■	■	■					
Bahrain	BH	■		■	■	■						
Bangladesh	BN	■	■	■	■	■		■				
Barbados	BB	■		■	■	■						
Belarus	BE	■	■	■	■	■	■	■	■			
Belgium	BL	■	■	■	■	■		■	■			
Bolivia	BO	■	■	■	■	■	■	■				
Botswana	BT	■	■	■	■	■	■	■	■			
Brazil	BR	■	■	■	■	■	■	■	■			
Bulgaria	BU	■	■	■	■	■	■	■	■			
Canada	CA	■	■	■	■	■	■	■	■			
Chile	CH	■	■	■	■	■	■	■				
China P.R.	CI	■	■	■	■	■		■				
Colombia	CO	■	■	■	■	■	■	■	■			
Costa Rica	CR	■	■	■	■		■	■	■			
Croatia	CT	■	■	■	■	■		■	■			
Cyprus	CY	■	■	■	■	■	■	■				
Czech R.	CZ	■	■	■	■		■	■	■			
Denmark	DE	■	■	■	■	■	■	■	■			
Dominican R.	DO	■	■	■	■	■	■	■	■			

Country	Code
Ecuador	EU
Egypt	EG
El Salvador	ES
Estonia	ET
Ecb	EC
Fiji	FI
Finland	FN
France	FR
Georgia	GE
Germany	GR
Ghana	GH
Greece	GC
Guatemala	GU
Honduras	HO
Hong Kong	HK
Hungary	HU
Iceland	IC
India	IN
Indonesia	ID
Iran	IR
Ireland	IE
Israel	IS
Italy	IT
Jamaica	JA
Japan	JP
Jordan	JO
Kazakhstan	KA
Kenya	KE
Korea	KO
Kuwait	KU
Kyrgystan	KY
Latvia	LA
Lesotho	LS
Lithuania	LI

Appendix B. *Continued*

Country name	Country code	(1) Objective	(2) Autonomy	(3) Decision making	(4) Appointment procedure	(5) Committee size	(6) Num. target	(7) Stability & supervision	(8) Sdds standard	(9) Index of economic freedom	(10) Corruption perception index	(11) Er regime
Luxembourg	LU	■	■	■	■	■	■	■				
Macedonia	MA	■	■	■	■	■	■	■ ■				
Malawi	MW	■	■	■	■	■		■ ■				
Malaysia	ML	■	■	■	■	■		■ ■	■			
Malta	MT	■	■	■	■	■		■				
Mauritius	MU	■		■	■	■	■	■ ■	■			
Mexico	ME	■	■	■	■	■	■	■ ■				
Moldova	MO	■	■	■	■	■	■	■ ■				
Mongolia	MN	■	■	■	■							
Mozambique	MZ	■	■	■								
Namibia	NM	■	■	■								
Nepal	NE	■		■								
Netherlands	NT	■	■	■	■	■	■	■ ■	■			
Netherlands Antilles	NA	■	■	■	■	■	■	■ ■				
New Zealand	NZ	■	■	■	■	■	■	■ ■	■			
Nicaragua	NI	■	■	■	■	■	■	■ ■				
Nigeria	NG	■	■	■	■		■	■ ■				
Norway	NO	■	■	■	■			■ ■				
Oman	OM											
Pakistan	PA	■	■									
Papua New Guinea	PP	■										
Paraguay	PR	■		■	■	■	■	■ ■	■			
Peru	PE	■	■	■	■	■		■ ■	■			
Philippines	PH	■	■	■	■	■	■	■ ■	■			
Poland	PO	■							■			
Portugal	PT	■	■	■				■ ■	■			

388

	Variable code	obj	aut	dm	ap	comsize	numt	sands	sdds	free	corr	err
Qatar	QA	■		■	■	■	■	■				
Romania	RO	■	■	■	■	■	■	■	■			
Russia	RU	■	■	■	■	■	■	■				
Saudi Arabia	SA	■	■	■	■	■			■			
Senegal	SE	■	■	■	■	■		■				
Sierra Leone	SL	■	■	■	■	■		■	■			
Singapore	SI	■		■	■	■	■	■	■			
Slovak R.	SO	■	■	■	■	■		■	■			
Slovenia	SV	■	■	■	■	■	■	■	■			
South Africa	SF	■	■	■	■	■		■	■			
Spain	SP	■	■	■	■	■	■	■	■			
Sri Lanka	SR	■	■	■	■	■		■				
Suriname	SU	■	■	■		■		■				
Sweden	SW	■	■	■	■	■	■	■	■			
Switzerland	ST	■	■	■	■	■		■				
Tanzania	TA	■	■	■				■				
Thailand	TH	■	■	■	■	■	■	■	■			
Tonga	TO	■	■	■	■	■		■				
Trinidad and Tobago	TT	■	■	■		■		■				
Tunisia	TU	■	■	■	■	■		■	■			
Turkey	TR	■	■	■	■	■	■	■	■			
Uganda	UG	■	■	■	■	■		■	■			
Ukraine	UR	■	■	■	■	■		■	■			
United Kingdom	UK	■	■	■	■	■	■	■	■			
United States	US	■	■	■	■	■	■	■	■			
Uruguay	UU	■	■	■	■	■		■				
Venezuela	VE	■	■	■	■	■	■	■				
Yemen	YE	■	■	■	■	■		■				
Zambia	ZA	■	■	■	■	■	■	■				
Zimbabwe	ZI						■	■				

Note: Columns (1) through (7) are based on data collected in 2004–2005-2006; SDDS as of end of 2005. ■ signifies that the data are available for the country in question. Columns (1) to (3) define "clarity," (4) to (7) define variables that influence "conflict."

389

Appendix C. *Coding of Select Governance and Socioeconomic Variables*

Code and expected sign	Explanation
obj = *Objective* –	The principal mandate or objective of the central bank: CASE 1–SINGLE target consisting of: inflation exclusively (explicitly mentioned with/without a numerical target) or a monetary target of some kind, or an exchange rate target of some kind = 1. CASE 2–MULTIPLE OBJECTIVES consisting of: inflation and some other economic variable = .5; other goals, namely monetary, financial stability as well as other objectives (e.g., economic growth/stability) = .1; other goals, namely exchange rate, financial stability, as well as other objectives (e.g., economic growth/stability). *Source:* Individual central banks through BIS's central bank hub, http://www.bis.org/cbanks.htm
aut = *Autonomy* –	Is the central bank independent/autonomous in making day-to-day monetary policy decisions? YES but this is NOT constitutionally mandated (i.e., not "organic" or part of the country's constitution) = .75; if the answer is YES to the organic part of the previous case = 1; if the answer is that the central bank is not explicitly autonomous = 0; the central bank is NOT autonomous but its role/functions are defined in the country's Constitution = .50 *Source:* Individual central banks through BIS's central bank hub, http://www.bis.org/cbanks.htm
dm = *Decision making* –	Single decision maker (e.g., governor/president) = 0; Group or committee decision making = 1 (if committee size is 6 or less); = .5 (if committee size is 6 or more). NOTE: decision making refers to MONETARY POLICY decisions and NOT decisions by an executive or senior board (that may make appointments or other decisions). NOTE: Please record committee size, and whether finance minister (or a representative) is on the committee, or whether there are outsiders (i.e., individuals who do NOT work for the central banks such as industry officials or academics). *Source:* Individual central banks through BIS's central bank hub, http://www.bis.org/cbanks.htm
ap = *Appointments procedure* –	Who appoints the CEO (i.e., governor/president) of the central bank: president/head of state of the country = .5; minister of finance, head of government (e.g., PM) = 1; Other (i.e., a committee of some sort defined in the central bank legislation) = 0. *Source:* Individual central banks through BIS's central bank hub, http://www.bis.org/cbanks.htm

(*continued*)

Appendix C. *Continued*

Code and expected sign	Explanation
numt = *Numerical Target* −	Is there a numerical target the central bank aims for, whether in the central bank law or as part of a publicly announced quantitative objective? If YES, and its inflation = 1; if YES and it's a monetary target = .25; if YES and it is an exchange rate type objective = .50. If NO or there is NO target = 0. *Source:* Individual central banks through BIS's central bank hub, http://www.bis.org/cbanks.htm
sands = *Financial System Responsibility*	Is the central bank responsible for maintaining "financial system stability," "financial soundness," "banking system soundness," or "stability" and/or supervision of the financial/banking system? STABILITY only? YES = .5/NO = .25 SUPERVISION only? YES = .25/NO = .75 STABILITY and SUPERVISION = 0 *Source:* Individual central banks through BIS's central bank hub, http://www.bis.org/cbanks.htm
SDDS	Does the country in question adhere to the IMF's special data dissemination standards? YES = 1; NO = 0 http://dbbs.imf.org/Applications/web/sddshome
CORR +	Corruption Perceptions Index as measured by Transparency International. http://www.transparency.org/ policy_research/surveys_indices/cpi
FREE −	Freedom house ranking: 2 = free, 1 = partly free, 0 = not free http://www.freedomhouse.org
ERR +	*De facto* exchange rate regime classification scheme of Levy-Yeyati-Sturzenegger (2005): 1 = Inconclusive; 2 = Float, 3 = Dirty, 4 = Crawling peg, 5 = Fix http://www.utdt.edu/~ely/papers.html

Index

Printed in the United States
By Bookmasters